BACK
HOME

BACK HOME

A Foreign Correspondent
Rediscovers America

Mort Rosenblum

William Morrow and Company, Inc.
New York

Library of Congress Cataloging-in-Publication Data

Rosenblum, Mort.
    Back home : a foreign correspondent rediscovers America
/ Mort Rosenblum.
        p. cm.
    ISBN 0-688-07780-3
    1. United States—Description and travel—1981– 2. United States—
Social life and customs—1971— I. Title.
E169.04.R67 1989
973.92—dc19   89-31158
                                                                      CIP

Printed in the United States of America

First Edition

1 2 3 4 5 6 7 8 9 10

BOOK DESIGN BY KATHRYN PARISE

For Sweet Gretchen, Again
And For Richard Boardman

Author's Note

For years I envied reporters who got to cover the United States as foreigners. They wrote about the richest and most diverse country on the planet, the shotgun rider of the free world, where a kid could make his first million before his senior prom. Like them, I was a foreign correspondent. But for me, America was only home.

My specialty, instead, was bizarre corners of the world. And late one night a French reporter told me about a city at the edge of a desert. Its inhabitants lived on grease and plastic; they decorated themselves with blue rocks and chokers made from scorpions encased in Plexiglas. Its stark hills and rare cacti were fast disappearing under bulldozer blades. The place, in what he called *le Far West,* seemed strange enough for me. What difference did it make if it was Tucson, Arizona, where I had grown up and gone to school?

Twenty years had passed since I left Tucson for a war in the Congo. After reporting from 145 other countries, I decided to go back and look at my own with the same optic. Finally, I could report on my country as if it were Burundi.

I had an advantage over real foreigners. Not many of them grow up knowing why a chicken enchilada rivals the Lord Buddha as an object of devotion. On the other hand, my objectivity might be in doubt. But it seemed like a fair point of view: Time and absence had made me an outside insider; I could love it and leave it all at once.

Contents

CHAPTER 1
The Big Fruit
13

CHAPTER 2
Monopoly on Boardwalk
40

CHAPTER 3
Stockbridge to Boston
60

CHAPTER 4
Blue Ridges, Black Holes
85

CHAPTER 5
Dixie and Parts South
106

CHAPTER 6
Down on the Bayou
151

CHAPTER 7
Forget the Alamo; Remember J.R.
176

CHAPTER 8
By the Time I Get to Phoenix
196

CHAPTER 9
Rockies: To Hell You Ride
218

CHAPTER 10
All the Gold in California
242

CHAPTER 11
Okie from Muskogee
281

CHAPTER 12
Indian Country
296

CHAPTER 13
Heartland: The Kansas City Milkman
312

CHAPTER 14
Hoosier Hysteria, Bluegrass Fever
347

CHAPTER 15
Motown to Graceland
361

CHAPTER 16
Portland to Portland: Last Frontiers
384

CHAPTER 17
Below the Beltway
412

Acknowledgments
447

BACK HOME

CHAPTER

1

The Big Fruit

You can select from three hundred ports of entry to the United States, unless you can fly a darkened Cessna below radar, in which case your choices are infinite. You can paddle in behind the salmon to a customs officer on the Columbia River. You can try Progreso, Texas, where you'll wonder if the bridge took you to the wrong country; even the streets of Belize seem paved with gold compared with Progreso's ragged row of dusty and rusty tin sheds. But to penetrate America, you've got a single choice: New York.

Outsiders spout preposterous twaddle about New York. Every Belgian and Bangladeshi has clear ideas about skylines, muggings, weird mayors, traffic, greed, genius, endemic rudeness, unexpected kindness and large apples. And each New Yorker abroad, hearing these gross generalities, beams with pride. He knows they all fit.

As an outsider I was no small source of twaddle. But I'd lived in New York once and knew a little of which I spoke. I suspected that New York was the place to part the curtain for a good look at America. Miles and months later I knew I was right.

From a distance New York seems a separate country, an international crossroads, different from other places where real Americans lead normal lives. It is an image New Yorkers love. In fact, the city faithfully reflects the rest of the United States. No generality about "Americans" is true, and yet hardly any is false. New York is the sum of all American traits and habits gone wild. Up close it is Middle America on speed.

It has its singularities, of course. For one, pastrami jet lag.

*

Pastrami jet lag strikes down Americans who travel too far away from their natural habitats. I had suffered low-grade attacks every time I visited New York. The last episode, however, got me to thinking.

There was a classic pattern. I'd land at Kennedy, dump my bags and head for the Star's Deli on Lexington Avenue. After a Johnny's Special—pastrami, corned beef, Swiss cheese and coleslaw—I'd try to sleep. At 3:00 A.M., just as some trained armadillo was doing backflips on Channel 11, stomach pangs and assorted malaises would attack. Jet lag is bad enough. Deli-flavored, it is murder.

The last time, however, my sandwich was delayed. Signs of distress flashed across my face. Fatigue and anxiety clouded my mind; reality started to fade. The waiter, sensing crisis, hollered over the counter: "Hey, the customah is waiting." Back came the reply: "Tell da customah ta drop dead."

This was New York all right. It struck me, after twenty years of reporting from foreign countries, that my own country was about as foreign as any I knew. It was time for a good look.

I had left the year before 1968, a naive schmuck of twenty-three sent to report from the Congo in the middle of a war not even the participants could figure out. When Robert Kennedy was shot, I was in some jungle without a radio. During Vietnam I was closer to Khe Sanh than Kent State. I spent the sexy seventies with Latins who take their grandmothers along on the first date. Later, when we the people supposedly crawled away somewhere and then came boisterously back, I watched through the looking glass. If it was morning in America, I was somewhere in the dark.

Except for brief home leaves, I didn't know my own country. To me, it was mainly an ideal, a counterbalance to all the venality, ignorance and hatred I reported from other places. That's how it seemed when I left. Now, like Rip Van Winkle, I was waking up again.

Some things were obvious. In France you can see through men's socks; in the United States you can see through the coffee. But the undercurrents ran deeper than most Americans wanted to look. We suffered from what the Europeans call a short memory. One good swift invasion of a small nation, and we are the best. A lousy few days on the Olympic ski slopes, and we are in decline.

We had an unbelievably bad sense of proportion. Every third person I met, hearing I lived in Paris, fretted about terrorism. From 1981 through 1988 four times more Americans were crushed by vending machines at home—eight—than killed by terrorists in France. New Yorkers killed that many every two days.

Approach and itinerary took some thought. Criticism, I quickly found, rubbed people wrong. Americans had coined the word "nay-sayer." As a foreign correspondent, an outsider, I would say what I saw. As an insider coming home, I would say what I felt. There would be nays with the yeas. On where to go, Paul Theroux, a neighbor who poked regularly into other people's societies, had some advice: You don't have to eat the whole pie to see what it's made of. But the American pie, partly fruitcake, has a lot of little pieces to taste. It would be a long trip.

I started in the summer of 1986, in New York, as America was preparing to celebrate the centennial of the Statue of Liberty.

Absorbing Manhattan is like sticking a fork into a wall socket. Only the well insulated, or the comatose, avoid sensory overload. After a day of New York traffic and manners, at seven-thirty, I ended up spitting fire near the United Nations. B. B. King was on at eight o'clock at Lincoln Center, and friends were saving me a seat. I'd have to stop first at the Drake Hotel. The street gods gave me a break, and a cab appeared. At the hotel I asked the driver to wait two minutes. New York had taught him, a recent immigrant, only four and a half words: "You pay now!" and "Fuckin'—A." We parted on poor terms.

At seven fifty-five, one abandons hope for transport on the East Side. People approaching hysteria milled about, awaiting the Taxi Miracle. Too much had gone wrong. I did not ♥ New York. I wished the heavens would open and a giant high-top sneaker would smash the city to applesauce.

Desperate, I flung myself at Brendon, the Jamaican doorman. "Are you going to let me miss B. B. King?" I asked.

He pondered briefly and replied in an island lilt: "We cahn't have that now, cahn we?" He snapped his fingers, and the steam escaping a nearby manhole was suddenly a silver Cadillac slightly shorter than Malta. Brendon leaned in and ordered: "You take care of my man now." Six minutes later, at Lincoln Center, the driver wanted only five bucks.

My friends had a box over the stage. A gospel singer warming up the audience was backed by six women with lungs of saddle leather. Energy built quickly and grew geometrically. Soon I was squirming.

Then clapping. And then, like everyone else in the place, I was standing on my seat, howling with glee and gyrating like an adder on angel dust.

I had seen nothing like it. In Vietnam I'd been on the wrong end of B-52 strikes. In the Soviet Union I'd gazed at the innermost windows of the Kremlin. I'd seen earthquakes and hurricanes and angry French waiters. But this was different. Corny be damned, this was the gut energy of America, and there was no power to match it.

Liberty Weekend was no party to miss. No one can fete a piece of rock like the people of Superlative City, especially on nonstop live national television. On July 3, I was on a rooftop in Brooklyn Heights overlooking the statue with a Sony television set at my feet.

President Ronald Reagan waxed on about our greatness. We were the dream of huddled masses yearning to breathe free. America, he said, was keeper of the flame of liberty. President François Mitterrand of France, sitting nearby, had the grace not to remind him who had supplied the matches. That France gave the statue to symbolize shared beliefs, and to remind us that the French had helped us win our revolution, was not a main theme. No one mentioned the New Zealanders and Costa Ricans and others who treasured equal freedoms. Such nuances clutter the emotions.

Before long the moment got to me. A crowd of immigrants on the same island where my father landed from Russia—praise the Lord, I could not help thinking—were about to take their swan dive into the melting pot. A little Vietnamese girl explained she was happy to be an American because, back home, the Communists were "ill mannered." The ceremony was dignified, even thrilling. Cameras focused on faces reflecting what my father must have felt. The chief justice intoned a solemn oath, passwords to the most powerful, the most prosperous and the most proud nation on earth.

Among my friends and countrymen, I watched the screen and felt tears form. Suddenly the picture flicked and changed. Some jerk in a huckster smile was selling trash bags. I was home again in America.

Everywhere someone had a pitch. Some eight hundred thousand people and I went to an evening concert in Central Park. This was the place every Lapp reindeer herder knows is hostile territory. But it was a family party. Pressed by crowds, I tripped over a young couple seated on a blanket; the man's right arm made a swift movement toward me. Oh, please, I thought, don't let him be one of those maniacs with a .357 magnum. He brandished a spicy duck wing. "Hungry?" he asked. His wife, meanwhile, poured me a paper cup of chilled white wine. Policemen wandered around, saying things like "Please" and "Don't ask me; I'm from Queens."

Pleasantly, peacefully, we listened to Beethoven's Ninth. Then, just before the Glorias, the Burger King air force attacked. A noisy little plane buzzed the concert, passing back and forth flashing hard sell. I wondered if the hamburgers were as tasteless as the advertising. The music was free, but some entrepreneur was not about to let it go without a commercial. That, people assured me, was what makes America great.

Enterprise was all over the streets, but it was not necessarily free. Among those offering junk emblazoned with Miss Liberty's sacred armpit was an Oberlin College student who had spent June stenciling T-shirts. He had sold $150 worth when police threw his shirts into a garbage bag marked "Evidence." After the fine for selling without a license, he figured he was $500 in the hole.

Money always talked in America, but it has learned a whole new vocabulary. Most statue restoration funds came not from kids' piggy banks, or taxes, but from corporate donors who hired a piece of the glory. The committee tried to ban a Budweiser commercial hailing the moment; Stroh's, having paid, was the Official Beer. ABC bought the whole weekend for ten million dollars. The people up there with the Reagans on Governors Island were not descendants of Miles Standish or crippled Medal of Honor veterans or winners of a liberty lottery; they were the ones who could pay the five thousand dollars.

Also, we seemed to have vastly enlarged our capacity to believe our own hyperbole. All week the papers profiled immigrants who had made it: the Thai-girl-rescued-from-a-shark-by-the-Seventh-Fleet-who-safe-in-her-adopted-country-now-teaches-Nebraska-grandmothers-to-make-better-apple-pies. Each moving tale made readers feel good about themselves. America's doors were open to every wretched soul who cared to knock. Only aspiring immigrants, faced with years of waiting, felt the heft of our regulations. Polls showed most Americans wanted it that way.

In the Boston *Globe* I read about Nellie Zuñiga in Los Angeles. She was working at the crowded Department of Motor Vehicles one morning when a gang of armed men burst in, blocked the doorway and herded everyone who looked Latin against the wall. In the parking lot some of them pulled Latins out of cars. One threw a boy on a car hood and chained his wrists. Women cried. Others froze in hushed silence. "They were hostile and aggressive," Ms. Zuñiga testified in federal court. They were U.S. immigration agents, conducting routine "area surveys."

Witnesses said federal officers peered into homes with flashlights, sought entry without warrants and pulled people off buses and trains. Virginia Zepeda was in bed with her husband when agents tried to remove the window screen. She showed one intruder her San Bernardino birth certificate. "He looked at it and threw it down on the bed and said it wasn't any good, and if he wanted to he could arrest me," she said.

This was America. Her case was reviewed; a judge determined the agents had no warrant and her birth certificate was fine. But that did not reduce the terror of the moment. Or the implications. Agents looked for "illegal aliens" by the same criteria the Gestapo had used to root out Jews and Gypsies. Anyone with black hair and a decent suntan might have to prove his citizenship, even if his family had been Americans since Coronado.

The Liberty Weekend mood left no time for reflection. Souvenir sales were brisk, down to the Statue of Liberty toilet seat covers and pictures of the hallowed lady in Madonna underwear. A popular item was a large plastic hammer for hitting yourself on the head, a typically New York amusement. Taboos were forgotten, like the one about not riding the subway late at night.

The Lexington IRT was a rolling party as festivities aboveground began breaking up. Strangers laughed and danced between stations, inviting each other to parties. Neither muggers nor cops bothered one guy drinking a sixteen-ounce Budweiser, beaming broadly to himself at some private joke. He wore a dinner jacket, shorts : baseball cap reading "Hurt me."

You can't make up your mind about a place like this. Brimming with cheer, I stopped for tokens at Columbus Circle. The guy in the booth, in a Yankees cap and a dirty flowered polyester shirt, was adding numbers. I gave him a ten-dollar bill and asked for four tokens. He slid out the tokens and returned to his sums. I asked for my change, and he ignored me. I asked again, louder. "I gave it to you," he insisted. The man behind me said he didn't. The attendant scowled and counted out his cashbox. Then he shoved six ones at me. "Everyone tries that . . ." he muttered. I asked if he was apologizing. His filthy look suggested he wasn't. A bored transit cop had watched it all.

Reading and listening, I knew I was supposed to feel proud. Newsmagazines declared us the most generous, the most capable and the most popular nation on earth. "We are a people on a pinnacle, gone giddy with our greatness," observed *U.S. News & World Report.* In celebrating the centennial, "we swept ourselves to new heights with our love of our land and our lore." On Channel 4 Gloria Rojas referred to France's gift to us as superb and *extraordinaire.* Fitting terms, she gushed, "whether about the fireworks, the country, or ourselves."

New York always warms to a party or a crisis. It is best seen in its workaday lunacy, when grime streaks the glory. With time and sturdy shoes, you can cover the world in New York. You may miss a Masai manyatta or the odd cargo cult, but there is hardly a society you cannot sample between Brooklyn and the Bronx. The trick is to figure out what you are seeing. Five cultures can hang out together on the same street corner.

Whenever some foreigner begins, "You Americans . . . ," I try to imagine which New York park bench he has in mind. There is one in Battery Park I could recommend to anyone who needs his stereotypes shattered.

On a summer Sunday a man I would have sworn was Papuan strummed an indeterminate stringed instrument and belted out "Wake Up, Little Susie." He shifted into something vaguely Spanish, and a lady of fifty in a Chiquita Banana outfit did an Iberian break dance with castanets. Off to the side, an old man danced a shuffling schottische by himself, wearing a polka-dot clown suit and a brace cap. He was, I guessed, Chinese or Irish.

The singer had some pals with him. They spoke Spanish among themselves and only halting, accented English to others. Dominicans, perhaps. Or Salvadoran refugees. One came around with a hat, and I asked him in Spanish where he was from. He seemed puzzled at the question. *"De aquí,"* he said. From here. He was an American who lived in the United States. I was the foreigner.

This would be some job, cramming Americans into tight paragraphs and chapter headings. The United States, after all, was an undiluted sample of the human condition around which we put borders and a national conceit. "American" did not differentiate us much from "people." Even more, the United States did not fit neatly in with those geopolitical ordinal numbers that had come into fashion.

We are First World all right, a free industrial society in which a worker can buy a toaster without missing lunch for a month. Americans of that primary world are the ones Europeans picture when they talk about chewing gum.

The Second World is reserved for the socialist bloc mostly, but we qualify. A lot of perfectly good Americans believe that unbridled capitalism is not the best way forward. The FBI isn't supposed to read their mail, but it does.

The surprising part is the Third World, the overlapping but distinct communities a correspondent would label "developing" anywhere else. Some immigrant clusters are as easy to see as if they had customs posts and national airlines. Emerge from the subway at Atlantic Avenue in Brooklyn, and you have crossed the Green Line into East Beirut. Somewhere around Mott, Broadway dissolves into the South China Sea. Native American settlements—the Navajo Reservation, for instance—are clear examples of separate nations. Poor people form definable pockets of "underdevelopment" in city centers and in rural backwaters. Mostly, however, our Third World is a subtle network of microsocieties and individual attitudes blended into the whole.

America is no longer a melting pot. It is a stir-fry wok. Whatever new ingredients are added to the rest, each retains its particular flavor and shape. But a certain uniformity is cooked in, giving us common characteristics, standards and frames of reference. You can say "American" without defining color, income bracket or education level and still come up with some workable generalities. You just can't get reckless about it.

From Battery Park it is a short walk north to Trinity Church. Eighty years ago Henry James took an inside outsider look at America and worried over the brownish black little church that was such a powerful symbol. It is just as well that he is not coming back again.

James was distressed that Trinity's superb steeple was dwarfed, and its graceful proportions obscured, by the buildings rising around it. Today architectural travesty is the least of it. For a man who treasured symbols, James would not have missed the irony of the paltry trickle of quarters landing in the collection plates compared with the hundreds of millions of dollars secreted away a few yards down on Wall Street by Christians, Jews and nonspecific believers in the American way, all feeding richly on the nation's trust.

The rest of America notices Wall Street in sporadic waves. There are insider trading scandals when a few people are caught in specific instances of public betrayal. The Dow-Jones average rockets, or plummets, when greed and fear lose their running balance. Someone makes a movie, or writes a book, and tongues click appropriately. The Securities and Exchange Commission and public prosecutors prowl around the corridors. The honest bankers and traders seek to keep their houses clean.

But every morning at nine-thirty the Big Board lights up and Wall Street lives a life of its own. Members of the little community, untroubled by grand extraneous themes like right and wrong, deal in reality. In business, wrong means illegal; an honest man is one who breaks no law. The other stuff—widows and orphans, do unto others and all that—has awkward aerodynamics for a fast track. Any good lawyer can demolish a moral argument. Something has to anchor the flotilla of intangible ethical issues. On Wall Street what matters is performance. The only phrase in America heard more often than "Have a nice day" is "the bottom line."

Garry Trudeau had it right when his inside trader character did some word association. What's the opposition of "wrong"? "Poor."

That this is hardly fresh insight seems cause for alarm. Everyone knows it, yet it gets worse and worse. In 1831, before Alexis de Tocqueville even got off the boat to begin plumbing America's depths, he noted a conversation with an American businessman: "Mr. Schermerhorn, who is nonetheless greatly infatuated with his country, told me the greatest blot on its character was the avidity to get rich and do it by any means. There is a multitude of bankruptcies, and they do not sufficiently damage those responsible."

Citizen Kane's old Jewish accountant, revealing some human revulsion to greed in business, observed that it was easy to make money if that's all one wanted to do.

These days one does not sneer at making money. It is how you keep score. Lee Iacocca, commenting on the more than twenty million dollars he earned at Chrysler in 1986, observed: "That's the American way. If little kids don't aspire to make money like I did, what the hell good is this country?"

Graduates of the School of Business Administration at the University of California, Berkeley, were given a similar, if cruder, en-

couragement in the 1985 commencement address. The speaker was
Ivan Boesky: "I think greed is healthy. You can be greedy and still
feel good about yourself."

Boesky, a high-flying arbritrager at the time, was making millions
no one would ever accurately count. A comfortable guess is that
they were well in excess of the hundred million dollars he was later
fined for inside trading.

The hoary phrase "inside trading" fascinated me. In a broader
sense, Wall Street is an insider's business. The illegal part is when a
guy with confidential information warns his brother-in-law in advance that some parasite is about to infest a particular company.
Such high sums are involved, and the technology and intelligence
are so complex, that the market belongs to the pros. The ranking
players take losses, too. But they are in the hunt. The rest of us are
back behind the trees, trying to follow the fox by listening to the
wail of the hounds.

A glance at the mechanics of Wall Street suggests that it is impossible to control illegal trading. Secret documents are seen by far too
many secretaries, clerks, typists and printers, not to speak of senior
partners. Besides a few overworked investigators, all that really protects outsider investors is Wall Street's sense of ethics. That means
each firm should have a compliance officer and a security system so
that colleagues can police one another.

To see how all this works, I talked to a man who was sandbagged
for blowing the whistle.

"This is off the record," the man said to me at least three times;
he knew Wall Street's power to take revenge. But he was helpful
and, I learned via other sources, truthful. We'll call him Whistle.

Whistle was a senior executive, and the compliance officer, of a
major investment banking firm. He discovered that a young colleague ran an insider trading ring, involving others in the firm.
He recorded a boastful admission from the culprit and then reported him.

"I immediately resigned, realizing I could no longer work there,"
Whistle said. And he has not gone to work for anyone else.

"As soon as you say anything, they destroy you," he told me. "They
can afford the best lawyers. They go back and find anything they
can about your personal life, your finances. They distort things, in-
timidate people, anything to discredit you. There is nothing you can
do against it. Even if you can afford the legal fees necessary, you
come out of it wrecked. Who is going to buck the system under
those circumstances?"

The morning we spoke, *The New York Times* carried a little item back in the finance pages about a guy whom federal authorities had tracked down and arrested. He was indicted for forty separate counts of illegal dealing, for earnings well into the millions of dollars. He was the first person to be convicted in a trial; others had pleaded guilty and bargained with information on their associates. He got two years.

Whistle was outraged. "You know what forty indictments cost the state? And that's all he was sentenced to. They sent a very disturbing message to anyone who wants to get rich the easy way. You tell me crime doesn't pay."

A few months later Boesky was sentenced; he got only three years. He trimmed his own penalty by snitching on everyone he dealt with, a substantial community. By some estimates of his illegal fortune, each of his years in jail should be worth considerably more than Iacocca's fat yearly earnings. There is the loss of freedom, but Boesky is not breaking rocks in the Georgia sun. And there is the shame, provided one sees it that way. For some, it is a badge of glory, of success at a high-risk, ballsy business. If the numbers are high enough, you can be a folk hero.

The message seemed pretty clear: Crime pays just fine. The trick is not to get caught. If you do, sell your friends.

Boesky and the others broke laws. It gets trickier when something is merely wrong. Who says? Up in the seven-figure numbers, justification comes easy. Universities have started teaching business ethics. But what are they? At Columbia, Asher Edelman offered a reward of a hundred thousand dollars to any student in his corporate raiding class who could identify a tasty target. The dean was upset, but the students weren't. This seems clear enough from the outside: Right and wrong are now, like almost everything else in America, subjects for negotiation.

I was especially fascinated by corporate raiders. Any old Africa hand knows a parasite when he sees one. Raiders argue that by muscling in uninvited, they force a company to improve its management. Translated, that means executives strip down—"lean and mean" is the American way—by firing innocent bystanders, cutting quality and selling valued assets that are not "profit centers." Employee loyalty has no cash value. Social responsibility is a murky concept that costs money. Some win big, usually lawyers, brokers and insiders, and many more lose.

Wall Street had changed from a nourishing Nile into a raging flood-swollen torrent into which you stuck your toe only advisedly. People kept calling market manipulation victimless. But what about that sixty-three-year-old widow profiled in *Newsweek* who got whipsawed on options? From a comfortable $600,000 portfolio, she was suddenly $403,000 in debt.

One morning I called on Thomas Odhiambo, a Kenyan insect specialist who had just won the Hunger Project's Africa Award. I'd met him in Nairobi and liked him. His gentle, rolling laugh masked none of his anxiety about his people. Things were falling apart in Africa, and we talked about why. I mentioned corruption. He gave a heavy sigh and started to answer.

The irony took a moment to hit me. This was New York. Every time I picked up the *Times* some official was off to Rikers Island. The Miss America I used to watch beaming warmly on TV had taken the Fifth. Mobsters controlled the cement coming in and the garbage going out. Corrupt health inspectors thoughtfully drew pictures of rats to threaten restaurateurs who didn't know the English word for bribe. Unions, even some police precincts, reeked of Mafia. During the corruption trial of Congressman Mario Biaggi, a *Daily News* front page screamed THEY ALL TOOK.

And why pick on New York? By early 1988 more than a hundred members of Ronald Reagan's administration were under a cloud or in handcuffs. And that was not counting Irangate. When the attorney general appeared on television, you didn't know if he was representing law in America or, yet again, defending himself.

We have less corruption than Africa. But the Zairian cop making eleven bucks a month has to steal to feed his kids. A cabinet minister is expected to support a whole village. The big African thieves started at independence when there were no state structures to stop them. An American official steals only if he is a slimeball prepared to corrupt a system that can afford to be clean.

During his trial Biaggi blustered unrepentently. On conviction he wept. I doubted if desperate families in Brooklyn shared his grief.

I could see the same thing happening that I'd watched in Africa. People see others get away with something, and they want their share. Americans still feared getting caught. But more were catching on. Overworked prosecutors needed tip-offs, evidence and witnesses. Someone had to step forward. It wouldn't be Whistle.

On a trip to the airport a cabby named Robert launched unprompted into a lighthearted disquisition on the subject. He seemed to believe his own exaggerations: The whole town, and most of Albany, were in somebody's pocket. One by one, he listed industries, commissions, departments, real estate deals. It amused him enormously. We reached the terminal, and he threw up his hands with a loud cackle. "Hey," he said, "whaddya gonna do? Ain't my problem."

With the courts hamstrung, and individuals powerless, a sort of corporate martial law helps fill the void. Executives don't like crime, either from their own convictions or because it is bad for business. They tend to police their own shops. But they make their own bylaws. They can afford to be arbitrary. And with competition for good jobs, they need not take prisoners.

Following Whistle's lead, I talked to a lawyer who defends victimized employees. She advises most of her clients to forget it. One was a woman who had just left law school with honors. She was hired on Wall Street until her drug test came up positive. It was a mistake; she hated drugs. She proved the lab had mixed up blood samples. The firm told her to beat it. And if she sued, she should apply next to Burma. The lab was liable, but too much time had passed. She could not find a job because corporate juntas wanted to know why she wasn't already working.

True enough, New York is a great place to be rich or, better yet, rich and famous. *Spy* magazine offered some insight on this in a piece entitled "Ego Mania." It quoted some guy I'd never heard of—he looked like an overweight John Travolta with a crappy barber—who said: "I love it when you call and ask if you can have a table in an hour and they say, 'What's your name? I'll check.' They always come back sounding sheepish and say, 'Yes, Mr. Longo. When can we expect you?' "

I suspect this has always been one of New York's endearing traits. A few years ago I was at the Abbey Hotel and rang an old acquaintance named Sharon, a friend of a friend, to discuss a project that might interest her. She was a wheeler dealer in movies. Her machine took a message. When I finally got her, she said, "Oh, yeah, I didn't recognize the name, and I thought if you were someone important, you'd be staying at the Regency."

In New York money can buy a great deal of happiness. Breakfast at Tiffany's is no big deal to someone who dines at Le Cirque. A take-home wage of twenty-one thousand dollars buys three stuffed elephants at F.A.O. Schwarz, before sales tax. On occasion I've ridden in one of those obnoxiously long black Cadillacs that paralyze midtown traffic. You can't see us through the opaque windows, but we're in there, sipping champagne and making jokes about your frayed collar.

Money is a vital benchmark, and it seems to provoke few complexes among those who have it. That prize Tom Odhiambo won was for helping alleviate hunger among Africa's impoverished people. It was awarded at an intimate black-tie dinner for fifteen hundred with an engraved menu. That was how you raised money in America, I was told. But an African friend put down her last fork before she got to the truffled torte. "This is grotesque," she said. Still, she was used to it.

The rich are easy enough to find. Just turn on the television. I watched some frenetic-tongued Englishman ooh and aah over a party in New Jersey. The program in a series everyone else seemed to know about, had a thin plot: Malcolm Forbes spent a lot of money on catering, flowers, tents, favors and stuff.

Those at the other extreme are more numerous, but they can be harder to observe. Television has no *Life Styles of the Poor and Wretched*. Many discourage curiosity seekers in their neighborhoods. Names like Harlem and Bedford-Stuyvesant are uttered in fear or contempt by people who stay clear of them. For years the name I kept seeing was South Bronx. Foreigners knew it as the neighborhood that was so bad it could only be burned down.

In Paris, years back, I took a friend to see *Fort Apache, the Bronx*. In the film, based on the Forty-first Precinct, a hard-assed inspector provoked angry mobs to besiege the station. In the heat of it, two officers threw an innocent kid off a roof. Paul Newman, a good cop, ratted on his colleagues and quit, frustrated at trying to keep order among sociopaths. My friend asked if it was all that bad. I didn't know, and I wanted to find out.

Heading off to the South Bronx, I felt foolish at the tinge of fear I hadn't felt since crossing into West Beirut. This was the United States, but *everybody* told me what to expect in the South Bronx. I checked for visible jewelry and wallet bulges. At Bloomingdale's I descended into the subway. The number 5 train stopped, disgorging matronly aunts and Queens teenagers on their way to sample shades of lip-stick. I got on the train and went off to war.

The subway was worthy of any journey-into-hell adventure story. On a bad day the New York subway ranks up there with Air Mali and the Mogadishu airport as one of the world's worst transportation experiences. On good days it only stinks of urine and is shockingly unsafe. But the ride north was uneventful; I did not catch my scarf in the closing doors, and no one sold me to passing Arabs. I studied the ads to kill time. "Mr. Edelman," one began, extolling a firm of New York lawyers, "I had a serious accident. Do I have a case?" Of course, the answer followed: "If you are seriously injured in any accident, you may be entitled to a substantial sum of money." It reminded me of a bumper sticker reading HIT ME, I NEED THE MONEY.

It was a normal load: a gnarled old man, a young mother with a few kids in party clothes, a boy with chubby thighs in shorts carrying a game bag, and a teenager with a Grace Jones haircut and an El Salvador T-shirt. At 125th Street we were joined by an enormous man wearing wide red stripes, with a shaved head and a large spade beard. He was having a heated argument with himself. Nonstop, his voice boomed around the empty car, angry or amused, but consistently obscene. We all ignored him and hoped he would not ask us to join the argument.

For outsiders on the subway, it was hard not to think of Bernie Goetz. Race had to figure into his vigilante assault, but that did not seem to be the point. The four youths Goetz shot might have been green or striped. Anyone not used to the New York experience feels the overwhelming vulnerability. One is a pansy in a public garden, protected only by a little sign that says DON'T PICK THE FLOWERS.

Above the Bronx River, "subway" is a term of convenience. The train clatters down an elevated track over vistas of bombed-out buildings, weed-choked empty lots and urban moonscape. The Simpson Street station is a treehouse of metal girders and reflecting pools of steaming urine. I trotted down the steps, ready for anything.

Very quickly I began to suspect a little paranoia among my prior informants. Contrary to popular belief, black and Hispanic people had better things to do than hassle white strangers. At first glance, the South Bronx looked like a placid backwater neighborhood of Santo Domingo, with a twist of suburban Seoul. An old guy in Xavier Cugat sideburns and a T-shirt washed cilantro in a bucket on the street, listening to muffled merengue music from a transistor radio. Housewives picked among exotic fruits and evil-smelling sauces at a Korean grocery. A few regulars hung out at Z & T Pizza. Kids played at the curb, stepping around a young man with shaggy hair and a dirt-streaked bare white chest. No one paid any more attention to an intruder than people might have at Gramercy Park.

Finding the Forty-first Precinct was no trick. Hardly a beleaguered outpost of civilization in an urban jungle, it stood all alone on a block cleared away of burned-out buildings. It was no longer nicknamed Fort Apache; it was called Little House on the Prairie. The Forty-first is a scruffy Third World station house like those I'd seen in a dozen Southern Hemisphere countries: streaked blue walls and crudely lettered signs; a receptionist who studied my card a full minute to determine which words were my name. The difference was that no muffled shrieks could be heard from within.

Inspector David Velez, the boss, was happy to see me. The South Bronx had gotten a bad rap, he said, and he wanted people to know it was coming back. "You can get the scent of enthusiasm, that it has turned the corner and is coming back," he said. There was a drug problem, he allowed, although some other parts of New York were worse. Hookers flourished, whatever the vice squad tried against them. Leaving your Nikon on the car seat was not such a hot idea. But people had burned down about all the buildings they were going to. Juvenile gangs were less of a problem; kids went to school. Murders were mostly among friends and seemed to be decreasing.

Velez was not exaggerating. Whatever the South Bronx had been in the 1970's, some things were coming together. This was a long way from Leona Helmsley's suites, but investors sniffed a change. Real estate was beginning to move. Neighborhood watches cut down crime and built up pockets of pride. Windows displayed flowers among the security bars, and new parks were safe for strolling. After the rough years the cops were trying hard to build some links to the community. A few retired officers had formed the Fort Apache Boxing Club to give kids a little orderly violence.

I liked Velez a lot and asked about his background. His family came from Puerto Rico, and he grew up in East Harlem. His father died, and his mother went on welfare. Unlike the stock stereotype, she did not squander it on her boyfriend's booze. She sent her kids to school and taught them about helping others.

Inspector Pat Gonzales, the zone commander, dropped in. He had spent twenty-nine years working in the Bronx, and he thought the place was great. He still sees its southern zone as an integral part of New York, full of taxpaying citizens. "I remember when I was a kid, watching Franklin D. Roosevelt go through the Bronx on his way to La Guardia, in an open car, head back, fedora hat, cigarette holder clamped in his teeth," he said. "What a sight."

The South Bronx is now more than 75 percent Hispanic, not necessarily counting Gonzales. His Spanish father met his Irish mother in America. He wasn't thinking ethnic; he was looking at people going back to work. Some companies were moving in. Lots and buildings were beginning to quadruple in value. American patterns were holding, he reckoned. Things go in cycles; when there is a vacuum, something fills it.

Drugs were the worst police problem, he said. If you arrest one pusher, there are ten behind him. The big guys were somewhere else. To clamp down seriously, Gonzales said, authorities had to start at the source. And something had to be done to cut the demand, the potential users' original motivation.

I mentioned that I was seldom a supporter of my local police but that New York's Finest tended toward a certain panache. The day before, for example, I'd seen some motorist commit an intersection outrage worthy of the guillotine in Paris. A cop merely pounded on the hood and yelled, "Move it outa heah."

Gonzales laughed. New York cops have seen it all, he said. They can mess with only the important stuff. "You know, I see these guys in small towns who swagger around, with their thumbs in their belts. Where do they get the time for all that?" The key, he said, is caring about people. "I always tell recruits that this is a people job. If you don't enjoy dealing with people, be a garbageman. Go deal with garbage."

On my way out, I watched two cops bring in a pair of hookers. It was straight out of *Barney Miller*. One woman wore a lime green jogging suit; the other wore hardly anything. Both were joking with the arresting officers, not the least disturbed by the cuffs linking their wrists behind their backs. Velez's assistant, Captain Dan Hayden, nudged me. "Now you tell me that's not an art, to bring somebody in and make 'em smile."

The women would each get fined twenty-five dollars, or they might spend a night in jail if they were broke. Then they'd go out and earn it back. Some had been in scores of times. Hooking, if illegal, is an industry, and the South Bronx is damned short of employment.

For two hours I cruised the precinct with a C-Pop team. The Community Patrol Officer Program assigns cops to hang out with the public. The idea is to revive the old respect people used to have for the friendly foot cop on a beat. A lot of "How-ya-doin'" up and down the street suggested it had some merit.

Ralph Argiento did the driving and the talking. We cruised the bombed-out blocks, and he pointed out buildings that had been brought back. The trick, he said, was cooperative action to run out the druggies and restore some tenant pride. "It was like shoveling shit against the tide before," he said. "When the supers gave up, the buildings went." New managements have power to evict tenants who break the rules.

I asked what happened at night to cars parked along the curb. "Well"—Ralph shrugged—"there's one." He nodded toward a bare frame so badly stripped I couldn't tell if it was a Cadillac or a Yugo. "This'll amuse you," he added as we passed under the Bruckner Expressway. Thieves had dumped hundreds of stripped auto carcasses under the raised roadway. The city built a fence to discourage the practice. The railroad built its own fence to stop kids from rolling cars onto the tracks. But the gigantic graveyard remained, a monument to the fact that crime was not exactly stamped out in the South Bronx.

I saw no cabs in the Forty-first Precinct. "Well," Ralph said, "if you add up the number of cabbies who've been killed up here over the years . . ." How safe was walking the streets? I asked. "Look, you see mothers wheeling their babies, old people, no problem. They belong here," Ralph said. "But you take a guy like you or me [he meant me; he'd been there twenty years, and he had a .38]. If he looks apprehensive, glancing over his shoulder, he's gonna bring out the worst in the nicest of guys."

With a philosophical shrug, he added: "You go into the jungle without a big gun, you're gonna get mauled."

Ralph was clear about his work. He did not hate criminals. "You got a job, I got a job—and so do they," he said. "As long as there's money to be made doing something illegal, someone'll do it. This would all be easier if crime did not pay. Unfortunately that is not the case." For all the improvement in the Bronx, he was not fooled about its flash point. We passed a detention center where youths had rebelled, and Ralph volunteered: "I don't mind saying this, and you can quote me. They tell me to be polite, careful and all that but, if there's a riot, to do what I gotta do. It's just like that."

Later, walking around on my own, I found the irony overpowering: an idle labor force, relative peace, cheap space, easy transportation. How could an investor miss? But like every other Third World country, the South Bronx was trapped in its borders. If there was no problem with visas or plane rides, its other two barriers were formidable: fear and ignorance.

Harlem was another surprise. It is no place to hang out with a bulging back pocket. But a self-possessed white might be more comfortable there than a black would be in some parts of Brooklyn and Queens. "The level of racial tension against blacks has grown to unbelievable proportions," remarked Diane Weathers, a black writer friend who came home shocked after two years in Rome. "Perfectly respectable-looking black men have given up even trying to hail taxis. If you're black, you don't ever try to stop a cabdriver on the uptown side of the street." One driver refused to take her to Harlem. "You have to, by law," she said. "I don't have to do anything," he replied, "but pay taxes and stay white."

Racial issues would take more reporting than I had expected. But first I wanted to separate them from poverty.

Finding the homeless is no trick in New York. Let your attention wander, and you'll trip over them.

At the Gucci end of Fifth Avenue, at Fifty-Third Street, a gaily colored poster advertised the Broadway production of *Les Misérables*. A few steps below the street was a scene beyond even the fevered mind of Victor Hugo. As I climbed down to the subway station, it took a physical effort to penetrate the stench of vomit and urine. Inert little bundles lay side by side along both walls. Occasionally one would twitch or turn fitfully. It was like the worst part of Port-au-Prince, but for two differences: There was none of the lively street life that lightens the load of misery in the Haitian capital; also, it was the middle of the afternoon.

No one paid attention to the spike heels and silk-stockinged legs that picked their way over the bodies. A transit cop, with no alternative to offer, surveyed the scene indulgently. Once a good-natured custodian slapped a wall near one group, and they all shuffled to their feet, scooping together their few rags of clothes, tattered blankets and cardboard mattresses. When the man moved on, they quickly remade their beds and went back to sleep. Those farther away did not bother to wake up.

One man, somewhere between seventeen and thirty, with filthy dreadlocks, lay lifeless under a threadbare khaki blanket. The sum total of his life was thrown loosely into a tattered plastic trash bag, a small one, tucked under his head. He had cruddy boots but no laces. A few guys had no possessions at all, not even the strip of grimy cardboard others used as mattresses. They may have had clothes somewhere else; I wouldn't bet on it. A few men were upright. One young black with vacant eyes held out a battered paper cup, without much conviction. I surveyed their faces, looking for the spark that might initiate an interview. There was nothing.

This was March, and it wasn't warm yet. After making a point of not blocking them out, I found the homeless in every underground passage. And the crazies. At Penn Station I watched a man in a brown suit stiffened with filth, young and able-bodied. He was absorbed in a fierce fistfight with a plastic trash barrel, and he was losing.

In every other industrialized society someone has thought of the bottom layers of the underclass. We offer something only to people who meet our strict criteria. Elsewhere varying safety nets provide medical care, housing, job retraining and family allowances. A homeless European can usually find a bowl of soup and a bed. In America down-and-out is a desperate business.

New York treated the crisis like an emergency, squandering millions by overpaying crooked landlords of welfare hotels unworthy of the rats and cockroaches they sheltered for free. Even for those who qualified, waiting lists for public housing averaged eighteen years. On the street some New Yorkers were generous. Others howled about the menacing eyesores that polluted their neighborhoods. From time to time, kids amused themselves by splashing gas on ragged human bundles and setting them afire.

I saw a piece in *The New York Times* suggesting muted outrage that a Soviet documentary focused on the poor and homeless. But no foreigners, however friendly, fail to notice them or shake their heads at our version of the human condition.

One Sunday morning I drove slowly through the far end of the East Village, looking for people with nowhere to live. Finding them was easier than I expected. On Ninth Street, heading west toward Second Avenue, two guys shuffled and staggered under a huge wooden structure the way ants carry home outsize burdens. It looked too worthless to have been stolen, and the guys looked too poor to be thieves. It was, in fact, firewood. The men were from a Rainbow communelet, part of a New Age hippie movement, that was having its usual fifty or so homeless to lunch.

Their tiny settlement was on a weed-grown lot, temporarily vacant, behind a bent and rusty tin door. A ragged tarp was strung over an open fireplace and a cleanly swept expanse of dirt. Some broken chairs showed signs of doubling as beds. The only dwelling was a rudimentary canvas tepee for two. Purple morning glories and sunflowers grew wild.

Caleb Beacon and his wife, Cascadas, seemed to be the heads of the household, although they took pains to explain everyone was equal. Caleb had done the world. He's been a hippie in the London production of *Hair*; he'd played flute in Johnny Carson's studio orchestra. Tattoos decorated his bare white biceps, and he wore a gaily colored crocheted Rasta hairnet. Cascadas had a nice smile and bad teeth.

I shook hands with a half dozen people around the fire. There was Red, who was black. He was a carpenter whose last boss took over his tools and Red's wages. "I got a self-destructive streak," Red said with a shy grin. "I guess I did too much wine and things. Sometimes I think I'm too sensitive for this world."

Manny was Hispanic and Italian. "He's our Woporican," Caleb announced. Manny smiled as though he had heard that one before; his T-shirt announced: "I Don't Give a Shit." "He used to have a job until he tried to stop some guy from getting mugged," Caleb added. Manny had worked for the city, cleaning up parks. He saw three Polish youths robbing an old man. He drove them off, flailing his spiked stick which was supposed to be only for spearing trash. They reported him, and he was fired for attacking citizens with municipal property. I did not check out the story, but Manny's eyes teared as he told it.

William Birdwell, Bird, wore a beret, a black raincoat and the owlish look of a Left Bank poet with writer's block. He had thought a lot about the injustices of society and the human price of others' greed. His basic message was that corporations and authorities wanted people to be beaten down, attached to their jobs and afraid to be different.

I brought up the word "homeless."

"I'm not homeless," Bird said. "I live on the planet."

"My home is my heart," Manny added.

Red snorted. "You're lying. I'm homeless."

I spent some time with Sunrise, a handsome but street-battered young man who announced, with a laugh, that he was a wanted criminal. His crime was sleeping out in front of the White House. Sunrise was part of the nuclear protest group that keeps a permanent vigil in "Peace Park," across Pennsylvania Avenue from the President. The cops took him to court for illegal camping.

Sunrise found he could no longer make a living by playing guitar for handouts. "In Washington you get arrested for playing on the street," he said. "It's the same on Bleecker Street. I see us heading towards martial law, and people are going to be railroaded into the system."

He shook his head, puzzled. "It's really scary. They are turning everybody into robots. You see people walking down the street with sad expressions. They don't turn their head one way or the other. They wear the latest styles, but what do they really have? Robots. Zombies."

The mood picked up when Stagger Lee stumbled into the fireplace. He repeated Sunrise's theme: "As soon as you start doing things for free, not supporting the system, they want you in jail. They want you dead. People like us are already gone, just living day by day."

And then Caleb: "Anything you do that makes you free, they want you in chains."

Stagger was all rough tattoos and incoherence until he pulled me aside. "You know where I can get poems published?" he asked. "I got a few things I'm working on." I asked if he had them written down. "No, but they're up here," he said, tapping his forehead. For the next fifteen minutes he declaimed moving and delicate verse about mystical Peruvian ladies, failing light and, mostly, living on the street.

The little kitchen served meals for free to anyone who wanted them. Cascadas and the others scrounged ingredients, paying token amounts to neighborhood grocers, who were regularly generous. They preached ideology of the Temple of the Rainbow. Drugs were energetically discouraged. "Shit, people got enough problems without that," Caleb explained.

One regular was a burly black man with a booming laugh. He wore huge earrings, a straw hat over a turban and a Monte Alban Mezcal "Eat the Worm" T-shirt. He and Stagger Lee and I did a rousing harmony on "My Girl" until none of us could remember any more of the words.

Another was Daniel Eggink, who wore a tie. Four years before he and his wife, a country singer, had brought their seven kids to New York from Haight-Ashbury in San Francisco. Their old car was stolen on the street, along with everything they owned. Now he printed greeting cards, using his daughter's drawings. He was the group's philosopher-spokesman.

The real problem in an increasingly desperate society, he said, was fear. "A third of the people are only one paycheck away from the other side of the line. They begrudge the homeless for not being next to them at their miserable jobs." People who might be of help ignore the homeless, he said; "The cruelest and most superficial people are those who've gone to college." And big business made it worse: "Corporations appropriate the land of marginal people and then defoliate. They want a dependent population, to keep people ignorant. New York is for the rich; if you make less than seventy-five thousand dollars, New York is not for you."

Daniel reflected a minute and concluded: "Basically the middle-class dream is a failure We have all been robbed of being able to take the mud and transform it with our dreams to meet basic needs and sell the excess. Once you could be poor with dignity. Now that is no longer possible."

I asked if he was worried about a new policy allowing street people to be carried off for psychiatric treatment. He was not.

"In New York dead bodies are swept right up," he said. "As long as you're alive, they'll let you rot in the street under the guise of freedom. If you don't even have the control not to foul yourself, you need help."

That was just before Joyce Brown was carted to Bellevue and had to fight hard to get out. Cleaned up, she was an instant media star. She did the talk shows, lectured at Harvard and took a job. A little later someone spotted her panhandling again, and she explained she'd run a little short of cash.

I mentioned her to a doorman I'd befriended, and he curled his lip. "You see, she's back on the street. That just goes to show you." I nodded, but I wasn't sure what that was supposed to show me. What I saw was a huge number of people in desperate shape, and they were inching steadily farther away from America's fabled taps of milk and honey.

A cheerier, lovelier New York emerged that evening, just as daylight faded and the first lights twinkled on. I stood at the corner of

Fifth Avenue and Fifty-ninth, watching horsecabs trot by the elegant Plaza Hotel. From that angle, between the southeast corner of Central Park and the handsome old buildings of midtown, New York is eminently approachable. Strollers ate Dove bars, fat sausages and Italian ices from sidewalk vendors.

Since the ancient Greeks and Romans, city planners have understood that proportion is the key to grandeur. In Paris only the Eiffel Tower and a few modern anomalies are taller than six stories. London and Rome allowed few high rises among their well-spaced monuments and parks. New York, by comparison a brand-new city, chose the drama and living space of a towering skyline.

In past trips I had always marveled at how well New York worked, with so many people piled on top of one another. The Empire State and Chrysler buildings were American Arcs de Triomphe. The World Trade Center and Wall Street served a particular function in the business end of town. Midtown skyscrapers seemed to fit together, staggered carefully for light and space. This time, as I looked down the canyon, something was wrong.

Tiffany's was dwarfed, and the old graceful facade of the Bonwit Teller was gone. An enormous pink and gold building had risen, blocking light, sucking up utilities and drawing yet more traffic into the midtown snarl. It was, I learned, the monumental erection of this guy Trump. I'd have to find out more about him.

Meantime, I went to see Dorothy Sarnoff, actress and personality-at-large, who seemed to have found the key to what pricks up people's ears in America. She was raking it in as speech coach and image maker to presidential candidates, business leaders, and celebrities in general.

Mrs. Sarnoff showed me some before and after tapes, quite amazing, of how she metamorphized executives and politicians into convincing leaders. They had not added a crumb to their knowledge, nor had they deepened their understanding of the human condition. They had simply straightened their shoulders, projected their voices, changed their ties, combed their hair and exuded confidence.

Her formula is simple. For American audiences, the delivery of a speech counts for 50 percent of its persuasiveness. Personal appearance of the speaker counts for 42 percent. Only 8 percent is content—that is, what the speaker has on his mind. Abraham Lincoln looks funny and was a pretty awkward speaker, I mentioned. "Yes,"

Mrs. Sarnoff agreed. "I don't think Abraham Lincoln could have been elected President today."

This whole matter of government by gagwriter was something I would explore. But a reasonable foretaste was emblazoned across the sweatshirt of a guy I saw later that day: "The secret to success is sincerity. Once you can fake that, you've got it made."

Henry James called New York the "miscellaneous monster," and eighty years later he was right on the mark. New York chuckles off every adjective you care to sling at it. It defies or confirms, at whim, every cliché connected to it.

You can find anything, but shopping is a military campaign. At a Fifth Avenue electronics store I bought a phone. Pressed for time, I swallowed the friendly salesman's line about the best price in town. When I saw it much cheaper everywhere else, I went back. The salesman was willing to exchange it. The manager laughed at me. We had words. He smirked and reminded me what an imbecile I was. If I was so cheap, I should have shopped around. I asked his name. "Dick," he said. "With a capital *D*." I'll say.

Later, seeking the best price, I went to 47th Street Photo. Its counters were tended by Hasidic men in long spit curls who scowled as though customers were interrupting Talmud class. A cashier shoved back my change, letting me know he knew I was a cheap schlemiel. Then he gave me a form to fill out. It asked if I had found the service cheerful.

Space is tight and bargains are hard to find. Some guy in Brooklyn was selling condos for thirty-seven thousand dollars. But all you got was a BMW-size patch of concrete between white lines. No sink, not even walls. It was a parking condo.

In the miscellaneous monster the news is often bad, thick with acts of stupid, selfish cruelty. But if you're keeping score, there are a lot more good things to say. You never know what you'll find behind a desk or through a door. Ingrid Schroeder, for example, is a handsome blond executive of a metals brokerage firm. During her spare time she saves African rhinos. On a trip to Zimbabwe a few years back she was distressed that the black African rhino was at the edge of extinction in the wild. Worse, hardly anyone was doing anything about it. She quickly organized a foundation and raised enough money to equip Zimbabwean rangers with a communications network.

The Central Park where James loved to spend an evening was

long ago declared off limits because of muggers. A decade ago guys walked around on Sunday afternoons shouting, "Co-caine. Co-caine. Joints in bags." But now strollers face more risk getting run down by power walkers. If still dicey, Central Park is about the liveliest, and among the most charming, little patches of recreational real estate in the world. I've seen nothing close.

Some Dixieland music brought me to the Bethesda Fountain. The On-the-Lam Street Band, with a one-armed tuba player and a noisy drummer, featured Jenny Romaine, who did the Charleston on four-foot stilts. In a top hat and Victorian skirt, she twirled and kicked with vigor. "I'll sing 'Lady of Spain' if we get a human sacrifice," she offered. I left before someone took her up on it.

Nearby I found the skaters. Now here's your good old American greatness, the Sunday afternoon roller skaters in Central Park. They are an ad hoc bunch that assembles to wheel endlessly around on a patch of asphalt. But there is something about their energy and humor, their easygoing color-blind manner. And there are some incredible skaters.

A Bruce Springsteen look-alike cruised by, in khaki shorts, bare chest and crimson baseball cap, enraptured by the sounds from the huge white tape player on his shoulder. A few times around, he led a little black girl, shaky on her skates. Mostly he just whirled and dipped and grinned. A guy in a stovepipe hat and spandex tights circled the asphalt with a stack of flash cards, displaying a different "Be Cool" message each time around.

I mentioned this transformation to my friend Olivia. And she told me how, in broad daylight, kids pulled her off a bike and smashed her jaw to steal her purse.

In New York nothing is ever only one thing or the other. On a last night in town I went back to Lincoln Center. No magic limousine appeared this time; I took the subway at Fiftieth Street. On the crowded platform a black man shouted obscenities at two caterwauling women, friends of his. At the top of their lungs, they discussed their mutual sex lives and alleged infidelities. The man pranced in circles, lunging at the locked gate separating him from the women. The crowd watched, half amused and half scared that shooting would start. "How many niggers you have to fuck for that car?" the man bellowed. At that a well-dressed black stranger started to intervene. Then he thought better of it.

A few moments later I was in the genteel opulence of an auditorium watching the premiere of a New York City Ballet Company festival. With thrilling flair and agility, dancers blended the classic and far-out experimentation. I tend to like my entertainment with car chases. But this was to die.

New York, any visitor has got to conclude, is no Big Apple. It is a fruit basket. You can find anything in it, from rotten to forbidden to the sort of stuff Eve must have fed Adam.

One sturdy outsider's image is that New York is the front row of the First World. Slick engineering, the renewing miracles of technology, keeps it humming. Power blackouts are over in hours and talked about for decades. I was surprised when my friend Bob Stebbings said his neighborhood's phones were out. We'd planned a party and a lot of guests had only his number.

Bob, a lawyer, asked questions. Someone had sliced cables, and crews went home without fixing them. Days passed. Phones worked briefly and died again. Bob remonstrated, along with everyone for blocks around. Hostile lines formed at pay phones.

This was New York, I kept thinking, where nothing vital stays broken past lunch. But Bob and I, pals from Brazil, did what you do in Rio. We waited. In three weeks service was back to normal.

With New York, you never know when to stop. But I had a sign. At the Drake, again, I emerged one morning and saw a long line of waiting cabs. The doorman was Sonny this time, and I said: "Gimme some guy you hate. I'm not going far." He laughed hard at that. It wasn't particularly funny, but he had figured I finally had caught on to the Big Fruit. It was time to move on.

CHAPTER

2

Monopoly on
Boardwalk

New Yorkers especially seemed to enjoy sheltering under the term "out of." It suggests unpremeditated amusement, safe from reproof, as in "I was out of my mind." Most Americans have to settle for Out of Control. But New Yorkers have their own category: Out of the City. On a Thursday in New York I riffled through the *Times* to see where people might go that weekend. Assorted Wagnerfests and dahlia petal jamborees did not seem sufficiently out. Then I saw an ad for Atlantic City.

Most of us learned our first blind greed from the Monopoly board, and all those properties are for real in Atlantic City. I had not been there since 1965, before the gambling. Since I had just come from Monte Carlo, it was a natural. Besides, I could find out more about Donald Trump, whose name was on everyone's lips, including his own.

As it turned out, I hit the jackpot even before getting there. On the phone the reservations lady announced, "Oh, you'll have a tough time finding a room. It's Miss America weekend."

I had thought the Miss America Pageant was abandoned when Bert Parks qualified for Medicare. Occasionally it crept into the news, like the time the judges finally gave the title to a black woman and then took it away when too much of her appeared in *Playboy,* and she displayed un-American lesbionic tendencies. But if it was not a coronation to stop the presses abroad, the pageant could still pack Convention Hall.

The procedure took all week. State queens rolled into town with retinues numbering deep into the hundreds: distant cousins; third-grade teachers; hairdressers; old boyfriends and new hopefuls; a vast backwash of general hangers-on. All were enthusiastic, but my eye caught the contingent from North Carolina. Young men in thin ties waved huge banners lettered LEAPIN' LORI, over a broad-jumping frog with blond hair and a slash of crimson lipstick. It looked like a sketch some Muppet designer had abandoned as too hideous.

Lori Boggs, Miss North Carolina, did not resemble a frog, and I mentioned this to one of the young men. Was she at least French? "Well, see," he explained, "in the parade she wore these frogs on her shoes, so this sort of distinguishes her from all the rest."

The Georgians' ensign was a large peach, predictable but easier to understand. I asked a small knot of peach bearers if they knew the candidate. They did. One of them, Miss Georgia's aunt, explained why it was all over but the shrieking. "Other girls are just as talented," she said, "but there is something about Kelly. The whole state is pulling for her." There was something about Kelly, but forty-nine other delegations had the same thing to say.

Fever was in the air. At Bally's casino I saw a blonde hovering over the roulette wheel, cautiously betting part of a modest salary. In the interest of science, I asked: "Aren't you Miss Iowa?"

She beamed brightly. "Do I look like her?"

Miss Iowa was Korean, I think, but why spoil the fun? She had spotted me for a man of taste. "Dead ringer," I replied, and moved on without cashing in my winnings.

I had arrived just in time for the last night before the pageant and wondered whom I would have to bludgeon to get in. Then it occurred to me to try the box office. A bored clerk, who might have been selling bus tickets to Asbury Park, had a pile of balcony seats. The talent inside was superb, if unexpected. Patricia Brant of Louisiana manipulated a pair of dummies that simultaneously sang "Row, Row, Row Your Boat" and yodeled. I watched Miss New Mexico as a swan and Miss Vermont pound away on drums. Miss California told jokes, and Miss Hawaii did a sexy torch number. A few seats away from me a lady dozed over her binoculars. A *fin d'époque* air hung over the half-empty hall.

But the next night's finale was something else entirely. Television cameras converted Convention Hall from a giant bare hangar with seedy seats and dirty floors into a high tech fairyland where dreams come true. Young men scrubbed red, stiff in rented tuxedos, escorted women dressed as if they expected to be called onstage as alternates. One aging gentleman steered along a walking wedding cake, who teetered precariously on skyscraper heels. Every seat was filled and wired with excitement.

To an opening swirl of flashing legs and color, Gary Collins exulted, "Where else could this pageant take place but in America?" as though other countries' women had hairy underarms and were best seen in public under paper bags.

But Collins was right. Besides the fact that Albania was not likely to select a Miss America, it was a uniquely American experience. Up in the cheap seats, I watched on a giant screen the faces of fifty women who surged down the gangway. It was thrilling. If I had been seventeen and had no mustache, I might have yearned to be up there. The girl in the seat next to me certainly did.

Her name was Rita, and she was ten. She had moved to Virginia from Iran about the time Iranians with money fled the Islamic Revolution. Rita had persuaded her parents to drive her the four hours to Atlantic City because she wanted to know how to be a beauty queen. She was not bothered by any possible exploitation of womanhood; she thought it was neat. As Rita contemplated the elaborately clothed and coiffed contestants, I asked her what she thought. She reflected a minute and replied: "They have to give all that stuff back when it's over, don't they?"

I surveyed the back balcony and tried to read the faces. The Golden Girls in the third row were no problem. Five grandmotherly ladies in leisure suits of washable synthetics beamed during the musical numbers and dabbed their eyes at the emotional stuff. Also, the second-string claques for state delegations were easy to spot. The puzzler was Red Tie.

A man of about sixty, with a wide red tie resting at a forty-five-degree angle over his ample paunch, sat stolidly through the proceedings. His face was fixed in a Churchillian scowl. I could not figure out why he was there.

The pageant wore on, striking every American chord anyone could remember to toss in. When they dragged out the purple mountains' majesty and the fruited plains, eyes moistened all over the hall. Not Red Tie's, however. He remained frozen in his imitation of a pit bull.

After a while the juxtapositions left me exhausted. One minute someone onstage was tugging at my emotions; the next, some phony-looking guy on camera was selling me pizza flour. A big production number thumped on: "The Heart of America." Then the pageant hostess said: "And now a message from this heartbeat of America." It was Chevrolet, with a slogan that was markedly close to the theme. I had the feeling that if Hyundai had come up with the bucks, it could have been at the heart of America.

Finally, the climax neared. In the evening gown showdown, the contestants had their only chance to show the public they could talk. Organizers dropped the interview part as too boring, and the questioning, which accounts for half the points for the crown, was done off camera with the judges.

Each woman squeezed in a few words about her goal in life. Miss Somewhere bubbled, "I'd like to teach the world to sing, in perfect harmony," and a kid behind me announced, "Hey, we sing that in kindergarten." One contestant, named Robin, said: "This Robin's gonna to fly." This Mort's gonna throw up.

My money was on Miss Hawaii, but she looked a little too dark and smoldering for the national mood. It was close enough: Miss Michigan, the winner, was a pneumatic blonde with blue eyes, but her name was Kaye Lani Rafko. Her mom, apparently, was into Hawaii. For talent, she did a fiery Polynesian hip dance, banging the stage with balls on thongs.

It was a real good American choice. She really did work long hours as a nurse for the aged, and she wanted to run her own hospice for AIDS victims. Her colleagues, far from being jealous, traded around shifts so she could get her hair done. She had dreamed all her life of wearing the crown. And she was witty, smart and damned nice-looking. The place went wild. Except for Red Tie, whose expression did not change a bit.

A sponsor, of course, had the last word. With everyone's tear ducts still flowing, and the great American heart beating with the warmth and dignity of the moment, some announcer declared: "Never let them see you sweat."

Crowds swept from Convention Hall in postpageant euphoria. A lucky few went to the grand ball. Most headed for the gambling tables. I had only one thing on my mind: Where was Red Tie? In the crush he had melted away before I could find out who he was, why he was there and how come he was having such a miserable time. Suddenly I spotted him standing alone on the main floor below. He seemed antsy, however, poised to disappear forever.

I summoned all the skills acquired in ten years of French ski lift lines. Elbowing, twisting and charging, I bolted down the escalator, eluded security guards and found my man. Slowly I sidled up to him. "Who's on the button?" I asked, pointing to a pretty face pinned to his lapel.

Red Tie turned his stony features on me for a brief moment. Then, for the first time that night, his face broke into a lovely, warm smile. Without the slightest suspicion about the importuning stranger who had not introduced himself, he started chatting as though we had been pals for life.

"Miss Louisiana," he said, "I've been a friend of her grandfather for thirty-five years. That's why I came over from Pennsylvania. Wouldn't have missed it for the world. And the wife died awhile back, you know. Any excuse to get out. Boy, it was some show."

Boy, was I a jerk. Red Tie, in fact, was a jovial, friendly man, a retired Westinghouse maintenance engineer who made the best of living alone. His name was Horace Warnner. "With two *n*'s in it," he added. "Only a crazy Dutchman would have a name like that. Most people call me Dutch."

Dutch had settled in Beaver, Pennsylvania, near Pittsburgh, and was thrilled to hear I lived in Paris.

"We lived all over the world," he said. "You know, people don't want to hear about it, though. They can't visualize anyplace else. Some of them in Beaver have never been more than thirty miles north, thirty miles south, not even to Pittsburgh. You try to tell them about conditions down there in Central America. They don't want to hear it. I can't believe people are like that."

It was a big theme with Dutch, and he went on. "I've been to four Rio carnivals, but they don't want to know about it." He shook his head in disbelief as if to add "the poor suckers."

The pageant was telecast without a hitch, and viewers had no hint of the noisy sideshow out front. NBC engineers had brought their strike Out of the City. For weeks the NBC employees' union had been picketing 30 Rockefeller Plaza. General Electric had taken over the network, and employees wanted a better deal. In Atlantic City their posters featured a well-fed pig in an elaborate hairdo with the banner MISS GE.

But Samuel Gompers had come and gone in the American labor movement, and strikes were not fazing the faceless corporations. Too many people wanted jobs, and the idea of solidarity with strangers, or taking a step back for a few steps forward, no longer fitted with the American way.

As eager crowds arrived for the pageant, a young engineer tried hard to harangue them. He explained what was going on in American television and why a lot of vital issues were at stake. He evoked the historic fight of organized labor and the rights of the workingman. Most of all, he condemned those who crossed picket lines in New York and now in Atlantic City, effectively torpedoing negotiations. The problem, he shouted, was scabs.

Two teenagers watched for a few moments, wavering between amusement at a grown man making an ass of himself in public and boredom at a message that did not penetrate. "What's scabs?" one asked. The other shrugged, and they went in to watch the show.

A few weeks later the NBC strike collapsed. And then a wider circle of people learned about scabs. Suddenly it was not the people behind the camera on strike but rather, in a different fight, the stars themselves. American Football was paralyzed. Players decided that only a united show of force would better their conditions and increase their cut of the owners' profits. But the owners weren't having any united shows of force.

Money and the chance of brief glory attracted enough reserve players to keep teams on the field. Fans knew the difference. But too many people had lost the imagination to do anything else with their weekends. They were hooked, and methadone football was better than cold turkey. Not many cared about the hardships of players already earning fat salaries; even fewer stopped to reflect on the state of American organized labor. But, especially when guys like Joe Montana, everybody's hero, crossed the line and trampled the strike, "scab" became a household word.

Convention Hall sits on the Boardwalk right next to Trump's Dump, a hotel-casino that blows "gaudy" and "garish" right out of the dictionary. It is officially Trump's Plaza, not to be confused with Trump's Castle, farther out of town, which makes the older Plaza look like a UCLA dormitory.

For all the glitz, the first impact is not visual. It is the overpowering stench of rancid grease. This is slightly unfair to Trump's housekeepers. Most of the Boardwalk, in fact much of modern America, reeks of outdated french fries. But it seems shockingly out of place amid the gold foil tinsel, blinking klieg lights and plastic chandeliers.

Once in the casino, one quickly adjusts to Trump's Grease. The place is packed with people, night and day, and a lot of them are having a real good time blowing away money. Some even win. Regulars pump coins into two and three slot machines at a time, expressionless whether the noisy little boxes feast on their upcoming mortgage payment or spew forth a windfall. The real action is around the roulette wheels or, even more, the craps tables.

"Ah, les craps," Prince Louis de Polignac had mused not long before, in Monaco. For years, he had been chairman of the Société Bains de Mer, which runs the Monte Carlo casino. We were discussing gambling styles. "The Americans are so, uh, demonstrative," he said. "When they win, they go 'Ouuaaou' and 'Youpiii.' Such exuberance. Whereas the European calmly takes what comes and seldom displays his emotions."

Prince Louis said he loved Americans, but he could not avoid the slight sniff that automatically accompanies the phrase *les jeux américains.* The "American games" include craps and blackjack, but the term is redolent of the slot machines that junk up Monte Carlo's Old World decorum. Under the romantic frescoes on the scrolled ceilings, tinny machines spit forth five-franc pieces. Coins run cheap little electric roulette wheels, with an adenoidal Japanese computer voice intoning, "No more bets, please," instead of the traditional *"Rien ne va plus."* To bring back some old elegance, the SBM decided to sacrifice the Café de Paris, banishing to that fine old brasserie *les jeux américains.* Once again, serious gamblers would have to brave the appraising stares of security gentlemen to penetrate the inner sanctums.

But it is a losing battle. The SBM manages to run the casino at a loss and has no choice. Some fancier *salles* may be restricted, but the lucrative machines are staying. And anyone can play, black tie or dirty Levi's.

Trump does not lose money, and he takes his Monopoly seriously. He set out to add Resorts International to his pile, thus giving him control of a third of all casino and hotel space in town. And not without immodesty. From the Plaza one reaches Trump's Parking Lot by a simple covered walkway over Pacific Avenue. It is hardly longer than Venice's Bridge of Sighs and far less remarkable. But it is Trump's. Down below a billboard crows: WHO ELSE WOULD HAVE BUILT A BRIDGE ACROSS THE PACIFIC? Hirohito came to mind.

To glitz up his bridge and parking garage further, Trump designed a waterfall that would be set against open space. The only problem was the space he had in mind was occupied by a restaurant equipment store owned by Harry Stein. The Steins had been in business in Atlantic City for ninety years. A *Newsweek* profile on Trump describes the negotiation session. There is a little browbeating, ending with "The alternative is I preclude you forever. Once I don't buy it, I don't believe the property will have any value. The gravy train is leaving the station." He tells the Steins to call his New York office. "You wait," he observed later on, "they'll come around. They always do."

This sort of deal making was the basis for a boastful ghostwritten autobiography. Reviewer Jonathan Yardley raised a point I was wondering about:

> There's an ample amount of noisy mouthing-off about wheeling and dealing, at which Trump regards himself as an artist, but there is relatively little about the nitty-gritty. On a couple of occasions Trump remarks in passing that construction is a rough business, but he has nothing—repeat nothing—to tell us about how construction gets done in the snake pit of crime and labor that is Manhattan, nor does he have anything revealing to say about the realities of construction and daily dealing in the world of casinos.

If I hadn't known much about Trump when I started my trip, I was hearing about little else. He smirked from every magazine cover. Talk was he would run for President. The *Newsweek* piece carried Trump's view: " 'I'm not running for president,' he says, 'but if I did . . . I'd win. There, I said it. I didn't think I would, but I did.' " He had won something: *Spy* magazine voted him number three on its list of the nation's "most annoying, alarming and appalling people, place and things," right after Ivan Boesky and Ronald Reagan.

Trump, forty-one then, had amassed about three billion dollars. He boasted to the *Newsweek* reporter, "There is no one my age who has accomplished more. . . . Everyone can't be the best." This is best? Let us be fair. Most of us could use three billion dollars and would be pleased with ourselves for having made it. But does that represent unmatched accomplishment? Can he comfort the dying with skillful nursing? Can he make people laugh, or think, or sort out troubled lives? Can he even do a fiery Polynesian hip dance, banging the stage with balls on thongs?

That, in fact, underlies the real difference between gamblers in Europe and America. Most Europeans take it casually because all that is at stake is how much money they'll take home, if any, when they finally tire. Win or lose, their societies will still judge them more on what they have to say, and on who they are, than on what they can spend. By Trump logic, in which money is how you keep score, the right slot machine can start you on your way; success could be just a jerk away.

A lot of the Atlantic City Monopoly board is still owned by other people. The Boardwalk itself remains unbowed, but the ornate old Steel Pier has been scrapped. In its place is an ugly multistory mall which vaguely resembles a ship. A sign downstairs advertises late-night dining in nautically named restaurants. At 9:45 P.M. on a Friday, however, all I found was the ubiquitous grease smell. The mall was nearly deserted and silent but for a dragging Muzak tape of generic big band noises.

At Captain Young's Seafood, a few waiters were wiping up tables. One looked stunned when I ordered something to eat. "You want to eat dinner tonight? But it's almost ten." I asked why they closed so early. "It's very seasonal here, and the season stops at Labor Day," he explained. What time did they close in summer? I asked. "At ten," he replied.

With everything else locked up, I was back at Trump's. At the all-you-can-eat smorgasboard, a gum-cracking cashier took my money across an ink-streaked linoleum counter. I piled a plate with taste-less crab legs, watery shrimp and soggy salad. For quantity, it was a bargain.

By day the Boardwalk teems with people, as always, but it has changed drastically. Saltwater taffy now comes from Philadelphia, packed in boxes with six lines of chemical ingredients listed on the side. I asked one man if his taffy was fresh. Offended, he replied with hauteur: "We get deliveries twice a week."

The hot new industry, after casinos, is T-shirt shoppes. One featured a shirt decorated with molded plastic, it had ribs gaping open around a blood-red wound and a reasonable facsimile of human innards. It read "Organ Donor." This, I complimented the guy behind the counter, was the most disgusting T-shirt I'd ever seen. "I don't know," he said. "I like the one back there with all the holes blasted in it that says, 'Who farted?' "

Away from the beach, the Monopoly properties have few takers. Scruffy homes suggest hard times and a rough life. Off Baltic, I passed a school with a large sign taped by the front door: THE USE OF BASEBALL BATS IS PROHIBITED.

Atlantic Avenue is a depressing strip of urban decay. Faded signs on the few old buildings hint at better days. Most of the new signs read PARKING, with arrows pointing toward the casinos. Great chunks of the old row houses and shops have been demolished, leaving jagged edges on those still remaining. One precarious structure, naked amid nonspecific empty lots, houses a Mexican restaurant. Another displays the shards of a marquee for the Apollo Theater. Just about the time Atlantic Avenue starts looking nice, you are in Ventnor.

One happy exception is Abe's, a fine old seafood joint that still smells like fresh oysters after fifty-three years. I had two lunches in a row there, and good as the food was, the best part was Dolores Bachen, the waitress. She grew up in Atlantic City and then left it. She had returned recently after a long absence. It was hard on her.

"I couldn't believe all the casinos," she said. "My husband and I came back to the old Steel Pier area, and we cried. Down at Atlantic and Texas, that was the old Savoy. We had our wedding dinner there. It was such a nice supper club, with dancing, and all of Atlantic City would go there for a nice evening."

I later saw the corner; it reminded me of West Beirut.

But Dolores had made peace with the casinos. Her son was a pit boss for Trump, rising fast in the organization. She gave me a paper her son, Steve, had written in ninth grade, in 1981. Gambling had gone on since Christ's killers rolled dice for his robe, he noted. There were serious drawbacks, but casinos breathed life into a moribund city. "Therefore," young Steve ended, "the conclusive facts are in favor of casino gambling."

Dolores thought so. "We have to have them, we need something bringing money into this city," she said. "Look down the street, what a shame it all is. Look at how people are living in this town. It was that way before, and without the casinos, it would have been terrible."

I asked if enough money from the casinos was filtering into Atlantic City. Dolores shrugged. "Look, you've got to crawl before you can walk. This will take time." How much time? I pressed. She shrugged again. "It will come. But I don't know if it will be in my lifetime."

That was the looming question in Atlantic City. In a larger sense, it was a basic question in modern America. What were the casinos— or big businesses in general—putting back into societies around them? The figures are one thing. In 1987 casinos reported $2.8 billion in gaming revenues, and they gave back a lot in taxes. Not counting spin-off employment, the casinos hired forty thousand people. They attracted thirty million visitors. But I had learned long ago to distrust numbers. I tried to get a feel for Atlantic City contrasts.

At midnight on a Saturday, I started at the upmarket end. All over town I had seen vans from Harrah's emblazoned with the slogan "We're Going to a Better Atlantic City." I followed one. Harrah's was more subdued than the nearby Trump's Tower; it was merely gaudy and garish. Both sit out on the bay, slightly removed from town, in a little cocoon of opulent prosperity. If some patrons were poorly dressed, taste, not poverty, was to blame. Many glittered with diamonds, and a few cruised the floor in twenty-five-thousand-dollar gowns. In either casino one feels like a fir needle on an overdecorated Christmas tree.

Out of the City people, past the point of numbness, seemed hardly to notice the money they spend. At Trump's I was amused to find the Four Freshmen, who were freshmen when I was. But even as Four Perpetual Graduate Students, their harmony worked, and they were a good act. In the lounge I saw a mature New York woman slug her husband's upper arm to get his attention. "You wanna watch them? They go on in five minutes." He mumbled something and, bleary and bloodshot, lurched off to the tables.

Casino anterooms were thick with twenty-four-hour tellers, human and electronic, for people who forgot to bring enough money. Sordid little pawnshops on Pacific Avenue advertised "Cash for gold," usually not much of the former for the latter.

The next morning I looked at the other extreme. It was easy enough; I walked a few blocks around my rented condo, an islet of luxury on the north side. Atlantic City's North End is a mini-South Bronx. Houses are wrecked and empty, in separated clusters on vast weed-grown empty lots. Some rows of homes were so forgotten that the city did not even cut away the curbs to allow access to them. If apartheid was gone in America, here was a ghetto that lingered on.

Of the twenty-six people I counted in and around the Thriftway, one was white, a Jewish matron trying with little success to collect money for the hospital's heart wing.

Farther on, downtown, an amiable cluster of bums stopped me for a handout along Pacific Avenue. All were white, and their patter was the usual: Jobs were scarce and everyone had to eat. But I sensed a particular note of despair. I asked one if the casinos didn't provide the opportunity for work. He glanced at his ragged friends and turned back to me. For an answer he made a sound as if he were clearing something large from his throat.

Walking back to the condo, I couldn't get those haunting Kris Kristofferson lyrics out of my head: "Ain't nothing quite like dying, Sunday morning coming down." I walked past the ruins of an old-style farmers' market and what must have been decent housing in a more hopeful time. A few sullen residents glanced at me suspiciously. In the distance Trump's and Harrah's glittered. And I saw yet another van headed toward a Better Atlantic City.

Casinos tended to hire educated young whites, and a lot of them lived and shopped down the coast. That sort of thing was hard to measure. Even harder was to tell how much money ended up with the New Jersey mobs. *New York Times* reporters regularly traced Mafia families to Atlantic City. State officials took firm action. But this mob business, I could see, was an accepted part of American life, a sort of training aid for young prosecutors on their way into private practice. You fought it for form, but then, hey, what the hell. It was easier not to see.

I talked about this with two dinner companions, a hardheaded and softhearted entrepreneur and a softheaded, hardhearted lawyer. The businessman, worth scores of millions, had started with nothing. "No one threatened me or forced me to do anything," he began. I asked if he had ever tried to sell hot dogs in New Jersey. He laughed and shrugged.

The lawyer shot me a pitying glance. Didn't I know some things were the way they were? How could you challenge organized crime? When a guy with a small salary is asked for a favor in exchange for lots of money, nine times out of ten, he will do it. If not, he may get hurt. I asked if citizens couldn't apply pressure, vote some funds, and demand results. The lawyer smiled a little. People's little victories against the system succeeded in making them feel good for only a while, he explained. Meanwhile, things usually got worse because even bigger crooks took the place of those brought down.

"That's the most depressing thing I've ever heard," I remarked.

"I know," he said, now grinning broadly. "I hate it."

Before leaving Atlantic City, I found some more people who were not following the Harrah's vans. Four streets in from the Board-walk, my eye caught a huge weathered sign reading TIMBUKTU, flanked by the words "Food and Drink." It must have been a sort of urban general store, but I did not get the chance to find out. The place cried out to be photographed, so I circled and parked on a side street. Something told me to leave the door open and the key handy.

I had on a battered leather jacket and dirty white sneakers; no one would mistake me for Donald Trump. Trying hard to look in-conspicuous, I rounded the corner and melted against a wall. Care-fully I slipped out a small camera and composed a long shot, across the street, at the storefront. Suddenly a voice froze the air: "Who's that mothahfuckah taking pictures?"

The tone scared the crap out of me. I'd been through hostile black neighborhoods all over Africa and in Jamaica. People had pushed me around and threatened me. But I had never heard such a harrowing blend of anger, suspicion and raw menace.

Within seconds the street had erupted. From a desultory Sunday afternoon torpor the atmosphere warmed to boiling. Heads shot out of doors. I saw a flurry of fists and the glint of steel and bodies headed toward me.

This was one for the sociologists. Was this about race relations in America? Was I the honky trying to exploit the brothers? Were some ant-size figures in my picture frame breaking a law? Or was it a hostile reaction to the widening gulf that separated blacks from the golden coast a few blocks away? I'd like to report that the consum-mate journalist stuck around to pose those questions. But that is not what happened.

Slow and cool, I sauntered back to the corner as though I hadn't noticed the turmoil. Out of sight I ran like a son of a bitch to the car, threw it into gear and laid thirty feet of rubber down the Mo-nopoly board.

*

For a contrast, I headed Out of the City for the Amish country in Pennsylvania. The film *Witness* had reminded me of the sober little communities I'd admired since a brief visit in 1965. Who but the Amish could circulate from Bird-in-Hand to Intercourse to Blue Ball without cracking a smile?

I had planned to start in Lancaster, the county seat, where farmers had gathered a few days earlier for an uncharacteristic protest against authorities. It was about a road, and I wanted to learn more. For the rest of Sunday afternoon I would make a quick swing through the old towns and farms. I was dreaming.

Highway 30, the old Philadelphia Pike that bisects Amish country, runs at the pace of chilled blackstrap molasses. Time had not changed the simple, handsome farms deep into the countryside. But the Amish towns were fast losing their character. Intercourse was always a wholesome little place that shrugged off outsiders who came to smirk at its name. But the prurient triumphed in the end; Intercourse has been screwed.

It was not the Amish. They had managed to keep their societies together, for all the lure of the fast lane alongside them. They shunned electricity and cars, but bent enough to accept diesel fuel and batteries. Their kids sneaked out to the barn for some transistorized transgression. But by and large, they kept the faith. The problem was the speculators. And all of us rubberneckers.

On a back road Mike Fisher explained it with no bitterness and only a touch of rue. He was my age, in full Amish gear: a Quaker oats hat, black wool pants and suspenders, simple white shirt, sturdy boots, a full beard and a look of earnest concern. He was sitting in a heavy front loader, working the controls with one hand and cradling his young daughter with the other.

"A lot of people are moving in," he said. "The old families with enough land to farm hand down their property from generation to generation. But a young man starting out can't really make it. Real estate prices are getting far too high."

There was no Amish reservation. Like-minded people had simply settled around Lancaster, and south into Maryland, as America moved west. They bought up farmland and populated little crossroads towns. Not many outsiders sought to move in, either for respect of others' ways or because it was damned hard to find a drink. That is changing. Property goes to the highest bidder, and Amish farmers are not noted for hardball leveraged buy-outs.

Mike's place was probably a century old. A comfortable no-nonsense house sat by a perfectly kept farmyard, with a solid barn put up with the neighbors' help. The shed doubled as a two-buggy garage. Everything was weathered wood and fieldstone, redolent of horses, hay and hard, clean living. But across the narrow road a developer had put up two houses fit for Syosset, Long Island. At night they blazed with electric lights; by day fat station wagons came and went among the horse-drawn buggies.

It is an aesthetic and spiritual problem but an economic calamity. As farmland dwindles, the Amish need other ways to survive. That means yet another shoppe or foodstall for the tourists. With people eager to sell them something quaint, Out of the City crowds pour in by the busload. The saturation point is near—or was passed sometime back.

"People just stop and gawk," Mike said. "My dad lives on a farm south of the highway. Three or four tour buses at a time park there. People stare and point. We just figure it is a fact of life."

The Best Western Intercourse Motel books up fast. Kids line up for Abe's Buggy Rides. The few old feed stores and churches are lost among an undergrowth of plastic and neon signs. By an inevitable equation, the more people come to look, the less there is for them to see. In fact, beyond the occasional person in Amish dress—either dazed by the turmoil or playing at it like a trouper—I couldn't figure out what people had come to see.

At the Blue Ball Farmers' Market, in search of fruit, I stumbled onto a Fellini set. A few forlorn stalls offered farm produce packaged in plastic, Safeway style. Almost everyone else sold sugary, greasy Amish junk food. I squeezed sideways among people in grotesque attitudes of feeding. An enormous man in plaid pushed soft ice cream into his mouth. Fat little kids wolfed down Polish sausages and sticky candies. One stall regretted, "Sorry, we're out of fritters," but huge stacks were available farther along. Outside, a trail of trash and goo led from the exit door to the line of tour buses.

Benign neglect once left the Amish to live their old way in peace. Now they are caught in the middle. "The law says that buggies have to pull over for motor traffic," Mike explained. "But they don't maintain the shoulders. People pull off the road and block our way. We have a choice of going into the ditch or stopping until they finish their pictures. Horses can get real impatient."

I learned about the road. State engineers planned a four-lane thoroughfare to relieve Highway 30. But most Amish did not want it. It would cut a swath through their lands, dividing the tight-knit society into two. And it would eat up even more precious farmland.

Mike, among others, was not worried. The state legislature was Democrat, and Lancaster County was Republican. The money would go elsewhere, as it did with the Goat Patch. He meant Highway 23. A freeway-size roadbed had been graded, but then it was abandoned. Now goats graze on it.

But something had to be done to get traffic around the farm country, Mike concluded. Highway 30 was a black ugly line, like the vein that runs down the back of a shrimp. And you could not avoid it.

Saying good-bye, I asked Mike if I could photograph him with his daughter. He looked pained, caught between courtesy and disapproval of yet one more jerk with a camera. "You can take it from across the road, but I won't pose for you," he said. I apologized for even suggesting it. And I wished I were dead.

I made one more stop in Pennsylvania. A sign pointed to York, and I turned off. For some reason, the name stuck in my mind. It was obviously not for the beauty of downtown York. I could see the little city was once a charming example of early Americana, with white steeples and handsome row houses made by carpenters and masons who loved their work. But block after block was decayed beyond the point of repair. Successive generations had decided that old means Sundays spent on sanding shingles—and no space for a TV den. After a while the "undesirables" moved in, and wealthier families evacuated to tract houses in the suburbs.

Incentives might have helped. But as areas deteriorated and houses emptied, authorities raised taxes to compensate for the loss. I met a man named Jim who had sold his downtown house for forty-five thousand dollars and had paid eighty-five thousand dollars for one in the outskirts. His property taxes remained the same.

The two-hundred-year-old town center was a hodgepodge of restored buildings lost among plastic and glass. Old squares had been razed to clear ground for office buildings in nondescript modern. At the Capitol Theater Bogart was back on the marquee. But in its setting the old movie house was no treasured relic of gracefully advancing time; it was just another seedy building awaiting the wrecker's ball. For me, a wayward citizen coming home to check out the national heritage, the effect was like a punch in the stomach. Not to pick on York; with a few happy exceptions, I found the same thing over and over.

We Americans never learned from Europe that preservation means protecting the atmosphere, not just separate elements. It is a complex process of blending new with old. The trees, paving stones, signposts, proportions of space and weathered patina are as vital as each building. Standard federal and state codes for street corners and setbacks and lighting are a threat. Laws and review boards are of limited value. With free enterprise, only combined voluntary efforts, at the extra cost of using real wood and brick, can save a living environment.

The Île St.-Louis in Paris, a little island in the Seine, fits the full range of a high tech society onto its narrow streets. Traffic flows; construction crews are at work constantly. And the island looks the way it did in 1630, when the last few buildings went up. One reason is strict ordinances. But mostly it is because people like Madame Turpin, the fruit and vegetable lady, refuse to use pocket calculators, let alone neon lights. They attach a value to quality and tradition.

Parisians can afford it. What happens when prosperity goes, when factories close and people are squeezed too tightly for such luxuries as external aesthetics? The answer is in Prague, a depressed capital run by godless, tasteless Commies. It is the best preserved, and perhaps the most beautiful, capital in Europe.

Driving out of York, I racked my brain for what it was that had made me stop. Then I saw it. Painted across a factory off the road were the words "Harley-Davidson." If a little scrawny for the Hell's Angels, I had grown up a closet motorcycle bum. York was where Harley Hogs were made.

The plant was closed, but I heard a thundering chorus of seventy-four-inch engines. The local motorcycle gang had gathered for beer and barbecue before heading out on a Sunday afternoon adventure. What the hell, I figured, Hunter Thompson got himself beaten senseless for *his* book; I waded right in.

The first guy I found wore a black leather jacket that did not quite cover a middle-age spread. He was a schoolteacher. The club was not off to rape and plunder outlying villages, he explained. They were on a poker run to raise money for muscular dystrophy. Jesus, what was America coming to? A poker run, he explained, is a rally where a rider stops at five bars. At each one, he picks up a card— and anything else he cares to—with clues to find the next. Or something like that.

At the Harley-Davidson Museum an old biker named Ed Gumper led a tour among motorcycles going back to stone wheels. He showed off the first knucklehead engine blocks and teardrop tanks. There was a streamlined little blue job that did 136.183 miles an hour at Daytona Beach in 1936. There was also a 1958 Duoglide, Elvis Presley's favorite bike, still the pride of the Harleys. It was green. "Green is an unlucky color," Ed explained. "You come around a bend in a bunch of trees, and oncoming motorists don't see you and crash right into you. Unlucky."

Later, I learned, Harley was an outpost in the deficit wars, and Reagan himself had flown in for a combat photo. Harley had been making fifteen thousand bikes a year in the mid-1960's but needed cash to grow. In 1969 it got conglomerated. The American Machine & Foundry Company bought Harley and pushed production to thirty-seven thousand a year. But no one would touch the suckers. AMF insisted on putting its own initials on Harley fuel tanks. What self-respecting wild person would terrorize a town behind the name of a bowling pinsetter? Vaughn L. Beals, Jr., joined the company and, unable to get AMF funding to improve quality, took it private in 1981.

But by then Honda, Suzuki, Kawasaki and Yamaha were dumping heavy bikes on the American market. Beals got federal authorities to impose a 49 percent tariff, to be reduced over five years. Thus protected, the company thrived. In the fourth year Beals asked Washington to drop the shield early. Harley's big "1," in red, white and blue stars and bars, was all the protection he needed. Reagan loved it.

The rest of the story is that Harley may have crippled motorcycling in the United States. High tariffs put smaller Japanese bikes beyond the range of a lot of potential new riders. Since hardly anyone starts out on a Harley Hog, fewer bikers are in the market. As it is, the society is getting older and paunchier, more prone to four wheels and cruise control. Paul Dean, editor of *Cycle World,* made that point to *The New York Times.* "In many ways," he said, "Harley shot itself in the foot."

As I drove back to New Jersey, a new subject imposed itself. It came in through the window somewhere near Elizabeth, an ungodly chemical stench. I thought about waste, the whole range from toxic to solid to human to simply generic noxious. Back in 1965, when I worked in Newark, I often wondered what would happen when we suddenly woke up treading filth. It seemed we were about to find out.

During 1987 the world watched in disbelief as a forlorn Long

Island garbage scow cruised six thousand miles, over three months, looking for a place to dump 3,186 tons of garbage. Television commentators in uncounted languages lingered on the irony: Americans were finally up to their ears in their own mess, and now they were looking around for other people's backyards. Finally, Brooklyn agreed to burn it. But what next? Within five years, experts said, a third of U.S. municipalities would run out of landfill space. By the turn of the century the country would have nowhere to take out the garbage.

By 1988 America was spending fifteen billion dollars a year to haul its waste, and that brought an additional problem. Garbage attracted the cockroach element. Prosecutors across the country were investigating mob connections, bid rigging, price-fixing and illegalities of every manner.

Corporate garbagemen took their lumps. At Waste Management, Inc.'s 1987 annual meeting in Oak Brook, Illinois, the chairman's recitation of his company's glories was interrupted by a strident voice. From a tape recorder in a locked briefcase, which Greenpeace had chained to a seat in the audience, the voice listed Waste Management's legal and environmental problems.

The volume was a big enough problem. Industry figures suggested it would cost someone one hundred billion dollars to dispose safely of all the toxic chemical waste lurking around American factories, not to speak of possible radioactive slag heaps and other mysteries too fearsome to think about.

The crisis was stuck at the NIMBY (not in my backyard) stage. New Jersey officials howled at the New York filth that washed up regularly on beaches from Sandy Hook to Cape May. New York authorities said if anything got away to New Jersey, it was accidental. Pennsylvania and New Jersey battled over Philadelphia ash, which someone then wanted to dump in Houston.

A single big incinerator could have burned that Long Island scow's whole cargo in a day. But apart from the $250 million initial cost and the huge power bills, incinerators produce toxic ash and pollution that are as bad as the garbage. That leaves dumping it in somebody's water.

To an outsider, this all seemed to be something worth worrying about. Not everyone agreed. An activist pushing for recycling told *The New York Times* of a San Bernardino, California, woman who remarked: "Why do we need to change anything? I put my garbage out on the sidewalk and they take it away."

But garbage slicks, not noted for respecting borders, poisoned more of the environment each week. Scientists found our errant trash as far south as Antarctica.

I moved on to New England but kept a watch on the garbage. In the summer of 1988 so much medical waste washed up on Long Island beaches that some had to be roped off. Debris included vials of blood tainted with AIDS. The beaches had hardly reopened when an electrical failure backed up New York's master sewer. The beaches of Staten Island and Brooklyn were closed, polluted with human waste. New York, incidentally, produces 1.7 billion gallons of sewage a day.

"I do believe this period of the 1980's will be remembered as the time the planet struck back," observed Stephen Joseph, the New York City health commissioner. Unless, of course, the planet is merely clearing its throat for what it is really about to tell us.

CHAPTER

═══ 3 ═══

Stockbridge to Boston

We expatriates can be a sorry lot, for all the advantages of our voluntary status as innocents permanently abroad. The worst is that few of our countrymen back home can spell the word and therefore misconstrue its meaning. For them, it is expatriot. For leaving America, we didn't love it. Or we are floating in a stateless void, Americans no longer and not quite Europeans of any type. We are, as my cousin Steve terms us, Europinos. *Merde.*

Watch the eyes of any blue passport holder whenever "The Star-Spangled Banner" is sung on foreign soil. Lids flutter by the time the singer struggles to the top of "so proudly we hailed." Moisture collects at the rockets' red glare. By the time it gets to the part where the flag is still there, teardrops are starting to roll. This applies to every American overseas, even lawyers. Hell, some of us even get soppy at the theme to *Hill Street Blues.* But you've got to be a Europino to know that.

That thought hung heavily as I looked around critically. Americans bridle at criticism and mistrust things foreign, expatriate friends warned me. When reflecting unpleasant evidence from somewhere else, you are a balanced reporter. Back home, you are committing treason.

Bob Braverman, a Duke University professor and frequent European traveler, had made a study of this particular subject. "Americans fear and distrust foreigners," he said, "and you live among the enemy." A friend named Kathleen was a victim. She chanced upon a French pal at Kennedy Airport, and she called out, *"Bonjour."* And a passing stranger, a woman her age, whirled around and said: "Bone joor, yourself, ya little bitch."

The signs were ominous. I once wrote an article for a Colorado weekly about why France had refused overflight to American planes en route to bomb Libya. It was simple reporting, with no personal opinion; I merely noted the French had their own reading of things. A friend on the paper told me: "Gee, Mort, everyone is going to think you're a traitor." She was obviously one of them. I asked why. "You live there and speak their language; you're on their side."

That bothered me for days. Were Americans losing the ability to see themselves objectively, to understand that others had their own legitimate viewpoints? Foreign correspondents in Washington gained stature back home by spending time penetrating America. Their readers, even those who felt they lived in superior societies, knew they were part of a larger world. They knew prosperity and security depended on other nations. If only for self-interest, they were curious about how others perceived them, and why. American sensibilities, however, seemed to taper off sharply at the borders.

I decided to test this in New England, especially in that Boston suburb which Britons see as the other Cambridge. It was obvious enough that the ports, mill towns and farms of Massachusetts were the early cornerstones of America. But I had other motives. Like all expatriates removed from the constant wash of the new, I clung to faded bits of the old for comfort. My little kernel of tapes includes "Alice's Restaurant" and vintage James Taylor. On autobahns, autoroutes and autostradas, I was awash in nostalgia for a stretch of road I knew nothing about: the turnpike from Stockbridge to Boston.

Heading north, I turned off the Connecticut Turnpike toward Stockbridge onto Route 7. "Turned" is not quite the verb; "wallowed" is better. Hertz had rented me a cocktail lounge on wheels. On a straight, wide road, I stomped the pedal to the floor, and the lumbering mass of natural resource picked up momentum. The needle inched up to seventy-five miles an hour, a speed at which West German police stop you to ask why you are holding up traffic. I remembered Americans frown on fast driving and slowed to sixty-five. It was not enough. The red light I passed was following me.

I pulled over. In my youth the smart thing was to walk back to the cop for a polite chat, saving him the trouble of getting out of his car. I started to bound out the door. A booming voice echoed from the birch tops: "Stay in your seat!" Great hokum, I thought, God is working for the Connecticut State Police.

The man had a loudspeaker on his car roof. I sat still, paralyzed from the shock. After four minutes of messing with his computer, he sauntered forward. No amount of *CHiPS* reruns seen on African hotel videotapes had prepared me for that moment. He was an ambulant hardware store. The full circumference of his belt was obscured by canisters, sticks, whistles, leather sheaths and a pistol the size of a small mortar. He had perfected a hip roll, banging together his weapons in a catchy cadence.

"Roll down your window," he ordered. That is not so easy in America. I had to start the engine to do it. Surely he would shoot me for attempting to escape. I handed him my pink French driver's license.

"What's this?"

"A driver's license," I replied, adding a slight accent to each second syllable. I was ready to burst into "Sank 'eaven for leetle gulls" if it would have helped.

"You know," he said with blatant glee, "if I write you up on this, I would have to put you in cuffs and take you down to the station, and you would have to post bond."

France, he explained, was out of state. He looked hard at me for several long moments and slowly reached back for the cuffs. Or his pistol. He was having much more fun than I was. Then he added: "But I guess we don't want that."

No, no, I agreed. We don't.

"I'm just trying to be a nice guy," he said.

For a horrible second I felt my hand reaching into my pocket to seize some stray bills. I caught it in time. The cop flicked on some hidden power source to light a blinding Have-a-Nice-Day smile. Then he walked away.

In Stockbridge a few people remembered the scene of the Alice's Restaurant crime, where Arlo Guthrie dumped the Thanksgiving garbage and provoked his tangle with Officer Obey. But times had changed. Once again, the local hero was Norman Rockwell. The master illustrator had lived and died in Stockbridge, and a little museum displays his most famous works.

Far more than I had realized, Rockwell had captured the changing moods of an America long past. He enshrined the ingredients of a holiday table, the millhand waxing his Studebaker, the shopkeeper boring his customers to paralysis. When he depicted a little town, it was all there: grandmothers' fresh bread, kids' slingshots, barber poles, prom corsages and a smartly snapping flag.

He caught the triumph and anguish of a little black girl going to school behind the bayonets of the National Guard. With his *Family Tree*, he gently mocked poseurs who flaunt pedigree that might not stand up to scrutiny. There is a touch of the tarbrush in all of us, he reminds, and cold winter nights narrowed the gap twixt *Mayflower* and native American. And, Rockwell makes clear, it is all to our credit.

One classic work depicts the old farmers' crossroads town in early winter, alight for Christmas. Wood-frame shingled homes are lined up next to shops with familiar surnames stenciled across the windows. But few of the families of the illustrator's favorite models can afford the place anymore. Rockwell's Stockbridge is now an Out of the City mecca where rich people come to hear good music and potter around in their fenced-in bits of country.

On weekends, traffic chokes the town. Shops feature self-conscious displays of country wares meant for people not likely to stay around past Sunday night. Before leaving Stockbridge, I plunged into my theme. On the veranda of the Red Lion Hotel, I talked to a friendly young couple. A political science teacher and a painter, they were from Cambridge. We covered the world in general, and I steered the conversation to culture shock. I tried to explain how it felt to come home from a strange culture to find a strange culture.

Making the point with feeble irony, I nodded toward the tide of people surging by, a rich blend of ruddy-cheeked blondes in satin jogging shorts and overfed fathers in plaid polyester. "There are so many *Americans* here," I said. It was supposed to be a joke.

The woman's response was quick, frosty as a Dairy Queen special: "Fortunately *you're* here to balance it out."

In a very short time it was clear that Braverman was right. For good measure, this was driven home later in France, when I was finishing up this book. At a dinner party the host asked why I chose to base myself in Paris. For a correspondent, I replied, Paris is a world hub.

It attracts exiled leaders, political movements, terrorist groups, international agencies, peace talks, business moguls and assorted other newsmakers. It is handy to Europe, Africa and the Middle East. I could have made a similar case for London. An American asked the obvious: "What about New York?" Whatever its power and excitement, I said, New York was too politically insular. Like other Americans who covered foreign news, I found it out of touch with the world.

My host's mother, an alert woman of eighty who was visiting from Los Angeles, took all this in. When I mentioned Paris had terrorists and New York did not, she murmured, "Thank God." For her, this balance sheet of a reporter's needs was a showdown between America and the Rest of the World. When I finished, she flashed uncharacteristic hostility and observed: "You've been in Paris too long."

Our thin skin, apparently, is nothing new. James Fenimore Cooper died bitter and exhausted from the fury he stirred with a hard inside outside look in 1835 after coming home from long absence abroad. H. L. Mencken wrote: "He began, ironically enough, as an apologist for [his countrymen], and while he was abroad as tourist and consul he wrote a great deal of soothing stuff on the subject. But when he returned home . . . he was led to reexamine the evidence, and the fruits of that reexamination, being bitter in taste, got him magnificently disliked."

On the subject of irony, Mencken himself went down pretty well. He was taken as a lovably colorful old curmudgeon by the people he described as that "glorious commonwealth of morons." Mencken was no traitor; he stayed home. No one seemed to mind that he did so, he wrote, because only in the United States could he feel so superior.

History suggests some explanation for touchiness. The United States had barely emerged from its first war with Britain when it got into a second one. And it was touch and go whether the war would instead be against France, America's first ally. When Cooper wrote, the Constitution was not yet fifty years old, and the country was gearing up for war against itself. For the rest of the century Americans glanced nervously over their shoulders to see what their friends were up to.

In Mencken's time the United States helped allies win World War I. But the Americans got in late and only reluctantly. They suffered no damage at home, while much of Europe was bled nearly to death. American businessmen profited during the war and, with the world in shambles, dominated international commerce. Entrepreneurs built railroads, steel mills and financial networks at home but inspired no universal admiration; they had not been called robber barons for nothing.

Mencken, pushing it perhaps a trifle, wrote of American foreign policy: "Its habitual manner of dealing with other nations, where friend or foe, is hypocritical, disingenuous, knavish, and dishonorable, and from this judgment I consent to no exceptions whatever, either recent or long past." The American people, he added, "constitute the most timorous, sniveling, poltroonish, ignominious mob of serfs and goose-steppers ever gathered under one flag in Christendom since the end of the Middle Ages, and [they] grow more timorous, more sniveling, more poltroonish, more ignominious every day."

That was 1922, and we probably got better with age.

America came out of World War II well enough. Hitler did not think enough of the distant nation to worry about it, and as he expected, isolationists hung back. But after Japan took the decision for us, we built ourselves into a world power at lightning speed. Frenchmen still weep at the American cemetery on Omaha Beach. We built the bomb and, right or wrong, had the courage to drop it.

The bold and hugely expensive Marshall Plan rebuilt Europe. American leaders displayed energy and innovation in a world emerging from shellshock. A brave young President faced off the Russians over Cuba and committed America to rolling back the Communists in Southeast Asia. And that's where most of us came in.

A popular analysis among us aging baby boomers is that America began to slip during the Vietnam War, which, by coincidence, was when we started watching. The stage was set for disaster when a clandestine assault on Cuba ended up in shambles on the beach. We lost our young President under circumstances as humbling as they were tragic. And then the Communists did not roll back in South Asia. Still smarting from losing a war we did not have to fight, we had to watch in impotent rage while loony ragheads held our embassy hostage. Elsewhere, foreigners who ought to owe us gratitude were snickering at us.

But according to the analysis, Ronald Reagan and a conservative shift turned the tide. We conquered a foreign state, even if it was only a Caribbean flyspeck which citizens confused with a city in Spain. People could say, "America is back."

We reporters love these facile sweeps through history and handy anecdotes; like Bible extracts, they can support almost any thesis. Seen from the outside, however, America was not back; it had not gone anywhere. Older societies see history in centuries; any setback is merely a blip in the continuum. We tend toward a shorter memory, and we lurch from incident to incident.

I left the United States before its reported decline and never felt it necessary to apologize for being an American. Most foreigners see us for what we are, 250 million individuals, with all the strengths and failings of human beings elsewhere. A lot of them love America. And hardly any believe we are a superspecies deserving of a league of our own.

The Mass Pike leaves a lot of time for musing. I remembered a quote, somewhere, by the Mexican novelist Carlos Fuentes: "What Americans do best is understand themselves. What they do worst is understand others." That was a key. Damned near every problem we get into is because we do not try to look at things through other people's eyes. I made a note to explore how this affected matters of state. But on an individual level, it was evident.

American travelers, who will discuss their wives' ovaries with anyone they happen to pass in an airplane aisle, rankle at foreigners who are rude or cold. The French, especially, are not effusive to strangers. But neither are the British or most other Europeans. Or Asians, for that matter. The difference is cultural and, most likely, historical.

European societies long ago worked out the nuances of tight living space over centuries; Asians have been at it even longer. People live and work in buildings that were old before Paul Revere learned to ride. Class is no mere synonym for cool; it can determine at birth who will make it and who will not. Intense conversations are conducted with eyebrows, shoulders and corners of the mouth. Tradition, culture and history weigh heavily on every aspect of life.

A European or an Asian is likely to greet a stranger with neutrality. No capital is offered or asked. Small judgments are made, and warmth or coolness is dispensed accordingly. A professional relationship may remain stiffly formal for decades. Or a friendship may grow quickly. But once human contact has been established, it is likely to be sincere and solid.

Americans, unencumbered by such baggage of form, do it the other way around. They leap upon strangers like St. Bernard puppies, all feet and enthusiasm. They begin with first names and arms around shoulders. Homes are thrown open immediately. But with all the capital up front, it risks being eaten away in a rapid and mysterious manner. To get beyond the initial encounter and build true friendship can take more work than the Old World way.

The American approach is more fun. "Have-a-Nice-Day" trips too easily off the tongue, but most people who say it would just as soon see you enjoy yourself. That is pleasant for one coming from France, where the typical stranger could not care less if your day included a shower in boiling oil.

It reflects the open American spirit, which lies beneath the energy, creativity and love of risk that built our nation. But it also accounts for the angst that torments us. Individually and collectively we need reassurance. We want to be liked. With shallow roots in history, with no established social order, each passing world event must be a reaffirmation. If not, it is a defeat.

Abroad, these feelings are exaggerated. Some Americans, tossed about in strange seas, cling to any countryman who drifts by. Others, aghast at being seen as innocents abroad, shove them away with boat hooks. Europinos tread water in the middle. In Nairobi a stranger in funny shorts accosted me as I checked out of the Mount Kenya Safari Club. "Hey!" he greeted me. "How much did it cost you?" I said it was a group rate. "But how much?" he persisted. Then he began firing questions, at ease that he was not importuning. We both were Americans among savages.

Two days later we were on the same plane. "Hey!" he said, across thirty seats full of non-Americans. It was as if he had found his old college roommate. I resolved not to be rude, but I had work to do and said so. A week later I flew into a tiny camp in the swamps of Botswana. There were three other guests, and he was one of them. In fact, he was a nice guy, with a lot to say. He just had a highly developed idea of affinity group.

The turnpike from Stockbridge to Boston is one of those long, wide runways, so handy when you're in a rush and so boring when you're not. I was neither, so it didn't matter; I was only following James

Taylor. The Berkshires were not dreamlike on account of the frosting. It was still fall. But they were beautiful, and suddenly I wanted to get in among some trees. That was when I discovered that on big American roads they chain up the trees.

It got to be ritual. I would pull into a Rest Area, park on the Pavement, walk on the Concrete Sidewalks and then come to the Chain. Or the Cable. Or the Curved Metal Barrier. I could never determine the purpose. The obstacles are never too high for a small human or a large animal to leap without effort. But they are always built with that expensive-looking American solidity. They cannot seriously be intended to keep a deciduous cohort from assaulting motorists (POPLAR PUMMELS PONTIAC: TRAIL OF LEAVES BETRAYS SUSPECT). Is it simple anal compulsion? I'm sorry, fellow Americans, but *that* is weird.

I made a brief diversion out of Stockbridge. An ad in the local paper invited, "Try the Nude Experience," so I did. Nude beaches were common in Europe, but Americans seemed more ambivalent about taking off their clothes in front of strangers. I wanted to see what went on at Birch Acres, "The Natural Choice."

The ad promised a swimming pool, a sauna, a restaurant lounge and camping facilities on "119 scenic mountain acres for sunbathing." It was all there as promised, but the ad had made no reference to the condition of facilities. A rough snack bar dispensed basics to a light crowd of leathery people. At the rudimentary pool I found nothing to report. Had I been looking for volleyball players to pose for those sunbathing magazines we secreted away as kids, I would have left unfulfilled.

But ogling was not the point, I was assured. A leaflet advised, "The primary role of Birch Acres is to provide a wholesome atmosphere in which people may practice social nudism." It listed a few prohibitions: weapons, disturbing the tranquillity, photography, walking uninvited through campgrounds, smoking in the clubhouse nonsmoking section, pets, glass containers, predicting rain, littering and sex.

Just before I left, having broken none of the rules, I spoke to a guy sitting alone on the rusty set of swings. This was freedom, he explained, the return to the natural condition. He waxed convincingly on the honesty of naturism. It is, above all, the abandoning of conventions and taboos, without fear or shame. The man said he was from Albany. Wasn't there any place closer? I asked. "Well, yes," he said. "But I prefer coming here. Nobody knows me."

I rolled happily into Boston. Just before I moved overseas in 1967, my sister led me on a weeklong pig-out: steamers and lobsters, thick soups and great chunks of roast beef hanging over the side of the plate. Ever since, the name Boston had me salivating like a conditioned laboratory hound. Despite a worrisome trend toward tofu, Boston was still a great eating town.

Besides shellfish, Boston was full of universities. I went to see Gary Marx, professor of sociology at the Massachusetts Institute of Technology, whose work I had always admired. Not that I read a lot of sociology; he is married to my cousin Phyllis.

Gary was studying fraudulent identities. With the sudden omniscience of computers, some people found they had to disappear to avoid paying for past mistakes. It was simple enough to create a new persona by feeding false data into the computers, he said, thus electronically becoming someone else entirely.

That was one of the great paradoxes of our society. Like no other people in the world, an American can live on the margins, with no identity papers or official registration. Police might question a ragged-looking stranger, but no one is obliged to say who he is. At the same time, without papers and an official identity, a person is obliged to live on the margin. He cannot work or drive a car or handle anything but the cash he dares to keep on hand. Once he has acquired his paper identity, it follows him everywhere.

Gary was also looking at police undercover work, the secret infiltration of organizations to gather evidence against suspected wrongdoers. That, he suggested in a book on the subject, left some unsettling room for abuse.

On any issue Gary is carefully measured. He always reminds me of ballast in a ship. Wherever an argument pitches, he will roll you back to center. My plan was to fill a notebook with pithy guidelines about where America was headed. Instead, I got a single, highly serviceable line: "Be leery of wise people bearing generalizations."

I observed that Americans these days seemed to crave rounded corners. In the interest of order, people preferred to knock the edges off anything that might cut, even wit. Risk was left to a small few; most people wanted safety, security, no surprises. Gary did not perceptibly disagree. If they could manage it, I added, they would even control the weather. Here the ballast shifted. If that can save people from the dangers of storms, he said, why not?

Here he had me. I knew why not. But how can you argue it is better to let people die? Months later Jonathan Raban came to my rescue. In a remarkable little essay called "Cyclone," the English writer described a killer storm that smashed the coast of Britain. He concluded:

> *It's so sad!* people said, trying to quench their smiles—for they didn't feel sad at all. They were thrilled by the magnificent destruction of the wind; it was as if the world itself had come tumbling down, and even the shyest, most pacific people in the crowd felt some answering chord of violence in their own natures respond to this tremendous and unlooked-for act of violence in nature itself. . . .
>
> A black-and-white striped Parks Police van patrolled the bank . . . its twin loud-hailers yawping about *risk, responsible* and *in your own best interests;* but its presence only added to the air of carnival. Whoever you were, the wrecked landscape had something in it for you personally. For some people, it was simply an enjoyable reminder. . . . They'd gotten away with it; they were survivors. . . .

The grandmother I shared with Phyllis Marx was a survivor in the most fundamental sense, the reason I took my America seriously. Anna Rosenblum grew up in the White Russian town of Borisov. She went to work at the age of eight, gluing together matchboxes from dawn to dark until her fingers bled. She hated the czar's injustice, and about the time she was old enough to do something about it, Lenin came along. Anna and her husband, Albert, fought the revolution. Albert was killed—by typhus or Polish mercenaries—and Anna did not want to go where the revolution was headed. She hid her five kids for two years and then got them all to America.

At Ellis Island the health inspector took one look at a sore on my father's scalp and ordered him back to Russia. Had Anna been one to take no for an answer, I'd have been doing my foreign reporting for TASS, not the Associated Press.

My father, a gangling teenager named Martin, learned English at the back of a class of snickering first graders. The oldest in the family, he brought home the first paycheck. When war came, Anna paid along with everyone else; her youngest son, Matthew, was marched to death as a Japanese prisoner in the Philippines.

None of Anna's ten grandchildren was raised as a flag waver, but each of us knew what the Fourth of July was all about.

This whole business of school and upbringing seemed to be a major problem. The world's continued health depended heavily on intelligent, literate Americans, with a clear sense of their relative worth. It was not comforting to read the latest results of student surveys.

My impression was that Americans learned little about the world, including why they should care. I had talked about this in New York with Cheryl Gould, who returned from reporting in Paris to NBC headquarters. As senior producer of *Nightly News* she set the agenda for what a lot of Americans knew about the world. "The biggest threat is not the bomb," she said. "It is Americans' ignorance."

Her thoughts were echoed by my old pal Jo Menell, a documentary filmmaker who grew up in South Africa and wound up in Bolinas, California, via England and Salvador Allende's Chile. He is about as perceptive an observer as I know. He was blunt: "The most dangerous thing in the world today is the ignorance of the American people."

Dutch Warnner, ol' Red Tie in Atlantic City, had dismissed most of his own generation as blind to the world. If that were to change, it would depend on the kids.

A sampling of Massachusetts junior high school kids found that half could not locate their own country on a blank map of the world. In a Hearst Corporation survey, in a nation that opposes communism 45 percent of young respondents thought "from each according to his ability, to each according to his head" came from the U.S. Constitution, not Karl Marx.

Later a Gallup poll for the National Geographic Society found fewer than half of Americans tested could not find Britain, Japan or South Africa. A third could name no North Atlantic Treaty Organization countries, and a tenth thought we were in the Warsaw Pact. Three quarters did not know where the Persian Gulf was, and half could not name the country with all the fuss about Sandinistas and contras.

"It is a good thing our ancestors found their way to America, because twenty-four million Americans, one in seven, can't find the U.S. on a map," the society president, Gilbert Grosvenor, said in presenting the results. "There is a shocking lack of geographical knowledge throughout this country." Of all nine countries tested, only in America did the older test group do better than those of college age.

And the problem was not only knowledge of the world. A National Endowment for the Humanities study of eight thousand American seventeen-year-olds came up with hair-raising stuff: For example, 68 percent could not place the Civil War in the correct half century; 43 percent was far off on the dates of World War I. Some thought Columbus discovered America after 1850; a third said it was after 1750. Jamestown, according to 38.5 percent, was settled after 1800.

Some might argue they weren't alive back then. But a third dated Watergate before 1950. To a lot of kids, McCarthyism means Gene, not Joe, and only 42 percent knew about the un-American witch-hunts. Altogether, they scored 54 percent correct answers on history, including accurate guesses on the multiple-choice questions. Teachers regard 60 percent as passing.

Half the kids knew that Samuel Gompers was first president of the American Federation of Labor, and that is encouraging. But among the other half, a lot of them thought it was J. P. Morgan. For some reason, 83.8 percent knew about "Tubman," just below the score for Thomas Jefferson. (I thought that was a pretty impressive score for William Tubman, that lovable old bandit who ran Liberia until 1971. It was, in fact, Harriet Tubman, the lady who helped slaves escape to the North.) Hitler was identified by 87.4 percent; but only 53.6 percent knew about Joseph Stalin, and I know teachers whose kids spell it Stallone.

In literature the results were worse. Only 40 percent knew which poet wrote *Leaves of Grass,* and fewer still could situate William Faulkner in a region of the United States. The seventeen-year-olds were asked, "In which novel did a 16-year-old boy expelled from school go to New York to find himself?" They were offered *Catcher in the Rye;* they preferred *A Tree Grows in Brooklyn,* two to one. But the frightening part was about U.S. population. Few understand where Americans had come from, or why, and how they dispersed themselves around the country. Barely half knew about the Dust Bowl droughts of the 1930's. They did no better with the present: Only two in five realized that significant numbers of immigrants had come from Latin America and Southeast Asia over the past two decades. Even among Hispanic teenagers, the score was only 61.2 percent.

"In our schools we run the danger of unwittingly proscribing our own heritage," wrote Lynn A. Cheney, the endowment's chairman.

In a later math and science survey of thirteen-year-olds in six countries, Americans came in last. The report, funded by the National Science Foundation and the Department of Education, found 78 percent of South Korean students could solve two-step math problems, compared with 40 percent of Americans. Results were similar in science. American kids were outshone by students in Britain, Ireland, Spain, and Canada.

At the same time bookstores regorged copies of *The Closing of the American Mind* and *Cultural Literacy*, delving into what our kids no longer knew. Opinion was divided. Lee Mitgang, education writer for the Associated Press, regarded this sort of thing as a gratuitous slander of kids. American children are neither dumb nor lazy, he told me. But their interests are shaped by the wider society around them.

My colleague Mike Goldsmith, a generic European, pulled his son, Andrew, out of American schools when, at the age of eleven, he didn't know the capital of Spain. "I knew that when I was five," Mike grumbled to me. A few years later I spoke to Andrew about it. "We didn't learn much in school in Washington," he agreed. "But I had more fun."

One question that American seventeen-year-olds blew totally was the site of the colony Winthrop and the Puritans founded. Less than a fifth knew it was Boston.

In fact, not a lot of physical evidence is left of Boston's earliest days. There are the treasured landmarks. Some of the old port has been restored. Some little storybook neighborhoods spill off Beacon Hill, off the splendid public gardens. But the American car has burrowed into the city like a fat mole in a small lawn. Although Boston is one of those few American urban centers where you don't need a car, everyone seems to have one anyway. Wide gashes of traffic carve up old neighborhoods. Somehow the scale is all wrong.

Back when Bostonians were pitching tea in the harbor, the city shaped itself neatly along the Charles River and up the hills. As in the European cities they fled, settlers built streets wide enough for carts and carriages. For a century and a half, houses, churches, offices and public buildings assembled themselves in stately splendor. When automobiles ran horses off the road, Boston made room.

That was our general approach. Europeans dealt with the new

age by making small cars. We got out the wrecking ball. Where new cities grew up around the traffic that spawned them, the effect is different. In Boston old church spires are dwarfed by concrete flyovers. Ugly girders and vast asphalt fields of no-man's-land break up architecture we will never see again.

In Boston people flung around the term "gentrification" in a variety of ways. Some seemed pleased to think of themselves as gentry. Others spoke the word with such heat they were snarling by the fourth syllable. I knew what it meant already, from New York: Old cities were being restored, and old tenants were being elbowed out to the fringes where they could pay the rent. For me, both a professional liberal and an architectural conservative, it was a tough call.

Out in Mandela, Massachusetts, feelings were not ambivalent. Bitter residents blamed a lot of the growing desperation on vanishing homes for the poor. But it went much deeper than that. I had gone there because of an article I had seen in Paris. It mentioned a new rap song on black radio. When a few controlled many, and poverty was like a slap in the face, the words went "Mandela, Massachusetts, is the place to be."

The place was a handful of old Boston neighborhoods: Roxbury, Mattapan, Dorchester, the South End, Jamaica Plain, Columbia Point and the Fenway. A lot of residents, mostly blacks and Hispanics, wanted to secede. Their 12.5-square-mile city would be named for Nelson Mandela. It would take in a quarter of Boston's land, a quarter of its 620,000 residents and 98 percent of its blacks.

In the article, organizers of an unsuccessful referendum insisted it was no symbolic gesture. "This doesn't have to be about race," said Curtis Davis, a thirty-three-year-old architect. "It's about power." He was inspired by the 1983 incorporation of East Palo Alto, a largely black and Hispanic area near San Francisco. He wanted more municipal services and a louder voice in local issues.

Bruce Bolling, the first black president of the Boston City Council, opposed secession but said, "It is an expression, a poll. It forces you to look at the inequities and say we need fundamental change in Boston."

When I drove into Roxbury, Nelson Mandela did not seem very

far away. I felt the same tense awareness I remembered from Sharpeville, in South Africa. More than race, however, the tension was over drugs. During the week before I arrived, ten people had been shot dead or stabbed to death in turf battles over drugs. Dealers were brown and white, as well as black. The Puerto Ricans hated the Dominicans, and the blacks and whites didn't think much of either.

In the old days Mandela's neighborhoods were genteel suburban settlements, with wood-frame homes set back in yards, low brick apartment buildings and rows of shops and offices on the main thoroughfares. A few diehard families still painted their white picket fences and swept off their stoops. By some estimates, however, half the people in Roxbury were "substance abusers."

On one hand, druglords enforce peace to encourage the stream of outsiders who drive in to buy. On the other, desperate locals steal what they can, often violently, to pay for their next hit. Police seem to ignore them all, except for occasional sweeps on selected areas. Altogether, it is a weird mix of Westchester and war zone.

At the corner of Parker and Tremont, dozens of tense young men with agitated eyeballs surged up to my bright red Chevy, with no apparent concern that I might be a cop. Some hollered out prices. Others gave me a sharp nod, a street sign meaning: Whatever you want, I got. I did not pause long to chat, figuring that if they got questions instead of sales, someone might start shooting.

Down a block-long street called Sonoma, known locally as Murderers' Row, only a few desultory blacks lounged against car hoods. The real action that day was along Centre, better known as 16 Ave because its dealers' specialty was one-sixteenth-ounce bags of cocaine. The price had dropped to $40, down from $175 around the mid-1980's, reflecting ample supply to meet a growing demand. Jails are overcrowded and court calendars are so backed up, I was told, that only egregious violators need worry. Most keep their wares in plastic bags under the tongue, and they spit them out upon payment. If spooked, they can swallow the evidence.

I watched a large group dealing drugs on the steps of a lovely old church, buyers and sellers alike ignoring the laughing kids charging among their legs on tricycles. Some dealers use their own children as salesmen, and a few hide drugs in baby carriages, assuming that no one would believe anyone could be that perverse.

With a few simple inquiries, I surveyed my options. I could score heroin of varying quality at several locations. Or there were the shooting galleries, crack houses which specialized in quick hits at low cost. Instead, I went to the Tobin Community School to look for Mandela residents who were not on drugs. I found Ronnie Bell and Kevin Schlehuber. Lifelong Roxbury residents, childhood friends and basketball rivals, they were a prototype for a black-white buddy film about growing up in the ghetto.

Ronnie, at twenty-five, was program director for the city school. He coached the under-fifteen basketball team to city championships and spent most of his spare time helping push youngsters away from drugs. "These kids don't have any heroes, no real role models except pimps and dealers," he said. "They see these guys dress well, drive good cars. If they go to jail, they come out and try to live right, but then no one will give them a break. Once they start to go bad, they're finished. When I think of all the kids I grew up with who are either in jail or dead . . ."

Kevin, a year older, is athletic director at Tobin. A former Mr. Massachusetts, tall and hard as stone, he has not yet had to use the serrated bread knife he keeps in a small bag. "I've lived here all my life," he said. "They're not going to hassle one of their own. But you never know. Before, if you got into a fight, it was just a fight. Now you see little kids carrying nine millimeter pistols."

The three of us drove around the neighborhood, and they pointed out the large hospitals moving into what is becoming the new medical center of Boston. "All those hospitals put a lot of people out of their homes, turning them to drugs because of depression, and now they need the hospitals," Ronnie said, not amused at the irony. Hospitals bought up houses for the land under them. And there was some more gentrification.

Pressure to take drugs is everywhere, Ronnie and Kevin agreed, and not only among the poor. At parties people laugh at you for refusing dope. A lot of users extol the thrill. I asked how they had turned out so well. Both replied simultaneously: "Parents." Their families had instilled values that stuck with them. Ronnie's mother worked hard at different jobs to make sure her son had enough dignity and lunch money to resist temptations of the street.

Kevin's father, a retired mailman, held together his clan of seven kids, who still ebb and flow around his well-kept little house. They call him Cheese. "We were married thirty years ago, and we made it work," he said. "I decided, What would I do at fifty-two, drinking in a bar, sulking, if I screwed it up? This is a good home. But today, with this drug scene, it's no place to raise kids." He had just seen a young black, an old friend of the family, who dropped by dressed for work. It was his first day as a cop. "What a job," Cheese said. "To kiss your wife good-bye each morning in a bulletproof vest."

Volunteers like Kevin and Ronnie were spreading the word around Mandela: There was a better way than drugging yourself to death. With only spotty policy and court action, however, no one needed to add the corollary: If you don't mess with drugs yourself, you can own that Red Porsche Turbo convertible over there by selling them. And this was America, with another side to every issue. One Roxbury wall proclaimed: THE FASCIST ATTACK IS WORSE THAN CRACK. PISS ON DRUG TESTING.

Later I cruised Route 128, the high tech trail. Governor Michael Dukakis was running for President, so lots of people were talking about the Massachusetts Miracle. Dying mill towns had attracted hot new technology firms, hard and soft, slicing into unemployment and raising the tax base. State programs taught workers new skills. Altogether, seventy-two thousand jobs were created in four years; after four years with the nation's highest unemployment, the rate dropped to 2.9 percent. It was an achievement all right, a clear example of American flexibility in the face of despair. But "miracle" seemed to be pushing it.

High tech jobs that appeared overnight would not necessarily be around in the morning. The old way—the forty-year employee who raised his son to be foreman—went with the scrapped machinery. The new firms hired well-educated, upwardly mobile specialists. Companies depended heavily on government contracts. A shift in the wind could blow a dozen of them away.

But they were clean, prestigious and responsive to local communities. Towns like Lowell and Taunton were reborn because of them. And the example was there for towns across the country.

Watching high tech in action, I thought of Charlie Chaplin in *Modern Times,* tumbling helplessly around in a society of our mechanical and electronic creations. That worried me a little. In fact, a lot of trends were starting to worry me. I wanted to celebrate the good stuff but also go for the throat. Both were important. Yet any artificial balance would be precarious. I'd report what I saw. In the end I'd offer not a kick in the groin but a shot in the arm. For this, I could use a little expert help. With Chaplin in mind, the obvious choice was Marcel Marceau.

For two generations a silent white-faced Pierrot named Bip had lived inside Marceau, watching Americans with critical affection. Each year Marceau and Bip visited some corner of the United States and looked back at the people looking at them. Past sixty-five, Marceau was a philosopher, painter, author and generous friend. In short, the perfect magic mirror.

"I love Americans," he pronounced. "Their enthusiasm, their openness, their energy and generosity set them apart. It took me ten years to be accepted in Paris, to be taken into the closed intellectual and social circles. In America it took a month."

Chaplin's *Modern Times* sometimes weighs on Marceau, too, these days. But he thinks we are going up the down escalator, as it should be. "The more we advance, the more we go back," he says, of Western society in general. "The greatest civilizations end up going backward." In a longer term, which is how he looks at things, he is comfortable with the directions he sees. "There is an endless wave that renews itself in America," Marceau said. "I have confidence in intelligence and memory. Time restores values and puts in place what should be."

Curiously enough, a different French observer in a different time made the same remark. That was Alexis de Tocqueville's conclusion.

The United States, I knew, was littered with former colleagues who had moved home. It would be fun to compare notes. In Boston I found Barry Shlachter. Barry had worked for AP in Tokyo, Pakistan and East Africa. He sneaked across the Afghan border to interview captured Russians. He had covered the Ethiopian famine and the killing fields of Uganda, as well as Angola and Mozambique. It was Barry who had found Beryl Markham the aviatrix, all but forgotten in a corner of Kenya, and alerted readers to her. He had just finished as a Nieman fellow at Harvard and was looking for work.

"The first shock coming home is opening folks' refrigerators and seeing huge amounts of things no one will eat," he said. "Or going to the supermarket and seeing four of five kinds of the same product." I nodded gravely. Once I flew home on vacation to Tucson, coming directly from a famine refugee camp in the Sudan. Two days after watching mothers beg for a single aspirin to comfort a dying child, I walked into a discount drug palace. The bottles stretched for half a city block: orange-flavored, kiddie-size liquid for tummy aches; automatic-release, heart-shaped, safety-sealed capsules for sniffles.

But Barry worried more about a smug lack of curiosity. No one cared about what he had seen. Not once did a Nieman fellow, the cream of American journalism, ask about events abroad. Nor did anyone else. His family and friends expressed only a little polite interest. He had brought back a tape he made in Afghanistan, a rare firsthand account of why the rebels were fighting and what they were up against. "My parents listened to this tape I made, with people getting shot in front of me, and they asked, 'Why are you getting so emotional?' "

A main reason, he had decided, is television. "TV creates a reality shift. One's own experience can't really compete with the fake excitement you can see on television." Even more, television provided a volume switch. By turning it down, a crisis or a threat faded. You could be as emotional or as detached as you wished. Then you switched it off entirely and even the picture disappeared.

I saw Arnold Zeitlin, a friend with whom I'd covered the Biafran war in Nigeria. Since then he had been AP bureau chief in Pakistan and then the Philippines. Ferdinand Marcos expelled him for reporting too well. He moved to Boston with his three kids. Arnold discovered what Barry did. He was a slight oddity, not up-to-date on *Moonlighting*, but safe enough to talk to on other subjects.

I'd last seen Jide, Arnold's adopted Nigerian son, when he was a little kid. Since then Jide had been a high school football star, an honor student and a soon-to-be-rich investment banker. He was an American, not an African. But then there are those cycles. I wanted to talk with him, but he was off to Africa. After a business trip to Johannesburg, his fires were lit. He was getting, as Barry Shlachter's parents might say, emotional.

Finally, I visited Richard Eder, an inside outsider's hero whose job was to reflect intelligently on books for the Los Angeles *Times*. We'd first met in Venezuela, where he was a real correspondent and I was an importuning cub fresh out of the box. As *New York Times* bureau chief in Paris he wrote the sort of insightful stuff that left the rest of us muttering in envy. We lunched at a pleasant little Italian restaurant with excellent food. When the coffee came, I reached for my pipe. The waitress appeared instantly and began hemming and hawing, in obvious pain. After a moment I got the point; she didn't want me to smoke. I was confused at first because she was so nice about it. After a short time home I knew the score. Extract the merest leaf of tobacco, and people descend upon you like magpies on popcorn. Light a pipe in a restaurant, and people stare as though you had deposited your penis on your mashed potatoes.

Something serious was going on here, and it seemed not to be about smoking. Few smokers opposed nonsmoking sections, and only a piggish minority refused any polite request to desist. I could understand people's concerns; I hated cigarette smoke myself. But the evidence of danger was, at best, thin.

If a diner sat near a constant smoker for 398 hours, he would absorb the nicotine equivalent of one cigarette unless, of course, one of them finished dinner first and left. In an office that same equivalent takes six and a half weeks, at six hours a day. That was according to the International Technology Corporation of Torrance California. Britain's Froggert Report said the secondary smoke risk was slight. K. Uberia, the West German biostatistician, called evidence inconclusive and conflicting; there may be no danger, he concluded. A French expert, Robert Molimard, defined the risk as "relatively low." Another, who asked not to be named, dismissed most concerns as "hysteria" in America.

In most of Europe, free and perfectly mature societies accepted that a good cigar was as much a part of a proper meal as a fork. Cigarettes, though banned in some places, were regarded as a personal affair. Civilized discourse determined the balance.

Obviously some danger existed. But there seemed to be nothing to justify the moralizing, the self-righteousness with which one group of Americans—majority or minority—was exerting its judgments on another.

The right to clean air seemed a little much to ask. If it flies, at least we might add freedom from screaming kids, body odor and obnoxious voices. Secondary child noise has got to cause stress, which, the surgeon general advises, is serious stuff.

Eder had reflected on the issue. "It is a kind of a nineteenth-century censoriousness," he said. "People permit themselves to say the most incredible things to strangers." He thought it was a reaction to years of hostility to having to endure things, smoking being only the most easily attacked. Now that a lot of Americans had tasted blood on this victory, what next? Censoriousness was an acquired taste. I added the general subject to my list of things to watch.

*

The Christian Scientists' mother church is no place to bum a cigarette, but it seemed like a monument to decent people who hold on
to beliefs without trumpeting them. I spoke at a seminar for the
Christian Science Monitor and took a close look. Before I went abroad,
the Christian Scientists to me were a sect of people who ran reading
rooms. Then, in Africa, I lost a friend. The *Monitor*'s Nairobi bureau chief died suddenly. Doctors said it was because he refused
medicine for a tropical disease. His family and the church thought
otherwise. I wondered about people who could fly in the face of
science at such risk to their lives.

Mary Baker Eddy founded the church in Boston in 1879. Her
Science and Health with Key to the Scriptures lays out the principles of
divine healing. Sin and illness are to be overcome only by the mind.
But unlike the followers of some religions with answers to major
questions, the Christian Scientists do not push their faith on us reluctant infidels. Instead, they push world understanding, an awareness that cultures see things differently but share common problems.

The *Monitor*'s lobby offers what may be the most illuminating vantage point on the world to be found anywhere. It is a huge walk-in
globe, the Maparium. From a long, transparent catwalk, visitors look
up and down from the center of the earth. The acoustics are dramatic; a whisper over by Bolivia reverberates from the Ukraine. The
lighting is like stained glass. But the message is in the perspective.
If you look out from the core, the United States is only a small
patch on the earth's skin. Africa is much larger. Countless islands
cover vast expanses of sea. Russia and its Asian republics are at once
distant and menacing. Mainly, the Maparium shows, the world takes
some figuring out.

Though too fond of dirty words and doctors to be a Christian
Scientist, I appreciated the *Monitor*. It was discouraging to see that
American life being what it was, the paper cut itself badly in a
scramble for readers. A thought kept recurring from one of the
books I had read on what Americans don't know.

In *Cultural Literacy*, E. D. Hirsch cites the Jefferson quote on which
all of us reporters were weaned: ". . . were it left to me to decide
whether we should have a government without newspapers, or
newspapers without government, I should not hesitate a moment to
prefer the latter." But Hirsch added the line that most of us had
never known was part of the deal: "But I should mean that every
man should receive those papers and be capable of reading them."

*

A short ride north of Boston, I-93 passes a large sign: NEW HAMP-
SHIRE, LIVE FREE OR DIE. Immediately after, another sign says SPEED
CHECKED BY AIRCRAFT. Up ahead, just after a toll booth, the state
monopoly liquor store and some dire warnings about seat belts, there
is something called the "State Safety Rest Area."

I stopped briefly in Manchester, New Hampshire. Above the urinal in a restaurant men's room, someone had posted that morning's
editorial from the *Union Leader*. It damned Ted Turner for reporting that young Soviets liked working in Siberia. He did not say, the
paper argued, that their tour of duty starts with a midnight knock
by the KGB and a ride in a locked boxcar. The writer was not fooled
by any of that *glasnost* nonsense. Where you live free, by the rules,
or die, Dr. Zhivago was a foreign correspondent.

Next door a gigantic sporting goods supermarket bulged with the
paraphernalia of active leisure. My reaction was mixed. I felt a little
awe for a people so devoted to fresh air and their own pleasure, so
capable of producing all those toys to help in that pursuit. But I
also remembered my talk with George Schaller, the naturalist, who
was taking a break from tracking snow leopards in Tibet. "The waste
and overdevelopment, you see it the minute you reach Kennedy
Airport," he said, nostrils flaring in disgust. "Americans pamper
themselves, eat so much, use so much. They talk about going into
the wilderness, but they know exactly what they'll find when they
get out and where to get help. Most wouldn't last two days in the
real wilderness."

A carefree-looking young customer in shorts came in, and I
eavesdropped as he chatted with a clerk in a hey-screw-it sort of T-
shirt. "They tore up my dashboard and got the radio . . . probably
got forty bucks to buy one hit of crack."

At a self-service gas station the pump didn't work. Then I saw the
sign: PAY FIRST. I told the man I wanted to fill the tank; I didn't
know how much. He said, "Gimme ten or fifteen. What you don't
use, you get back." Doesn't anyone trust anyone? I asked. He glowered. "Those are my orders."

Freedom, Bobby McGee had observed, was just another word for
nothing left to lose. I hurried on to Vermont.

It was the wrong time for summer camps, unfortunately. Back in
Europe, my friend Dennis Redmont's son Rodrigo had told me about
his experience in Vermont. He was reared in Rio de Janeiro and

Rome, in polite society. At camp, when bananas were handed around, he peeled his the way he was taught. With a knife and fork. The poor kid's life was miserable after that.

"These kids can be so spoiled, so *cruel*," a young camp director had told me on a plane. Her place, in northern Pennsylvania, attracted a mix of rich kids and others who were helped out financially. "Parents who feel guilty about abandoning their children send candy in lavish packages, and the kids can be so selfish. Our rule is that everything gets shared. But someone will say, 'My dad paid a lot for this.' and I'll say, 'Well, fine, but what about your friends who don't have any?' And he'll say, 'Why doesn't their dad buy *them* some?'"

I also did not call on Aleksandr Solzhenitsyn, who had gone from the gulag to the Green Mountains. He stayed behind closed doors and emitted ungracious observations about America's bloated self-indulgence and lack of fiber. Ah, but Vermont is beautiful.

In the little town of Bristol I told a shopkeeper that the place hadn't changed a bit. I'd meant it as a compliment, but she seemed a trifle miffed. "We have new streetlights," she pointed out. True, something was off. Tacky modern globes on wrought-iron poles now lined the classic weathered-brick main street.

Also, Johnny Tomasi's tiny sprout house had become a barn. When I'd been there a decade earlier, he was a kid with a new wife, Susan. They'd messed with a few sprouts, to make a living. Now they were shipping eight thousand pounds a week. They had kids and a big house with an American flag on the porch.

Cruising the back roads, I saw fewer of Vermont's distinctive old barns and farmhouses than I remembered. Ugly plastic Harvestore silos, emblazoned with American flags, broke up the view. Vermonters were fighting a losing war against wealthy yup-class people who dismantled barns to have weathered wood for their new homes. Those huge yellow wheel cheeses fell victim to health laws. Cheese had to be sealed in plastic. Little else was done in the traditional, time-consuming way.

Beverly Red, who had made her fortune turning out furry little "vegimals," retired early into the country to raise two kids. She worried about television. A touch of *Mister Rogers* might be good, she said, but she saw kids getting passive, short of attention and bereft of imagination. "Children learn by physical involvement, by doing things," she said. "People think children are modern, but they're always the same. Instead of all this propaganda about Russia, they should just stick the kids together, and we'd work it out in a generation."

I talked to Bev about American kids. I had noticed many seemed thoughtless and undisciplined compared with most other societies. Recently, in a small crowd, a fat little boy had screamed, "BOO!" in my left ear, straightening my hair. But he was addressing his father, and I was merely standing in the way. He had not been taught to pick up other people on his radar. Yes, Bev said. It was the obvious result of shoving children off in day-care centers, plunking them in front of the TV and palming off gifts and indulgences for real attention.

When I mentioned lax drug enforcement in Roxbury, Bev told me about friends in Middlebury who had bought a head shop fifteen years ago and made it into a clothing store. Police had just raided them for drugs. They found nothing; the couple didn't use them. Not to be put off, police confiscated the roach clips the new owners used as clothespins. Since cops spent eight hours in the place, the word in Middlebury was enshrined in stone: Those drugs dealers had been busted.

Bev had clipped a newspaper item about "zero tolerance." U.S. customs officials had stopped a University of Vermont student at the Canadian border and found traces of marijuana, smoked months before, in a corncob pipe left in the glove compartment of his van. They seized the van.

In the Vermont hills, things seem pretty clear. People were nuts beyond the Green Mountains. I headed into Burlington, to the airport. The city was overbuilt and full of people in ties, to hear locals tell it. But it was not exactly the cold big city. At a Kentucky Fried Chicken the counterman greeted me like an old pal. "You hear [somebody's] Tavern has a new owner?" he asked. I said I hadn't. "Well, see you next week." No such luck.

CHAPTER

4

Blue Ridges,
Black Holes

Before moving on, I went back to France to catch my breath. I was covering the United States the way I would Africa or Western Europe: a series of planned forays, with room to make a wrong turn after a scent. I would end up in Washington, but I wanted to stop there before heading into Appalachia and the South. In full presidential primary campaign, reeling from a silly season of foreign adventure, Washington was the way Rome must have been about the time someone noticed Hannibal's elephants.

Flying into Washington's Dulles International, after New York's John F. Kennedy, is like arriving in a different country. *Business Traveler* ranked JFK the world's worst airport, after Lagos, Nigeria, and that's not the half of it. But it is never boring. At JFK I was mashed into a shuttle bus full of Cadillac dealers returning from a European fling, awash in duty-free bourbon. A woman under a precarious tower of platinum hair, wearing drill-punch heels and a "Hello!" tag mentioning Florida, cracked Doublemint in my ear. She fitted only partially into a silver lamé tube top; her pants might have been baked on at the dealership. Gum notwithstanding, she chatted intimately with friends at the far end of the bus.

Dulles brought me to another world. Crowds moved smoothly, free of bovine overtones. We landed with no stackup, and a huge pod rolled up to the plane. People filed inside and sat down rather than hog the doorway as they do in Europe. I hogged a seat by the door and began tapping at my computer. "Neat machine," said a gentle voice next to me. "Are you writing your impressions of life?" My neighbor was the flip side of the Florida blonde, a flight attendant in mufti, with a prim little bow and a high collar. Her sensibly done brown hair framed an angelic face, and she moved almost apologetically. She was one of those sweet, wholesome heroines on the Sunday night Hollywood classics the French like so much. Her name was Elizabeth. I said I was writing about America, and her eyes lit up, preparatory, I was sure, to saying, "Gee whiz."

Instead, she said: "The society has gone to shit. These cocksuckers, I had to move to the Midwest to get away from it. . . ." With a little encouragement, she told me about being a stewardess on an American airline. "Boy, you sure see it in my job. All they care about is money, comparing what they've got with what other people have. And bitching about the smallest things. And spineless? They're always telling me to tell another passenger something. I always want to say, 'Why the fuck don't you tell him yourself?' "

She referred frequently to gonads and their environs during our brief chat. Elsewhere I might have thought her virtue easy. Most cultures tend to draw clear lines around who is a lady. In fact, she was probably a sweet, wholesome heroine with colorful language. Then again, I wouldn't bet on it.

Americans can't seem to decide what to think about sex. The subject, I hoped, would recur during my travels. But mass hypocrisy seemed evident. In New York street corner kiosks offer stacks of *Screw* magazine with phone numbers for as many sleazy, risky encounters as an overcharged adventurer could possibly handle. I picked up a copy of *Harper's* which had reprinted the style sheet for *Penthouse* letters ("asshole," "peehole" and "blowjob" are single words; "butt-fuck" takes a hyphen). At Dulles there wasn't a *Popular Sperm* in sight.

In a crowded newsstand I browsed through magazines racked up neatly behind high Plexiglas panels. A section of the top row, I noticed, had been painted black. If you are five feet eight inches and stand on your tiptoes, you can just make out the upper half of three familiar words: *Playboy, Penthouse, Playgirl.* To buy one, the process is simple. You leap up like a stunted forward trying out for the Washington Bullets, make a grab for the top of the desired magazine and yank ferociously. I tried it; it's not so bad. The only problem is the crowd of people who stop to watch.

In America, I was finding, you never knew what to expect.

At the post office a jovial black woman made a colossal effort to get my package onto a departing truck. Ah, I reflected, the land of efficiency. Then I talked to the guy behind me. He was lined up to buy a two-dollar money order. He had business in Charlotte, North Carolina, and needed a list of addresses from the Chamber of Commerce. "They won't take a check," he told me. "They say it takes them six weeks to collect on checks, and so many of them are bad. No one trusts anyone anymore."

These matters of trust and efficiency were coming up often. So was racism. Washington at the time was talking about football. I heard Dan Rather announce that the third black quarterback in a week had started in the NFL, a new record. It seemed a pretty weird thing to keep records about. I had thought that after Jackie Robinson had opened sports for blacks in 1947, white players were happy to have the help. In racially mature America, were we still counting colors?

Earlier I had watched Ted Koppel's jaw drop when Al Campanis, the Dodgers' director of player personnel, declared blacks were not suited to management. They were better at sliding. Koppel gave him another chance. No, Campanis said, blacks weren't cut out to be executives. Campanis had championed black players and didn't seem to dislike them. Instead, this was the sentiment I recognized from South Africa. It was not racial hatred; you could deal with that. It was the ingrained belief that the poor benighted race was permanently disadvantaged, destined by its creator to be a shade lower on the human scale. The odd Jesse Jackson was a happy exception. Some of your best friends could be black.

Cases, subtle or flagrant, arose in strange places. FBI agents tormented a black colleague. Mysterious threats warned he would be castrated and his wife raped. He was a "black devil." When he complained, the victim said, he was punished while his colleagues were promoted. Only persistent legal action and national publicity brought corrective action from the FBI, the elite guard of our freedoms.

Then there was Cheryl Tatum's hair. Ms. Tatum, a cashier at the Hyatt Regency Hotel restaurant near National Airport in Washington, restyled her hair in cornrows. The tight braids, favored by some of Africa's most beautiful women, not to speak of Bo Derek, were gathered back in a pageboy. But, she told *The New York Times*, she was fired for contravening Hyatt policy on "extreme and unusual hair styles." She quoted the personnel director, who did not deny the remark, as saying, "I can't understand why you would want to wear hair like that, anyway. What would the guests think if we allowed you all to wear your hair like that?"

It's the "you-all" that scares me. Any corporate vice-president could slime out of that one. "You-all . . . cashiers." Or "you-all . . . people on the night shift." Never mind that white women's punk spikes went by unchallenged; this was about hair, not skin color. With subtle but deep-seated racism, in either direction, you never know where you are. And it is one of those areas where there is no being an outsider.

After a short flight to New York not long before, I was leaving a crowded plane when a large woman began hollering at me. She was black. "Don't you know any better than to hit a small child?" she demanded. "Aren't you going to apologize?" In the jostling, apparently my briefcase had bumped her son, who looked up, smiling, puzzled by it all. I gathered my breath to apologize, but the woman wasn't having any. "Is that how you treat another person?" she bellowed, finding her range. "He didn't do nothing to you." I ached to apologize to the kid. His mother barreled on, her voice rising steadily. "Maybe you'd like me to hit *you* and see how it feels," she said, waving a meaty paw under my nose.

By then deplaning had stopped. Passengers were staring, most of them looking at me as if I were the grand dragon of the Georgia Klan, having just set fire to Uncle Tom's Cabin. Was this a racial incident? Likely. It is not my practice to clobber small children under any circumstance; mothers, I might make an exception. Funny how this society works. Had I managed to rid myself of insidious racism and sexism, I would have belted the lady in the chops.

Racism, though no small issue to those at the wrong end, was not the only thing happening in America. I did not want to get obsessed with it. But I was beginning to see the problem had proportions I had not realized. Racial incidents were one thing. But ingrained racist thinking involves the fundamental way we Americans look at ourselves.

When South Africans threw apartheid back at me, I hooted them down. We had abolished discrimination. Plenty of color-blind Americans and mixed couples led happy lives. If there were lingering problems, it was only natural. People alive today had grandparents born into slavery. It took time. But it gnawed at me. I watched an interview with James Baldwin, not long before he died an embittered outsider in southern France. He said waiting for equality had taken all his grandfather's time, his father's time, his time. He fixed the reporter with a hard stare and demanded: "How much time do you need?"

The South Africans, at least, have a deep political fear. A black majority, with different values and ways of life, could dispossess them from land they have settled since the 1600's. They see nowhere else to take their families and their culture. Right or wrong, it is cause for concern. American whites face no such menace. When we discriminate, it is simple ignorant inhumanity.

I flew into Charleston at dusk, and a familiar feeling overwhelmed me. It was that anxious revving of the senses which works at travelers who approach strange, remote countries as failing light filters the features below. I had felt it all over the Third World: Sparse lights suggest the shape of a small city. A broad incandescent ribbon traces the freeway hastily finished for some forgotten major event. Smokestacks identify someone's absentee industry. Little tin roofs mark the workers' quarter, and sprawling estates reveal where the money is. A few military aircraft were visible by the small airport terminal. By the time we touched down, I was steeling myself for customs and immigration.

Like most Third World capitals, Charleston has stylish new buildings among stately old ones, cultural trappings and a lot of people who bristle at the suggestion that they inhabit a backwater; it has hard-edged men who know what they don't like. But the place exudes a slow-lane charm, transcending the bluebloods and rednecks at its extremes. At the Hertz counter a young woman did a certifiable double take at my address and allowed herself the kind of "Gee!" people ridicule in big cities. "You live in Paris," she reflected, sighing audibly. She thought West Virginia was beautiful, but she was none too happy at never having been out of it.

Holed up in one of those chain hotels that look the same everywhere, I watched America celebrate the Super Bowl. It was not much of a game, but people seemed to take the results seriously. In Washington people hung by their knees from lampposts, screaming and spraying Asti Spumante at strangers. In Denver grown men and women looked as if their airedales had been abducted. The victorious District of Columbia was just up the road. But we were all somewhere else.

Early in the morning I drove to South Charleston, to which one drives north, and then followed the interstate to Huntington. It was a grim ride.

Living better with chemistry has its price, and West Virginia is one place it is paid. Along a lovely, lazy river an unbroken string of stacks spews noxious fumes into mountain air. You could damn near run a car on river water. Things are improving, industries insist, but the Environmental Protection Agency cannot bring back hillsides gashed away in strip mining or mask the industrial sprawl.

People have to eat, obviously enough. But that is one of the tragedies of West Virginia. For all the man-made ugliness, it is not producing enough paychecks. We screwed up paradise trying to do nature one better. Either the profits did not go back to staying ahead of nature or someone forgot to notice how the world was changing. Or maybe it wasn't such a hot idea in the first place.

I headed south along the Tug Fork River, and not too far along, I was back a century in Kermit.

A few tubes of neon and some cheap modern roofing disguise Kermit as just another nondescript American town strewn casually between a two-lane blacktop and a creek. The odd police car prowls resolutely over the more passable roads. But no one traveling more slowly than sixty miles an hour is fooled.

Not long before I arrived, the feds had finally closed down the town's most prosperous boutique. It was a ratty little mobile home, a pebble's toss from the police station, where customers lined up outside, rain or snow. When business was good, a sign went up OUT OF DRUGS. BACK IN 30 MINUTES. It was a retail outlet for dope. Kermit's other main industry was arson. Most of the town was empty lot by the time I got there; insurance companies had begun to catch on.

This was not the America we outsiders had come to expect from the sitcoms. Or maybe it was. The drug shop—and the volunteer fire department—were just a few services of the Preeces, who made the Hoggs of Hazzard seem like the Waltons. There was Wig Preece, the old man, and his wife, Cooney, known as the brains of the family. Another dozen or so Preeces helped run Kermit. Their bar, a sort of Cheers with sidearms, was named the C & W, for Cooney and Wig; regulars affectionately called it the Cut and Wound.

I wanted to talk to the Preeces, but they were just about all in jail: mother and father; two daughters and their husbands; a third daughter and her boyfriend. One young Preece was freed, but he came back to Kermit and stole some checks from city hall which he forced a local merchant to cash. Then he spent the proceeds on video games at the grocery, and he was out of touch again. One jailed son-in-law was the town police chief. His only deputy was also behind bars. Altogether, prosecutors got sixty-five convictions and no acquittals from the drug ring, the Mingo County political machine and the money around both.

Kermit, it seems, was always like that. It is smack on the Tug Fork River, which separates a very dry county in Kentucky from a very wet one in West Virginia. As in the days of moonshine, not so long past, the state liquor store does 60 to 70 percent of its business with visitors from over the border.

When the Civil War erupted, an officer named McCoy from the Kentucky side remained loyal to the Union. West Virginia did not secede, but a Hatfield from the neighborhood joined the Confederacy. Bad blood followed.

I drove around slowly, wondering how to penetrate the town without anyone deciding to penetrate me. Then, just across from an abandoned truck marked "Fire Department," I noticed a For Sale sign. A friendly man named Tom was selling his house.

Tom had bought a bigger place in Kermit, where he had lived all his life. When I remarked that he must like it, Tom snorted. "Look at your car. Look at mine." I looked. After a few hours in the West Virginia mountains, my hood was thick with yellow-black coal sludge. Tom's looked as if someone had been sick on it. "It's a nasty little mudhole, and I hate it," he said. "I just can't afford to leave."

In Kermit, he explained, the mines were nonunion and flourished. He made eighty thousand dollars a year as a night foreman, and his wife, an administrative worker, earned another fifty thousand dollars. Tom had seen some of the world; his baseball cap read "Vietnam Veteran and Proud of It." But he was a miner. "That's what my daddy did, got mashed up just over there," he said, pointing south. "Broke his back in three places."

When I asked about the Preeces, Tom chuckled. "Well, they were real nice to the town," he said. "Debby, over there, she ran the ambulance service." A lot of people think that straddling the law is part of the folklore, he added. "They'll be missed around here." Had the crackdown dried up the drug supply? "You can still get whatever you want, as much as you want."

Instead, I went for breakfast just over the Tug Fork in Lovely, Kentucky. Tom had told me about a new restaurant. It turned out to be the L & B, the sort of business that fortifies your faith in people.

Barry Webb, a thirty-one-year-old coal miner and cosuperintendent of the Calvary Temple Baptist Church Sunday School, had just opened the place with his wife, Linda Lou Kirk Webb. Also prominent was Alexandra Lynn Webb, aged two, responsible for a major dessert's being named gaga cake.

"How are you enjoying nasty country?" Barry offered as a greeting, pegging me for what I was. He was used to outsiders, especially reporters. In 1963 President Lyndon B. Johnson went to Inez, up the road a few miles, then the seat of the poorest white county in America. The coal boom changed all that abruptly until the bust, in the late 1970's, when the region's nouveaux riches were poor again.

"What bothers me is that they all look down on us, they think we're all hillbillies," he said. "They just look at the people who don't care, in those shacks and all. Most people around here have good things, want good things, like everywhere else."

Barry splits his time between mining and running the L & B. Linda, a beauty queen of recent vintage, is cook and decorator. "We just decided to jump in and try it," he said. Friends, relatives and hungry strangers keep the place humming, with a permanent conversation that stews like a stockpot. Someone mentioned lawyers, for example, and ol' Harmon Germer chimed in.

"I kin tell you about lawyers," he said, and he did so for a half hour. Also judges. And Omaha Beach. Basically he said his grandfather had left him a large piece of land that mining interests had cornered. He had been fighting for it eight years. "Money talks, and here there is too much money," he said.

Harmon needed the land. He'd spent twenty-seven years in the mines, and he had too much coal dust in his lungs to scramble for a living. He was off to North Carolina for some fresh legal talent. "I ain't stopping," he said. "That's what they want you to do. They want you to quit."

I also met a young woman from Kermit and asked about drug dealing and assorted illegalities.

"You know about it, and you don't know about it, if you see what I mean," she replied elliptically. "Some people think they run the county. They're your neighbors, and they don't bother to hide it. I'm twenty-four, and it's been going on as long as I've been around."

Rural Appalachia, Barry Webb notwithstanding, is not like everywhere else. Some kids reach their teens without seeing a fork. There are some nice houses and new cars. But gravity-defying shacks of rotted planks and twisted tin bear a comfortable familiarity to the outskirts of Rio de Janeiro, Lagos or Manila. Battered mobile homes perch on rocky tops of hills as if they had been dropped by sky-hooks. South of Kermit, the countryside looks more like Haiti than the United States, except that the people are white. And there is far more trash strewn around. Plastic garbage catches in branches, as year-round foliage. In the Third World people find some use for every bit of rusted auto corpse, exploded mattress, trash bag or sar-dine can they can find. In the West Virginia hollows such items are lawn decoration. All this says nothing about human dignity and ba-sic values. But this is poor country.

In Williamson I stopped for lunch with Wally Warden, editor of the local daily, who ought to have a drawerful of Pulitzers. He broke the Kermit story. He has no illusions about mining. "My father is the size I am, a big, healthy brute, except that he can't breathe," he said. Half of the county's retirees are on disability, many with black lung. But he is not quite sure what to do about it. Many families are only a few food stamps away from starvation.

"Awareness of what coal mining does to the environment is tem-pered by the awareness that there is nothing else," he said. "Once we made a complaint about a muddy road. The result was they shut down the road for seven days while they cleaned it up, and people didn't work."

Some mine operators turn off their scrubbers at night, when in-spectors can't see pollution spewing from their stacks. But, the op-erators argue, they need every penny they can squeeze to stay in business. Maybe not. But in a larger sense, West Virginia shares one of the Third World's worst problems: However obvious future dan-gers might be, the crisis at hand takes priority. As Wally Warden put it, "You don't look ahead that far. You look at tomorrow."

I was about to turn up into the hills when I saw a road marker pointing right. It said MATEWAN. A popular film had shown how mining companies crushed the unions in Matewan, during the 1920's. What had happened since? I pulled up to a little storefront office marked "United Mine Workers of America" and talked to David Phillips. He had liked the film a lot.

"The conditions are the same, but more so," he said. Mines were still using hired thugs, armored cars and questionable legal tactics to break strikes. Surely, he was exaggerating; twelve people were shot dead in May 1920. Mary Harris Jones, Mother Jones, talked of "industrial slaves and their masters." The atmosphere might be different, Phillips said, but unions still could not get a fair shake. "What has not changed," he added, "is greed."

But the union question is hardly so black and white. Membership is way down, and some miners say it is because inflexible leaders have priced labor out of the market. Strict contracts opened the doors to foreign competition. Yes, but . . . In a different way, arguments resembled those outside Convention Hall, where NBC technicians struck the Miss America Pageant. Organized labor had given workers dignity and a shot at the American Dream they might never have gotten. Corporations do tend toward greed and callousness. Greed, however, cuts both ways.

The only thing that seemed obvious was that big companies had figured out today's America: The average worker is not anxious to take a step backward to help some stranger, even if down the road it might mean helping himself.

On my way out of town I stopped by a front porch that seemed left over from the set of *Deliverance*. A bearded young man sitting on the broken steps, among comatose dogs and cats, watched me narrowly. He said nothing to several requests for road directions. A woman with steel teeth three steps down was more helpful, if hardly more friendly.

"Not many jobs in town," I remarked.

"Ain't much of nothing," she said, ending the conversation.

The next lady I addressed might have been the friendliest person on earth. I'd stopped to photograph a general store and gas station, with letters dropping off the Ashland sign, and I noticed movement inside. In hopes of avoiding a shotgun blast, I decided to go in and introduce myself. Betty Francis had no shotgun, and if she had, she would never have found it. After twenty-seven years, her store's counters were shapeless heaps of everything from gum boots to Gummi bears, with the odd bear trap and boat hook thrown in. The mess amused her immensely, and it didn't seem to bother any customers. "Pleasing you pleases us" was written on her bill, and that was no idle boast.

By coincidence, she was the mother of Wally Warden's ace reporter and something of a newshound herself. I asked about a sign up the road that said HATFIELD CEMETERY. There was an old Hatfield hanging around somewhere, she thought, and she gave me some directions.

Awhile later I found two old gentlemen rocking on a porch and asked if they knew Aunt Ginny Hatfield. They did. She was up in a hollow, with a hip injury, and she would be one hundred and one the next month. One man, who seemed to know a lot about her, started a fresh story. "Well, one day Mother got up—" Mother? He was Elijah Hatfield, seventy-four.

"Well, them McCoys, we're no more enemies," he explained. "We outlived 'em all. Some of them lived just over there until six or seven years ago," he added, pointing to a house within pistol range across Route 52. "Good people."

Aunt Ginny was the oldest survivor of the bunch, but in fact, either clan could marshal a small army should the need arise. McCoys populate eastern Kentucky. Elijah Hatfield alone has seventeen kids, including one born when he was sixty-four, and as many nephews and nieces. But no one can still work up any rancor over the old feud. Neither the Hatfields nor the McCoys are even sure of the details. "They claim it was over a hog," Elijah offered.

He fitted the part perfectly, in long underwear, which he scratched periodically. A rascally twinkle illuminated his tales of whiskey and women. Personally I preferred his electric spaghetti. It seems stray dogs had been hounding his garbage, so he rigged up a booby trap. He filled a pail with linguine al pomodoro only a stray dog would approach. If one stuck his nose in the bucket, however, he received enough current to persuade him henceforth to lunch elsewhere. Pesto control.

Hatfield had worked in the mines thirty-seven years. I asked about his lungs. "Don't have any. Stay out in the air all the time." His pal Buddy Belcher, also had been brutalized by coal mining. But like almost everyone along the Appalachian ridge, he seemed sad at its passing.

"There's just too much unemployment," Belcher said. "At least they get the checks now, and food stamps." People could move away, he allowed, but they don't. West Virginians love their land and take pride in what outsiders think is tough terrain. "We got land that goes up so you can farm both sides of it." Belcher laughed. "But I'll tell you, if they cut them checks off, everything'd starve to death."

I pushed on to find Aunt Ginny. At a bar on the way four youths stopped their pool game to give me careful directions. The only words I could understand were "gas station," and that's where I found her, in a house across from a gas station.

Aunt Ginny was born Zettie Ferrell, and she married Epp Hat-field just after the turn of the century, when McCoy was a dirty word. But she was not one for dirty words. "I remember the hoeing and planting and the singing," she said. "We had a fine life." When I asked what else she recalled, she declaimed three pages of a poem about a mother's love; she had memorized most of her old Mc-Guffey schoolbooks.

She beamed with pleasure at the intrusion by a stranger. "I'm happy to meet with any friendly people," she said, squeezing my hand. When she confirmed that she would be one hundred and one in a few weeks, I mentioned Willard Scott. He and Aunt Ginny were made for each other. But she looked blank. I explained who he was, as much as that was possible. "I don't care much about TV these days, except for the preaching," she said. "I'm sorry, I don't know Wilbur."

Gary, West Virginia, is a place to remember when holiday speakers fog up in rhetoric. It shows, on one hand, how fiercely Americans will fight adversity. But it shows also how deeply needless adversity is ingrained in the American way. Gary is a coal ghost town, but its ghosts are still living there.

Since 1902 Gary had shipped metallurgical coal to Gary, Indiana, where it was used to make steel. In the 1950's it was the leading coal-mining region in the country. Suddenly America was going out of that line of business. Almost from one day to the next U.S. Steel locked up and went home. Gary's fifteen thousand people were left with no visible means of support and a water system that oozed brown sludge. That was in 1981. When I arrived, the population was below two thousand, and all but the disability checks were drib-bling away to nothing.

Driving in early one morning, I asked where to find a cup of coffee. I was directed back down the mountain to Welch, from which I had come. A small supermarket still operated, but just about everything else was in Welch, including the mayor of Gary. There were no streetlights; electricity cost too much. The pool hall had closed down when out-of-work miners had no more money for side bets. Mostly Gary was occupied by pensioners, widows and people like the one-legged Vietnam vet I met who rarely left his mountain-top farm. And miners who refused to believe that the latest dip in

Gary's boom-and-bust cycle was almost certainly the last.

I had been briefed the night before by a friendly couple who had settled in Welch some years earlier. In such a small place, in matters so touchy, neither wanted to be named. In contrast with farming, they had explained, mining took from the land and gave nothing back. It produced a curious mentality, a class of people willing to extract wealth, with little attachment to the land itself. "People came here to make money and go," the wife said. "They didn't want to make their marks here. For zoos, parks, museums, you go to Pittsburgh. They put their money up there, not here where they made it. There is no culture here but coal. They have a Coal Festival, a Coal Queen. I think sometimes if I see another lump of the stuff, I'll blow my brains out."

But this is West Virginia. Miners themselves would rather scrounge odd jobs at home than go make ax handles in North Carolina. "They expect it to start again," my friend continued. "They believe it. They think they will be coal miners again, but they won't be."

Gary, Welch and the rest of McDowell County are in the same boat. On the first day of every month the post office is ankle-deep in envelopes ripped open by anxious people, and each month the envelope snowfall diminishes. On welfare check day, housewives line up at food stores behind carts stacked high with pinto beans and Pepsi. Drug dealers bustle along on their rounds. Within a week you can track each new dollar down Main Street. Most of the time jobless men have nothing to do but bully their kids, belt their wives and eat too much.

Health care is limited. Just before I got there, three people were hurt in a car wreck, and two of them had to be flown to Charleston in a helicopter. Heart attack victims must decide whether to take a chance on a road trip to Bluefield, if they can afford it.

With little money and less motivation, schools are inferior. There is not a movie theater in the county, and the nearest bus stop is an hour and a half drive away. Few kids have any notion of nearby Virginia, let alone Nicaragua. Their fathers notice foreign wars when they're about coal. A local vocational school equips young men with mining skills they will probably never use. And no one sees any alternative. Tourists show scant interest in a place where the only historical markers recall mine disasters. Local authorities were delighted to attract a state prison. The Welch daily newspaper is campaigning to use abandoned coal mines for storing nuclear waste.

Ron Estep, the pragmatic mayor of Gary, knows exactly what faces his battered community. "It is as bad as it can get in terms of the economy," he said. "The long-term implications for coal are good but not for people living here. The future is highly technical, robotics. Jobs created will require sophisticated college graduates with degrees in engineering. The average blue-collar miner has got to satisfy himself that his job is done. He is going to have to start over."

He also knows why it happened. "We have been a captive market, and we've lost out. We saw it coming. The state government had reports on the situation in the 1960's, but nobody paid any attention. Every bit of it could have been avoided."

Estep, who now runs a government-supported training program to turn miners into everything from chefs to computer specialists, has given the recent past a lot of thought. Though too polite to phrase it so bluntly, he faults American ignorance, arrogance and apathy. No one read the writing on the wall; no one even bothered to learn where the wall was located.

"If Japan could take our resources, bring them halfway around the world and sell steel here cheaper, you knew something was wrong," he said. South Korea, Taiwan and others started late with fresh technology. American producers stuck to old ways and steady markets until they were too far behind to compete. Then they walked away, toward something else. But their workers could not follow.

Federal and state authorities might have planned ahead, he said, but then they never do. "Democracy is a crisis-oriented system," Estep said. "We really don't look at a problem until we have to." This, he acknowledged, is nothing new. But he was just warming up. "The problem here is that people do not exercise their rights to go out and demand what they need. We should be directing those who should be lobbying for us. People know for a fact that this is a democracy, so they don't worry about what that means. Less than thirty percent get out and vote. Until the Depression this was a republic. Now we have macho politicians. You can't have a democracy without accountability."

The mayor of Gary paused to catch his breath and then shook his head at how simple it ought to be. "Their own destiny lies in their own hands, and they're not doing anything about it."

Even more than Gary, Davy drives home the tragedy of West Virginia with the force of an air hammer. It is up a long, winding road from Welch, in a time and place of its own. All along Main Street dogs laze in boarded-up doorways of clapped-out buildings. At the lone gas station I stopped to talk to Nelson Keaton, the owner. After thirty-three years in the mines he had decided to try something else. But, at long last, Davy seemed to be giving up the ghost. "Looks like people are leaving, all right," Keaton said. "I'd get out, too, if I could sell."

Keaton's son, John, at twenty-five, wasn't so sure leaving was the answer. "I been outa state three times to work," he told me. "I just can't make it. Besides, when you do go, you don't know nobody. . . . Better to stick around home."

An old man in a baseball cap heard me announce my purpose. "Son," he volunteered, "you sure picked a poor state to write about." His name was Arthur Green, and he'd been a miner. I asked if he had suffered from it.

"Emphysema, tuberculosis, alcoholism, one lung, pin in my hip," he replied. "Not much else can be done to me but put me in the ground." He'd worked all over the country trying to put his four kids into school. Finally, he decided to come back to Davy, because he was born there. I asked how long ago that was, expecting to hear a figure near retirement age. "Forty-one years," he said. He was four years younger than I was.

A young woman sat in her car, nursing a baby, and we talked about the future. "That's the school over there," she said, pointing to a roofless, blackened hulk covered in graffiti. It burned down in 1979, and town fathers used the insurance money to pay off teachers' back wages. Now Davy's few remaining kids, underfed and badly looked after, make a twenty-mile daily round trip to Welch.

Driving down the hill, I reflected on the trip from Charleston. The desperate conversations resembled those I'd had in two dozen developing countries around the world—except that McDowell County was not developing and no one was giving foreign aid. It was still morning, and I was clear-eyed and professional, picking over the evidence to analyze yet another godforsaken corner of the globe. Arlo Guthrie rumbled from the radio, and I stopped to listen. "Good mornin', America, how are ya? Don't you know me, I'm your native son? . . ." All of a sudden I couldn't make out the road.

If I'd left home naive, twenty years of watching the world pick at its sores had cured me. West Virginia was devastating not so much because of poor people stuck in their tracks, which was bad enough, as because of all the Americans who would argue with me. Especially those in West Virginia. Psychotherapists talk often of people's refusal to accept the unacceptable. But reality muscles through, acknowledged or not.

After a look at Appalachia, one's mind no longer automatically attaches the adjective "black" to underclass. Poverty often has a racial, or at least an ethnic, tinge to it. There is "white trash," but surely even impoverished Klan members can afford clean sheets. By some calculations, a quarter of all American children under six live in poverty. Decent, hardworking, God-fearing Americans, white, black and otherwise, stare routinely into the face of starvation.

A nation that likes to see averages can easily misplace poor people. When economic indicators rise or fall, we select general terms: sluggish, healthy, recessionary, booming. But, on a per capita basis, a single Donald Trump can mask one hell of a lot of jobless West Virginians.

The question bears asking: Are we really so well of, so singularly generous, prosperous and free in an otherwise faltering world?

In bald statistics, according to the Urban Institute in Washington, American children lived in worse poverty than those of at least seven other industrial nations during 1988. In the United States 17.1 percent were in families below the poverty line. That was twice the West German rate and three times that of Switzerland. In Britain, with all of its unemployment, the level was 10.7 percent. But the real difference is even greater.

True enough, no other country offers such opportunities to make a fortune. In Europe and Japan too many obstacles stand in the way: tradition; government regulations; unions and inflexible workers; restricted markets. In the land of equality anyone can trot onto the field and score a touchdown. But when Rousseau and Jefferson declared all men are created equal, they were not thinking about football.

At best all men have equal access to the playing field. Many, however, are born without spikes. A lucky few are given the secret game codes. Some are more willing to knee a groin when no one is looking. The American way allows scant opportunity to sit quietly on the sidelines. Everybody plays. The losers are hauled off the field so as not to obstruct the game.

By our rules, everyone must score. What if illness outstrips health benefits? What if college tuition gets out of hand? A layoff? Eviction? A simple slip in the mud can mean losing. If losers don't starve, they sit out the game, marked by humiliating labels, such as "welfare mother" or "unemployable." Anyone can get back on the field—we are famous for going bankrupt one day and bouncing back, unsullied, the next. But what about slow people or sick ones?

Here we might shift the American metaphor from football to footwear. You are supposed to get out of a rut by pulling yourself up by your bootstraps. Try it the next time you're wearing boots with straps on them. Better yet, try it barefoot.

Every other industrialized country, except South Africa, provides free health care. Most pay for higher education as well. European unemployment benefits go up to 90 percent of the last salary, and workers can retrain at a token cost.

Sweden goes the farthest, with crib-to-crypt welfare. Everyone gets the same benefits to avoid social stigmas. The state provides a safety net below which no one can fall. Anyone can use that as a trampoline and grow rich; many do. The society, famed for its productive industry, is not especially burdened by layabouts. Conservatives say that taxes are too high, that the state goes too far. But even the right wing defends the basic system.

What America can learn from Sweden is open to question. It is a small, homogeneous nation spurred on by a Lutheran work ethic. It is hardly as creative, as freewheeling, or as much fun as the United States. For some Americans, Swedes are a bunch of Commies. But one thing is crystal clear. There is no Davy, Sweden.

There is no Pigeon Forge, Sweden, either. After seeing the bleakest part of Appalachia, I went to Dollywood, a vast amusement park on the theme of a poor kid growing up to be Dolly Parton in the Smoky Mountains of Tennessee. It was a tough trip.

For the American Dream, Mountain Variation, it is hard to beat Dolly. I love her myself. She is in my road tapes box, along with Jerry Jeff Walker and Jesse Winchester, and is most likely as nice as her friends say she is. Dollywood, for all the plastic hoke, has its charm. Real purple morning glories climb over split log fences among the sparkling brooks and stands of pine. Johnny Appleseed's tin-pot hat was made in a Newly Industrialized Country of Asia, but musicians play dulcimers they made themselves, and craftsmen patiently demonstrate skills their fathers started to forget.

Mike Rose, peering through little round glasses over a full red beard, was banging on a glowing piece of wrought iron. He was born nearby and, after studying sculpture at the University of Penn-sylvania, decided to be a blacksmith in the Smokies. "I had my own business but spent most of the time running around chasing down bills," he said. "That's why I ran off and joined the circus." He meant Dollywood. He could earn a lot turning out coat hooks but decided that made him just like some machine in Taiwan. Instead, he pre-ferred gargoyle-topped canes and fancy fire pokers. He seemed happy enough, but not many people spent money on handmade quality. "The only way to get rich in this business," he said, "is to sell blacksmith tools to aspiring blacksmiths."

Dollywood has brought jobs and tourist gold to the bottom end of a depressed chain of mountains. The park employs 2,000 people and attracts 1.5 million visitors a year. Then again, talk about your mixed blessings.

Pigeon Forge and, worse, nearby Gatlinburg loom as chilling monuments to what happens when greed, bad taste and lack of forethought combine with a particular distortion of the American idea of family fun.

The process was dead simple. Visitors loved the down-home charm of Gatlinburg, which had thrown itself haphazardly astride a raw, rushing mountain creek. Word went around. Builders brought in warmed-over plans and bulk plastic. Creekside rooms earned more, so the river disappeared under overhanging terraces. Every junk food chain and wax museum mogul in the region smelled the ac-tion. Gatlinburg was masked by garish signs hawking cheap imita-tions of what had been obliterated. All that was left were two rickety footbridges, sealed off as too dangerous for modern America.

"It was greed, ra't down," observed Ted Wright, an antiques dealer who feared the same would happen to his own nearby town, Town-send. "I cain't understand people not able to think about protecting what they got that has value."

Local promoters argue that the nearby Great Smoky Mountains National Park is as beautiful as ever. The park attracted 10.2 million visitors in 1987, nearly three times as much as the Grand Canyon. True. And a tree grows in Brooklyn. Nature was doing its part, whatever man screwed up around it.

In America there seems to be a pathological draw to the celebrated. Dollywood began as a minor-league park called Gold Rush City. In 1986 Parton, whose personal solid geometry is better known than the Smoky Mountains', negotiated partnership. She pops in every month or so, her pals perform regularly and her name is carved on every tree.

I revealed myself to be a shameless sufferer of it. Strolling around, I followed the sound waves to an open stage where a thin blond woman emitted rock and roll. A sign declared FREIDA PARTON. Her ample bosom were credentials to the family, but she was distant and severe. I sat down on the front bench next to a chinless young man in a FABULOUS FREIDA sweat shirt, who watched her with desperate devotion. When her eyes fell on me, she broke into a wide, sunny smile. Clearly I had lit up her life. Ugly pride suffused my spirit.

The groupie next to me was rattled. He was devastated by jealousy, but then I had been anointed. He shifted imperceptibly closer to me. "Is that a cousin or sister?" I asked him.

He was horrified at my ignorance, and his reply was a rebuke: "That's Dolly's little sister!"

A few minutes later Freida paused to sign autographs. I went up to talk to her, and the sunny smile returned. Poor woman, I thought, how can I break the news that I am already taken? We chatted amiably. Before leaving, I said I was out of cards but told her my name, adding, "In case you remember it."

She chuckled. "I don't know why I would. I meet a thousand people a day."

Not far away, to the southwest of Knoxville, is the Tellico Dam. Remember the snail darter? Back in the 1960's the Tennessee Valley Authority decided the region needed yet another lake. A mere two-hundred-million-dollar earthen dam on the Little Tennessee River would produce one. No one was quite sure why it was needed. Recreation and industry were mentioned vaguely. The loss of prime farmland, or the proximity of other lakes, made no impression. The TVA, the last surviving dinosaur of Franklin Roosevelt's New Deal, had started to move. The project took on a life of its own.

Moving families from beloved farms merely took some hard, mean dealing, but there was plenty of precedent. The Cherokee problem was tougher. Lake waters would submerge traditional Cherokee burial mounds. This was the heart of old Cherokee country, and the lake would obliterate the still-unexplored traces of the centuries-old sacred capital. But Indians, particularly dead ones, were no obstacle. The TVA would move the bones.

Mere beauty was no contender. Fishermen insisted the Little Tennessee was among North America's best trout streams. Any philistine with a free hour could see how lovely it was, glinting silver among the trees and rocks of Smoky Mountain foothills.

But the snail darter nearly did the trick. Ecologists argued the two-inch fish would disappear. The river was its only habitat. Court battles raged; millions were spent. In the end the TVA went ahead anyway.

In *Indian Country* Peter Matthiessen described how John Duncan, a Republican congressman from Tennessee, "used a whole bag of procedural tricks to sneak an unseen, undescribed, and undebated amendment past his unsuspecting colleagues in just forty-three seconds." In the Senate, he said, Howard Baker, also of Tennessee, lined up scant support, asserting that the dam was vital for energy and that the future of the snail darter was assured. The Philadelphia *Inquirer* called it "an abomination of irresponsibility . . . a towering symbol of almost everything that is rotten in the District of Columbia."

After all these years people still didn't like the dam, and by the time I got there, some were starting to hate it. At the time, Matthiessen pointed out, it was clear someone would make a lot of money when all the condemned land went back on the market. Sure enough, the TVA had sold back chunks of land to developers who had their eye on the yup class in Knoxville.

"I figure we got about three hundred dollars an acre, maybe a little less, back in 1970," remarked a retired gentleman who had to sell sixty-eight acres of what is now prime lakefront property. After visiting the Tellico Village sales office, I calculated that he could buy back similar land at roughly a hundred times that. Of course, that would include golf rights, utility hookups and such amenities as a security force to protect him from the neighbors.

"Ain't much you can say about it," the man said. "We used to it by now." He asked that I not give his name. "I've got to live with the TVA."

In Knoxville a TVA official, who was even more concerned about anonymity, acknowledged that the lake served no purpose. "You know, those engineers in the West Wing, they're builders. Once they got going, they had one goal in mind," he said. "Our excuse was that Congress ordered it, but that's no reason."

The engineers had gotten going on seventeen nuclear power plants, meantime, but nine of them were scrapped. I didn't want to rub it in, however. That morning the TVA had to shut down its Sequoyah nuclear plant, recently restarted after thirty months' paralysis. A new director had just fired half of the executive staff. You had to sympathize with a power company that was losing money after fifty years of taxpayer support.

The Tellico Dam, if history now, told me a lot about how things work in America. Authorities recognized environmental value if lobbyists were there to rub their noses in it; votes were at stake. But then again.

The snail darter, meanwhile, showed up elsewhere in 1980, and "that damned little minnow," as Tennessee legislators called it, was doing fine. "That fish was a crock." Wright, the antiques dealer, chuckled. "You cain't eat it, you cain't sell it, you cain't fuck it. This was about something more. If you'd ever fished the Little T, you'd understand. It was the ultimate."

The Indians are mostly forgotten. The remains of 191 of them were gathered from 285 sites and reburied out behind a museum by the lake. Carroll Hamilton, who runs the museum, wished it hadn't been necessary. "That's supposed to be progress," he said. "I don't see it that way, and most of the people here don't either."

The displays are nicely done, but it is a vastly depressing place. Little signs on the mass grave plead PLEASE KEEP OFF THE MOUND. Few visitors pause long enough to notice how the first Cherokees described how the world began: "All was water. Bears went out and brought up soft mud to make earth. It was held by four cords. When they broke, the earth would sink back into the water and all would die."

CHAPTER

5

Dixie and Parts
South

Some people find God in Carolina. I found Reeboks. At those rare times we got together, my nephews Jon and Rich Gellman eyed my foreign feet with concern. I'd wear zip-up boots. Or Japanese running brogans. But when I showed up in some fruity Italian jobs, they could take no more. They bundled me off to a Chapel Hill mall and, for an unbroken hour, schooled me in high and low tops, blacks and whites, Velcro and the geometry of arches and ankles. I emerged in a gleaming white pair which Rich thoughtfully camouflaged in filth. Finally I looked like an inside insider.

In three years Americans bought enough pairs of the funny-looking, comfortable shoes to make Reebok the nation's most profitable company. Annual profits increased by 200 percent. Chairman Paul Fireman earned fifteen million dollars in 1987, not the sort of wage you associate with shoe salesmen. The British only invented Reeboks and wore them quietly. But as with pizza and the Walkman, Americans gave them Life. By 1984 the American subsidiary had bought out the eighty-nine-year-old parent company.

This exuberant expropriation of imports tends to frost the hell out of foreigners. Americans who swear by Michelin radials are amazed to learn that France exports tires. A Swedish friend visiting America met some guy who, wanting to be friendly, pointed to a train. "This is a train," he said. "Do you have trains in Sweden?" People bragged to her about mobile phones, which the Swedes had pioneered while Americans were still fumbling for dimes.

On *L.A. Law* a prosecutor paraphrased "a great American": He disagreed with his opponent but defended his right to speak. Voltaire, dead for some years, did not sue.

But if buyers forget who made what, sellers don't. The U.S. deficit was climbing toward $180 billion, a third of it with Japan alone. Living abroad, I had learned about that the hard way, but people at home were catching on fast. U.S. authorities let the dollar's value fall. That cut our prices, and we sold more. It also closed off the world to budget travelers and brought home Americans trying to start businesses abroad. Those countries that had pegged their economies to the dollar were out of luck, as were foreign investors who had banked on America.

It was some spectacle, that toilet paper greenback, symbol of a rich nation hustling credit to cover its consumer excesses. Back home, I could see again the depth of our potential. The problem, complex at the top, seemed simple enough at the bottom.

Jesse Jackson reduced it to a campaign gimmick. He'd ask for a show of hands from owners of a foreign-made video recorder? All hands went up; Americans made no VCRs. How many owned an MX missile? Fewer hands. He did not explain how to repel Russians with a remote channel changer, but he made his point: "We ain't making what people are buying."

More, people aren't buying what we are making. Americans love imports. And we sell too little abroad. Few other societies share the American sense of proportion, and we are slow to adapt to others' tastes. When we hit big, someone copies our product, with a new twist and a lower price. Our growing service industries provide jobs but little foreign exchange. Defense exports invite a whole new set of problems. Ron Estep had laid it out in Gary. As in Brazil and Sudan, our debt was rising. Self-indulgence would carry a price we had not begun to calculate.

But in economics there is always an on-the-other-hand. Some specialists argued that borrowed capital broadened our base. All we needed were brains and energy. I had seen plenty of both. Properly shocked, we could restore the balance and surge on to new prosperity. Or had some fatal flaw dulled our cutting edge? The Research Triangle, that patch of Tomorrowland between Raleigh and Durham, was a good place to find out.

Something in the ozone of the Research Triangle tells you that America is in no danger of slipping into the Stone Age. On a vast plain of bunkers and glassed-in offices those nerds from the high school Slide Rule Club are now doing acrobatics on mainframe computers. Security is brutal in the Triangle. But with a little warning, I stuck my head in the door at Northern Telecom.

For an hour Kathy Gritton took me from one maze of wires to another, speaking to me in tongues. She flung open steel doors to expose printed circuitry and miniature hardware of supreme complexity. We looked at experimental phone booths you would need a bazooka to vandalize. Single-minded technicians paid no more attention to her well-turned ankle than did the winking computer screens. This was serious shit. Everything had a name, or an acronym or a number, and she knew them all.

Essentially we were in a room with thirty million dollars' worth of gadgets to make sure telephone switching equipment worked as it should. Units were tested on up to six hundred thousand calls an hour, which is more hold buttons than most New York secretaries can handle. Elsewhere in the building people were busy. Northern Telecom was a crucial player in a scramble for a multibillion-dollar government communications contract.

I was convinced. Jesse may be right, but the condition need not be permanent. If someone would sort out the priorities, U.S. industry could make an MX missile that tapes *Moonlighting* on its way to Armageddon. But then, there was a hitch here I kept forgetting: Northern Telecom was Canadian.

All the people I spoke to there were American. Northern Telecom's investments were pumped into the U.S. economy, and its taxes went into American treasuries. So big deal, right? What if the company was Japanese? This stuff begins to get tricky. I'd met some men with steel plates in their heads who were still a little nervous about foreign intentions.

That's what struck me at the Research Triangle. I expected fancy technology. But I hadn't realized how vital it was for Americans to give some coherent thought to foreign investment. Every Canadian, on average, owned a square foot of Manhattan. Britons, Germans, Koreans, Saudis, Nigerians had big money in every field. The multinationals had always been a synonym for big U.S. business. For years I had seen countries deal with American money. The smart ones used it as a resource, built with it and passed strict laws to protect what they defined as their own interests. Now investment was coming the other way, fast. And few Americans seemed prepared to think about it constructively.

*

That night, in my sister Elise's comfortable living room in Chapel Hill, I thought once again about Ron Estep. When he said Americans were shaping their destiny by default, he meant more than the money. I had seen our blind spots put the world in danger, but I had not realized how much was obscured. Grenada, even after our enforced call on it, was almost a total blank.

On *Frontline,* Seymour Hersh documented four years after the fact how our Keystone Kops invasion had endangered the lives of American medical students it was supposed to rescue. Having been there not long before we invaded, I was fascinated. Nearly everything Hersh reported about the assault had been covered in the weeks that followed it—and generally ignored.

An appealing young rebel, Maurice Bishop, had deposed a despised dictator on the relaxed little Caribbean island. Most people liked him enough to excuse his tepid Marxist philosophies and tune out his barn-burning speeches. Even Bishop laughed off the rhetoric. "It's sand dancing, mon," he'd say, meaning it was as deep as tracks on the beach. The private sector flourished. Americans, even journalists, were welcome without visas.

Before the invasion I had inspected the secret air base. A cop directed me to the best angle for pictures. It was a strip of blacktop to replace the pocked, tiny runway at the wrong end of a forty-five-minute pothole course across the island. Dependent on tourism, Grenada would starve without a decent airport.

Bishop tried hard to deal with Reagan. But he was a Communist. Needing an airport for tourism, he turned to Cuba. That, for Washington, was a secret plan to build a base for arms shipments to Nicaragua. As she told Hersh, former Ambassador Sally Shelton-Colby had advised Washington that the menacing naval base Reagan invoked was a broken-down fishing wharf.

If Bishop was too extreme for Reagan, he was too moderate for hard-line cronies. Radicals used U.S. distortions about Grenada as justification to remove him. In a power struggle Bishop was murdered. General Hudson Austin took charge and swiftly assured six hundred Americans at St. Georges Medical School they would be safe. He opened the supermarket for them. At the time a U.S. force was steaming to the Middle East. Instead, it went south.

U.S. intelligence knew so little about this menacing adversary that paratroopers were dropped into antiaircraft fire, the only serious resistance. Troops were given 1978 Grenada Tourist Board maps. When they raced in to save the students, most were not there. The school's rector had rushed to Washington to pinpoint two campuses. But no one told rescuers about the second campus. It took the Eighty-second Airborne Division four days, against token opposition, to cover a distance students jogged in an hour.

The first night Reagan declared victory. His listeners included most of the students, stranded and frightened by the danger Operation Urgent Fury had created. Reagan said stockpiled arms had been found, ready to sow havoc. He paused and, in his dramatic heavy breathing, announced: "We got there just in time."

The arms cache, reporters later found, was some relics going back to Spanish-American War days, with some modern weapons for the Grenada militia. The CIA never released its assessment, leaked later, that there appeared to be nothing for export. The Cuban militia was mostly bulldozer drivers, and only a few Grenadian defense force troops fought back.

We went to war almost blind, against an enemy we did not understand, in spite of counsel we did not heed. We killed 45-Grenadians, including 21 mental patients we bombed by accident, and 24 Cubans. We lost 19 dead and 119 wounded. As we realized four days too late, we could have rescued the students within minutes by helicopter, if that had been even necessary.

But the administration wrote its own history. It banned reporters from Grenada for the first two days. Four sneaked in, but they were lured aboard a U.S. Navy ship with a promise of a telex line. They were, when you cut away the niceties, imprisoned. Public relations officers told us how Grenadians reacted. Cameras missed U.S. troops—heirs to the men who had stormed Iwo Jima—experiencing "morale problems" when the campaign lasted past dinner. Or refusing to advance toward supposed hostages until air cover was assured.

By the time reporters learned what trouble we had conquering an island with fewer people than Yuma, Arizona, Americans were celebrating their greatness. Few noticed Loren Jenkins's story about the last patient in the mental hospital we bombed. The man, still dazed from the carnage, summed it up better than anyone: "They're crazy out there."

The real message was lost. We had stomped on a roaring mouse, revealing ourselves to be militarily incompetent, politically reckless and unable to apply our own intelligence data. We risked lives we meant to save. We were proved to have distorted the facts. When our allies dissented, we rounded on them. But that did not temper their judgment.

The final irony was predictable. The Americans, having run off the Cubans, finished the airfield. Grenada needed tourists, we said.

The aftermath was so much drivel for the Sunday morning snore programs. Polls showed a majority of Americans were perfectly happy to be informed by field commanders and government public relations people. Reporters were too arrogant as it was; it served them right. Few Americans seemed to care that if reporters weren't there, they weren't there. What stood out were the photos of jubilant young Americans kissing their home soil. It was just extra detail when many said, on reflection, that was because they were happy the whole business was over.

A year afterward Reagan boasted about the success, concluding: "America is back."

Hersh's program clarified some points. He interviewed a U.S. spokesman whose darting eyes suggested the administration was not after new facts. Other reporters noted that taxes and inflation had soared so high there was talk of voting in the old dictator. U.S. aid totaled little more than the seventy-five-million dollars spent on invasion. The turmoil scared off tourists and investors. And the island's best little inn was absorbed as the U.S. Embassy.

But if people didn't care back then, they cared four years less in 1988.

In the shady sections of Chapel Hill small wars in faraway places take on a certain abstraction. For people on Robin Road, mayhem is what happened in the Murder House, and that was years ago. Someone was killed in a family matter. Anyone on Robin Road could give it to you, blow by blow. For a long time the place was empty. When someone moved in, dark rumors said the real estate agents withheld the grim details.

It reminded me of a remark by Jorge Luis Borges when violence in Argentina was killing people by the thousands. He reminisced about the old days in his Buenos Aires neighborhood of Palermo, when the rare murder victim was talked about for months. Above all, Borges said, people knew his name.

But the Murder House faded in time. Chapel Hill, like Buenos Aires in the good old times, lived beyond the Key Line. The arbitrary frontier was getting to be a standard measure for me. Everywhere I asked people if they locked their doors, when they had started to lock, and why. And I was curious if once securely turned, the key was left under a geranium pot where even a burglar who couldn't locate America on a map would find it. Tracing the Key Line would tell me a lot about modern America.

Elise is the sort who gets up early to water her ferns and feed her cats and then drive a long way to work, humming. She watches the world carefully, only partly to know what craziness her brother might get into, but she doesn't worry about it. She has faith in people's good instincts. Her circle of friends would be a pretty good cast of characters for a book I noticed called *What's Right with America*. In fact, the author should have come to her wedding.

For a brief moment, I shelved my detached observer status to put on a yarmulke and give away the bride. But—Elise will forgive me— I was reporting. We were in the flower-choked backyard of a dog-loving, hard-playing blond young doctor, Elise's daughter, Randy, with a dozen benches full of beaming guests of various colors. The service was partly in Hebrew, a language I had last used to tell soldiers not to shoot at my photographer. Little things were important. I could leave my camera on the back seat of the convertible. I didn't wonder if anyone boiled the water.

The company included relatives from all over the country who had made good lives for themselves in a dozen different fields. True, there were a couple who still talked about *schvartzers*, but they'd lived in Hymietown. All in all, it was a warm, inspiring reminder that there was plenty right with America. But no one needed me to tell them that. Mr. and Mrs. Gordon Light went off on a honeymoon, and I went back to poking under the rug.

Elise, among other things, was press secretary for a gorilla. She was marketing director for the North Carolina Zoo, at Asheboro, and Ramar was her star. The zoo was a fine example of public and private money wisely spent. An ersatz African plain and a walk-in aviary gave visitors a feel for how the animals would be living if not behind bars. Elise knew every rodent personally and attempted to make introductions. I slipped away to watch the patrons.

As a conservation loony I was heartened to see so many kids

dragged around by parents and teachers. At the white rhino enclosure a little girl yelled, "Hey, look at the rhinosaur."

One mother observed, "That's big hogs, ain't they?"

Just about everyone mentioned that rhinos were large animals. A lot of them were in no position to cast aspersions.

This question of weight is difficult. Genetic disorders and thyroid problems are often to blame. But let us not avoid the issue. Too many Americans are fat, and some are shockingly and dangerously obese. Obviously many people exercise and look great; I noticed that. In fact, at that extreme we probably have the most fit aerobic subclass in the world. At the zoo, however, they were not in the majority.

I had been warned. My Australian-Swiss friend Paul came back from Michigan, and I asked what struck him most. "The big asses Americans have," he said. "They are gross. Even if people are slim at the top, they bulge out in the most alarming fashion. It's the junk food. You can't imagine what they stuff down themselves. Their idea of breakfast is one croissant and three sticky buns. All sugar."

Fair or not, it is what visitors notice. Even before I reached New York, I watched a little girl on the plane. By the Azores the aisle around her was littered ankle-deep in candy wrappers. When the meal came, she speared her steak and bit into it the way a warthog might. It was strong stuff.

At the zoo I watched two grotesquely misshapen parents, with a ten-year-old son as round as they were. They might have been jugglers. Between them they balanced two quarts of Coke, several hot dogs, a large box of indeterminate starch and sugar and something that looked like a picnic basket. Everywhere I turned, people whose thighs billowed out of shorts were trailing waste.

Specialists tell me the southern diet is especially fattening. But it is not only the South. The surgeon general reported in 1988 that thirty-four million Americans were obese. And I could see why. Everywhere I went, people gave me grease and sugar. Mainly, it was the proportions and the frequency. Falling into step, I found myself swelling like a tick. At movies the popcorn tubs could be plumbed to be Jacuzzis. Soft drinks in cups were sized like olives, small being large enough to douse a forest fire. About every twenty minutes someone was saying, "Let's go get a pizza." I, a fully formed American happy to be back, was always saying, "Sure."

Fortunately there was the North Carolina Zoo to remind me what might lie ahead.

My particular problem was that I had just spent a few months in Africa watching kids die for lack of a handful of grain. There was no immediate connection. Some American giving up his second Twinkie was not going to save Sudan; the world was choking in excess food that poor people couldn't afford to buy. Also, I wasn't there to preach. But somehow, the contrast between people stuffing themselves with food that was killing them and others dying for lack of any food at all made me shudder.

Preaching, in any case, would not be out of place in Carolina. Jim and Tammy Bakker's Heritage U.S.A. was the second most popular theme park in America after Disneyland. Unless you count passion plays and swing sets on a Galilee motif, there is little to do and less to see. As near as I could make out, it was popular because the Bakkers convinced people it was where God took his rec-vee on the weekends.

Jim and Tammy were not in when I got to Heritage U.S.A. In fact, the place was not even in Charlotte anymore. When the embarrassment started, townsfolk suddenly remembered it was in Fort Mill, thirty miles south and over the South Carolina line. The head shepherd had been caught diddling Little Bo Peep, telling her it was in aid of the flock. More details filtered in. The innocent victim had squeezed Bakker for at least $160,000 in hush money and then exposed her chaste bosom to *Playboy,* for $1 million more. PTL, supposed to mean "Praise the Lord," was rendered often more as "Pass the Loot." Or "Part Thy Legs."

From a distance the God-in-a-box industry of televangelism always seems like some bad joke Americans at home are playing on expatriates. It is not really happening; they are only trying to scare us. Up close, it is not so funny.

The most casual look at America reveals how vital religion is today. We have long since given up nature as a guide to right and wrong. A lot of elected leaders, civil servants and corporate directors don't seem to know the difference. Parents and teachers have lost much of their old authority. For believers, that leaves only God. And a lot of people want to reach God so badly they'll follow any flimflam artist who claims to have an open line.

And if Sunday morning television is any guide, they must want to reach God awfully bad. I got my first look at Jimmy Swaggart after he began flinging stones at Jim Bakker but before he slipped on his own slime. He was hard to take seriously. But his name fit perfectly, a blend of swagger and braggart.

Swaggart was in high spirits, fresh from revealing how Bakker had soiled the cloth in a Florida motel. The thing to keep in mind, he said, was the power of prayer. Carried away with his message, he let his voice rise to a whine. Perspiration flowed. Then he lapsed into a little story. He was on the road, praying aloud in his room, when the motel phone rang. A woman next door had heard him through the wall and recognized his voice. He comforted her in God, he said. "Together," Swaggart thundered, "we raised our voices to heaven." Suddenly he paused for a half second, and his brow furrowed imperceptibly. "It was on the phone," he added hastily. "I never saw the woman."

The next time I saw Brother Swaggart, he had gotten his. It was his first time back at the electronic pulpit after admitting doing something dirty, never fully explained, with a prostitute in New Orleans. He was no longer thumping the Bible; he fondled it gently. He spoke elliptically about the power of forgiveness. At the end he fixed a doe-eyed gaze on the camera and said, "Thank you. Thank you. Thank you." Something about that scene, the abrupt shift from hollering hypocrisy to a pathetic plea for sympathy, made my gums ache.

That was not the last time I saw Swaggart on TV. Off the air at home, he was down in El Salvador, thumping a Spanish-language Bible via a hellfire interpreter who managed to get across even the weeping and gasping. After the bananas and bullets, we were sending down our biblical toxic waste.

On another Sunday Jerry Falwell was educating his followers about the intricacies of foreign affairs. His was another show entirely. He avoided histrionics and suits that glowed in the dark. He used only two syllables to say the name Jesus, and he talked about the day's news as much as ancient times. As such, he exuded credibility, and he clearly wielded clout. An evil conspiracy stalks the world, he explained. It was inspired by the devil, but its application was left to that foul trinity Hitler, Stalin and Gorbachev. I don't know what else he said; that's when I switched to *The Flintstones*.

At the PTL motel outside the gate of Heritage U.S.A., I followed arrows on hand-lettered notices taped to the wall. The "Bring the Bakkers Back Club" had an office down in room 110. I opened the door to a paralyzing cloud of perfume emanating from a woman who occupied a lot of space behind the large desk. In a powerful voice, booming and rasping at once in a thick drawl, she asked what she could do for me. I told her, and she immediately began opening and closing file cabinets.

The Reverend Inez Brown, of Austin, Texas, had documentary proof that the devil had done in Jimmy Bakker. She riffled through papers carefully, with three fingers arched in the air. "I made a mistake and put nail polish on my fingers," she explained. As she thrust newspaper clippings and handbills at me, I tried to follow her rumbling discourse. Jerry Falwell, the wrong kind of Baptist, was the villain. Tammy Faye, such a lovely woman, would pull through.

My mind wandered. The motel walls were decorated in mono-chrome computer art, mainly a portrait of Mrs. Brown and another of the Bakkers over the legend "We love you, Jim and Tammy." The stench of perfume was deadening. Mrs. Brown explained on, pausing alternately to unstick her fingers or sip from a liter-size mug of Coke. She mentioned someone: "He was one of the best hellfire and brimstone preachers there ever was."

About then a good-looking young man from Atlanta stuck his head in the door. "God bless Jim and Tammy," he said by way of greeting. "I just wanted to say I love 'em." Then he left, and so did I.

Heritage U.S.A. was a disappointment, but then, I'm no funda-mentalist. It is a large park littered with papier-mâché backdrops for passion plays and souvenir shops selling bumper stickers with slogans like "When the going gets tough, the tough go to Jesus." It was winter, and only diehards were around. I sneaked out of the television show studio audience after five minutes and wandered into the Total Learning Center in search of a phone. A very nice lady, Betty Cannon, sat behind the reception desk.

"It was literally like someone died around here," she said, recall-ing the first news of scandal. "But we asked the Lord to see us through, and he did." She had come five years earlier with her hus-band, a pastor, and found peace. "This is a place where the body of Christ can come together as part of the Christian world," she said.

Mrs. Cannon was no fire breather. Calm, assured, she explained how people of all religions were aiming for the same place. Heritage U.S.A. was a peaceful spot where they could meditate, congregate and find glory in God. "This is his ministry, and he will not allow it to be put under." Attendance dropped a little, but the scandal made the place famous. Foreigners came from everywhere, not always to pray. "We've been made fun of," Mrs. Cannon said, "but the Lord said this would happen. By persecution, you know I am coming."

She repeated my name. "Are you Christian?" I said no. "I know you are Jewish," she replied, "but there are Christian Jews." I decided to save her some trouble and move on.

I walked a garden path to the Upper Room, a pasteboard replica of a vaulted Jerusalem chapel, furnished lavishly with boxes of Kleenex. It contained Plexiglas bins stuffed with a half million miracle requests. I read one slip of paper: "Please pray that I can read the Bible. I am blind." There were also thousands of photos of people who reported on their miracles.

The main hotel was a high-rise slab with a Hollywood antebellum facade tacked on. Its interior had plastic wood antiques, spindly iron fancywork and a soaring atrium in exuberant bad taste. The theme was celestial southern, but it looked as if, with any decent blow, it would be gone with the wind. But, the skeptical visitor had to admit, the blow had come, and it was still there.

A jovial black doorman in white livery, Lee Noble, thought the place was great. "I came down from Philadelphia to check this out. God just opened doors for me." Now he was opening doors for God.

In North Carolina I followed the case of a twenty-one-year-old man named Michael John Shornock. The papers called him Rambo. He had been jailed for theft, and he escaped. Recaptured, he was later paroled. But police wanted him about some stolen guns. Shornock was not going to be caught. He made the papers when he forced a woman to heat up some spaghetti for him; he shot her pit bull to get in. He fled on her son's motorcycle. A month later two men robbed a bank and wounded a policeman in their escape. The next day a sheriff's deputy stopped a car for littering, and the driver shot at him. That night gunfire broke out at a party. Police suspected Shornock was there. They found the bank getaway car. Shornock, they said, was a bank-robbing litterer who had shot at a cop.

A manhunt began at Sugarloaf Mountain on November 23. A day later Shornock was cornered in a cabin. He escaped in an exchange of shots with highway patrolmen. By November 25 Shornock had melted into the woods. A survivalist, fiercely defiant of bars, he would run forever. The posse got too close, however, and Shornock shot a deputy in the face. He got away.

This was high drama. Old Fort police officers said that a few months before, Shornock had asked to check into a state mental hospital. He called himself Rambo. The hospital released him under that name without identifying him. An old friend said he had the potential to do anything in the world but, at seventeen had told her, "Everything is going round and round and round, and I can't catch it." He had wished he'd been born three hundred years earlier. Captain Faron Hill, of the Cape Carteret police, said, "He hasn't harmed civilians. I don't think he would if he didn't feel threatened. But police officers threaten him."

I knew how it would end. I had seen it in *High Sierra* when Bogart got himself surrounded on a bare mountainside, at the end of a career of bank robbery. Someone would say something like "We hated to do it, but we didn't want any of our boys hurt."

The Charlotte *Observer* announced, on November 27: POLICE KILL SURVIVALIST IN MOUNTAIN SHOOT-OUT. Captain Hill, who had been after Shornock over three years, told the paper, "There was so much desperation. . . . I don't want to see nobody die, but I don't want to see any of us die, either."

Who could say? Shornock was a hard case all right. People blamed the hospital, which denied he had been there. But that was a sidelight. Such Rambo manhunts were not so rare. And especially when there were no hostages, it seemed as if fleeing the law meant capital punishment. I talked this over with Calvin Trillin, who, if irreverent about chicken à la king, is a student of killing in America. "There is only one level of response," he said. "You bring in more and more guns."

Savannah is one of those great old towns that have held on to some heritage. Partly the city was too depressed to renovate. But in the early 1950s, when the city tore down the splendid old Farmers' Market to build a hideous parking lot, citizens rose in arms. A group of women formed the Savannah Foundation. A Historic Review Board was given power.

"People all over the country have reached a point where they want to preserve old things." John Jordan told me in his antiques shop in an original cotton warehouse. "Values are on the rocks, and people feel more comfortable if they belong to a group with an attachment to the past. Savannah is way ahead because there is so much to clean up."

All over town people have restored antebellum mansions on graceful parks, refitting shutters and shoring up iron balconies. The old wharf and Cotton Exchange breathe history, a crumbling line of mossy bricks, elaborate ironwork and weathered wood. Cobblestone lanes and steep stairways layer down to the water from a line of handsome magnolia-choked buildings on the main street.

The city's main project was bringing back the riverfront. The whole area was cleaned up and let to businesses catering to tourists. The original train, renamed the Riverstreet Rambler, still plies the wharf. It carries tourists along with freight, blaring rock music as it puffs by.

"The riverfront has to have an economic base," Jordan said. "They sure as hell are not going to be shipping any more bales of cotton. What do you do? That's the problem we had. Total depression. Those old buildings just sat there, economically decadent."

He seemed to be apologizing. The whole idea sounded great to me; I pictured a line of old-style craftsmen beating on iron and cranking out fresh ice cream. Then I went to take a look.

After passing a few moldering buildings, the Rambler disappears into a tunnel that wasn't there before. It is a huge salmon loaf bearing a large sign HYATT REGENCY SAVANNAH.

On the other side the new part started. In one window I saw a disgusting life-size robot in a white suit and vest, white hair and mustache, with a face from congealed latex of an unhuman hue. "Har, har," boomed a cryptometallic voice from somewhere within, "don't be afraid of these Injuns. Won't harm you a bit, har, har, har." Grotesque eyes were set into orangish pink dough shaped into a permanent smirk. "Come on in, come on in, my name's Mark Twain." The voice delivered a fractured version of southern history, touting guided tours of Savannah.

That it was a long way from the Mississippi or that Samuel Clemens would have shot the man responsible was beside the point. One may argue that I am not seven years old and should not be a killjoy. But it just seemed that the real Mark Twain and the characters he left us, like the real old Savannah, ought to be enough to enrapture a seven-year-old. The mindless patter was obscured by a competing din. In the next window a pirate and his parrot were selling the same tour in whining voices. Over and over, all day long, the same stupid half jokes pierced the atmosphere of one of the few old southern ports Americans might still enjoy.

I hurried down to the Brass Wheel, hoping to find some old boat fittings. A woman at the counter smiled broadly, anxious to help. But all I found were brass tsetse flies, cute nautical sayings on phony wood, brass ashtrays you could pierce with a thumbnail and shelves of nonsensical made-in-Taiwan geegaws.

At an old bar, gutted to make room for a fast-service snack outlet, I met an amusing couple from Atlanta. They loved Savannah and had extended their vacation to stay longer. They told me about a restaurant called the Pirate's House, installed in three adjoining houses, among the city's oldest.

The food and service were good. I decided not to notice the plastic, Formica and cheap decor that masked the two-hundred-year-old walls. On the way out, though, I stopped to read a cutely lettered sign over a hole in the ground: THE EERIE UNDERGROUND CHAMBER WITH ANCIENT WALLS OF HANDMADE BRICK. THE MYSTERIOUS ARCHED TUNNEL ENTRANCE (NOW SEALED FOR SAFETY REASONS) WAS UNCOVERED BY WORKMEN IN 1962. WHO IT WAS CONSTRUCTED BY, WHEN AND FOR WHAT REASON ARE STILL UNKNOWN. COULD IT BE AN ENTRANCE TO AN OLD SECRET PASSAGE STILL UNDISCOVERED? COULD IT HAVE BEEN PART OF A DARK, DARK DUNGEON? WHAT DO YOU THINK?

What do I think? That someone should simply figure it out and restore it for its intrinsic historic value and not hoke it up in some jerky, coy manner. Ancient is Babylonia, or Greece and Rome, not the plantation period of the South. It's a fine idea to fire kids' imaginations about the past, about mysterious holes in the ground and forgotten epochs of pirates and escape routes. But how can kids grasp hold of history—or develop a solid feeling for their heritage—if pandering grown-ups constantly bury the real mystery in a thick slush of hoked-up cuteness? And don't any adults still want honest evidence of their past?

Up the road in Georgia a little city named Athens protects the handsome neoclassic homes built by early statesmen during a revival of interest in the ancient. Such unrewarding indulgence has gone out of fashion; curiosity tends to stop beyond immediate memory. A diminishing percentage of Americans seem to share Socrates' conclusion that the unexplored life is not worth living. Or Plato's subsequent observation: A society that puts to death a Socrates has got to have problems. I wondered if somewhere down the road I'd find some convenience store offering economy-size, no-deposit bottles of Diet Hemlock.

Longing for reality, I headed into downtown Savannah and found Ferrebee. Rather, he found me. He stopped me under a statue. "You got a dime for a cup of coffee? It costs seventy cents." I extracted a handful of change, and we probably hit it halfway. "Oh, thank you, thank you," he said, performing an elaborate bow. He wore a little straw panama and a big beard. Ferrebee launched into a detailed account of Savannah history, along with an unexpurgated version of his own biography. Unfortunately I did not understand a word of it. He does not speak too clearly. If I read his hand gestures correctly, though, he was once a champion golfer.

On the road out of town, my peripheral vision picked out a battered, faded sign reading RIB HUT, OLD-FASHIONED PIT BAR-BE-CUE. I slammed on the brakes. Inside, it was raw-plywood, butts-in-the-urinal authentic. Someone had managed to stain the stainless steel. The menu was a collection of scrawled signs on the walls. One noted, THE SWEETNESS OF QUALITY OUTLASTS THE BITTERNESS OF COST. A few desultory patrons watched *Guiding Light*. I sat at the counter next to a homemade plaque that said NELEASE FEGGINS, IN APPRECIATION FOR BEING A WONDERFUL MOTHER AND GRANDMOTHER. And cook.

Mrs. Feggins has run the place for twelve years, with help from her five kids. Her spicy, smoky ribs, pork or beef, defy words on paper. A Kentucky Fried Chicken has set up across the road. Large sedans headed out of town tend to veer toward the familiar colonel rather than the half-boarded-up red Rib Hut. That, I am told, is a nationwide pattern. But Mrs. Feggins, for one, is not worried about fast-food chains. "I got all my old customers and a lot of new ones," she told me. I'll be back.

Down the road and over a bridge is Hilton Head, perhaps the most famous golf course society in America. I went over to see Irv and Florence Hoff. To get to them, I had to penetrate Sea Pines, their particular corner of paradise. That required a stop at the Pass Center. A polite lady phoned my hosts. With elaborate care, she traced huge numerals on a card; I had three days. "Do I get arrested if I use this on the fourth day?" I asked, making a weak joke. She thought a moment and said she would check. Out front, a security guard emerged from a large Ford. He had a bulging stomach and a yellow stripe down each leg. He wore no gun, but the American flag on his sleeve gave him authority enough.

Actually I could have bought my way in for three dollars. Sea Pines is troubled by riffraff who use the beach. A steep entry charge, it is believed, will at least result in a better class of garbage left on the sand.

Inside, Sea Pines is a splendid little enclave for people who have done well with their lives and want to enjoy the time they have left. Golf, dinner, light gardening and sundowners with friends make up the daily schedule. The world arrives each evening with Brokaw, Jennings or Rather and each morning with the *Wall Street Journal*. Local affairs, the most important news, are well covered by the Hilton Head *Packet*.

David Stacks, just finishing up as managing editor of the *Packet*, was a little miffed that every reporter who came through called the place posh. There were, after all, a lot of normal people who ran the businesses, cleaned the pools and fixed the air conditioners. Many of them lived on the mainland and commuted. It was, he agreed, an insular little community. "But we are part of the world," he said, enthusiastic about the teleprinter that kept the newspaper up to the minute. "It is the most exciting thing in the world to sit in a bean field in Beaufort, South Carolina, and read about U.S. jets screaming over the Mediterranean fifteen minutes earlier. One reason the *Packet* is successful is that it tries to be a national and international paper."

Another reason, of course, is that it is a lovable little journal in a protected place. The first issue I saw carried a line from Edna St. Vincent Millay, in big letters above the nameplate: "O world, I cannot hold thee close enough!"

Hilton Head was just another of South Carolina's Sea Islands, forgotten by everyone except, of course, by a few thousand black farmers and fishermen who had made their lives there. Then, in 1956, it found itself the subject of an American Dream. A young Yale law graduate named Charles Fraser took over five thousand acres from his father, General Joseph Fraser, and formed the Sea Pines Company. He realized that Hilton Head was halfway between the rich people's winter headquarters above New York and their summer mansions in Florida. If the island had a decent golf course and fancy accommodations, they might stop off awhile. He whipped up the Hilton Head Classic tournament and got NBC to televise it. The star, Arnold Palmer, was just making it big. Hilton Head was on the circuit.

With a new bridge to the mainland, the island developed fast. Money ebbed and flowed, with various operators behind it. By 1977, after a few years of recession, the Sea Pines Company was $41.8 million in the red. It was about then that Bobby Ginn, a twenty-five-year-old University of South Carolina dropout, started a condo project at Sea Pines Plantation. On Hilton Head a plantation is a golf course with fancy homes and shops around it. Cotton is scarce; even the golf clothes tend toward brightly patterned synthetics. But plantations are numerous, and by 1985 Bobby Ginn had cornered most of them. With much grinning and backslapping, he was king of the island.

Ginn's financing was a package of loans and guaranteed debts, secured by a precarious pyramid of properties with assessed values that raised a few eyebrows. Cash did not flow. Before 1985 was out, bumper stickers appeared reading HONK IF BOBBY OWES YOU MONEY. The next year Fraser pressed the Citizens & Southern National Bank of South Carolina to apply pressure. Ginn found partners, who, pretty soon, forced him out. Then it got complicated. To figure it all out, I realized, I would have to skip Texas, California and the North.

When the lawsuits started, no one could find the pricy corporate jet. Questions arose about banking practices, appraisals, high salaries and assorted other dealings. Hilton Head Holdings had two hundred lawyers involved, charging up to $350 an hour; the judge got irate when legal fees went higher than the amounts being disputed. Bobby Ginn, with his neatly rolled parachute now unfurled, was still smiling.

During the 1980's Hilton Head's population rose from 11,300 to about 20,000. It grew to thirty shopping centers and twenty golf courses, linked by well-surfaced, landscaped roads. In that period the sheriff's department increased from six men to a hundred. The new sheriff, a tough ex-marine named Morgan McCutcheon, does not like disorder. To protect a national governors' conference, he had frogmen deployed off the beach. Crime is rare. There was a drug arrest, but that was after an undercover agent worked hard at the bust; she was a good-looking dispatcher who told a desperate young admirer she would not go out with him unless he brought her marijuana. There are hardly any murders. But even little enclaves like Sea Pines are high above the Key Line.

Florence and Irv lock up tight even when they buzz off for a quick bottle of milk. In fact, prospective burglars are few. Repairmen and service people buy an annual pass to come onto the property, an expense that ends up on their bills. Outsiders, if welcome, do not feel unnoticed.

Most of the island's original settlers have cleared out, the first ones gnashing their teeth over how much their neighbors got later on. But not Virginia Bennett. She would not sell at any price, and her reluctance did not stop developers after the scent of money. In her eighties she lived alone in her tumbledown wooden house on three acres, ringed by multistory luxury condos.

Conservationists note a limited concern among the well-to-do, for whom the issue of environment still smacks a little of troublemakers. But they all want sighing pines and birds along the fairways. Besides, someone has come up with a bumper sticker that gets 'em where it hurts: NO WETLANDS, NO SEAFOOD.

The Hoffs took me for seafood at the Harbour Town Grill, an elegant Sea Pines clubhouse. The lobby features a relief mock-up of early golf in the United States, circa 1786, the roots of Hilton Head's Heritage tournament. It might be today, with men in funny hats and colorful clothes selecting clubs from leather bags. Instead of electric golf carts, however, they had Negro slaves.

Mostly Irv told me about Joe, the barber. Joe starts work at 5:30 A.M., clipping the golfers and construction workers. Then he knocks off early to pursue other interests. Like tomatoes.

"Ol' Joe taught me how to grow tomatoes," Irv said, in a rare admission; he is a proud and accomplished grower. "See, you take a fifty-five-gallon drum and fill it halfway with wood shavings soaked in Nutrisol. Then you put in dirt. When you plant the seeds, you got to jump back fast, or the plants will hit you in the eye. Yeah, and you've got to keep the drums away from telephone lines. I'm telling you, you need a ladder to pick tomatoes."

Joe's tomatoes were nothing compared with Atlanta. It was the third fastest-growing metropolitan area from 1980 to 1986, its population jumping 20 percent to 2.6 million. From 1982 to 1987 its annual job growth rate of 5.7 percent was the nation's highest. Hartsfield

International handled more flights than any airport in the world. Huge, flashy malls offered class and quality. There was fine art and good food. And only Newark, of America's large cities, had a higher poverty rate. In Atlanta 27.5 percent of the population was poor.

It is Hotlanta, sin city of the South, and it is the sedate capital of the Bible Belt. Atlanta is, as travel brochure writers like to say, a land of many contrasts. Personally I was there for the American shrine. I wanted to see Coke Tower.

For better or worse, nothing says America in the world like Coca-Cola, and missing its headquarters in Atlanta is like not visiting St. Peter's when in Rome. For me, the twenty-six-story building was less the Vatican than it was Omaha Beach. I was fascinated by the Cola Wars.

A few years earlier I picked up a book entitled *The Other Guy Blinked* by a guy named Roger Enrico, who made carbonated sugar water of a different name. The first words put me on guard: "How does a person who runs a company like Pepsi-Cola USA find time to write a book?" That would depend on the book. I could imagine Solzhenitsyn: "How does a person who mines salt all day and writes in his own memory without a mainframe IBM or ghostwriters or secretaries find time to write a book?"

Enrico explained why he thought he and his Pepsi troops out-hyped Coke: They were "smarter," "shrewder," "faster." He seemed worried lest the reader get the wrong idea: ". . . it may seem, in these pages, as if Pepsi is a company that creates advertising, and oh, by the way, we make soft drinks, too." Then he devoted the rest of the book to advertising and image making.

Coke had it all wrong, he said. It relied on "rock-ribbed American values," small towns, parade, picnics. "All good stuff—we use some of it ourselves—but deadly in the soft drink business if that's your dominant image," he wrote. "Use" was the word that stuck in my mind. For Enrico, the key is that he persuaded Michael Jackson, who nearly went the other way, to do commercials for Pepsi. "If we're new and bold and challenging and a lot of fun, what's left for the other guy?" The product maybe?

As the Pepsi man explained, Coke couldn't handle the pressure. It panicked and junked its birthright, the century-old secret formula, to bring out some new goop called New Coke. It was a disaster. And Enrico proclaimed, "After eighty-seven years of going at it eyeball to eyeball, the impossible actually occurred: The other guy blinked."

At some distance from the battleground I contemplated this object lesson in light of the book I was about to undertake. Basically insecure, I have little control over my fluttering eyelids. Coming home to face America was an exciting challenge. But, heaven forfend, what if I blinked?

In the end Americans proved themselves to be less sheeplike than Enrico's philosophy implied them to be. A lot of people thought about it and decided what they liked to drink was more important than what Tina Turner claimed she drank. The old stuff came back as Coke Classic, and customers embraced it in greater quantities. Pepsi won out in 1985 but not in 1986. Overall, Coke had 40.3 percent of the U.S. market share in 1987, compared with Pepsi's 30.2.

"People were loving the classic Coke but were drinking something else," observed Roberto Goizueta, the guy who blinked. "Now they are loving it and drinking it."

But it would be a long war. In the United States alone the annual retail take on soft drinks is $35 billion, nearly as much as the state of California spends or earns in a year. That means a single percent share point is worth $350 million. On a typical July Fourth, Americans drink a billion cans of soft drinks. Then there was the rest of the world. In 1987 Coke earned more in Japan than in the United States. It outsold Pepsi three to one overseas. New foreign markets would be the next battlefield.

Before I was admitted under the giant marble dome of Coke Tower, a pleasant receptionist asked my name. She typed it into the computer and studied the screen. I panicked. On the way from Savannah I had drunk an RC Cola. The computer would know. Some time passed, and I was given a numbered badge with my name in large letters. I'd been accredited with less fuss to cover real wars.

At one point in the visit I glanced toward the business end of the operation, where scientists monkeyed with the Formula. My escort looked nervous and directed me to the souvenir shop. Next time I'll stick to easier targets, like the Kremlin basement.

At that particular moment Atlanta was gripped in a cultural crisis. The conservative governor had pushed through a law making it illegal to serve liquor where there was nude dancing. This was a real blow because no city has strip clubs like Atlanta.

Cheetah III was a large, cheery barn full of long counters and sturdy tables on which dozens of well-built women acted out a trip to the gynecologist. Each dancer started with what she might wear to bed on a honeymoon and ended up, in most cases, with only a garter that doubled as a cashbox. It was the kind of place that feminists hate. The dancers I talked to, however, seemed to like it a whole lot.

Bouncers gently propelled to the street anyone who failed to exhibit couth. Hustling was strictly forbidden; most of the women were married or otherwise committed. A cheerful and energetic dancer could earn enough to send her kid to Radcliffe, although most choose not to. The clientele was thick with businessmen and professionals, well dressed and mannerly, enjoying a quick belt on their way home. Most other clubs were similar. The Tattletale sponsors an annual golf tournament, and the proceeds help battered women.

I wondered about the sort of people who felt privileged enough to write their prejudices into law, proscribing others' pleasures. No one was closing down the Cheetah III or the several dozen other places like it. But if no longer bars, their only raison d'être would be to enable guys to gawk at vaginas. Beer and spirits lent a cheery atmosphere, enlivening the conversation and warming the air. However much Atlanta might like the stuff, things would not go better with Coke.

There was a comeuppance down the road. Most people figured the measure was to clean up Atlanta well before the 1988 Democratic Convention. Two weeks before delegates arrived, however, a court stayed the order. That gave reporters a fresh angle. The whole country had a fleeting glimpse of forbidden fruit.

There were worse problems, however. Racism, for example. Andrew Young, more than a "black mayor," was a statesman and diplomat of wide experience. Police leaders were black, as were a majority of urban leaders. Even the archbishop was black, the first in America. No one bothered to remark on that anymore. So many people talked about the New South, in fact, that I wondered if the old one, at long last, had faded into folklore. Some researching turned up an Atlanta telephone number, and I called it. I got a voice on a machine, one of those semiliterate redneck voices that ring hard, like buzzard droppings on a tin roof: "You can read it in the Atlanta *Constitution* and see it on the television news . . . AIDS is killing niggers by the thousands. . . . Niggers are helping it along with their sharing of needles and free love. Keep up the good work, niggers. AIDS is the new white hope. Praise God for AIDS. This is Daniel B. Carver, grand dragon of the Invisible Empire of the Georgia Ku Klux Klan. Please leave a message, and I will call you back."

I said that my name was Rosenblum. Ro-sen-blum. He did not call back, and I was just as happy.

In Paris I had heard over and over about Forsyth County, just north of Atlanta, which has had no black residents since a wave of racial violence three generations ago. News footage from Cumming always focused on the old white courthouse and young white faces. I'd formed an image of a wisteria-choked antebellum hamlet, lulled to sleep each night by the chirp of crickets and the gentle crackling of burning crosses. The last thing I expected was a plastic-roofed, overpaved stretch of suburbia.

Sheriff Wesley Walraven, a former Eagle Scout and biology teacher who dislikes cattle prods, was as gracious as he could be to yet another reporter come to all-white Forsyth County. Most of his work was keeping track of outsiders, black and white, who trucked in from somewhere else to demonstrate. "It's getting so that if you want to get on TV, you come to Forsyth," he said. Nothing specific kept blacks out of the county, he said, except maybe fear for their lives. "We don't burn schools, like they do in Pontiac, Michigan. But people tend to go to folks where they feel comfortable," he explained. "It's a social issue."

Walraven saw change coming. "The reason that folks don't like each other is that they don't know each other," he said. "The society is becoming more homogenized. There's a black man staying over at the motel, working here."

It all seemed plain enough to me. Cumming was a bedroom community for Atlanta with some normal people and a fair number of racist morons. What black person in his right mind would want to live in such surroundings, except to prove a point? I was anxious to examine racism in the Deep South, but I was not deep enough yet. This was not discrimination; it was simple, stupid exclusion.

Norman Baggs, a bearded bear of a man who edits the *Forsyth County News*, has no illusions. "We certainly have not resolved the racial problem, and I don't know if we ever will," he said. But he saw some value in the repeated demonstrations. "White supremacists often think everyone else agrees with them. This gives the average man the chance to stand up and tell the racists and bigots to go to hell. There are forty thousand people here, and probably thirty thousand would go out of their way to welcome anyone."

What worries Baggs is the reaction from elsewhere. "That really opened my eyes, the scary letters we received from all over the country. 'Run 'em out, kill 'em.' 'Don't let the niggers run over you like they did here.' People in Pennsylvania called here, looking for work. I really think it's worse in the North."

Even more, he is concerned at the turn in old-style racism. "In the last couple of marches there were Nazi flags. There is a new paramilitary character, with some survivalists. The skinhead attitude really scares me. There is a definite area of hatred, and you just can't get there. I guess you tell yourself it's not out there, but it is. I see a real resurgence of racial problems all across the nation."

He sighed heavily and finished his thought: "It's not laws that will do it, but personal attitudes. Now there is a bitterness over expectations that never came to be. We were naive to expect anything else."

Soon I was deep enough in the South to see what Norman Baggs was talking about. From Atlanta I drove through Tuskegee to Montgomery along Highway 80, Alabama's Via Dolorosa. Montgomery is a charming old city left behind by cotton. The antique passenger train station is an excellent restaurant. The freight depot, restored with equal care, is a hotel. And a gleaming white State Capitol still reflects the glory days, right up to the Confederate flag flying defiantly from its dome.

When I arrived, the flag was at the center of a storm. A black legislator had scaled a fence to take it down and been arrested for trespassing on state property. A lot of whites sneered at the gesture, and some were downright ugly about it; why disturb a harmless souvenir of history? Other whites, and most blacks, said that was the whole point: that too many people had forgotten the Civil War was about slavery.

The intellectual argument was that even a century from now a Nazi flag would not be welcomed over the Reichstag in Berlin. Closer to home, the pit-of-the-stomach feeling was that some southerners' attitudes had not changed all that much since the Stars and Bars were flying for real.

An outsider learns immediately in the South that words are worthless in any discussion about race. When someone begins, "Now don't get me wrong," you know it is time to run for the exits.

Rather than ask about racism, I decided to try testing the wind on my own. I started with Sunday morning services at the Dexter Avenue King Memorial Baptist Church, in the shadow of the state-house flag. It was Martin Luther King's old church and still a symbol of the old South.

Except for an aging Norwegian with an Asian wife, I was the only white guy there. No one appeared to notice. A woman came around with a guest book. Later in the service she welcomed each visitor by name. She came to my signature, which resembles a profile of the Himalayas, and gamely attacked it. "Uh, Nort . . . Rosselbum." I was standing by then. "Rosenblum," I said. "I'm not much at penmanship." Every head in the place had turned to me. The woman invited all guests, Nort Rosselbum included, to join the church, and I felt among friends.

A man behind patted my shoulder and handed me a hymnal which fell open to "We Shall Overcome." I had a queasy moment of déjà vu. I had come to the South believing that we had overcome, in the 1960's. Having been back awhile, I realized how distorted a view one can get, looking at one country from another. It is worse when one of those countries is your own. All of this makes reference by comparison a risky business. But sitting in church, I sensed a strong whiff of Soweto.

The hymnal's preface asserted that liberties taken with inspirational music had aroused "an alarming concern." It concluded, "There should be a marked difference between music in nightclubs and that of churches, and even passersby should note the distinction." The pastor and his flock had taken note; the service was deadly dull. But people threw themselves into prayers about forgiveness, patience and Christian values.

Afterward Norman Walton introduced himself. He was a history professor at a local black college, and he showed me the murals downstairs depicting Dr. King's life. I asked how he thought it would be if King were alive. "He'd still be fighting today," Walton said, with no heat. "Maybe it was never meant to be over. You just make the adjustments you can."

From Dexter Avenue I drove southeast for half an hour to visit Martha and Glen. I'd met Martha briefly up North, and she urged me to phone if I got to town. When I did, they both bubbled over with warmth.

"Southern hospitality" was one of those empty phrases to me, like "northern efficiency," until I got to Glen and Martha's. They were disappointed I had a hotel room and horrified when I had to miss dinner. If anyone really drank mint juleps, I'd have been given them by the bucket. Martha drove me around the county, tracking down friends and sources for me and explaining the facts of southern life.

She wore old Levi's and a mink coat, wheeling her big sedan down narrow lanes through some of the most beautiful country in the world. She showed me where the local gentry hunted foxes and put their dogs on field trials. Glen was off after birds in the woods nearby. We whizzed past a flat pasture with a limp sack hanging from a pole. "That's our international airport," she said. "Don't laugh. It's got a wind sock."

Martha had lived abroad, and she traveled widely; but she always came home. "I wouldn't trade this for anything in the world," she said. "There's no place like it to raise kids."

We passed a lively-looking roadhouse. "That's Funk Junction," she told me. "It used to be for whites."

Bullock County was 80 percent black, but the big homes and the old stores were owned by whites. Blacks seemed to inhabit shacks and trailers, as in the clichés that were supposed to be outmoded. I asked about race relations.

"You know, people say, 'Send 'em all back to Africa,' until they start thinking, 'Well, except for Tom and Sue and Mabel and ol' Zeke,'" she said. "There are some very fine colored people down here."

Martha took me to Union Springs, a movie-set county seat with a brick courthouse, stately but seedy storefronts and blossom-fringed old houses. We stopped at one of the two Methodist churches in the town of ten thousand. It was the one which people said would probably accept blacks if anyone pushed the issue. The other would not, period.

The Reverend Asbury Wolfe—"Mr. Woof," as Martha called him— seemed sad that no blacks were in his congregation, and he found it awkward to explain why that was so. I asked him instead about teenagers.

"When our young people go to college or get away from here, they don't tend to come back," he said. "There is nothing to come back for." Bullock County had been a thriving part of the Cotton Belt, but that was all over. If soybean and cattle farms kept some old families going, they provided few jobs. Essentially, he concluded, it was a desperately poor place with little future.

Prodded slightly, he pressed on: "Values have changed. In the entire American society morals have changed. Young people are a lot more materialistic. They want to make money. And sports. We're going too far to the extreme. It's like in the Roman days, with big arenas. We've become obsessed. I just spoke to a young fellow in the third or fourth grade, and I asked, 'What's your goal in life?' He told me, 'To be an athlete. For the money.'"

He paused a minute and concluded, "This has hurt us. It has hurt us a lot."

From church we drove to a tidy building south of town. "That's our little school," Martha said with some pride. It was, more precisely, an academy, one of the many private institutions built in Alabama immediately after public schools were segregated. No blacks attended.

Bullock County's public schools had 3,500 black pupils and 250 white ones, she said. "I'm not a racialist, but I do want my children educated. You just cannot send your kids to public schools. By April fifty-four girls were pregnant in the high school. It's pitiful."

But, I asked, don't separate schools for whites drain off resources which could make the public school better? She eyed me narrowly. That was one of those chicken-egg questions outside liberals like to ask. Some time passed, and she answered obliquely: "Racial problems are much worse in the North, where they don't know how to live together. We have been getting along well for a long time."

Later on she asked whom I planned to see in Montgomery. I mentioned the Southern Poverty Law Center. It is a private group run by an Alabama lawyer to take on egregious civil rights violations. Not long before, the center had helped a Mobile woman sue the Ku Klux Klan for seven million dollars after her son had been lynched. But Martha did not like the center. Her face contorted. "What do you want to see *them* for?" she asked. "They come down here and stir up trouble. If they don't like things here, they can go home. If we don't, we are home. I don't know if they've got enough sense to walk around."

It was a distressing pattern. This was a charming, warmhearted woman, a good mother and surely a loyal friend. We were having a great time, so long as we avoided the Subject.

I had to get back to Montgomery, but she invited me to a party at the Union Springs Country Club the next night. Another friend in the room had mentioned some velvet pants, and I joked that I might wear those.

"Lemme explain something to you, Mort," she said, with a deep chuckle. "Don't wear velvet pants. And don't tell them you've been to the colored church. This is still the rural South, and our veneer of civilization is quite thin."

The party started out fine. Hostesses flew to my side and showered me with greetings. Their husbands pumped my right hand and deposited a fat glass of bourbon in my left. People wanted to know about Paris and New York and, mainly, what I thought about Bullock County. I stuck to distant topics and had a good time. The crowd grew to about two hundred, and laughter echoed. After a while a man about forty, with intelligent eyes, introduced himself as the local judge. It was time.

So how are race relations here?

"Oh, fine, fine. I think we're making a lot of progress."

Then why are the only blacks in this room carving roast beef and pouring gin?

"Well," he said, "these things take time." The Junior Miss Pageant in Montgomery was integrated a few years ago, he said. That was progress.

What about the schools and churches?

"You know, if you go to a black church, you won't be welcome. They really don't want to mix."

I told him about Dexter Avenue. He smiled warmly and remembered he had something to tell his wife.

After that, the *R* word arose only in passing. I talked to a sharp-witted old woman who had run the elementary school for decades. She thought American geography and social studies education was shocking, especially in that part of Alabama. Kids didn't learn anything because the teachers didn't know anything. A businessman told me about trying to survive in a cotton ghost town; it was not easy. Finally, it was time to go.

Glen had reached a comfortable state of *in vino veritas,* and he was expansive on the way home. The three of us liked one another, and we'd been to a good party. He wanted to make things clear for me as a final gesture.

"Hell, all this talk about race problems," he said. "My niggers are doin' fine." He mentioned a longtime employee, part of the family, to whom he'd lent six thousand dollars. "I'd do anything for him, and he is devoted to us." Glen added, "He's doin' just great, the black stud of Bullock County. . . ."

I lapsed into morose silence. Their affection for specific blacks was genuine, as was most South Africans', and it was often returned. That was how it worked. The black stud of Bullock County, I knew, thought the world of them. However much I'd filled the role of outside liberal, I had not come to change anyone's system. The truth was that my friends' approach to a complex old problem made me real unhappy. But it was a complex old problem.

It was easier to take sides at the next stop. I spent the morning with the Klanbusters. The Southern Poverty Law Center was set up in 1971 by Morris Dees, Jr., an Alabama lawyer who made a fortune in the direct-mail business and decided to do something with it. He was joined by Joseph Levin, a law partner and fellow graduate of University of Alabama. After some early successes someone burned the place down. The tide of sympathy mail contained enough checks to build a huge new center, with a library and computerized files. There were no more fires.

Dees, the son of a cotton plantation overseer, explained his view of Klan members to *American Lawyer*: "They're losers in life in many ways. The average rank and file members are not that zealous. They're good folks. They're just people who have a bias against blacks, but they're not basically bad human beings. They would have been good labor union members if the labor unions got there first."

Not all the center's lawyers and investigators thought that Klan members were such good folks. A racially mixed group, the center's staff came from back East, elsewhere in the South and Alabama. Joe Roy, chief investigator, was a former Alabama cop.

Roy's tactic was to go after the money. Putting a Klansman in jail might be a moral victory, he knew, but keeping him there was no easy job. The law might punish the few who went out and hurt someone, but it left unscathed the secret society that sent them. "When you start seizing old Billy Bob's pickup and taking away Bubba's family farm," he said, "they start to get the message."

The center's victory in Mobile established the fact that Klan assets could be seized because of members' actions.

Roy was heading to Hemphill, Texas, one of those tiny East Texas backwaters near Louisiana. On Christmas 1987 Loyal Garner, Jr., thirty-four, had driven two friends just across the state line to retrieve a car. Police arrested them, passengers included, for driving under the influence of alcohol. Then, according to charges, three officers deprived Garner of his civil rights by beating him to death. Garner's friends said they all had noisily demanded to make a phone call. Officers beat up Garner in his cell and then took him to another room, where he moaned as beatings continued. Battered and blood-soaked, Garner was dumped back in his cell, where he breathed heavily, without moving, all night. The next morning deputies took him to the hospital in Tyler, where he died.

Peter Applebome of *The New York Times* interviewed a white friend of Garner, in Florien, Louisiana. "To put it mildly, I think Junior Garner was one of the finest men I ever met, white or black," said Stan Self. "That's what bothers me so much about this, that it could have happened to anybody, but you'd never think it could happen to him."

In the glare of publicity, Sabine County indicted Hemphill Police Chief Thomas Ladner and two sheriff's deputies, Bo Hyden and Bill Horton. The charge was not murder but civil rights abuse, which carried a penalty of five years in prison. Center lawyers said the judge refused to disqualify jurors who admitted contributing to the officers' defense fund. In a short trial the three said they had had to beat their prisoner in self-defense. The witnesses, they said, were only prisoners. A jury of eleven whites and one fearful black woman found them not guilty.

The Southern Poverty Law Center put faith in a murder trial scheduled later in Tyler, in the next county over. But after the Sabine verdict the case was thrown out, on grounds of double jeopardy. The law officers went free. Center lawyers planned to have their own trial. On behalf of Garner's widow, six children and parents, they filed for major damages against the three men, the town and the county. As Dees and Roy said, they were going for the money.

The center kept thick files on the Klan as well as on scores of other white supremacist, survivalist, neo-Nazi and generic lunatic-fringe groups. Its investigators knew that "fringe" was a misleading term. Not many were needed to wreak havoc on a society. Extremist membership went far beyond the diehard rednecks and burnouts I expected to find.

Across the country, the center knew, tattooed young skinheads preached themes like "White Unity" and "Niggers Suck." Near San Francisco skinheads putting up an anti-Semitic poster flung a youth through a plate-glass window when he interfered. Sacramento skin-heads nailed a former gang member to a board, crucifix style. Their roots were in England, but like Reeboks, America took them over. John Metzger, the twenty-year-old son of Tom Metzger, a Klan alum who headed the White Aryan Resistance, told *The New York Times*: "We've been working with them for two years. We've been able to be an influence and fine-tune their perceptions . . . filling a void in their lives."

At a trial in Fort Smith, Arkansas, in 1988, the former leader of the Covenant, the Sword and the Arm of the Lord testified that his pals had considered dumping enough cyanide into the water sup-plies of New York or Washington to kill a half million people. "The ones who would be killed would not really matter," he quoted a colleague as saying. "It would be a good cleansing."

As it was, he said, white supremacists committed murders and tried to blow up utilities to spark civil upheaval. Extremist right-wing groups worked out the plan at Hayden Lake, Idaho. The idea was to establish an all-white state in the Northwest.

Along with ethnic deviance, most groups also targeted homosex-uals. In one poster a sheeted Klansman points outward in the cele-brated Uncle Sam pose. "I want YOU, queer," it says.

Not many were linked, but they formed a broad brotherhood. An unofficial bible, a novel called *The Turner Diaries*, detailed how the Jews had finagled control of the country, guns were banned and all right-thinking men would rise up to rid the nation of all blacks, Jews, socialists, fags, dogs and Bolivians. Poking through the cen-ter's files, I could see it was nothing to laugh off.

I cut myself too tight and had to miss the Coon Dog Memorial Graveyard. The fifty-year-old cemetery, tucked in the woods of northern Alabama, featured a statue of two dogs barking up a tree. More than a hundred coon hounds were buried under elaborate headstones. "Black Ranger," said one. "He was good as the best and better than the rest." The time to go was Labor Day, when coon hunters gathered for speeches, buck dancing and, its being Ala-bama, a liars' contest.

Instead, I settled for evening barhopping in Montgomery. It didn't take long. At a place called Cheers, a name I had seen before, some gentleman in black leathers was unduly interested in the tempera-ture of my neck. I moved on.

Honey for the Bears was in a crumbling red-brick building down-town. For a dollar you could be a member, thus circumventing a lot of Alabama liquor laws that make you go thirsty on Sundays and all. A sign threatened jail and dismemberment to any rowdy persons, but the condition of the furniture suggested no one read it. Behind the bar was Lily, a kindly, timeworn grandmother with a cascade of red curls. She wore a *Miami Vice* jersey under her lumberjack shirt and smoked a cigar. She was pure Alabama. Once she followed her husband to Houston and was sick from the day she got there. "I was tired all the time, had no energy, just sick," she said. Finally, doctors decided to operate. Lily figured if anyone was going to cut on her, it would be someone back home in Montgomery. As it turned out, she was cured by stepping off the bus in 'Bama. That had been thirty-four years ago, and she hadn't gone anywhere since.

At a fancy bar nearby, near closing time, I chatted with a friendly young woman. She was the bartender and also a mind reader. "I haven't had sex in six months," she said. It was not an invitation. "I'm terrified of AIDS. You can't be too careful." Once, she said, she found the perfect partner, a handsome, amusing man who liked her a lot. Just to be safe, she stuck to platonic dating for a few months. Then, one night, she went to his place.

"We were getting pretty friendly when I saw this photograph of him and another young man," she recalled, with a slight shudder. "I questioned him, and he finally admitted he'd had a homosexual experience. That was it, I said. I'm outa here."

In a strict sense segregation was over in Montgomery. It was just that people had worked out who was where. Countless exceptions blur the line, but no one in good faith denies it. The Montgomery Country Club didn't take Jews; they had their own club nearby. Blacks went to neither. A lawyer told me about a group of northerners visiting town to scout business sites. At a country club lunch stop the lone black man among them was left on the bus. I tried to get his name to find out what really happened. Did white delegation members leave him behind? No one knew. It was just another of those incidents.

In Columbia, South Carolina, the facts were clearer. Charles Savage had returned to his native state as the International Business Machine Corporation's top local man. He was shunned by good clubs and the golf course around the corner. His kids were insulted on the school bus and not invited to the white kids' parties. He quietly transferred. The Washington *Post* focused on the case in 1987, when Columbia promoted itself as "the Sun Belt's emerging city." A lot of whites reacted harshly to racist holdovers. But from the window of the all-white Summit Club, members could sip bourbon and look out at the Confederate flag atop the State Capitol, just as in Montgomery.

As anyone who read newspapers in the 1960's knows, Highway 80 heads due west from Montgomery to Selma. King led blacks and whites down its center, on the first freedom marches. Civil rights workers were shot dead by its side in response. Potbellied sheriffs with riot guns and ax handles swore no niggers would be equal while they were on watch. And they were right. Today sheriffs between Selma and Montgomery are niggers, and you'd best not refer to them that way.

I set out to see John Hulett, sheriff of Lowndes County, but was running late. At a run-down gas station I stopped to telephone him. The owner sat at a small desk, moving his lips over a column of numbers. His neck was deep crimson. Howdy, I said. He made a noise like a junkyard dog that had missed breakfast. I made a needless purchase and asked for the phone. "Ain't got none." I pointed to a black thing with a dial on it. "Private." Could I just make a short call down the road and pay him? "Don't know what it costs." He shuffled irritably to signal he was done making conversation. I thought again of *The Turner Diaries* and Klan ideology. Maybe too many of his cousins had married each other, and I was being harsh. But if this was the master race, we were in deep trouble.

The sheriff's office in Hayneville looked like a West African spoof of *Barney Miller*. An aged gentleman in a shabby coat snoozed in a chair, his feet flung over the counter. Two women made desultory attempts to shuffle papers but kept getting sidetracked in a raucous conversation with a perpetrator, obviously a repeat offender, who I think was being instructed to book himself. He left on his own to go post bond. After fifteen minutes a woman noticed me in the tiny room and shambled over with a chair. "Watch out for the wall," she warned, too late. "You'll get that white stuff on your clothes." Then I was taken in to see Hulett, and it all made sense.

Except for once in a while, things just don't get nasty in Lowndes County, and Hulett, nearing retirement, was not one of your gleaming-shoes MP types. He had been sheriff since 1971, when black people, who make up 70 percent of the county, realized they had the right to vote. Macon County was the first to elect a black sheriff. A handful of others followed.

I asked him how blacks and whites got along in Lowndes, one of the poorest counties in the country.

"We talk about some improvement, but there is not too much, socially," he said. "The churches are totally segregated. Recently I had my first chance to go to a white church, to talk about crime. It was only for business. Whites come to our church, but we don't get a chance to go to theirs. I suppose blacks could push. But I feel the white community should open its arms." As in Bullock, there was a private school for the whites.

Hulett laughed easily, but the statehouse flag incident did not amuse him. "So many people said it meant nothing. We like to say if you don't understand, hush your mouth and let those who do understand do the talking. How many people want to come here when there's a Confederate flag over the Capitol?"

The system is still loaded against blacks, Hulett said. Whites want more than their fair share in reapportioning districts. Federal investigators harass black voters. White farmers who accept seven hundred thousand dollars in federal subsidies begrudge a poor black mother her two-hundred-dollar welfare check.

That last point bothered him a lot. "These rich farmers are living off the federal government, but when it comes out in the papers, it looks like the welfare mothers are taking all the money." For all the subsidies, he added, poor farmers can't get a thirty-five-thousand-dollar loan to improve their crops.

The daily harassments bother him. When he goes to Montgomery in uniform, sheriff's deputies treat him like dirt until they find out he outranks them.

"When I look back, I am disappointed, I am really disappointed," Hulett said. "I didn't think then that in eighteen years we'd have these problems. No one has really come forward to make that real effort."

As a younger man he stood guard in Birmingham to keep Klan thugs away from black schoolgirls. "The same type of guy is here today," he said. "I can see a lot that goes on that is the same."

The challenge, he said, is to break the cycle. As sharecroppers blacks fell farther behind in debt. After a while they lost their confidence and then their dignity. "A kid who grows up without a bathroom, who walks up the road and comes home to build a fire for cooking, he knows he's a little different. A mother who can't read or write, how can she teach her children?"

But he was not optimistic. "The reason we're on the bottom is because it's designed for us to be on the bottom," he concluded. "And people don't want to work together to do what has to be done."

Thirty-five miles down the road, in Wilcox County, Prince Arnold runs a different kind of sheriff's office. It clicks smoothly along under the watchful eye of a beautiful young receptionist. I arrived unannounced, and Arnold, like no one else I met in America, inspected my press card before sitting down to talk. It was an experience.

I started by asking why Wilcox County was so poor.

"Slave labor," he replied. "They want domestics and farm workers at fifty dollars a week, and if you bring in opportunities, those people will leave you. I been here all my life, I know it. Cotton was a free-labor type of activity. That's where rich people made all their money."

At thirty-six Arnold respected Hulett as a mentor but took a different tack. When I mentioned his colleague's remark about whites opening their arms, he snorted. "You don't have to love me. You don't even have to like me. Just give me a chance. Blacks in 1988 don't want to fight; they want opportunities."

Rather than ask questions, I just tossed him cue words.

Schools: "Public schools are ninety-nine percent black. We might have twenty white kids out of three thousand students, all from poor families. Time! This is 1988, and it still takes time."

South Africa: "Whites in South Africa and this country think we are inferior. Mostly they are afraid of what we can do. Look at Doug Williams [the Super Bowl had just been played], how many records he broke. He's a quarterback; that's a smart man's job. We blacks, we're supposed to *catch* the ball."

The economy: "We're poor as the devil; there is nothing here."

Drugs: "That is a big problem, like everywhere. The stuff comes from another country. They ought to be able to handle it."

Black voters: "Now they write about Haiti, all these election problems. It's the same problem we have. People are cheating. A lot of blacks just don't go to the polls. They don't want to be cussed at."

I stopped him there. Was he saying that election fraud and harassment remained a problem in Alabama?

"Sir, let me tell you something. It is still going on. Yes, sir, and if they say it is not, they are lying."

On the other hand, Arnold said, the last decade had been easier than he expected. In 1978, as a coach and an art teacher with no experience, he succeeded a man with a cigar and a big stomach who had run the county almost since the Civil War. Four white men started the race, but Arnold won by two hundred votes. "They cheated, they lied, everything," he said. "People have what they call a sacred position, and they don't give it up easy," he said. "If you dethrone a king, he is going to fight you."

When I asked if diehard Klansmen caused a problem in Wilcox County, he bobbed and weaved. "Let's just say with a black sheriff, they don't make a lot of noise. Man, now I'm not going to overlook some things that were overlooked before."

Leaving Alabama, I stopped for dinner in the little town of Jackson. A pretty black waitress named Joan was killing herself for her customers. During her break we chatted about life. She was thirty with two kids, and she had just moved from Sacramento.

"In California they're so sneaky. They pretend they're not prejudiced, but they are. They never give you a break. Here they don't hide it. I'd rather someone be up front; then you know how to deal with him. Alabama is the best place; you know where you stand."

At the southern end of the state she lived in a mixed compound and sent her kids to a mixed school. "I love it here," she repeated. "I can't stand California values. One thing I can tell you is that people are coming back to the South. In the big cities you can't take your eyes off your kids. They'll snatch 'em. New York has garbage in the streets, and you've got to live in a slum. Sacramento, it's rotten, rotten."

That, I was finding, was what happens when you try to make neat packages of a nation of 250 million people. Racism was a big subject for a quick measure. If some whites wanted their flag, the Birmingham *News* had editorialized: "Take the thing down, put it in a museum and shut up about it." Segregation academics were still thriving in rural, backward areas, but they were weakening fast in much of the South. Prince Arnold was going to the Democratic National Convention in Atlanta, joining a contingent of blacks who had never had such political clout in America.

But the National Urban League in Atlanta had just reported blacks had lost ground during the 1980's, with average family incomes dropping from the 1970's. Nearly half of black households were headed by single mothers. Black scholars reported that urban problems had worsened, the gulf had widened, since the 1968 Kerner Report warned, "Our nation is moving toward two societies, one black, one white—separate and unequal."

The U.S. Census Bureau was clear: In 1986 the national poverty rate for blacks, 31.1 percent, was nearly three times that of whites; 42.7 percent of blacks under eighteen were classified as poor. Black unemployment, 13 percent, was two and a half times the whites' level. In 1968, when all minorities were counted together, the jobless figure was 6.7 percent compared with 3.2 percent for whites.

But racism was ground you could not survey by numbers. A reporter could be guided only by his oldest tool, feel. For a little help, I consulted Gary Marx, my cousin the sociologist. He had studied race relations since the 1960's, when he fought hard for civil rights. His heart has not hardened since, but he is fiercely scientific about drawing conclusions. I got no emotion out of Gary, and he wasn't calling it either way. I said I was amazed to find so many elements of South Africa in the American South. He dismissed that out of hand. I harped on the lack of progress; he reminded me of how different things had been in 1967.

Of course, the gap was wide between our situation and the political terrorism of apartheid, where blacks were officially subhumans. But I had heard too many South African whites to ignore the similarities. They name a few "wonderful colored people" and insist that blacks are far better off under benevolent care than they are under corrupt black leaders. It is just that blacks, as a persuasion, are not quite up to real people.

In America we had come an enormous way since 1967, no doubt about it. Since 1867, however, I was not so sure.

Caleb Beacon and his cat relax in the kitchen-library-family room of their outdoor Rainbow communelet.

Sunday afternoon skaters on the patch of concrete south of Bethesda Fountain

Central Park on a Sunday

This was the only shot I got off of the Timbuktu before the street erupted around me. Those guys in the picture, and an uncounted number of others, were headed immediately afterward in my direction.

Sheriff Tom Anderson of Gary, born and raised in the holler. His tie tack is a pig, he notes with some pride.

Lee Noble came down to Heritage U.S.A. from Philadelphia and, he said, "God just opened doors for me." Now he opens doors for God at the PTL hotel.

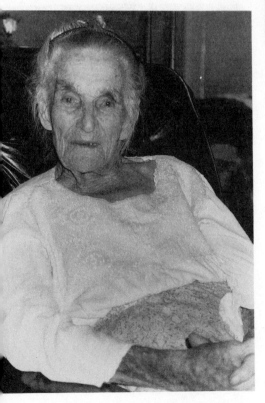

Aunt Ginny Hatfield, born Zettie Ferrell, is the oldest survivor of the old feud with the McCoys. But she's not sure what it was all about. She is over 100 and has never heard of Willard Scott.

Bullock County was pretty dry in 1967,
and C. B. Williams lost his cotton crop.
His family and friends decided to give
it proper last rites.

Harold and Myrtle Bigler. As I shot
this, Myrtle laughed. "Well," she said,
"you've got a picture of the two old
cronies who live in a muggy old cabin
in the woods."

Bernard Blanchard and net, with crawfish near Catahoula, Louisiana.

A Cajun fiddler and a New Orleans office worker on holiday warm up at Fred's on a Mardi Gras Saturday morning in Big Mamou.

The plea to customers at Fred's. On good days, you can't see it for all the people standing on the tables, booths, jukebox, chairs, or cigarette machine.

Down there, if you have something to say, all you need is a back bumper, and there are plenty of those in Texas.

A gentleman stands by the polished doors of the Menger Hotel, San Antonio.

Gunfight at the O.K. Corral, in the style of modern Tombstone. Not long ago, you could lie back under a tree and fill your mind with scenes of the old shootout. These days you fork out cash and leave your imagination outside.

Part of what's left of Rico, Colorado

An old stone bank, later the Elks' Club, is now one of the town's numerous T-shirt shoppes.

En route to Cutler and Nancy Umbach's llama farm near McCall, Idaho

Beverly Hills cop and amused friend from Japan

Breakfast at Disneyland

The hungry i, San Francisco's old
folksinger haunt gone topless

CHAPTER
6

Down on the Bayou

Deep in the Swamp, among the water hyacinths and alligators, Harold and Myrtle Bigler lived alone at the beginning of time. High water had carried off the house they had settled into back in 1946. Now they shared a beached steamboat cabin, with no toilet or running water, that was towed in by barge. Sometimes they splurged and ran the generator, for lights at night. The nearest neighbor was a long boat ride away, and Harold, at seventy-eight, couldn't see the submerged stumps too well. Myrtle saw fine, but she was slowing down at eighty-eight. Anyway, the nearest—and only—neighbor was Alcide Verret, who was just about ninety. He didn't have a phone or transmitter either, and he had no more use for newfangled medical nonsense than the Biglers. But Harold and Myrtle weren't exactly alone. Lurking under a doily near the wood stove were Vanna White and Willard Scott.

With only a couple of fresh batteries, the Biglers could tune in to America: *Three's Company, Eight Is Enough*; *Superior Court, People's Court* and *Night Court*; *Miami Vice* and *Hollywood Squares*. But they don't. "I just watch the news," Harold said. "That other stuff is not for me." Myrtle wouldn't even go that far. She could not figure out why three people sat there making inane remarks to each other, rather than explain what people needed to know to stay safe in their swamp, so she gave it up.

"You know," Myrtle told me, "one time the lady in the office [on-screen] was telling the news, big news about riots and things some-

where—the names of those countries, I can't think of 'em—and then
she said to the man next to her, 'Aren't you glad you don't live in
that world?' And he said, 'A-men.' " Myrtle, looking puzzled and a
little exasperated, added, "What world do they think they live in?"

Myrtle had never been beyond Morgan City, a grown-up settlement at the bottom of the swamp. But eighty years of exercising a
sharp mind taught her that events in places she couldn't pronounce
affected her as directly as the level of the Atchafalaya River. The
box under the doily apparently hadn't caught on to that.

Television, mostly, was what brought me into the swamp. There
were other reasons. I'd always been fascinated by the Atchafalaya
Basin. This was Cajun country, and I had wondered how an isolated
old French-flavored culture faced up to a sudden new hope that
had blackened fish on every menu in SoHo. I wanted to know what
impact the Army Corps of Engineers and an oil boom had made on
the fragile wetlands of southern Louisiana. And there was Mardi
Gras in Big Mamou.

But television was the overriding theme in America, at every level.
Experts insisted that it shapes what we know, how we think, who we
are. Was there somewhere back in the far reaches of America a
forgotten subculture that managed to survive from week to week
without *Monday Night Football*?

A set of happy coincidences led me to Harold and Myrtle. I had
heard about Greg Guirard, a Cajun photographer-philosopher, and
arranged to meet him. Then I chanced upon Andrei Mikhailov-
Konchalovsky's *Shy People*. Barbara Hershey plays a resolute swamp
woman who keeps her family riveted to old ways. Jill Clayburgh, a
New York photojournalist-bitch and distant relation who tracks her
down, resolves to impose the present. Hershey's character breathes
love and hate; Clayburgh's, who couldn't manage either, preaches
warmth. At one point Hershey scowls. "You city people, you're warm,
like dishwater. You got to be hot or cold."

At the film's climax Clayburgh knifes crazily through the bayou
in an aluminum skiff, careering off cypress stumps and into the air.
As it turned out, it was Guirard's boat; he was lying in the bottom,
yelling, "Slow down." Guirard, as technical adviser, took Hershey
out to meet Myrtle so she could feel the part. She ended up spending all her free time slamming down the 'Chafalaya just to hang out
with them.

By the time I found the Biglers I was richly acquainted with the film's main character: the swamp itself. Louisiana bayous are hot and steamy, but not before breakfast on a rainy February. A craw-fisherman and coiffeur named Bernard Blanchard ran me out in his open boat. For two hours we sliced the frozen fog, and my chattering teeth drowned out the forty-horse Yamaha outboard. Eerie shapes materialized from the mists and then suddenly evaporated. We inspected the crawfish traps Bernard had tied to cypress stumps in the back channels. Wet and miserable, I loved it. But I had the uneasy feeling that I had better enjoy it while I could. For messing up primeval peace, there is nothing like oil rigs, greedy politicians and the Army Corps of Engineers.

Greg had briefed me on outrages to the Atchafalaya Basin, but seeing it was a shock. Centuries-old cypress forests were cut to stumps, sticking above the water like wrecked fleets of ships. Logging had stopped, but trees that survived the woodcutters had suffocated, their roots covered by silt shifted by dredging. As happens when nature is messed with too much, the ecosystem had started to shift, and no one was quite sure of its direction.

On the wider bayous Erector set oil camps replaced the wooden hamlets abandoned by swamp people. Broad gashes were cut through the swamp to ease drilling and oil rig traffic. On one new channel I leaned over the boat to pull two Styrofoam egg containers from the water. What a world. We trash our last natural sanctuaries to produce yet more petroleum for unnecessary packaging that can never find its way back into nature.

Harold and Myrtle were natural as anything left in the swamp. But they were the last remnants of a vanished breed. When I asked Greg how many people still lived in the swamp, he shrugged. "I know three." The Biglers were two of them. Until the 1940's there were maybe six hundred. In an outboard age even the old-timers preferred an easier life in town. Anyway, most said rising water and oil rigs had taken away too much of what once kept them there.

Alcide Verret, the third old leaf clinging to the vine, was Cajun, with roots deep in Louisiana. But Myrtle's family was from Fort Wayne, Indiana. Her father settled the backcountry when the wide bayous nearby were narrow channels and much of the water around was lush land. The family home washed away long ago, and the Biglers had pushed their home farther back five times since then.

I dropped in unannounced, and Harold was messing with firewood in the pelting rain. He was happy to see Bernard, and at the
magic word "Guirard," his smile spread to a wide grin. "Go on in,"
he ordered. I did. Myrtle was waking up in bed in the corner of
their large single room. She had heard no introductions; all she saw
was a desperate-looking, shaggy stranger approaching her bed. She
beamed and chatted for a few moments before it occurred to her
to ask: "Now, who are you?"

The Biglers could have cleaned up as stand-up comedians, mercilessly ragging each other with ferocious good cheer. "Here," Myrtle said, taking over when Harold failed to spark a fire in the stove
we huddled around. "Y'all are trying to warm up the heater." Myrtle was a pretty woman, with gray curls and eyes that actually twinkled. Harold looked like a small aging eagle with Coke-bottle glasses.
Even close up, his reedy voice sounded as if he were trying to reach
Paraguay. Myrtle called him Ol' Loudmouth.

Harold tended toward strong views. I mentioned doctors. "Used to
be in the old days, they'd try to get you well so you could go back to
work and pay your bill," he said. "Now if you get sick, they keep you
there. You want to be healthy, then try to stay away from doctors."

A few years back Harold stopped cold turkey after smoking a
pack and a half a day since he was eighteen. Mainly he was fed up
with spending forty dollars a month on cigarettes.

On retirement homes, he snorted. "I'd rather go to jail than to an
old folks' home. I believe they treat you better." We came back briefly
to TV. "How do you like them weather birds?" he began. "At six
o'clock they say there's going to be such a wind. You see any wind?
They're nothing but a bunch of bums, drawing a salary for nothing.
To say a few words."

He was not happy about young people running around and not
getting married. Neither one was impressed with values or styles
that followed the 1950's. When Guirard's daughter brought a long-
haired boyfriend to visit, Harold grinned his grin and hollered, "I
don't know whether to shake your hand or kiss you."

There would be another war. Myrtle was clear on this point. "Definitely another war. My grandfather used to say that as long as there
are people, there was going to be a war."

Harold broke in. "It's going on right now, some kind of sneaking
war going on right now. . . ."

Harold had slogged across the Philippines, fighting Japanese. He
had rambled all over as a youth, but in 1946 he decided he had

seen enough. He married Myrtle and moved to the swamp, a trapper, hunter and fisherman.

"I've always been satisfied," Myrtle said, explaining, not boasting. "We've never had lots, but now we have a good income." That included her minuscule Social Security check and Harold's army pension. She noted with a rueful chuckle that her father once owned the land from which oil companies have extracted fortunes. He sold it in 1922 for a thousand dollars. "I'm glad I didn't have a lot of money," she said.

Harold chimed in, as he usually does: "You had a lot of money, you'd be dead today, worrying about keeping it."

I asked when they last saw a movie. "Oh, let's see"—Myrtle mused— "it was in Morgan City." Harold remembered James Stewart played a shrimper in it. We decided it was about thirty years earlier. For a while the Biglers had a tall antenna and a big TV, but they found nothing on it worth the generator fuel. They preferred looking at the world straight in the face or at the photographs kept in fat scrapbooks and stuck on the walls.

They listened a lot to the radio. Myrtle had heard a country song that hit her hard. "It talked about these people who lived in a muggy old cabin in the backwoods," she said. "It goes, 'Joe, come on in here, get out of that mood you're in.' About children's toys laying around and memories from a thousand years. Sure wish I could hear it again."

A mysterious force tugged me toward the kitchen: the aroma of split pea soup. Myrtle was one fine cook.

Before leaving, I took their pictures. They posed on the porch, slightly serious. It was the Grant Wood scene but with real warmth and no silly pitchfork. "Well," said Myrtle, "you've got a picture of the two old cronies who live in a muggy old cabin in the woods." And she laughed real hard.

Alcide had gone to town, but I saw an article on him. He'd lived alone, he had said, because that was how it was meant to be. He was married, back in 1929. He told the reporter: "My wife went to the store to get kerosene for the stove, and they gave her gasoline. Blew her plum through the partition." A second wife died of a rare disease. On the third try Alcide's bride had a heart attack before the wedding. "I decided the Good Lord wanted me to stay by myself. I said, 'Well, forget it.' "

Instead, he threw himself into cooking. His pumpkin pie and swamp sludge coffee were famous all the way to the Gulf.

In *Shy People*, as tension mounts between the old and new, the symbolic bridge is a battery-powered television, not unlike Harold and Myrtle's. The daughter-in-law wants one desperately; the mother knows what it will mean. Conflict erupts in a single violent moment. After seeing as much of American television as I had by then, I understood the drama.

America is anywhere the tube is. Isolation is only the time it takes to get to the nearest people. But on a Georgia sea island, in the back hollows of West Virginia, on snowed-in Vermont farms—or in midtown Manhattan—the agenda is the same. With some local nuances, the same commercials interrupt the same newscasts and the same mind-numbing stream of programs. Everyone is exposed; more homes have television than indoor plumbing.

Stronger-willed people can tune it out. I, for one, am a real sucker. Like when someone sets peanuts in front of me, I consume with no particular pleasure and hate myself later. Most people are that way. By the time the average student finishes high school, he has spent thirteen thousand hours in class and twenty thousand hours in front of the TV.

You've got to wonder. *Love Connection* sends people on a date so afterward they can demolish each other coast to coast. "Well," I heard one gallant young man remark of the woman on camera with him, "I'm not into the wide-bodied scene, Chuck. . . . She's just a basic California type of blonde, an airhead."

Or *The Newlyweds Game*. One morning the host asked four couples which of their friends was best suited to be centerfold in "the Bow-Wow Journal." All, without hesitation, named whom they regarded as the ugliest woman they knew. Earlier a husband was asked what item in his house would likely be accepted by the Smithsonian. He replied: "What's the Smithsonian?"

One afternoon I heard, "Racial Gang Rape—Next Geraldo." I remembered Geraldo Rivera from several smash-and-grab foreign stories, and I watched his melodramatic talk show. It was about why stars, including his truly, took risks. Why do we do it? he asked, rhetorically. Why do we put our lives on the line for a story? To illustrate his risk, he showed a photograph of half the population of Pamplona running before the bulls, with a microscopic Geraldo among them.

(Not long afterward Geraldo fans got to watch their hero in live action. In a program on racism and neonazism, one guest began choking another, and the place erupted in flying chairs. Geraldo got clobbered in the nose, and the camera lingered on him, ducking down out of the action, hands over his head.)

I saw some good stuff on *Donahue,* but one teaser sniffed: *"Ménage à Trois,* They've Done It—Next Donahue." Back in the 1960's, I thought, no one was shocked at a *ménage à fifty.* Were we going backward?

Then there was Morton Downey, the one who called liberals "pablum pukers." His show was *Lord of the Flies* come to life. I watched one discussion about whether beauty queens were exploited, a fairly stupid topic considering the wide room for opinion on the matter. He yelled at one guest, "Most women wouldn't vote for another woman, especially if she was like you." The audience made coyote noises. Downey's home station was trying to count his show as a public service. Maybe so, if we ever need civil defense training against atomic assholes.

Whole afternoons of soaps didn't surprise me. But I saw newspapers which ignored a minor world war in the Persian Gulf give over a quarter page daily to synopses of each fictitious continuing crisis for distressed viewers who had to go out and had forgotten to program their VCR.

For *All My Children* one day, a paper noted, "Cliff let Pilar move into his house and agreed to help her raise funds for her people, who are still fighting for freedom in their South American country." I wondered how many people marked the difference in their minds when the story line went: "Ollie let Adolfo move into his safe house and agreed to screw his people to raise money for . . . ."

This struck me as a chillingly serious issue. From what I could tell, a lot of people had trouble drawing lines between fact and fiction, news and comment, program and commercial. That did not seem to worry the networks. New shows made drama out of real life, and vice versa. TV was reality. Richard Dysart, the actor who plays elder statesman on *L.A. Law,* was in hot demand to speak at legal conventions, and lawyers consulted him earnestly, as a senior colleague. "Boy," he told a reporter, "that tells you the power of television." And how. Law school applications had jumped 15 percent, just the way journalism did after Watergate.

Later on I saw an item posted in a teachers' lounge somewhere: More shots were fired on one evening of television than by a large metropolitan police force in an entire year.

When you do NBC's *Today Show*, among others, you sign a statement that you have used no inducements to get invited. That is reasonable, since you can sell a lot of anything by a brief appearance. One morning I watched Willard Scott, after doing the weather, gush on about a new hotel at Disney World. On location he raved about the service and the food and generally pronounced it the finest place in the universe, in his habitually enthusiastic way. Soon after, he was selling dog food in a real commercial.

You can learn a lot about America from *Today*. For example, I watched Shari Lewis and a hand puppet named Lambchop cover the Bible in sixty-second sketches. Next, Lewis said, she and the talking potholder would be doing one-minute Greek mythology.

What you don't learn much about on *Today* is the rest of the world. In New York I had gone to see Steve Friedman, who had been executive producer for eight years. He was a proven gauge of what interested Americans, at least before breakfast. I wanted to know if people cared about foreign news. Yes, he said, if they are shown how it affects them. What about Chad? No, he replied, with a grimace, Americans would never care about Chad.

As we talked, a ragtag Chadian army was routing a Libyan garrison, killing or capturing four thousand of Muammar Qaddafi's occupation troops. A small force overran fortified positions, attacking in trucks on open sand. Libyans fled in panic, leaving a billion dollars in Soviet-made missiles and aircraft. The clear lesson was no surprise to anyone with sources extending beyond the Reagan White House.

Qaddafi ruled a stretch of desert with the population of metropolitan Denver. He amassed hardware, but his troops could barely use it. He could have been dissuaded from terrorism by discreet action. Instead, invective bordering on hysteria gave him status he never would have achieved on his own. The U.S. bombing of Tripoli strained the Atlantic alliance. Had a Libyan missile scored a lucky hit, we would have paid heavily for needless machismo. But it went down in history along with the Grenada invasion, a swift stroke against tyranny by a no-nonsense leader who restored his nation's flagging honor.

Under the circumstances, there must have been a few Americans at least as interested in Chad as where Elmer Toops took Lydia Freem for dinner on the *Love Connection*.

*

When American television turns to news it cares about, nothing can touch it. The film *Broadcast News* was an amusing look at a linguine-brained anchorman, but it was no inside story. It is not easy, wrapping up the world in twenty-three minutes each night, and no newscaster is happy trying to do it.

You've got to admire these poor bastards who work with the whole world kibitzing. So much television is entertainment that people forget reporting is a grim business. When public servants refuse to level, reporters have to insist. It is not pleasant to watch, but life is like that sometimes. I'd like to meet the meat-packer with enough guts to make hot dogs in plain sight of the people expected to eat them.

This came up in early 1988. Dan Rather asked George Bush a few pertinent questions and ended up splattered all over the papers for weeks afterward. It was simple enough. Bush, who was Vice President, was believed to know more than he admitted about secret arms sales to Iran and an illegal transfer of the proceeds to our proxy army fighting Nicaragua. That had undermined American diplomacy and jostled the Middle East power balance. Wars started that way. Even if Bush had no part in it, he had been in the next room. And he was running for President.

Rather asked for answers. Bush cried foul; he had not expected that kind of question. Rather persisted. Bush dodged with a remark about a dispute Rather had just had with his network. As hard as Rather tried, we got no answers from our Vice President. Instead, Rather was deluged with rebukes. He was disrespectful to, gasp, a leader. Who did he think he was?

That was not how I remembered America. Somehow, raising one's voice had become a worse crime than refusing to explain how one might have risked all life on earth. The White House had sullied a nation's name. Who elected the President and Vice President? Who paid them? Didn't anyone want accountability?

Had we lost the point of our democracy, that we wanted no kings who rose above the people they served and that we were supposed to notice when an emperor wore no clothes?

I clipped two letters about the episode. One was from a Ted McDowell, who wrote to the Hilton Head *Packet* urging that Rather be fired: "For a few sleazy moments, Dan Rather lifted the lid on the cesspool side of network news. His savage attack on the vice president during a live interview represents a new low in unfairness, sensationalism and bias."

The other, to *Newsweek*, came from a South African: "All I can say is that I wish we had a Dan Rather in this country."

The frightening part about broadcast news was how little of it was devoted to the world beyond America. To cut costs, the networks pulled home crews and correspondents. Local stations could fill in the gaps with syndicated material from independent sources, they reasoned. But local broadcasters had even less interest in spending good money on foreign coverage.

Thus truncated, the world was no match for the painstaking presence of the people who talked about it. Finishing this manuscript, I watched the *CBS Evening News* for a week. At the time, after a generation of crushing socialism, Burma was shaking itself awake. Ne Win stepped aside, and there was turmoil over his succession. One night, when almost every newscast in Europe started out with murderous riots in Rangoon, CBS dwelt on domestic matters for seventeen minutes. Burma then got forty-five seconds, but no names were mentioned. It was only foreigners making trouble over something. I imagined the sign-off: "This is that guy who reads the news. Good night."

However well television news was done, it could offer little more than a working index of main points, with only selective depth, for anyone who wanted to follow world events. Saying you get your news from television is one of those moron oxen William Safire writes about, a contradiction in terms.

One night, deep into the *NBC Nightly News*, after a feature on politics with a clip from *The Best Little Whorehouse in Texas*, Tom Brokaw said: "A group of scientists in Antarctica today presented new evidence supporting the theory that chemicals used in industry are creating a hole in the ozone layer of the atmosphere. This loss of ozone has scientists alarmed because it could let dangerous radiation from the Sun reach Earth." Then he went on to something else.

I happened to be visiting the studio and asked a producer why the item was so short. He replied, "Well, we didn't really understand what scientists were reporting, so we decided to wait until they got back." Reasonable, but unless listeners followed up, they were ripe for the solution offered by Interior Secretary Donald Hodel: Wear a hat and sunglasses.

*

Executives from both sides insist that television and newspapers do not compete. But don't believe them. They mean television and newspapers should not compete, but each scrambles for the attention of busy minds on the move. *USA Today* combines traits from both—an NBC friend calls it the paper for people who think television is too difficult—and has a devoted following. Yet the *Wall Street Journal*, which looks like railroad tracks, grows steadily in circulation. Most other papers aim for specific regions, and I was just starting to digest them. But I quickly developed a warm spot for the trash weeklies.

Sometime back the good old *National Enquirer* went straight, depriving faithful readers of its boy-trapped-in-refrigerator-eats-foot sort of journalism. One issue I saw focused on "the Seven Dwarfs," everyone's nickname for the Democratic presidential field in early 1988. The *Enquirer* asked people if they could name more candidates or more dwarfs. The dwarfs won. Winners of their category were Dopey and Gary Hart.

But there is the *Weekly World News*. It is comforting to pick up a paper that declares in war-size headlines: CANNIBALS SHRINK SPACE ALIEN'S HEAD. That particular story explained in bold letters, "Wild savages on the island of Borneo ended a close encounter with a starship crewman by lopping off his head and shrinking it, says one of the world's top anthropologists." It also promised "Dramatic photo of creature's skull inside!" Hands trembling with excitement, I opened the paper. Under the headlines STUNNED SCIENTISTS MAKE DISCOVERY OF THE CENTURY! and CREATURE MAY HAVE HAD 2 BRAINS! was "an artist's conception." It showed an egg-shaped bald head with pointy Mr. Spock ears, barfing up puff adders. A large feather duster hung from each earlobe, and a double bank of fluorescent lights shone in hollow eye sockets.

Another *Weekly World News* announced, CANNIBAL CHIEF HAS A ROLLS! over a story beginning, "Wealthy, wild-eyed jungle chieftain Uru Urucatuagua rules over a ragtag band of near-naked Indians deep in the Amazon rain forest, an untamed land with no electricity, no roads and no gasoline. But loony Uru's grass shack is stacked to the rafters with . . ." The article explained that the "pea-brained potentate," otherwise described as the "slap-happy Indian," struck it rich from gold found on tribal lands. The source was "South American television correspondent Carlos Neagu," not further identified, who was quoted as saying, "All day long this big, ugly chief rides around in his silver convertible, honking his horn and screaming orders to his flunkies. . . . The guy's definitely a whacko."

My favorite was about the Seychelles, a little Indian Ocean island state with French roots, an English heritage, African blood and a socialist government. It once had a reputation for willing women. But reporter Joe Berger gave us the whole story: "Sizzling Seychelles is a potbelly's paradise, an idyllic island retreat where white sand beaches are littered with luscious, long legged belles—all desperately seeking a man with billows of blubber drooping over his belt!"

Seychelles women tend to dark hues and speak a colorful Creole. Berger found an unnamed "green-eyed goddess with a golden Seychelles tan" whose English mysteriously resembled that of a *Weekly World News* writer: "I could never fall for some skinny little runt and those oily lunks with their bulging muscles make me sick. Give me a tub of lard anytime."

I often think of Mr. Berger when someone says, "You American reporters . . ." Is he a pea in the same pod as I. F. Stone? The *Weekly World News* and the Los Angeles *Times*, like Geraldo Rivera and *The MacNeil-Lehrer NewsHour*, all are "the media."

Berger, and Izzy Stone, for that matter, could do their digging in peace. Too often, television required that even us pencil people work on camera. Presidential news conferences—no longer press conferences—were staged with the same care as *Wheel of Fortune*. No reporter asking a question, whomever he or she works for, was unaware of the little red eye.

Presidents played to the larger audience, not the subject at hand. These game shows took the place of serious dialogue with reporters, and even then they were rare. Mostly we were reduced to the humiliating, misleading process of correspondents shouting over a helicopter. And then a nation of viewers, mistaking it all for *Johnny Carson*, wanted to know why those louts were yelling at the nice man.

At least that's how it looked from the swamp.

Greg Guirard blamed television for crippling Cajun society. People saw themselves as backward in their patched clothes and hairstyles. Those who had been happy with old ways suddenly felt inferior. With new income from the oil fields, young people scurried to catch up. "TV put them in touch with everything," he said. "Now they buy the same toasters, the same bedspreads as everyone else. We found more people living the old way in the hills of North Carolina and Virginia than here."

In fact, I found Roy Blanchard dozing in front of the TV. Roy, Bernard's cousin, had been out coon hunting all night. He was a crawfisherman's folk hero, and we talked about the swamp.

"Yeah, it don't take much to mess it up," he said. "Like can tabs, remember those? They were killing more fish. But mainly it's the oil companies. It got worse when they started running out of oil. The state let the companies do anything, let 'em go right into your living room."

Canals were disastrous, he said. "When they make a cut, there can be a fifteen-foot difference in water levels. It is like funneling in sand." Crawfish beds, cypress roots and natural channels disappear in the process.

Roy's Cajun drawl sounded almost Mexican. "The other day a coon got my dog, man. Talk about a commotion." He used the same phrase to describe how an oil crew boat knifed his skiff in half, dumping him into the water in eighteen-degree weather on a pitch-black morning. The crew boat was on the wrong side of the channel. "Man, talk about a commotion."

Not long before I met Roy, Reagan had tweaked Congress about foolish spending. His example was grants for crawfish research. No one who had ever tasted Cajun crawfish bisque thought much of Reagan's speech. This was a crisis to dwarf the arms race.

"It's getting hard to fish," Roy said. "Bait is thirty cents a pound, and it was six not that long ago. And the price is lower. We used to catch only three-quarter-inch crawfish, but now these guys are going for half-inch. We tried to make them realize they were only hurting themselves, but finally, we had to go along."

Thousands of independent fishermen in the swamps depend on a small group of buyers, whom most suspect of cheating them. "At the end of the season they go on vacation for two or three months in their Cadillacs, and I barely make it to next season," Roy said. "But try to get a penny more, and oh, they complain. They don't cut each other's throats. They pay twenty-five cents a pound and get fifty cents, and you gotta put it on scale."

Bernard nodded gravely in agreement. He was blacklisted because he sold some crawfish directly from his boat. He barely broke even last year. Before, he spent the off-season fishing crab in the

Gulf, but his motor blew up. He would have to take a loan to survive. He caught Roy's eye, and they both grinned. "But we do it because we love it."

There will be crawfish. Producers raise them in ponds. That is the main reason why fishermen's earnings are so low. And so many chemical-fed catfish are grown in ponds that fishermen in the open swamp cannot find markets. "You almost gotta make an appointment to sell your fish," Roy said.

Supply is one thing. For Louisiana purists, it is a tragedy that their world might no longer produce natural crawfish and catfish.

The problem is bigger than fish. It is the old battle between man and nature. Greg's wife, Bubbles, has two photos taped to the refrigerator. She calls them their success story. The first shows the house of a man up the bayou who bragged about shooting beavers for the hell of it. The second shows the house smashed to splinters. During the man's absence, beavers gnawed a lone black willow, larger than anything they normally fell, and dropped it squarely onto his roof.

Talk about allegories. Louisiana is famous for its dirty politics, but not many people stop to reflect on the practical results of corruption and neglect. On a far grander scale, the state has been shooting figurative beavers for sport, and nature is exacting its revenge.

The Coalition to Restore Coastal Louisiana reports the state is losing fifty to sixty square miles a year. Greg, a consultant to the group, translated that to the American metaphor: "That is an area the size of a football field, every ten minutes." Some coastal towns now begin at Third Street or Fourth Street. Their First and Second streets are somewhere near Guatemala.

A report issued in 1987 gets right to the point: "It is now possible to contemplate that nearly all the extensive maze of coastal marshes, swamps, bayous, bays and natural river levees will have largely disappeared, consumed by the gulf, within our lifetime. . . . The state and the nation will either act now to save Louisiana's four million acres of coastal wetlands, 40 percent of the nation's coastal marshes, or lose them forever."

The worst problem, experts say, is that contractors were allowed to dredge up shell reefs that protected the coast. Short of rock and gravel, Louisiana used crushed shell for roads and building. Now the continental shelf drops off sharply, and silt from the rivers drops away, no longer repairing natural erosion. Salt water washes inland, killing plants that help hold the coast.

"If there is a serious hurricane, there is nothing to stop it," Greg said, shaking his head at the stupidity of it all. "These were very rich breeding grounds; a third of the nation's seafood came from here. It's killing all that."

The picture is immensely more complex. Since the Great Flood of 1927, the Army Corps of Engineers has built levees, dams and bypasses. Some of its works averted catastrophe. Others helped cause a few. Engineers seldom consulted less qualified civilians whose only connection to the job was that their lives and livelihoods depended on it.

Arbitrary decisions had to be made. The big levee, built after 1927, was to protect New Orleans. That meant the water had to go somewhere else. Morgan City, for instance. In 1973, when frantic crews threw sandbags on the levee to hold off floodwaters, national guardsmen kept a permanent watch to make sure someone with a load of dynamite did not alter the arbitrary decision.

Reading through the coalition's report, I stopped from time to time to ask, "Who let them do this?" Greg gave me that look. Didn't I know about Louisiana? Some people made fortunes, shared them strategically and moved on.

Had anyone caught on yet? I asked. Greg's wife, Bubbles, replied, "In the last election for governor the only strong ecology guy got four percent. You kinda go, 'Uhhh,' and throw up your hands." She added a rueful laugh.

We covered a wide sweep in the Guirards' generous kitchen. Greg explained that he was planting three thousand trees on a hundred acre patch of land his father had left him. He was distressed that so much forest had been lost, so like a sort of Johnny Appleseed with evergreens, he put a lot of his own money into planting. This was no holdover hippie or born-again visionary. He was simply a good man with what we used to call civic spirit. "I'd like to have a place where anyone can just stop and walk around and enjoy the trees," he explained, with an embarassed chuckle. "I've got a lot of strange feelings about landownership. I don't believe people should own land."

He and Bubbles were back after brief lapses everywhere. They had lived in Belize, Guatemala, the Carolinas and Virginia. Finally, they decided, Cajuns belong in Catahoula.

Greg is a master woodworker, but he found marketing hand-crafted furniture was too difficult in a society geared to mass-produced plastics. Besides, he wanted to spend more time in the swamp. He borrowed some money and published a book of his photographs. It did well enough to keep him going. Meantime, there was crawfish politics. Greg was pissed off at the clique of buyers who had a lock on local crawfishermen. He organized a bunch of independents into a cooperative that did its own marketing.

Bubbles, a teacher, was worried about schools. "No logic skills are being developed at all," she said. "Students are taught to repeat what is programmed by the teachers. Scores often better reflect how well a teacher has taught test taking than the material itself." Educational quality was appalling. If a student failed twice, she said, he was bumped up a grade anyway. "I am teaching adults who were graduated from high school who can't read."

No geography is taught in early grades, Bubbles said. "Kids ask their French teachers if they drove here from France." I asked why this was. Their daughter, Michelle, a college student home on holiday, answered in mock redneck: "We're Americans, the best; ain't gotta know nothing else."

This education thing was plainly serious. I kept getting the same answers. In Union Springs, Alabama, Sarah Ogletree, who had been principal of the elementary school for nearly half a century, said kids know nothing about the world around them. "It's pathetic, just pathetic," she had said. In Welch, West Virginia, it was the same. People were hardly more optimistic in Atlanta and Charlotte. "Pathetic" was the word that came up most often. Often it was "scandalous." Or "shameful."

We shifted to the impact of oil. "Before, there were four or five cars in Catahoula, a town of eighteen hundred," Greg said. "Then nineteen-year-olds went out to the oil fields, brought back their own cars and starting talking like Texans. The values changed. Some kid around here just spent fourteen hundred dollars for a gold chain and a medallion. He told his mother he had to have it." He paused and laughed. "I can't even buy spare tires." Old customs faded away. Hardly anyone can still slaughter a pig, Cajun fashion, the fabled *boucherie*. "And what did it all get us? We're still leading the state in unemployment."

About then a local workman named Ti' Frere stomped into the

kitchen, wearing camouflage shirt and tough boots, and we talked some more about crawfish. Crawfish are to southern Louisiana what sun, money and diet soda are to Beverly Hills; the subject arises often. Another visitor who arrived, by coincidence, was a crawfisherman. There was general agreement that messing with the swamp had damaged fishing, but no accord on how or why. Greg laughed. "There are five hundred experts in Catahoula, and none of them agree on anything."

I asked Ti' Frere about the Key Line. "I never lock my door," he said. "My mama and daddy never lock their doors." Greg and Bubbles agreed that it had never been a Cajun custom to lock up possessions. But especially where envy had set in and outsider visitors were common, times were changing fast.

We switched subjects fast, and I forgot to ask about the Catahoula hog dog. It is a blue hound that, when asleep, resembles an overbeaten rug. When it is not asleep, it is best to be something other than a nearby coon.

Going to Louisiana in February was no accident. For as long as I can remember, Mardi Gras sounded to me like America's best party, and I'd always wanted to go. But all anyone talked about was New Orleans. I decided to go see Fat Tuesday in Big Mamou, deep in Cajun country.

The first Cajuns—Acadians—reached Louisiana in the mid-1700's, when Britain threw them out of Nova Scotia. French, with Norman roots, they would not take the oath of allegiance to England. New Orleans was French, but its Creole society did not want poor cousins with funny manners. Cajuns settled in the southwestern wetlands. With the Louisiana Purchase in 1803, they became Americans. I'd spent time among them in 1985, researching a book on the French. And I couldn't wait to get back.

While other societies blended in a single pot, the Cajuns refused to melt. They remained a thin, flavorful sprinkle on top, like the filé on their beloved gumbo. *Les américains* around them tried everything, from whipping schoolkids who spoke French to heaping scorn on anyone vaguely Cajun. Most withdrew, proud of their culture but diffident among outsiders. Some honed sharp knives and sharper tongues. It was not wise to mess with a coonass. But the draft for Vietnam and, much more, the oil boom broke up customs. Television gave young Cajuns a new standard. Now that melting is no longer required, now that *les américains* smile when they say "Cajun," it may be too late. Or maybe not.

Fred's Lounge is a small raunchy building at the end of a block on Mamou's little main street. It comes right after Clouds, the Casanova Bar, Vickki's, the Brass Rail and a barbershop. Every Saturday it opens at nine o'clock in the morning, and by a quarter after it is shoulder to shoulder crowded with people already draining their second Buds. By ten you can hardly get through the door; by eleven, not even Mamou lifers want to try it, and the party spills into the street. Inside, too many people are perched on the furnishings for anyone to see the hand-scrawled signs reading PLEASE DO NOT STAND ON TABLES, CHAIRS, JUKEBOX OR CIGARETTE MACHINE. Those are normal Saturdays. During Mardi Gras it gets crowded.

Seasoned waitresses squeeze among the patrons, picking up empties and drunks. It takes a certain flair. One trick is to scan below the belt line, from behind. If any denim-encased lobes cease twitching to the beat, it is time to check for vital signs. Another is to listen. Each customer is expected to emit a joyous "EEEE-HEEEEEEEEEE!" at least once every five minutes.

Whatever the crowd, two islands of empty space are sacrosanct at Fred's. There is the center zone, where deadpan Cajun musicians project sounds to rouse the distant dead. A white-hot accordion, a fiddle, guitars and drums accompany singsong ballads about such classic themes as man's unrequited love for seven-foot mutant crawfish. The band's space is roped off, but the second sacred patch is protected by force of circumstance. It is Pascal's dancing room.

Pascal is a very large regular, loved by all. In motion, he is a frenetic beached whale in brown trousers, thrashing his head wildly from side to side, a crazed grin frozen on his face. He would overheat seriously but for streams of perspiration. He is amazingly light on his feet, a virtuoso of Cajun two-step, but only the unwise and full-size delivery vans fail to allow him clearance.

Shouting, I spoke to a a guy named Dale who was having a great old time. American money was worth toilet paper overseas, he said, laughing, but so what? "We got more stuff in the United States that we never see. No need to go anywhere else."

Two Mamou mamas grinned next to him. Do you get here every year? I asked one. "Sometimes every week," she replied.

I came out for air and watched some guy pissing a fat stream against someone else's pickup. Carnival had started.

In the alley a couple of black kids rifled through the garbage. It suddenly occurred to me they were the first I'd seen in Louisiana. Blacks live in their own part of Mamou and, apparently, take a separate-but-equal part in the carnival.

There is a fixed pattern in Mamou. Saturday is the opening round. By Sunday campers and trailers are scrambling for parking space, and dancers spill from the bars onto the streets. Monday night people wear whatever they have the imagination to think of and the courage to put on. But traditional gear starts with a colorful Conehead hat and an elaborate mask built on a wire-mesh frame. Streets are blocked off around bleachers and a bandstand. On Tuesday morning those still moving do the main event: *courir le Mardi Gras.* Local men on horseback troop from door to door and farm to farm, accompanied by raucous crowds of camp followers. At each stop they yell a Cajun equivalent of "Trick-or-treat." Back comes a chicken for the gumbo pot, or some rice, or moonshine, and yet more dancing commences.

For the hard cases, Fred is still the highlight. The 1988 Mardi Gras was the start of Fred Tate's forty-third season on the block. At seventy-five he was still popping tops off short necks and passing them across the bar. I asked him if he thought Mardi Gras and the culture around it would be safe with the next generation. "Yup," he said.

He might be right. One regular is Michelle LaFleur, twenty-one from nearby Eunice. Michelle identified herself as the great-great-great-great-granddaughter of Louis Arceneaux, Longfellow's tragic Gabriel. When the Cajuns fled Nova Scotia, it seems, Louis and his sweetheart, Emmeline, were separated. Louis thought she was gone forever, and he married someone else. Emmeline, not gone forever, pined away. Longfellow renamed her Evangeline and made her as famous as Juliet.

"A lot of my friends are getting back into Cajun music and dancing," she said. "I love it." But she spoke no French. Her parents, victims of the speak-English campaign of their generation, had not learned it, and she had not studied it in school. If she had kids, would she insist they learn French? "Probably not," she allowed. "But I'll teach them about their culture."

I broke for lunch at Janie's Cajun Deli; it was more a lube job, with greasy catfish, deep-fried vegetables and french fries. In the back room a nine-year-old kid hustled me out of a quarter at the

Goonies machine. He wore his camouflage baseball cap backward, like a Li'l Rascals character. I could hardly believe his eye-hand co-ordination at the video game. In the back reaches of southern Louisiana, he was a video kid, not into books or curiosity about the world, but a hell of an operator at the joystick. I felt I was watching the future: In twelve years, the kid would be a Top Gun fighter pilot, but he wouldn't be equipped to elect the man who had control of the start-game button that would send him scrambling.

As he left, I asked his name. It came out "Rab'ly," and it took a minute to register. Rabelais.

"Do you speak French?" I asked.

"No."

"Going to learn?"

"No."

"Why not?"

"No one to teach me."

Eunice takes its Mardi Gras more seriously. It is a family holiday, and Mayor Curtis Joubert shapes it as a buttress against sagging Cajun culture. On Saturday morning, while the rowdy crowd stomps at Fred's up the highway, a loyal little band assembles for a jam session at Marc Savoy's music store. Marc's door carries fair warning: NO SHIRT? THAT'S O.K. COME ON IN. NO SHOES? . . . NO CLOTHES? THAT'S O.K. COME ON IN. NO SOUL??? KEEP OUT! Inside, a small plaque notes: STRADIVARIUS BUILT 496 VIOLINS IN HIS LIFE, OF WHICH 3,000 ARE OWNED BY CAJUNS.

Whoever built Marc's fiddle, it sounds good. He sat down with an accordion player pushing eighty, a few other guys and his wife, Annie. "Chink-a-chank" comes close to describing the sound of well-played Cajun music, but it does it no justice at all. About the only other outsiders were two French musicologists, who sat down with accordion and bagpipe to join in.

The big show was that night. The town of Eunice had bought the dilapidated Liberty Theater and, with volunteer labor and private gifts, restored it to former glory. Every Saturday night it produced an old-time *Cajun Radio Show*, and this was the first Mardi Gras special. A local station had painted its logo right under the stage, a crawfish dancing in the shadow of a drilling rig. Nearby a slogan read, "Hit Kickin' Country."

I worried a little when a National Park Service ranger came out in a Smokey the Bear hat to do the introductions. Had I stumbled on to some tourist sound and light show? But he sounded right. He was there because the theater fell under the Jean Laffite National Historical Park. (Interesting how swashbuckling lawbreakers are heroes if they wait long enough. Will there be an Ivan Boesky Historical Park someday?)

First up were the great old-timers. It was fabulous. Aging couples two-stepped in wide sweeps, tripling their speed after someone shook out some cornstarch the way they used to do on barn floors. Next was the new wave, Waylon Thibodeaux and a half dozen young chink-a-chankers in matching red and black outfits. Waylon wore shades and a black cowboy hat.

Mayor Joubert was in his glory. He fought to preserve Cajun culture the way St. Louis carried the cross. He was, however, on tricky ground. He campaigned even harder to get the oil jobs back and to capitalize on the Cajun rage sweeping the country.

I had just seen a documentary in which New Orleans chef Paul Prudhomme rejoiced at the attention and at the Cajun's new wherewithal. "People can't live like they used to," he said. "They have telephones and light bills to pay. All the hoopla came at the right time. Food and music were being lost."

Seeing the natural joy at Marc Savoy's that morning, I wasn't so sure. People had said the same thing about Bali, the fabled Hindu island in Indonesia. Young people were not learning the dances, with their delicate hand movements and fearsome possessions by the spirits. Painting and woodcarving seemed on the wane. A surge in tourism brought back the old skills. But they were designed for an audience, and they lost something vital. It would be sad to see the Cajuns lose the spontaneity of music played for each other, which outsiders had to feel on their own.

It was the same thing with food. Adapting the classic recipes for alien tastes broadened the appeal, but it opened the way for shortcuts, substitute ingredients and all sorts of travesties ol' Alcide Verret, for one, would never allow.

There was nothing to worry about at the Liberty Theater. Music does not get more authentic. Between acts, someone announced a picnic: "Ain't no cotton candy, no hot dogs, no plastic beans, just an old-time Cajun festival." On the way out, generous local merchants served samples of homemade red beans and rice. I spent the next half hour copying the recipes.

It's funny how this stuff always comes down to a choice. Progress, or "growth," as chambers of commerce call it, has gotten to be synonymous with loss of culture and damage to the environment. But there seemed to be no reason why the Cajuns' good manners, rich humor, fabulous cooking, like their beloved natural crawfish and swamp, should be inconsistent with electricity and indoor toilets. With a bit of balance, the same man ought to be able to pilot a plane and paddle a pirogue.

After the show I went with friends to a masked ball. And then, looking for a raucous end to the evening, we went to a dance at a trailer park halfway to Mamou. My costume had been a silly red cellophane hat with a soft curled brim that got lost somewhere in my hair. As we walked in the door, a dour old gentleman snapped, "You cain't dance in that hat." He was right; I can't dance worth a damn in anything. But how would he know? Seeing how he was dressed, I knew it was no fashion critique. He pointed to a sign that forbade wearing a hat while dancing. Sure enough, everyone on the floor was bareheaded.

Why? I asked. Does it get pretty wild out there? "How can it? I'm the bouncer. Any trouble, and there's one place for them." Hats were banned because sometime in the past someone got hurt with a hatbrim. The insurance company paid, and decided to eliminate yet one more possible risk. On the way out I noticed the old guy's speed limit sign. It said 9½ MILES AN HOUR.

The last act was gumbo at the mayor's house. I mean, this was serious gumbo, cooked all morning in a pot big enough to dip a sheep in. Joubert and his family took turns at revealing gumbo nuances, down to trailing the last touch of filé across the top. Mostly we talked about the subject that had kept arising since I first got to Louisiana.

The mayor, formerly principal at the high school, described how the change came: "Kids were dropping out of school in ninth or tenth grade to earn thirty-five thousand dollars on an offshore rig. They'd take a welding course and make forty thousand dollars. Then they'd come back in a Cadillac to see the high school principal and say, 'Hey, Mr. Joubert, look how well I'm doing.' Everybody had all the things money could buy: a boat in the yard, swimming pool. Then the bottom fell out. Most of them have debts up to here."

He went on. "We have a little airport and had to build more hangars for all the Learjets. Now we're trying to rent out a hangar just to pay costs. It is tough. Talking about averages, we forget about all the human adjustment behind the figures. Lot of people just picked up and moved to Atlanta, or Nashville, just on hopes."

Joubert said the schools were working hard to whet curiosity among kids, to encourage interest in studies. High school students get a special Gold Card with a B average or better. They receive discounts and gifts from merchants who support the program. There is always a distinction known as AVIS, a very important student. "The schools and merchants got tired of waiting for Big Brother to do something about improving education," he said.

It all smacked of bribery to me, discouraging for the slow, but they liked it. BAD sounded better. Among the Eunice High School Badgers, BAD stands for Badgers Against Drugs. The students' association tries to persuade kids to shun dope. It reports some success.

I had to catch a plane, so I asked Joubert for a quick general assessment of the Cajuns' future. He was optimistic. "I was really worried for a while, but you can turn on the radio anywhere between here and Port Arthur, Texas, and you know you are in Cajun Country."

The Fontenots of Baton Rouge, visiting relatives, were not so sure, but they hoped the mayor was right.

"We have a lot of healing to do from the way *les américains* suppressed our culture," said Brenda Fontenot. "My dad was beat on the hands for speaking French. We were awful to kids who acted Cajun. I remember Teddy. . . . We laughed at him, persecuted him. Sometimes I want to go find him and hug him and tell him I'm sorry."

This came from down deep. She was highly educated, sensitive, a woman who had reflected on life and values, and she spoke with fervor.

"I'm so proud to be Cajun," she repeated. "There's just something inside of me that comes up, that makes me think of the past and say, 'I'm gonna get 'em.' " She paused to watch me get all this down on paper and then added, "It brings tears to your eyes to know someone cares about your culture and who you are."

A few miles from Eunice, I wheeled back onto I-10, clicking myself back into the American mainstream of rounded edges and clean closets. In any direction I could find whatever I needed, from a honey-dipped doughnut to an earthmover. But it struck me, all of a sudden, how rare it had become to find passion.

*

Later I realized I had outsmarted myself in Louisiana. I veered around New Orleans Mardi Gras as pointless mass lunacy in tight quarters, which is, of course, why I should have gone. My sister Jane went. She met some people who invited her to stay on Bourbon Street. Jane is not easily impressed and knows better than to feed my propensity to recriminate. But she could not hold back. "It was so much fun," she said. "The floats. People were screaming, *screaming*, 'Show us your tits.' 'Show us your dick.'" This was definitely not Jane. True to the two-source rule, I debriefed Idanna Pucci about Mardi Gras.

It seems that Idanna, a Florentine nobleperson but you'd never know it, had a great-grandmother who was the 1881 Queen of Rex. This says nothing to you and me, but it stops New Orleans in its tracks.

"There are no words to explain the social intricacy of New Orleans," she said. "It makes old Florence seem simple." Idanna was staying with a real estate magnate whose wife is of blue English blood with roots in Boston going back to the *Mayflower*. Everyone loved him. He gives generously to civic causes, and Prince Charles is his occasional houseguest. That is not enough for the Boston Club. Old family in New Orleans means old New Orleans family. But Idanna, an itinerant Italian, was swept into the Boston Club with full honors. Rex queens are never forgotten.

It works like this: New Orleans people are organized into carnival societies. The most prestigious is the Boston Club's Rex. The leading black society is Zulu. And each holds a parade of floats from which dressed-up people throw favors, notably strings of beads.

Idanna was invited onto a float and supplied with three forty-pound sacks of bead necklaces and a bagful of cheap red and black lingerie stenciled, "Happy Mardi Bra." Suddenly two million people were screaming and waving and clamoring for her to toss them something. "Fun somehow transforms itself into this incredible consumer horror," she said. "People want something, and they have to have it. It is an unbelievable power trip, on the float, being able to decide who gets something."

Each person throwing beads has to be lashed to the float to keep from being yanked off and digested by the crowd. The strong shove in front of the weak or yank prizes from their hands. Faces plead and cajole and threaten. People on the float tease and tantalize, making quick decisions about who gets the good stuff and who gets the crap. They command people in the crowd to strip off their tops or drop their pants.

"I was caught between a total power high and the worst nightmare of my life," Idanna said. "It was frightening. You make eye contact and throw someone beads and see a body leap up and grab it. You begin to hate it. You start hating this whole brutal populace and take revenge in the most sadistic way."

We are talking about dime-store glass beads.

"Mardi Gras is when people are officially allowed to let go," concluded Idanna. "To just let go that way on schedule is not human nature." The way she and Janie described it, all forms of person, straight, strange, transvestite, plaid golf pants, the lot, cram themselves so tightly into the French Quarter that no one could move. The fun they have is measured in the tonnage of garbage they leave on the streets. They all drink until they stagger senselessly, slur their words and vomit on their shoes.

Damn, and I missed it.

CHAPTER

7

Forget the Alamo;
Remember J.R.

I flew into Dallas clutching a newspaper clipping that might as well have said WORLD ENDS, NO SURVIVORS. It announced a new Texas state law against pitching a beer can out the driver's window. Bowing to outsiders' pressure, the Texas legislature ruled you couldn't drink while you drove. Everyone has his symbols of liberty: stone torches or cracked bells or whatever. Mine is the Texan's right to be an asshole and proud of it.

It was still Texas, however, and I need not have worried. There was the Bubba Clause. True, ol' Bubba wasn't supposed to hold an open beer behind the wheel. But he could hand it to his girlfriend or his dog before the Ranger sauntered up to the window. Seat belts were similarly covered. The feds would not give Texas any highway money without a seat belt law. The legislature passed one that exempted vehicles over a half ton, as in Bubba's pickup.

Growing up in Arizona, I had fixed ideas about Texas. We used to say, for example, that farther west we kept the bullshit on the outside of our boots. It was endless nothing: The sun is riz, and the sun is set, and you ain't out of Texas yet. In fact, hardly any of us had ever been there. Had we taken an honest look, we doubtlessly would have agreed with the unofficial hymn of those freedom-loving armadilloheads: There's no place like Texas.

The usual exaggerations aside, it is less a state than a continent that has not bothered to cut itself loose. Space is one thing. At Dallas-Fort Worth Airport, I nearly had to refill my tank before reaching the exit. In 1987 Dick Reavis of *Texas Monthly* went to London, Paris, Moscow, Athens, China, Egypt, Mercury, Saturn and Paradise, and he never left Texas. His National Tour of Texas, a hundred thousand miles, took him to twelve hundred towns.

But there is also diversity. Planning a Texas itinerary is like mapping out a Napoleonic campaign. Dallas and Fort Worth, hardly more than a hyphen apart, are vastly different. El Paso and Houston are in separate universes. Little towns are nothing like the cities, and ranches don't resemble farms. But it is all Texas. You can start anywhere, and I picked Albany.

Albany, Texas, has more Picassos than stoplights, two of the former and one of the latter. It is a nondescript little cattle crossroads up the road from Abilene, on flat prairie dotted with the odd oil well. Its fame comes from the intense pride its dwindling population of two thousand takes in coming from Albany. Each year a nightlong outdoor epic, the Fort Griffin Fandangle, draws busloads of senior citizens from as far away as Wichita Falls. It is some show, complete with longhorn cattle, buffalo and howling Comanches, taking Albany from primeval times to microwave chili. Like everything of its sort, it starts with horsemen parading the Lone Star flag so fast you can hear the pop in Oklahoma.

I loved the Fandangle. At first I was merely surprised that such a small place produced so many people who could sing on key. Then I was amused. I'd just read *Texasville*, and here was Larry McMurtry right down to the collapsing Whitney, where Albany saw its last picture show. Finally, I got caught up in it all. I mourned the last buffalo and the first barbed wire. I saw Fort Griffin shut down for lack of Indians to kill; I watched the railroad arrive, right after them scoundrel sheepherders. By the end of the night I knew every drunk who had staggered out of the Beehive Saloon from late last century until Shackelford County went dry.

In that outdoor arena a peaceful, easy feeling blocked out everything that wasn't Albany, Texas. Not only was I a long way from Paris, but I wasn't all that close to Abilene. Ronald Reagan once observed it was a two-day drive from Nicaragua to Texas. Maybe. But when you were heading the other way, it was about a million light-years.

Albany's Picassos are kept in the town jail, along with a Modigliani, a whole shitload of modern stuff and one of the world's largest

collections of ancient Chinese tomb figures. The jail had been re-
done as an art museum. I spoke to a curator there named Lee Heatly,
nineteen and blond, as mannerly and beautiful a woman as I'd ever
met, who was marrying an oilman and settling in Albany.

"Seems like in Texas people in small towns always go back to small
towns," Lee told me. "It gets on your nerves, but I wouldn't have it
any other way. They care. If you need something, somebody in Albany will give it to you." When I mentioned *Texasville*, she chuckled
and offered a few true tales of the lurid sort. "Nobody uses their
blinkers here because everyone else knows where they're going."

At dinnertime people are likely to turn into Fort Griffin General
Merchandise, a restaurant housed in two historic buildings moved
up from near the abandoned cavalry post. It serves what might be
the finest prime rib in America, marinated in herbs, onions and
peppers and then broiled in a mesquite oven. Ali and Nariman Es-
fandiary, the owners, are from Iran. They like it fine in Albany, but
they cross their fingers every time things heat up in the Persian
Gulf. Their father was a general in the shah's army, and they were
settled in America years before the Islamic Revolution. But that did
not stop Texas rednecks.

During the hostage crisis Ali was in the U.S. Air Force in Abilene.
"Every time I came home, my house was a different color," he said.
"People threw things all over my lawn, splashed paint, broke win-
dows. When I moved here, boy, I thought they were going to shoot
me at night. The cowboys, they can just push you off the road."
They did not, however, and Ali was doing fine.

But his art is suffering. He trained as a French chef and has to
hold himself back. "These cowboys don't understand a four-ounce
steak and a nice sauce," he said with a resigned shake of the head.
"They want meat. And that's what we give them."

On Ali's advice, and with Lee's help, I got myself invited to Watt
Matthew's ranch outside Albany. It was no trick; Watt is a classic
western gentleman who keeps his doors open. Somewhere near
ninety, comfortably wealthy, he still sleeps in a bunkhouse with his
men and rides out each day to check on his cattle. Lunch was a
simple affair: fresh catfish from the local creek, turkey tamales from
San Antonio and a buffet spread in the cookhouse, including bris-
ket, ham and peach cobbler.

The company included Aunt Lucille, bitten by a rattler at ninety-
four and off her feet a few days. I had no report on the snake.

Watt is the major patron of the Fort Griffin Fandangle, no surprise since his family pioneered much of the area. On the far reaches of his spread he has restored some of the oldest buildings in West Texas, including a settler's house dug out of a hillside. Artifacts range to Comanche arrowheads collected the hard way.

"Ranching is still pretty good in Texas," Watt said, but he seemed slightly troubled. "Hell," he went on, "we used a helicopter to get some strays out of the bush. I'm not proud of it, but it was so much easier."

It was good to find a purist.

The "Metroplex" is about as opposite from Albany as human habitation can get. The urbano-gastric term refers to Dallas, Fort Worth and a galaxy of unfortunate towns that managed to find themselves squeezed in between the two cities. Opinions vary widely, particularly in respect to Dallas. No small number of people think it is fabulously beautiful and exciting, destined to replace New York as the real capital of America. And others think those individuals should be strapped away in webbing, out of harm's way. One tends not to be neutral about Dallas.

I followed a friend's directions into Dallas. He said to look for the ugliest building on the skyline, and I was having a hell of a time of it. One had a hole in it big enough for an Airbus. Another looked like a stack of quarters. There was one with layers of sharply beveled roofs that, I discovered later, had a propensity to hurl sheets of ice at the sinners below. At nightfall the tallest one was outlined in green neon. Altogether there was enough mirrored glass for an entire subcontinent of narcissists. I liked it.

Later my friend took me on a bankruptcy tour. He pointed out which of the fancy buildings housed banks or businesses that had rolled over dead. He showed me the "see-throughs," new office towers where light streamed unobstructed from window to window because no one had moved in yet. And he told me about still-to-be-realized plans for the turnaround.

In the Metroplex and other big cities, I learned, one looks at the future. In places like Albany the focus is on the past. What makes people a little nervous is the present.

"You're writing a chapter on Texas?" some airline clerk back East had guffawed. "Better make it Chapter Eleven." His reference to the bankruptcy code was not too funny in Texas, however much outsiders might think Texans deserved it. In the heyday of the late

1970's, when money gushed and people back East could barely pay their power bills, a popular bumper sticker crowed: LET THE BAS-TARDS FREEZE IN THE DARK. In 1988 there was a new one: PLEASE, LORD, JUST ONE MORE OIL BOOM. WE PROMISE NOT TO PISS IT AWAY.

Houston was hit worst because it had little diversity, but just about every part of the state felt the impact. In Dallas whole ghettos of unfinished condos were bulldozed. One real estate developer put it simply enough: "Ain't nothing complicated. A whole lot of banks lent way too much money on stuff that wasn't worth shit." That was about it. When oil was plentiful and the price was high, there seemed to be no limit to the economy. Texans defined profit as getting money from the bankers and loss as having to pay the sons of bitches back.

Banks collapsed by the score. When federal law had prevented savings and loan companies from calling themselves banks, they came up with the word "banc." They joined the game, and soon after-ward a lot of them were bancrupt. Texas institutions led a national parade of failures that could cost the federal savings and loan un-derwriters something over eighty billion dollars. There are those who advocate letting the bastards fry in the heat, but such simplici-ties apply only to foreign affairs.

By the time I arrived in 1988 some levelheaded people were talk-ing optimism again. Burl Osborne, publisher of the Dallas *Morning News*, was convinced of it. Oil was one thing, but Dallas had a lot more to offer. He was probably right. In the longer term, it is hard to see how Dallas can't make it; it is far too brash to die.

Back in France, most people had a single association with Texas: "Souse Fork." In the course of reporting, I had heard J. R. Ewing speak a dozen different languages in scores of countries. The tele-vision program *Dallas* was so popular that Zaire and the neighbor-ing Congo had a small war over it. Separated only by Stanley Pool in the Congo River, authorities in Kinshasa and Brazzaville fight hard for listeners to their official television newscasts. One got the idea of using *Dallas* as a lead-in. The other ran fresher episodes, at an earlier time. And so on.

Before arriving in Texas, I decided to track down the ranch called South Fork and get permission to see the set. Talk about being out of touch with the American way. That was like asking if I could please visit Las Vegas. I suspected something when I turned off the freeway and asked directions at a convenience store. "Another one," the clerk shouted to her friend. I caught on when I got there and saw a giant pastel oil rig behind a building marked "Souvenirs—Gifts" at the far end of a great sea of cars.

South Fork was famous, and in America fame is money. Television crews and actors came in periodically and worked behind barriers, well out of sight. Meantime, the ordinary white ranch house, along with its simple paddocks and pastures, was a national attraction. People paid $6.95 to get onto ranch ground, where they saw a breeding corral marked "Mares Motel." On a separate $3 house tour, they got to walk into J.R.'s tacky bedroom instead of just looking in the window.

The only exit to the place routes visitors back into the gift shop. I brought some kitschy postcards to the register, and the young cashier sensed I was not serious about it all. Who buys all this junk? I asked. "You wouldn't believe it," she said. "Just guess how much that thing over there costs." She pointed to a fifteen-inch model of an oil derrick, a few pieces of straight wire soldered together. "Fifty dollars!" she went on, assuming correctly that I wouldn't come close. "Some guy actually bought one. I felt kind of sorry because we were all laughing at him when he left."

I extracted a notebook and told her why I was asking questions. "This place!" she said. "This is just a money spinner, just exploitation. I think it's terrible about the people who used to live here." She had already told me that story. South Fork had been a working ranch, among the few left within easy reach of Dallas, and the production company made arrangements to film there. People began stopping by the gate to gawk. Soon they pressed in from all sides. Finally, the family sold the place and left. Maybe they were happy to go; I didn't have the heart to call up and ask.

The other favorite spot in Dallas is the grassy knoll, the slope leading down from the Texas School Book Depository from which Lee Harvey Oswald shot John F. Kennedy. It draws a smaller, more respectful crowd, and for once, there is nothing to buy. The sixth floor is sealed off, but the city has carefully preserved the intersection. People stare at the spot on the road where the young President was hit. And almost every visitor runs a finger across the word "allegedly" on the plaque naming the assassin. Was the element of doubt because Oswald never got to trial? Or did someone know something he wasn't telling?

*

Dallas is not all glitz. At the Adair Saloon, a cherished spot for pink hamburgers and red necks, the trademark is a pox of congealed white lumps stuck to the ceiling; patrons amuse themselves by soaking napkins in beer and flinging them skyward. Parts of the city are stately, and others are elegant. But much of it looks designed by overfunded architects pressed to work without benefit of their morning coffee. It is the city of the future and proud of it.

Fort Worth, in contrast, has taken pains to retain its cow town character. Fine old buildings line central streets, surrounded by space and greenery. At night friendly yellow bulbs highlight the skyline. The city is sometimes forgotten in the shadow of Dallas. That is too bad.

I'd driven fast from Albany to Fort Worth, and the radar never beeped. In the good old days no one in his right mind bought a used car from a Texan. It could take a week to get out of Amarillo if you didn't stand on the gas, and there is nothing like speeding through a sandstorm to pock up a windshield. I had wondered if the national mood and federal regulations had slowed down Texans. They hadn't.

An attraction in Fort Worth was Mike Cochran, a wry western sage whose shortest version of "yes" is "mighty fine." On the phone he had promised, "I'll tell you some lies about West Texas, so you won't have to go there." I could hardly wait. We dined with most of the former Nairobi bureau of the Associated Press. Jim Peipert and Barry Shlachter had both gone to work for the Fort Worth *Star-Telegram*. Barry, whom I had last seen in Boston, was getting into Texas. He found plenty of refinement. In Abilene fourteen artists were working on the world's largest velvet painting, inspired by Manet's reclining nude.

But he was still in culture shock. "There is no interest at all in where I was abroad," he said. "It is like that part of your life never existed. People don't tend to be interested in you if you haven't gone to Baylor or TCU. They have their friends and are not all that anxious to make others."

Prowling the Stockyards, we came upon a sign announcing a performance inside by Ray Wylie Hubbard. Some readers may miss the significance here. But imagine a traveler to old Vienna, having forgotten where he was, finding a poster saying, "Tonight Only. W. A. Mozart." I mean, Ray Wylie Hubbard is the composer of "Up Against the Wall, Redneck Motha." And my good fortune had only began. After the concert Hubbard gave me a telephone number in Austin for Jerry Jeff Walker.

*

All of us have our heroes, and I've got two: the guy who invented warm *escalope de foie gras* and Jerry Jeff Walker. Ol' J.J.'s music has sustained me in the bleakest of times. On long Jeep rides into the African desert, I've had "Bojangles" coming out of Walkman ears from under a cheesecloth turban. I've run hard for borders with dashboard cassette players blasting out one of Walker's songs about running for the border. He was my kind of poet, the essence of hard living, faded Levi's, friendship and general craziness. I dialed his number with a trembling finger, and after some business with wives and secretaries, that familiar voice came rumbling out of the phone: "You play goff?"

I said I didn't. "Well," he said, "we'll just drive around in the cart." Fine, I replied, and booked a flight to Austin.

We met at the Barton Creek Country Club, a lavish Texas temple to leisure that hovered just beyond reach of the Grim Reaper. Jerry Jeff was wearing white pants and a shirt with a small animal on the pocket. It was not what I'd expected from the guy who wrote "Ramblin', Scramblin' ": ". . . Took three or four steps backward and gave her a dropkick right in the crotch; I believe in treatin' women gentle, but first you got to get their attention." But he was laughing at himself then and was still doing it.

"This is the booj-wah side of Jerry Jeff," he said, chuckling. It was no apology. Texas had tamed down around him, and he had clearly found himself another way.

"I used to be a boundary checker," he said. "The speedometer said a hundred twenty miles an hour, so that's what we went. The bottle said thirty-two ounces, so we drank it. Got to be like one of those oil sheikhs, too many shoes and shit. I just sort of slowed down and started acting with some sense."

The problem, he said, was the world was getting too crowded to be crazy in. "You know, when twelve guys throw stuff around, it's all right," he said. "When twelve million do it, you got some serious shit. That's Buckminster Fuller. If everybody at every level adopted integrity, we've got enough capacity."

He no longer messed with dope or Wild Turkey. His music focused on Django and Jessie, his kids, and on his wife, Susan. They shaped his life. "Swim, Django, swim!" he bellowed in between sentences, as we watched his son in a relay race. Later I followed him home. He had a Mercedes; but it was dusty, and the license did not read "JJW." We hung out for a while, and he played some new stuff, heavy on lines like "Take what life gives you." Little Jessie came in and wanted to know why he was always fooling with his guitar. He explained that he made some money writing songs. "Not as much as Willie Nelson," she said. He smiled. I showed her a battered tape of her dad's music that I had played all over the world. She thought I was a little weird.

We talked some more about life. Walker thought Americans tended to be wasteful and often foolish, putting greed ahead of good sense. An economic crunch had revealed a lot. "The things I thought were innate to Texas, the love of the land . . ." he said. "I found out they'd subdivide that ranch in a New York minute if they could make beaucoup bucks in it."

But he figured the country would find a balance. "That's what Americans do best, invent things. Then they bend 'em all out of shape and have to start finding the right level." As for Texas, "I think them old boys learned their lesson."

Actually, I discovered, Jerry Jeff was from New York. But so what? He headed off to watch a football game with Django, and I drove away feeling great, like some missionary from Paraguay who'd gone bowling with the pope.

In Austin I met Molly Ivins, another hero. She writes a column for the Dallas *Times Herald*, and she is one funny woman. Molly felt what she called the terrible human misery of the bust, but she saw its other side. "I was starting to miss a lot of things that made Texas a better place to be," she said. "It's nice to see things slowed down a bit, that there is time to exchange civilities."

The most important thing about Texas, she said, is that it's big. "There is a tremendous sense of no limit, it's all bigger and better and looser." In New York you can't get loose.

Texans, she allowed, are somewhat inward-looking. "You have to take Texas history twice to graduate from high school, so every kid can tell you the name of Sam Houston's horse at the Battle of San Jacinto, which I happen to know is Saracen, because I took it three times." She paused here for coffee. "Of course, I don't have the faintest fucking idea where New Zealand is."

But then, knowledge probably ought to be relative. I had just had a demonstration. At the clubhouse Jerry Jeff introduced me to two guys he called Coach and Earl. We talked for some time about golf. Earl, a very hefty black man, asked where I lived. "France." He mused. "You'll have to pardon my ignorance, but is that anywhere near Europe?" Something told me I should have been asking him the questions. Only later I found out he was Earl Campbell, who crammed the record books as a Houston Oiler. And Coach, for good measure, was Darrell Royal. As former head football coach at the University of Texas and inventor of the wishbone, he was more famous than France.

I'd had in mind to check out corruption in college sports while in Texas. Southern Methodist University was out of the athletic business for a while because of repeated nastiness over recruiting. It was hardly the only culprit. I asked Earl if football had cleaned up since the SMU scandal. "Yes," he said, "and I don't think it was that dirty before." He gave me a look that suggested we should go back to golf. Coach, comfortable that I was too stupid to put the question to him, just smiled pleasantly.

But I'd get into sports later. I had a lot of Texas left to cover.

Waiting for Jerry Jeff at the clubhouse, I overheard J. R. Ewing on the phone. Actually he was fatter and older, but I'd know that drawl anywhere. "We know we're gonna make awl," the voice boomed. "We just don't know how much we're gonna make. We'll Fedex you a couple of reports. You're gonna see some real good shows."

The man got up and strode past, sipping something from a plastic cup. He nodded on his way past, smiling to himself. Texas bust, my ass. He was not out to sell pencils from the back of his Lincoln Town car.

The Barton Creek Country Club was a good spot to reflect how important it was in America to situate time and tense when one speaks of fortune. It had passed through the empire amassed by John Connally, whose life was a perfect parable for the Lone Star State. Born to a tenant farmer in poor brush country south of San Antonio, Connally got himself an education and then a fortune. As governor of Texas, courageous and tough, he helped the nation absorb the shock of Kennedy's assassination. After sorting out the Treasury for Lyndon Johnson, he came home to make some money. He went bust, as big as Texas, owing $48.7 million with $13 million left in assets. And he took it like a Texan. Reporters in Houston watched him auction off the trappings of a lively life.

George Christian, his former spokesman, summed it up: "John

Connally rolled the dice and came up snake eyes."

But there were plenty of dice left in Texas.

South of Austin, the road skirts Texas Hill Country and crosses what are probably some fine-looking rivers. I couldn't say. All I saw were the obnoxious cement blocks that line bridges on America's interstate highway system. Driving the big roads is a lot like flying. It is fast, but you don't see much.

At San Marcos I just missed Bob Hardesty, the popular president of Southwest Texas State University. Governor Bill Clements, a serious Republican, had fired him in what Hardesty's friends were convinced was the sort of bald political persecution that shouldn't happen in America. In just over six years Hardesty had increased the school's endowment from four hundred thousand to seven million dollars, and he had obliterated its party image. Faculty and student groups clamored to keep him, and both denounced what they called petty politics. He had been a Lyndon Johnson speech writer, however, and his wife was an aide to the former governor.

The board of regents removed him, 5–4, in a bitter session. Reasons given seemed to conflict. "I'm concerned about after-the-fact scurrying around to assemble evidence against President Hardesty," observed Katherine Lowry, one regent. Another, Ed Longcope, read a statement saying fellow regent Ruben Escobedo had approached him in the men's room and said, "The governor wants Bob Hardesty fired." Nonsense, Governor Clements told reporters. He wouldn't know Hardesty if he saw him.

Mainly I was headed for San Antonio. As kids we wore silly-looking raccoon hats with dangling tails, the alleged headgear of a Tennessee thrill seeker named Davy Crockett. And we all knew of Crockett's heroic end. He got himself trapped with some Texas volunteers in a mud-walled mission called the Alamo. The general, Travis, scraped his sword in the dirt and invited those prepared to fight to the death to cross the line; others could get themselves killed more expeditiously by trying to sneak out the back through Mexican lines. The dark forces of General Santa Ana overran the place. When all was lost, one last defender was shot on the way to light the powder magazine, thus preserving for San Antonio one of the richest tourist resources in the West.

It was a good story, the kind we Americans love. No one worried that the only witness was a guy who bugged out early. For as long as anyone can remember, it has been enshrined as a Texas passion play. But it was wearing a little thin.

Some obvious questions dawned on people. Why was fighting Mexicans for Texas real estate such a noble pursuit? Who assigned the black hats to whom? Who was there first anyway? And for that matter, why weren't some Anglos picking the frigging cantaloupes?

Most of us Ellis Islanders had looked only peripherally at fellow citizens known progressively as Spanish, Mexican-Americans and Chicanos, when they weren't greasers, beaners and taco twisters. But then someone put them in a census column labeled "Hispanics." Along with Puerto Ricans, Cubans and assorted others, they numbered anywhere from eighteen to thirty-five million. They rivaled blacks as the nation's largest minority. They could swing a presidential vote. California, Texas and New Mexico, altogether 20 percent Hispanic, account for 81 of the 270 electoral votes needed to win. I was curious if we had stopped humming "Cielito Lindo" and started looking at Latinos as real people.

San Antonio was the place to ask those questions. The city's social and economic hierarchy was marbled richly with families of proud Mexican descent. Mayor Henry Cisneros, celebrated nationally for energetic leadership, was no mere token. People with Hispanic surnames made up 55 percent of San Antonio's population. But that included Roger Robles's four kids.

Robles, who sells Buicks, is one of those rocks that anchor our society: hardworking, devout, loyal and as American as *pie de manzana*. He was the friend of a friend. I rang him up, and he rushed over to ensure that I saw the San Antonio he loved.

He was heartsick over some of the overdevelopment, not only in San Antonio but beyond. "Here we had this great world to tame, and it was endless. And we never got over its being endless." But that wasn't the worst. Later, over Texas barbecue and beans, he frankly discussed his life's failure.

"My kids won't learn Spanish, I am very sorry to say," he told me. "We did everything we could but beat 'em. They grew up sitting there and watching *Howdy Doody* in the morning. Now they just aren't interested. They'll never understand me." By now they are grown, and he has given up. Robles is not alone in anguish. It is a story heard often in San Antonio and more often still in places where Mexican culture has eroded away.

"I was brought up with tremendous pride, to have the best of both worlds," he said. "We believed in the old values. Divorce was a

Protestant sin. Now I'm one of six kids, and I'm the only one with the original wife."

Robles spent nights doing volunteer work with Catholic Charismatic Renewal. And he spoke Spanish whenever he could. "The strongest part of our culture are the family ties, the traditions, the customs, and that is all tied into the language," he said. "If we lose that, we lose everything."

From what I had seen so far of Hispanics in America, he was describing a general phenomenon. Linda Ronstadt, daughter of a half-Mexican, half-German hardware merchant in Tucson, embraced the culture and recorded *Canciones de Mi Padre* (Songs of My Father). But speaking no Spanish, she had to memorize the words.

Hispanic surnames, I quickly learned, were a flimsy measure. I met a blond doctor named Rodriquez whose great-grandfather had come to Oregon from Spain only long enough to deposit his seed and his name. At the same time a lot of young Latinos were fiercely proud of their culture, language and literature. As might be expected, it was a personal choice that varied widely.

At the Alamo Molly Rios sold souvenirs depicting how brave Texans held off the brown horde. Her grandfather came from Mexico, but she was studying business in St. Louis with an eye on New York. "I don't speak Spanish," she told me. "The only time I think about my background is when I'm filling out applications for scholarships. Then, on every line: Hispanic, Hispanic, Hispanic."

Though I had never been to San Antonio, I had conjured up a perfect image from its reputation. It would be a elegant old Mexican city, with shaded plazas and Spanish colonial buildings set back in the graceful open spaces they required. Having seen what had happened to most other Mexican-style cities in the United States, I counted heavily on that image. San Antonio is nothing of the sort.

There is a lovely, gentle city under there somewhere, but it is losing its struggle against a grotesque overlay by developers with no sense of place. The famed River Walk has isolated sections of ironwork balconies and mossy tiles, but garish hotels and office blocks spoil the mood. Loving hands preserved the Mansion del Rio, an elegant hotel by the river. But the Palacio del Rio is a towering Hilton, a non-Mexican cement bunker whose name mocks what it masks.

The boat ride down the river is a trip to Hispanicland, with tourist cafés offering a mishmash of Xavier Cugat, mariachi and bullfight airs.

Friends who showed me around seemed distressed that I did not love the city as they did. I wanted to. Each time they pointed out a historic structure or a fascinating old facade, I peered at it with enthusiasm. But that was not the point of Mexican architecture.

The architecture, like the culture it belonged to, needed a sense of order, of tradition, of respect for values that withstood fast-changing trends. The old had been obliterated. What little of the new that was Mexican tended toward Taco Bell modern. I was pretty sure Santa Fe and a few islands were still intact, but they were not enough.

I wondered if San Antonio, like Puerto Rican and Cuban neighborhoods elsewhere, was a sign of the times. Statistics showed that the U.S. Hispanic populations were increasing five times faster than the national average. But evidence suggested that those new people would have a decreasing notion of the rich societies that produced them.

Other parts of old San Antonio were gone. Roger used to like Hipps Bubble Room, decorated inside along the lines of a Christmas tree. You'd get your drink sent down in a little train on the bar. That was torn down. But there is still the Esquire Bar. It is fifty years old, slightly younger than the women I saw cadging drinks, and is perfect old Texas funk. The bar is four thousand bottles long, seventy-five feet from end to end, and the ceiling is of elaborately beaten copper. The front entrance is appropriately sleazy, but the back door gives onto a leafy terrace that overlooks the narrow river at its most beautiful bend.

My small party included an attractive woman, and the private cop bouncer hung around our booth to chat. Do you ever have any problems in here? I asked. "Ha!" he replied, lifting his ample belly with two hands as though he were about to drop it on an imaginary troublemaker. A large .44 was strapped to his side, but personally, I'd be more worried about the belly.

His main job was to be sure everyone was twenty-one. This subject had just arisen. I was accompanied by Dave Sedeno, the local AP man, who looked older and wiser than his twenty-six years. At the previous stop, a fraternity party yuppery named Dick's Last Resort, some snotty young kid, probably only minutes over the limit himself, had demanded proof of his age. I'd forgotten about that aspect of America: You can die in a trench at eighteen and, coincidentally, decide whom to kill. You can get a drink at twenty-one.

*

The question of Mexican-Americans took a sharper focus farther south in the Rio Grande Valley. In San Antonio they had long since arrived. Down on the border it seemed as if they might never get anywhere.

Kika de la Garza's family settled in southern Texas when the *Mayflower* was still a bunch of uncut trees in Europe. He was elected to the U.S. House of Representatives, a Democrat from Mission, Texas, but he harbored few illusions. We talked about the new immigration law which required employers to demand proof of citizenship before hiring.

"I told my colleagues that if I put on jeans and a flannel shirt and walked down the road in South Texas, twelve guys would stop me and say, 'Hey, boy, where you going?' " His point was that the measure was discriminatory, sort of like the passbook law in South Africa. "There are plenty of blond, blue-eyed Mexicans who come up with no problem," he said. "It's only those of us who look like Benito Juárez who get the hassles."

De la Garza had thought a lot about invisible barriers; this was subtle ground. There were Mexican governors, mayors, judges, top officials. Nothing formal prevented a poor barrio kid from being President. Almost nothing. Mexicans still picked the cantaloupes. It was not unlike the black's situation, we agreed. A black man might reach the White House next time around. But America's ghettos and rural slums would neither disappear nor change color.

"You can't explain it, but there is something holding us back," De la Garza said. "We only get so far, and then we stop. Maybe it is in our frustration. You guys, the media, set the standards for us. Hell, we don't even get to pick our own heroes."

Then he laughed. We were talking not in Mission, Texas, but in Brussels. As chairman of the House Agriculture Committee he was addressing the European Parliament. "You know, for a Mexican kid who started out shining shoes down in South Texas to be representing the U.S. Congress at an international meeting, that's quite a leap."

The Border Patrol chief in South Texas disagreed with De la Garza about discrimination. His name is Silvestre Reyes, and he is not blond. Everyone must show proof of citizenship to get a job, he said. Skin tone has nothing to do with it. Contrary to overall national figures, he saw a significant drop in illegal entries since the 1987 general amnesty which accompanied the immigration law.

The amnesty made citizens of 2.4 million people, added to 4 million legal immigrants during the first seven years of the 1980's. Counting expected legal arrivals, immigration authorities calculated the decade's total would match or surpass the 8.7 million arrivals during the peak period, 1900 to 1910. On top of that, at least a few million people could be expected to sneak over the borders. Most of the decade's immigrants would be Hispanic and Asian.

The cool numbers were fascinating. Asian-Americans had increased by 142 percent during the 1970's, and according to the Population Reference Bureau in Washington, they would double again to eight million by the turn of the century. Though less than a 2 percent minority, they would be as numerous as Hispanics are now by the middle of next century. Today 40 percent of immigrants were Asian; more came from the Philippines than anywhere except Mexico.

But Mexico still led the list. A lot of people across the border did not like it in Texas, but their choice was to let families starve at home. That was why, in 1987, Miguel Tostado Rodriguez climbed into a boxcar that was locked and left on a siding in the sun. He dug an air hole in the floor with his fingers, and he survived. Eighteen others suffocated. In Dallas a KLIF radio talk show mouth named David Gold expressed an opinion many Texans quietly felt: "They got what they deserved."

In light of the situation, federal officials wanted the borders covered. Reyes's agents found mostly Mexicans, but also every other sort of foreigner, from Swedes to South Africans. They just sneaked across the Texas border, defying electronic sensors and aerial patrols. Reyes, a professional, worried about this. What kind of way was that to run a country?

As much as illegal immigrants, the Border Patrol worries about drugs. So does Customs. But the grand old man of that domain is Kenneth Miley, head of the Drug Enforcement Administration's McAllen office. After thirty years on the border, there is nothing he has not seen.

"Come here," he said. "I'll show you something." I had a fair idea of what it was. When I walked into the outer office, a rich, pungent bouquet made it clear I had found the DEA. We headed smack into the aroma. Ignoring some minor seized evidence in a chicken-wire enclosure, Miley flung open a walk-in vault. I was nearly paralyzed by the fumes. In neatly stacked rows and haphazard piles, I saw six thousand pounds of the finest Latin American marijuana. Potent resin oozed from the dark bricks. Oh, maybe one time in school I had taken a hit with a future candidate for the Supreme Court. What the hell. I punctuated my questions with long, deep breaths.

At a thousand dollars a pound, the stockpile was worth about six million dollars, wholesale. That was just the recent seizures. The DEA burns the stuff regularly. I didn't ask where.

In another room Miley fiddled with a combination lock on a filing cabinet. A bottom drawer was crammed to its top with money. "There's a lot," he said, unnecessarily, hefting a stack of twenties the size of a concrete building block. There wasn't much cocaine around. On good days, however, agents in Texas seize two tons at a time of Colombian coke.

"The drug traffic is like water finding its own level," Miley said. "You stop it in one place, and the volume increases somewhere else. Now most of it is coming through this sector." He sketched a simple map. Successive crackdowns had added to the risk of smuggling through the Caribbean. Florida radar had discouraged free-lance pilots. Couriers on regular flights could not handle the volume. But there was that long, snaky border between Brownsville and Laredo.

At the time smugglers were hiding drugs in the floors of refrigerator trucks which crossed legally at checkpoints. Sealed neoprene bags foiled the dogs. It was a pretty smart move. Customs officials could spot-check but only by unloading the trucks. And hundreds came through each day. Already it was taking people up to four hours to cross into the United States from Mexico. All the checkpoints needed were mountains of tomatoes rotting in the South Texas sun.

Miley had a Puerto Rican deputy from the streets of New York who was still shaking his head over South Texas. At a party his son met a girl with a fat Rolex and clunking gold jewelry. "My boyfriend's a dope dealer," she explained. At some point she asked what his father did for a living.

"Er, he works on airplanes," the son said, picking a profession at random.

"Hmm," she said, eyes widening. "Could we meet him?"

In Brownsville I saw the picturesque old border town I was hoping to find. Old stone buildings anchored the main streets among ramshackle buildings meant to withstand the few seasons owners would spend before moving on. The permanent temporary squalor, shored up by some handsome construction in between, had solidified into a small city. Not long afterward I learned a cold lesson in why travelers ought to resist assigning other people to squalor so they can find it quaint. A Brownsville department store collapsed in a pounding rain, killing twelve of the people who had sought shelter inside.

Harlingen, a sprawling new-looking city that does not seem to have much point, is just up the road from Brownsville. President Reagan found a purpose for it, however. In one silly flight of rhetoric, he announced that Harlingen, Texas, was a mere two-day drive for Communists invading from Central America. He provoked little fear among local residents; many of them had seen that road. On the contrary, a lot of them loved the speech.

"It was wonderful," said a large woman named Doris, who sold forty-five flavors of shaved ice on the otherwise uninteresting main street. "Finally, someone noticed us."

The Rio Grande Valley is poorer and more desolate than Appalachia. Infant mortality is half again the national average, which, already, was higher than that of eighteen other industrialized countries. With 0.2 of 1 percent of U.S. population, Hidalgo and Cameron counties accounted for 10 percent of all out-of-hospital births. Doctors treated diseases found only in the Third World.

Among the 250,000 people in four hundred rural slums, unemployment ran to 50 percent. Altogether, a fifth of America's 57.9 million rural people were poor. But Commerce Department figures showed average annual personal income for McAllen-Mission at sixty-eight hundred dollars, the lowest in the nation. The levels were only marginally higher for Brownsville-Harlingen to the east and Laredo to the west. It was as if America had just sort of run out before it reached the border.

From the valley I'd planned to head up the coast. I wanted to visit the Hartes in Corpus Christi. Ed had recently retired as publisher of a bunch of newspapers, and he knew Texas. But mainly he and his wife, Janet, typified that hardy class of Americans who left few indentations on their parlor couches.

Every so often, in Kinshasa or Singapore or Paris, my phone would ring and a scratchy voice would announce: "Mort! Ed Harte! I got tickets to the Russian mud wrestling tonight!" Or: "Mort! Ed Harte. What're you doing for supper?" The Hartes generally had someone in tow, a minor head of state or a fleeing Bulgarian felon. They were not among those typical ethnocentrics people had been telling me about at every stop. But I had to move on.

Besides the Hartes, I also missed Houston. All I saw was the airport. If what everyone told me was true, it was just as well. I remembered Houston from the boom, falling all over itself to grow fast. Then it seemed like a nice place to live, but no place to visit. Now it had a drive-in immigration office and self-made near billionaires scrounging for work. Down on its luck, it didn't need me around to snicker.

In fact, I regretted not staying, all the more when the spirited Paris daily *Libération* ran two full pages a day for a week on Future City and what it meant to America. But then I had a few other lapses. Like Florida. This was, I was realizing again, a very big country.

At the Houston airport I found a new twist for the Morality Patrol. Someone had sealed all copies of *Playboy, Penthouse* and *Playgirl* in plastic, with their covers masked by white cardboard. Only the magazines' names were exposed, along with the bar code so the clerk could take your money. Nearby a gigantic display offered a swimsuit issue of *Sports Illustrated*. Its cover was far more revealing and provocative than any of the censored ones.

Even in Malaysia, where the government had hired young maidens to paint India ink blotches over pubic hair, I'd heard no one object to *Penthouse* covers. One could bend at plastic covers. Parents might not want their kids seeing what human bodies really look like. Eventual buyers might not want sweaty thumbprints on Eddy Adam's filter work. But cardboard masking any clue to contents?

Crotches or not, major skin magazines were among the few places left that devoted decent space to fiction and long articles on controversial current events. Besides, the dirty pictures have a following among voting citizens whose forebears also fought the British and wrote the Constitution. Censors would argue that the magazines remained on sale. But they excised the people's right to know what they were buying.

In the end the message was clear: An anonymous minority has decided that the magazines' millions of readers simply want generic jerk-off material and don't care, anyway, about words printed among the pictures. Then again, they might have a point. Such filth leads to downfall. Just ask Jimmy Swaggart.

*

Looking back, I understood why I blew off Houston. The American scale had begun to overwhelm me. Even in small to medium-size cities, no one strolled. The distances were all wrong. In most places, time and inclination weren't enough; you had to leap chain-link fences and sprint across fast lanes. Signs like WARNING: PIT BULL WITH AIDS discouraged recreational loitering. Cars had brought mobility to the society. But they cheated Americans out of that great pleasure of European, Asian and Latin American cities, the aimless meander among shopwindows, newspaper kiosks and cafés. I'd do Los Angeles, rested up, but I was not ready for America's fourth-largest city.

This scale business was strong stuff. When I went to school, Oreo cookies were friendly little brown things at the bottom of my lunch sack. Suddenly they were at the heart of a hostile takeover scramble involving a figure approaching the gross national product of Portugal.

Even in a spiritual sense, people were thinking too large; the finer points had dropped away. My Houston source was Sydney Rubin, an AP friend who ended up in France after covering the Rio Grande Valley. In Texas I tried to remember what she had told me to do. Instead, I remembered her sitting at the news desk one night with the bemused look of a shaken believer. "You know," she said, "I've been reading *The Mill on the Floss*. It just struck me. Nobody ever talks about morality anymore."

I couldn't recall much about *The Mill on the Floss*, but I was getting that same look. Although I was there to report on America, part of my purpose was to go home again. It was high time. From Houston I caught a plane for Tucson.

CHAPTER

8

By the Time
I Get to Phoenix

Forever the routine has not changed. When I say I'm from Arizona, someone says, "Funny, you don't look like you're from Arizona." Fast-talking, neurotic types with suspicious noses are supposed to come from New York. Arizona is for slow Marlboro-smoking cowhands. Whoever worked that one out has never been there.

Even when I was growing up in Tucson, there were a few Jews who did not convert to Protestantism to make more money running department stores. Back then Tucson was a relaxed old Mexican-flavored town to which you could safely send your sinuses. In Phoenix, the sprawling state capital, everything looked as if it were built yesterday, as it was. But Tucson had a soul.

Tucson began to change drastically on my watch, but I didn't notice. It wasn't so bad at first. A group of loonies called the Sunshine Climate Club tried to lure businesses and tourists without much success. Who would willingly come to a place where your steering wheel was a ring of fire for five months in a row and the year's three inches of rain all came on the same September evening? The sun was always there, but then some image maker thought up the term "Sun Belt." By then car air conditioners were in fashion. Tucson was finished.

The rape of Tucson is no mere figure of speech. One of the nation's oldest settlements, the only walled city in America, has willfully obliterated most traces of its past. Great chunks of unique Sonoran desert are stripped away—"peeled" is the developer's term—

for parking space and fairways. Centuries-old saguaro cacti were knocked over or dug up and sold quietly on a burgeoning black market. Natural dry riverbeds were lined with concrete, or their walls were gashed away.

Atrocious houses climb up the little peaks that once distinguished the town. Old Mexican neighborhoods and Snob Hollow, where the rich folks lived, are empty gaps between cheesy chain hotels in which nobody wants to stay. The original plaza is gone. Asphalt covers ancient Indian mounds. Traffic chokes the city and pumps fumes into air so poisonous and yellow that you can barely see the skyline once you have picked your way across no-trespassing land to the foothills. Eastern-style lawns draw down the water table and add exotic pollution to the air. Everyone has to have a swimming pool to fill regularly.

They tore down Ash Alley and the old adobes downtown, with their high saguaro-rib ceilings and verandas. And they destroyed all the dappled, magical soft light that took the edge off the heat and allowed oleander-scented breezes to circulate. Mexicans and Indians understood the climate—and the light. They never minded smoke because it just blew away. They cooked in fireplaces, over pungent mesquite, on the hottest days. Thick walls and tiled roofs were shaded by pepper trees. Clay ollas on the porch kept water cool.

A distinct feeling of something real and natural was left in trust to Tucsonans, who threw it out like so much trash. With it went the soul of the Old Pueblo, the nickname that stayed behind for developers to continue exploiting.

Now the streets were hot and harsh as sun reflected off glass and polished brick and rose off asphalt covering old dirt lots. People cowered from it, with their air conditioners, afraid to stew in their juices. However much Americans chortle at the mention of Timbuktu, those backward, funny Africans still understand what we have forgotten. You've got to go to Timbuktu to see what Tucson lost.

Some Tucsonans will howl in protest, especially those who display the newest bumper sticker: DOES YOUR JOB DEPEND ON GROWTH? They will point out what is left and a few things that have been restored. A new consciousness is coming to terms with past mistakes. You can still walk among old adobes, even if only law firms can afford them, and buy fresh tamales at El Rapido. San Xavier del Bac Mission is intact, still used by Indians. The Desert Museum, a zoo and botanical garden, is a gem; the University of Arizona gets high marks.

There is a civic spirit and warm weather, and it's a great place for a convention. That's all true. But Tucson has been raped.

Part of the tragedy is that it all happened without many people noticing it. Coming back briefly after extended lapses, I saw it as in time-frame photography. But there was no master plan to wreck the place. Developers sought permits one project at a time. Zoning was changed in patches. No one could object to just a little bit more. There was always the hammer: Growth meant new money in the community. "Whaddya, for no growth?"

Spurred by energetic marketing, Tucson tripled in size in the twenty years I was gone, to six hundred thousand people. That is as big as Phoenix had been, but Phoenix had doubled in that time.

Lawyers and businessmen made fortunes in land deals and then leveraged profits to build more ticky-tack in fragile areas. A friend of mine boasts how his company broke the ban on subdivisions in the foothills. Vast areas were closed off to hikers. The city council and Pima County supervisors, for reasons I've never understood, kept saying yes. In the end Tucson quietly salami-sliced itself to death.

For as long as anyone can remember, Tucson's artist was a cantankerous Italian named Ted De Grazia, who painted angelic children with big, soft eyes. He had built a little mission deep in the foothills, a lovely structure of adobe, cactus ribs and pastel colors. As teenagers we took our girlfriends up the twisting dirt road into the hills and read them poetry off the mission door; it never failed. After a while a four-lane road was cut past the mission, destroying its magic. By then De Grazia had built a studio complex closer to town.

The cluster of rambling adobe buildings, with beehive Mexican fireplaces, rich tiles and red clay floors, was in the best traditions of old Tucson. Fat prickly-pear cactus and wildflowers grew around its corrals and irregular walls. Artisans set up shop there, offering Indian crafts and southwestern finery. A succession of little old ladies ran great Mexican restaurants.

De Grazia's place was right on Campbell, the wide avenue everyone took to get up to the foothills, at the corner of Prince Road. It was the only thing within miles that did not look as if it had been built a week earlier in Cincinnati.

When the artist died, there was a fight over his inheritance. His second wife ended up with the property and sold it to Dean Cotlow, a developer. He had planned a twenty-thousand-square-foot office block to make a "dramatic statement" in Tucson, but he sold to Chevron for a self-service gas station. He, a native Tucsonan, told the local paper, "It makes me sick, but you gotta draw the line somewhere. . . . That almightly dollar rolled in, and you have to be practical." Bulldozers razed the whole complex, prickly pear included. Outrage followed, and the gas station did not get built. I drove by in 1988 and saw a raw empty lot with a For Sale sign on it. It was Ted De Grazia's last monument to Tucson.

The point of "growth" was not whether new people came. Even hard-line conservationists realized no economy could move forward without new life in it. Jobs were vital, along with the energy of new people. The question was what new people did when they got there. Bill Waller got to Tucson after I had gone, a newspaperman on the move from Chicago and St. Louis, with some time in Paris. The desert got him. He spent days at a time hiking the ridges, finding forgotten waterfalls and identifying wildflowers that showed up once in a decade.

Waller bleeds with every scrape of the bulldozer blade. Patient and deliberate, he refuses to get hot about the issue. "You can still find places that are untouched, still beautiful," he told me, after one of my sputtering tirades. "People don't want to do any walking. What you have to do is go a little farther than the average person."

He fights developers on their own ground. As a cofounder and activist in a committee against bad development, Waller follows each project carefully. He attends the meetings and asks the questions. There are times, I suspect, when his Zen peels back and he secretly yearns for an AK-47. But he sticks to his typewriter. He wrote in the *Arizona Daily Star*: "We need look no further than the landscape around us for our model of how Tucson should be as a city. Desert plants choose their habitat carefully, they take water sparingly and don't waste it, they grow slowly, very slowly, and they endure." They endure against time and nature; a bulldozer uproots them in a single pass.

To find out how it had happened, I went to see David Yetman, a Pima County supervisor who kept getting elected although he did not wear a tie. He knows well what happened to Tucson, and he feels bad about it. He fought hard against La Paloma, eight hundred acres of golf course and parking lot in the richest foothills land. "It passed, three to two, and the people who voted for it are gone," he said. "But it is not."

Yetman spread out his fingers and, in a heavy voice, explained the facts of life: "The problem is statutory limitations. We can only require so much. If builders don't ask for rezoning, they can do all sorts of things that are unconscionable. I can't imagine any effective design controls when they are only voluntary. We are not permitted by the state to do these things. We're still in the cowboy era, and cowboys don't have anybody tell 'em what to do. But they're not so much concerned about the range as how many gold-plated Stetsons they can buy."

Cowboys, he acknowledged, had long since become a figure of speech in Tucson. We were talking generally about the American way.

"What this really shows you, philosophically speaking, is that private property takes precedence over public property rights," he said. "What that really means is that a person who owns land has a greater say, even though it is destructive to the community. It seemed okay when there was plenty, and anyone had a fair shot at making enough money to buy into the dream. These days the dreamers are the land rapers, the Saudis and Japanese and the drug kings."

The county's response was to buy up as much land as possible. Ten million dollars were budgeted over a decade for open space. One problem was that private buyers had more money. The other problem was that Pima County had no say over incorporated towns. And every little settlement was incorporating to take advantage of developers' largess.

I asked Yetman how a city like Jerusalem could keep its character after thousands of years, while Tucson had lost its in a few decades. By coincidence, he had just been to Jerusalem. The difference was rigid restrictions; everything must be built of local stone and only in carefully selected areas. A few services were ignored—like sewers. You just can't do that in a modern situation.

But whatever is necessary, he said, the fight had to continue. "This is the best desert in the world," he said. "Scientists come here astonished."

We talked about another travesty. Campbell Avenue, running north toward the mountain from River Road, is one of America's loveliest stretches of road. It twists and dips through the rich desert, following the natural rise and fall of the terrain. But it was scheduled to be bulldozed, straight as an arrow, and widened.

"Governments are increasingly being held responsible for accidents," he said. "It happens all the time. When you have to pick between a road that is charming or one with no accidents, which do you choose? We have to change it, even if it means ecological devastation."

It was no longer people's responsibility to drive carefully; authorities had to post huge signs, install guardrails and straighten out curves. Insurance demanded it. That was why in 110-degree Tucson weather, signs on the bridges say WATCH FOR ICE.

The same phenomenon was freezing out small volunteer groups the county used to support. Pasar, which worked with alcoholics, had to come up with a liability premium out of a budget of fifty thousand dollars. It passed on.

The big Tucson issue is water. Scientists disagree about how much is left in underground water tables, but no one is very optimistic. "I claim that within a decade real restrictions will be put on water," Yetman said. "Long-term supply is very uncertain."

From that I steered him to a broader issue. Why couldn't Americans seem to think more about what their grandchildren would have to confront?

He drew a breath and cut loose: "It's difficult for some people to think beyond their next paycheck. Part of the measure of success for the American male is how much money you make. In that case, you don't dare look at your grandchildren. People are expecting unbridled affluence, having sacrificed production. That cannot last. We can't be affluent without somebody producing something. Expectations pervade every part of our society. But community services are not there. The goal is making money and buying electronic appliances."

It was striking how many people had said that as I traveled around, yet trends showed no signs of changing. After the stock market crash in October 1987, some spending went down. Madison Avenue adjusted a few dials. But the pitch shifted from greed to fear, two tines of the same fork. The tune would change again.

We were getting far afield, but I was learning things. Yetman was an honest elected official with wide support, and he was striking every discordant chord I had heard so far in America. Even the Mafia. He told me about a small farmer, in the back reaches of Pima

County, who had to pay off the mob to sell his fancy salad greens in New York.

I raised a final issue with Yetman. His county would be the second one hit if, as Reagan warned might happen, Communist hordes came swarming across the border. It was already a major conduit for drugs and refugees from Mexico and beyond. What did he think?

"The most positive single thing in the country was the vote to cut off aid to the contras," he said. "There is a broad knowledge that something is wrong. Something is fundamentally and spiritually misleading."

I mentioned I was looking into American involvement in the drug traffic, and in some ways, we resembled Colombia.

"We are not that much different from Colombia," Yetman said. "People don't get killed that much here. But you have a secret war, drug cartels, with proxy armies supported by the CIA. You have the State Department as a knowing partner. Connections that go high into the Justice Department. And nothing will be done. Sounds like Colombia to me."

At the University of Arizona, the Journalism Department had escaped from the basement of the old Liberal Arts Building. But the curriculum hadn't changed much. Students still learned there was no flexibility to editorial integrity.

On my first day there, in 1962, I was ready to rake muck. Miss Martin at Tucson High had taught me about lead paragraphs and dangling participles. I wanted to know how to pick the lock on the county clerk's files. Then Sherman R. Miller walked in, a half-smoked Parliament dangling from his lip, and told us about newspapering. He was a grizzled retiree from *The New York Times*, with a simple philosophy: Without honest papers, the world had no reliable basic data. Free choice would be impossible. Any newspaperman influenced by anything more than a fair reading of the facts was a notch below mass murderer.

The paper we put out, which Miller supervised, relied on advertising. But if an advertiser suggested a story even obliquely, Miller snorted like a rhino. A paper's main asset is credibility; everyone must know exactly what an advertiser buys and what he does not. That was the commercial part. More important was the editorial principle. An editor who tainted his mix by accommodating an advertiser, even as a personal favor, was cheating the reader. And if he cheated, and pretended he didn't, he was not only a hooker but also a hypocritical slimeball. This was not just Miller; it was the bedrock principle of American journalism.

But things had changed since I'd been gone. A preoccupation with immediate profit put pressure on editors for some flexibility. Advertisers buy more space if allowed the impression they are influencing editors, even if editors know better. Business executives scrambled for middle ground, inventing terms like "advertorial copy" and selling special advertising sections. I had had a bitter personal taste of all this.

Back in 1979 the owners of the *International Herald Tribune* in Paris invited me to edit their paper. I was enthusiastic. The *Trib*, jointly owned by *The New York Times,* the *Washington Post* and Whitney Communications, brought the best of American journalism to 150 countries. My only question was if I could work by Miller's rules. My new bosses were surprised I would have to ask.

With three mothers-in-law busy elsewhere, the *Trib*'s editor and publisher were left alone to find accommodation. The editor had to make the paper accurate and interesting. The publisher, who outranked him, had to make a profit. My position was vacant because the previous editor had objected to a program of "special supplements," editorial inserts on pertinent subjects, such as Niger or the Indian chemical industry. They were prepared by the advertising department but not labeled "advertising." But a new publisher promised to change that.

My first board meeting was not comforting. An American board member railed against classified ads for escorts. The owners' papers did not allow prostitutes to advertise, and neither would the *Trib*. The accountant noted, for the record, that the ads brought in $250,000 a year. That was not the point, the board member insisted. It was the principle. Weeks later the ads continued. I asked the publisher why. It turned out they brought in $400,000, not $250,000.

The supplements impasse was hopeless, and I held two final lines. They could bore, but they couldn't distort. And ad people could not discuss editorial matters. Afterward one salesman invited the president of Sierra Leone to "dictate" a supplement's contents. And so forth. But the publisher and I managed to settle the problem. He fired me.

The resulting heat helped clean up the supplements. But that was later. In the United States I checked out with the owners who had hired me, and they could hardly have been nicer. One told me: "You did a fine job, Mort, and I'm sorry. But you've got to understand that the *Trib* is in Europe. We do things there that we do not do here." I could see Sherm Miller's half-smoked Parliament wag up and down at the idea.

I went out to my old paper, the *Arizona Daily Star*, and found some comforting continuity. Judy Donovan, with whom I had explored Arizona ghost towns and whose father, ol' H. George Donovan, had defended Tombstone from defilers, was still writing editorials. June Johnson Caldwell Miller, a widow of Erskine Caldwell and an elegant lady far beyond that fact, was reviewing books. Americans are aware of things, she told me. But there was no great exchange of ideas. "Small, intense groups of people are talking to each other."

Overall, however, it was a sobering visit. I had left a smoky newsroom of clattering black typewriters, where a battered old-timer from Chicago sneaked hits from a bottle of Jim Beam in the darkroom. I came back to a carpeted salon of eerie green computer screens and respectful young reporters nibbling trail mix. The *Star* and the Tucson *Citizen* share a modern complex at the edge of town. The stately old pink downtown building I knew, with Mexican grillwork windows and smelly presses in the basement, is now parking space. But the real changes were inside.

Deadlines came with a slight increase in the clicking of keys. Each reporter, rewrite man or editor talked with his fingers, via electrons, in silent communion with his machine. Her, in fact, not his. Women were no longer chained to "the Society Page" and the telephone switchboard. To me, "rewrite man" is a job title unrelated to gender. But I found forgetting to make it "person" was worth my life. No copypersons hovered about to remind laggards gleefully what the editor had threatened to do with the gonads of anyone making the paper late again.

The trash barrels that had smoldered when confused with ashtrays all were lined in clear plastic Baggies. There were no ashtrays at all. Funny world. In a newsroom in Warsaw you could not write what you wanted. But you could smoke a cigarette.

Essentials were the same. Reporters took pains to spell names correctly. A thick sludge of press releases and routine sources was filtered into news. Occasionally the police radio cackled, and teleprinter bells rang, and pulses quickened. There were some fine pros at work, digging hard. But I couldn't spot a maniac in the place. Where was the guy who had almost killed me when, as the new kid, I did not know that when his wife called on Christmas Eve, I should not say he had gone home? Or the one who settled an argument with Allen Ginsberg by belting him in the chops? For Christ's sake, who was having any fun?

Worse, I got a sense that a lot of people there considered themselves employees. They were doing a job; if they helped the organization make more money, they might get raises. Jesus, didn't they get it? Theirs is a calling, a permanent challenge to push the world forward, to enlighten. The paycheck, puff, puff, was simply the wherewithal to allow them to keep doing it. I was getting dangerously weird. Ol' Sherm Miller came back again, on deadline when crap was flying in all directions and someone dropped a tray of lead. He jiggled the Parliament, meaning he was about to speak. "There's two kinds of people in the world: newspaper people and the other kind." Still? Probably. But I left, feeling like some kind of medieval monk.

As long as I was on a curmudgeonly nostalgia trip, I decided to go the whole hog. I went back to Peter Howell Elementary School to see how kids were taught about the life ahead of them.

What I remembered most about Peter Howell was trying to quit the Safety Patrol. I had joined because I thought girls would like the uniform, a white patent leather belt and a yellow tin hat. Pretty soon I was spending crucial moments after school stopping cars so the girls could take off with guys who weren't so dumb. I decided my duty lay elsewhere. But Les McQuarry, the principal, wasn't having any of that. "Are you going to quit everything you try in life?" he demanded, eyebrows bristling, in his voice of doom. In the course of that painful conversation, he said, "Anywhere you go in the world?" World?

Wise ol' Les McQuarry had been succeeded by Armando Alday, who might have been my classmate. He was a veteran of all levels of teaching who decided to return to elementary schools. In the years since I'd been there, Peter Howell had shifted to a new age. In my day apples were what mothers stuck in the lunch pail. Now tiny kids did acrobatics on Apples in the computer lab. Blond kids with progressive parents studied in Spanish-English bilingual classes.

Special course work helped pupils with learning disabilities. But geography and history had been obliterated, folded into a catchall called social studies, which dealt mostly with how wonderful our particular society was.

Alday took me to a fourth-grade class and introduced me as a visitor from France. How many of you know where France is? I asked. Most hands went up. I called on one little girl. Okay, where? "Next to Italy," she said. Meantime, there was a great rustling of pages as kids immediately went for the map. I asked what else they knew about France. "French fries," one girl said. A boy in the back waved his arm. "Lot of famous people." Could he name one? He screwed up his face a few moments and then beamed. "Jack Shellac."

I was floored. Where had he heard of Jacques Chirac, the premier of France, at that moment running for president? "I saw it in a cartoon," he said, clearly proud of my reaction. Jesus, I thought, a fourth grader who read the editorial pages. This presented me with a problem, of course. What about my thesis that schoolkids didn't know about the world? For weeks, all over the country, I recounted the story. Finally, I told it to Lee Mitgang, the AP's education specialist who thought kids knew more than people realized. Lee, however, was also a specialist in cartoons. "Blacque Jacque Shellaque," he explained. "He's a Warner Brothers character. He's from Canada, a fur trapper."

In other classes, teachers confirmed my worst suspicions. "Geography is their least favorite subject," a fifth-grade teacher told me. "They just are not aware of the rest of the world." I mentioned that some Alabama schools used books so old they referred to Persia. "Gee, that's awful," he said. He thought a moment and added: "Persia. That's Iran-Iraq, isn't it?"

Jerry Gallegos, a sixth-grade teacher obviously liked by his pupils, thought geography was seriously neglected. He did what he could to emphasize it, he said, but acknowledged that kids weren't wild about it. I asked what interested them most, and he showed me some essays. The class had been asked to write on the theme "I Wonder . . ." It sounded like a good idea, appealing to young imaginations. I picked up the first one, from John: "I wonder why I'm not rich. My dad is supervisor for the government and only makes $18 a hour. . . . I wonder why I have to go to school. . . ."

Another was from Joe: "The thing I'd wonder about is if there is going to be World War 3? I'd probably get blown up and if not, I would be afraid. Another thing I'd like to wonder about is how people get radio hams on a car antenna."

A teacher friend had warned me that what shapes kids in elementary school is what sticks with them. "Sixth grade is your last good shot," she said. "Then they become seventh graders and lawyers and are lost forever."

Later Alday agreed. If students were to acquire a taste for the wider world, it would have to come from elementary schools. "Children at this level are much more open," he said. "They haven't developed their prejudices, and you still have opportunity to reach their natural curiosity."

But Alday saw no movement toward teaching foreign languages or cultures at that level. "Our whole society is geared another way," he said. "We're too ethnocentric. When immigrants come to the country, little pockets keep their culture alive; that's one generation. And then they must learn the language. If not, they are always one of the others on the outside, looking in. Look at what we did to the Cubans in Florida, for heaven's sake. This was not an uneducated group of people. But they had to start all over again. I don't think we do that very well.

"We are Americans, so we don't have to learn about other cultures and peoples. They don't exist. Ask the kids in this school. Seventy-five percent won't be able to tell you their neighbor to the north."

Before leaving, I stopped in the library. A book called *Ethiopia in Pictures* gave fascinating background on a country where millions of children starved each year. In 1985 Americans everywhere were singing, "We are the world, we are the children." But no one had checked out the book, not even a teacher. There was another good book on American Indians, explaining who they were. It had been taken out twelve times in twenty years.

I skipped my old high school, but Deborah Latish, with a column for the *Citizen*, covered the subject. She pronounced herself horrified at some essays from high school juniors sent in by a proud teacher for citywide acclaim. The teacher had written "super" and "very excellent job" across papers like this one: "I feel were the best country in the world. Where else can you vote, everyone can and elect who ever you want to office. A nation where know one has to much power in the government where each branch checks and balances one another where the government is dezighed for one thing and one thing only to be fair and serve 'you' justice." This was because we had a constitution, "which latter included the bill of writes."

From time to time I had seen articles on cactusnapping, the damnable practice of uprooting unique desert plants for sale back East or in Japan. But the U.S. Fish and Wildlife Service had scored one for the other side. A couple vacationing from Oregon had gone to visit their favorite cactus, a nineteen-foot saguaro on the desert. They found an empty hole and called the cops. Federal agents tracked the cactus to a Las Vegas nursery, on sale for fifteen thousand dollars. The couple was flown down to identify it. The culprits were hunted down, and the couple got a reward. You've got to love a country where that happens.

But then there was Byrd Baylor's encounter with the Arizona Game and Fish Department. A writer of children's books and an Indian enthusiast, Byrd lives peaceably off in the desert. Her son, Tony, lives within shouting distance. Driving home one day, he passed a dead javelina, a wild pig, left by hunters. Her baby was barely alive. Tony's neighbor had saved four such orphaned javelinas and returned them to the wild. Together, Tony and the neighbor nursed the little pig. Trading off night shifts, they fed her every hour. Then she moved on to slivers of wild greens. After a few months she was nearly ready to go.

Tony walked out one morning, and a voice yelled, "Hit the ground, son of a bitch!" Seven heavily armed men ran toward him, threw him on the ground and handcuffed him. The hunter who shot the mother broke no law—it was pig season—but the guy who saved the orphan was illegally harboring wildlife. State authorities pay a $250 reward to anyone who turns in such criminals.

The Department of Public Safety came along on the raid. For three hours, while Tony sat in irons, officers looked for more javelinas: in his papers, in the ceiling insulation, in shelves and drawers and behind a poster. Visiting friends tried to call Byrd, in Tucson, but police refused to let them at the phone. Next the cops went to Byrd's house, on the same warrant, and went through her manuscripts, tax records, laundry and linen. They opened a tin of tea, dislodged a Virgin of Guadalupe and yanked a large plant out of its ceramic pot. Then they found some evidence.

Byrd had a thirty-year-old eagle feather, blessed for her by a medicine man in New Mexico. A smaller medicine pouch was decorated with a duck feather. And in a ceramic fetish box there were some other sacred objects: The posse scattered the contents on the desk, ripped out the feathers and left a seizure notice for "numerous raptor feathers."

Tony went to court and asked for a jury trial. He was told he could be fined $1,000 but would be let off for $120. He insisted on a trial. Authorities told Byrd they would not prosecute for the feathers. She asked if illegal seizure might be a reason. Later I asked her why she didn't go after the Arizona Game and Fish Department. Her lawyer told her to forget it. "They only have to plead honest mistake," she said.

Sure enough, I learned, the Supreme Court ruled, 6–3, that police and public officials could conduct illegal searches if they reasonably believed that their actions were constitutional. That came from a 1983 case brought by a Minnesota couple. FBI agents and police burst into their home looking for a bank robbery suspect. The couple said the guns terrorized their three young daughters, and when they asked for a search warrant, one officer replied, "You watch too much TV."

Looking for some good news, I picked up *City Magazine*. There were features on solid citizens, good at what they did, and listings that reflected a vibrant city with varied interests. I stopped at an article by Susan Day, who had done something I had thought of myself. She and her son had crossed Tucson on horses east to west, following the washes, the dry riverbeds.

A county park official told her it was possible but suggested she carry a gun. Some mean characters slept in the washes, especially by the train trestle. She wasn't worried; she had perfected the lipstick caper. Awhile back three men in a pickup tried to stop her on the highway, near where a lone traveler had been murdered. She scared them off by talking into her lipstick as though it were a radio mike. But she was uneasy about the wash. Someone had been shooting dogs from the banks.

For safety's sake, Day wore men's clothing, pulled a cap over her short hair and penciled on a mustache. She followed a route that had served the ancient Hohokam, Spanish conquistadors, Apaches, pioneers, cavalry troopers, cowboys, settlers, bandits and posses. The latest in line were people in office clothes, from riverbank condos, who stared down the cement embankments "as though we are lions in the lions' enclosure at the zoo."

All along, gray ugly cement encased the natural walls of dirt crags and cliffs. Growth had altered the floodplains, and a chunk of the desert city of Tucson was washed away in 1983. It was a freak flood, but it scared people. The banks were cemented. "What have we done to our old shifty washes, the riverine habitats of our wildlife, our own raucous, irrepressible roots?" Day wrote. "We decide we have gone too far."

At Campbell she and her son led the horses up a cement ramp, with a railing. Steel and concrete blocked the river. Day's horse spooked at light reflecting from a tall building. Back in the wash, she worried about approaching motorcycles. Not long before, bikers had swarmed around a mounted friend, roaring closer and closer, until her petrified horse managed to escape. But these bikers did not stop. The horses moved on through garbage and broken glass, frightened at flapping white garbage bags.

Finally, they reached the dreaded trestle. A man in a long dark coat watched but did not move. They threaded among the pillars under I-10, the overhead traffic deafening. There was more. But Day had done it. It was still the Tucson she knew and loved. Nothing to it.

I made a few last visits. On Broadway and Alvernon, near my old house, progress had obliterated Walsh Drug and its soda fountain. But that was hardly a surprise. I had found what might have been America's last mom-and-pop fountain in East Orange, New Jersey. It was run by Bill and Bridy Gavin. An old Coca-Cola spigot was intact, but nothing was in it. "If I used that, it'd be two dollars a glass," Gavin said, in a lilt he had kept in the eighteen years since he had left Ireland. "You can't afford the syrup."

He picked up a battered, and retired, ice cream scoop. "Half of that? Seventy cents! And that was in Jimmy Carter's time." He gestured to his empty open-top freezers. "A five-gallon tub of ice cream, twenty-three dollars and something. Then you start adding the electricity for the freezers. You can't pay it."

"These McDonald's milk shakes today," he said, "there's not a drop of milk in them. Oil, powder, cornstarch. Just air." He had been flailing the scoop like a conductor's baton, and he made a great arch to widen his scope far beyond milk shakes. "It's all make-believe."

But the Gavins' eight-stool luncheonette held out with grilled cheese sandwiches, candies and little packets of bobby pins. TRY OUR NEW CREDIT PLAN, a sign advised. 100 PERCENT DOWN. NO INSTALLMENTS.

Another offered an old Irish blessing about the sun in your face, soft rain in your fields, the roads rising to meet you and God holding you in the palm of His hand.

Walsh's was a real drugstore, but I remembered it because my second job was cutting Mr. Walsh's grass, right after my lemonade stand. Which was why I noticed a CNN item about a kid in Potomac, Maryland, who had parlayed his lemonade and lawn-mowing earnings into a kids-for-hire conglomerate. He was interviewed in a chauffeur-driven stretch Cadillac. "The only thing I can figure out is I've grossed a hundred thousand dollars since going into business," he said. He was hiring a tutor so he wouldn't have to mess with high school and expected to be grossing ten million dollars within a few years.

The Tucson stop was a tough one. Disappointments on Memory Lane do not qualify as reporting. I wanted to be fair. But familiarity is an advantage to a reporter if he removes his own feelings. With this in mind, I reviewed my thoughts. They didn't change; facts are facts. If of passing interest to the outsider in me, they were devastating to the insider.

After I had survived my first few hairy incidents as a foreign correspondent, I bought a small piece of land in the Tucson Mountains. One needed roots, I decided, and those were mine. Someday I would crawl away among adobe bricks and start the rest of my days with refried beans and green chile salsa. After a while I even added some portable roots, a turquoise Navajo bracelet that I wore all the time, ignoring those who assumed I was an aging New York hippie with an I Ching board.

In fact, I was born in Milwaukee. But my father moved us out to Tucson when I was three. He ran a bar in the old Mexican part of town. His Russian blood mixed well with the Latinos'. Every February he got out his Stetson and took us to the rodeo. After a while he bought Doc's Liquor Store and became Doc. Then he died. My sister Elise had moved away. I was in Africa. My sister Jane was still there, writing in the *Star* about Tucson's endangered environment. Our mother died in 1985; Jane went to San Francisco. Tucson, to me, was down to a patch of land, a turquoise bracelet and a clear idea of what had been a unique corner of America.

I drove out of Tucson without even glancing left over to my four little acres and made a mental note to reread Thomas Wolfe.

*

These days one forgets how small the world has grown. Back in
Paris, I picked up the daily *Libération* and saw a substantial headline:
GOVERNOR IN *LE FAR WEST,* EDWARD MECHAM, CORRUPT AND RACIST,
THROWN OUT OF OFFICE. His name was Evan, actually, but they got
the essentials right. When I lived there, our cross to bear was Barry
Goldwater. Today ol' Barry looked pretty good.

Arizona politics tend to swing widely in all directions. Bruce Bab-
bitt, the literate and broad-minded governor who preceded Mecham, might have made a good President. Some fine senators and
congressmen have come out of Arizona in recent years, along with
a few doughnuts. This is probably because the place is split among
old-time westerners who like things simple and honest, energetic
EVs (eastern visitors) who have taken root and chilled reactionaries
who have come to let their minds narrow in the sun.

Okay, so it's more complex. But in Phoenix, at times the fastest-
growing part of the country, it is no longer the old-timers' game.

Arriving in Phoenix, I headed straight for the Camelback Inn. In
school, when we drove up to Phoenix to impress ourselves, the
Camelback Inn was a pinnacle of anyone's success. It was a hotel set
within a country club for the richest of EVs and for the cream of
Phoenix people. I never had enough money in my Levi's, but then,
it didn't take Levi's. More, it didn't take Rosenblums.

Times had changed, but I checked into the Camelback Inn feeling a little the way James Meredith must have felt as the first black
at the University of Mississippi. I went to my room and picked up
the breakfast menu. The first item was lox and bagels.

Whoever had owned the Camelback Inn, had sold it to a man
named Marriott, whose biography was in the drawer on top of the
Gideon Bible. The core of the hotel had not changed, tiled-roof
buildings set low among paloverde trees, cacti and bright flowers,
all framed by jagged bluish mountains and a bluer sky. By a sparkling pool, guests turned a darker shade of pale. New units looked
a little suspect, but they were built in token Southwest fashion.

Inside the rooms you could tell instantly that Marriott had been
there. Or his pal Hyatt, or Westin, or any of those guys who buy
their building materials and ideas in bulk. Plastic woodlike furniture, with cheesy little scrollwork, sat against paper-thin drywall. The
ceilings were done in white sandpaper and something that looked
like congealed body fluids. The drapes, rugs and bedcovers were

petroleum-based. I feared if I breathed deeply, I'd be sterile for life.

This was it? On the Phoenix-Scottsdale line, just off Paradise Valley, in *le Far West,* which symbolizes everything real and manly/womanly about John Wayne America? Plastic curtains and pot-metal geegaw light fixtures?

But it was a fine hotel. It was me, not them. I would have to stop crashing about America like some crazed character in a Greek tragedy. The Marlboro Man had been nibbled to death by jackrabbits and buried in Boot Hill. His job has been taken by a hairstyled person in plaid synthetic who rushes over to tell you that your cigarette not only is unhealthy, obnoxious and illegal but also yellows the ferns.

Phoenix after twenty years is Rip Van Winkle run wild. I remembered when I first flew out of Sky Harbor Airport. A friend drove me to the door of the one-story terminal and parked at the curb. I walked a few steps to the plane, one of the few scheduled that morning. Going back, I descended an endless escalator into canyons of beaten copper and stone inlays, to a vast floor covered in a carpet of Indian motif. Rolling red letters on a black panel welcomed me to the world's eighth-busiest airport. Signs pointed to a six-level parking garage. And that was only Terminal 3.

The place was jammed. I noticed two guys in sleeveless undershirts stenciled "Mazatlan," in greens and yellows. One had on striped blue Bermudas and a Peruvian cowboy hat with a gaudy ribbon braided down the back. There were Levi's, white ducks, baggy shorts, black leopard skins, polyester pantsuits but, except for a few guys behind the check-in counters, not a tie in sight.

At the Phoenix bus terminal, by contrast, the exact same Milky Ways were still lined up at the nicked candy counter; someone had merely multiplied the number on the price tag. Nothing else had changed. The same Mexicans in cowboy shirts lounged on the broken plastic chairs next to haggard young mothers clutching vinyl tote bags and restive children. Someone may have swept the floor in the intervening years, but I wouldn't bet on it.

A few modern touches had been added. The battered old pinball machines were replaced by battered video games. Some scarred TV sets were affixed to a few chairs. The magazines on sale were gaudier and raunchier. But the same kid sat in the ticket window, with the pimple on his forehead still waiting to burst. He said it cost $129 to go to New York. I asked how long it took. "Two and a half days," he replied, adding helpfully: "It stops along the way."

At Sky Harbor I stopped at a high-tech long-distance phone with a computer screen. It promised to take three different credit cards in my pocket, but it lied. I tried other phones; none worked. Finally, I dialed "O." Nothing happened. Several minutes of scrambling to determine "access codes" got me a human voice. I asked what was wrong. "I don't know, sir. I've never used one of those phones, and we have no instructions. Find another phone." I located an old-fashioned kind and asked the operator to charge the call to a friend's phone. But there was no one home to verify.

After some searching, I found another kind of credit card phone. It jerked me around for a while, asked dumb questions about which brand of alphabet soup I wanted to use, told me my number was out of the "calling area," messed around some more and then cut me off. Exasperated, I called another operator. She was flabbergasted to learn I had no AT&T credit card. I was an outsider, I explained. She would send me the forms immediately; they would arrive in six weeks, and I would have a hundred-dollar limit. They never arrived.

All this would hardly bear reporting had it not happened, in more or less the same way, everywhere I went. In New Mexico, after a long hassle with an officious operator, I broke down and called collect. I gave her my full name. "Just a moment, Mort," she said.

In modern America you are not supposed to be upset by familiarity from strangers to whom you feel no warmth. This is sometimes hard to grasp. Once, in Zimbabwe, I had to make an urgent call to a lawyer in Denver. It took forty-five minutes to get a faltering line I knew I would lose any minute. The receptionist flooded me with the cough syrup of mechanical politeness, but I could feel she was toying with her hold button. She asked my business, and various other things, until I blurted: "Look, please put me through now."

Her voice took on injured tinge, but she was unshaken. "Are you at a pay phone, Mort?"

I took a drive around town, down Nineteenth Avenue past Brown's Colonial Mortuary and My Mother's Prime Ribs, Pizza, BBQ. And I ate at El Maya, a fine little hole-in-the-wall restaurant, remodeled in plastic bricks and beams, distinguished for two things: Nearby was the school where an Arizona teacher of the year was accused of child molesting. Also, Ava Gardner had been a frequent customer for a while in 1954.

It's a funny thing about Phoenix. People who like it tend to love it. Warm and dry, it is a vast playground of golf courses, tennis courts, art museums and galleries, fancy stores and chic boutiques. It is big enough to attract good theater and big-league sports. My cousin Steve travels the world regularly. No philistine, he loves a good meal and shot at the Louvre. Then he says good-by to us Europinos and hurries happily home to Phoenix.

But those who don't like it go for the throat. It is a soulless, endless urban sprawl, too big to be a comfortable little city and too small and landlocked to be Los Angeles. Traffic can be paralytic. The natural setting was long ago overwhelmed by hilltop housing and farmland turned into cheap condos.

For all the changes, affairs were still controlled by a tight little group known as the Phoenix 40, the old-line social lions and moneymen who knew what was in the closets. Real estate was an especially touchy issue, literally worth a reporter's life. Don Bolles of the *Arizona Republic* had dug too deeply, and he had been murdered. An investigative team of reporters from around the country never could find out who did it or who ordered it.

Another Phoenix distinction was from the Environmental Protection Agency. In 1986 the city had the nation's worst carbon monoxide pollution and was the worst violator of EPA regulations. Beyond Phoenix, the Phelps Dodge Corporation in southern Arizona was the West's largest producer of sulfur dioxide and pumped three hundred thousand tons a year into the air until the plant was finally shut down in 1986.

Down in the south, Tombstone still boasted it was "the town too tough to die." That was true, if you counted mummification in cheap, gaudy wax. I had always counted on Tombstone to fend off the Gatlinburg greed syndrome. For years it kept its flavor. The old Crystal Palace Saloon was just as the Earps left it except that someone had strung electric wire into the chandeliers. Boots still rang on the board sidewalk, and real mud crumbled off the walls. No longer. Historic preservation codes kept basic lines intact. But people had managed to dude it up anyway.

In the mid-1870's Ed Schieffelin went out prospecting in Apache

country, and someone remarked, "All you'll find there is your tombstone." By 1882 Tombstone was the rowdiest town between New
Orleans and San Francisco, with hookers, booze and a twenty-four-
hour saloon and whorehouse called the Bird Cage Theater. In 1889
it abruptly died when the silver ran out.

Boot Hill Cemetery, in that brief period, had filled up fast. One
marker read, "Here lies Lester Moore, Shot by a slug of a .44, No
Les, no more." But its prospective inhabitants took it seriously. When
the first man was buried there, a drifter named John Hicks, miners
scrounged up the only white shirt in camp for the burial. These
days rollicking tourists drop their ice cream cones on the graves of
good folks, in a manner they would frown upon in Forest Lawn.

Downtown the Earps and Doc Holliday had a half-minute gun
battle with some bad-ass ranchers that went down in history. The
O.K. Corral is still there, but nothing is left for imagination. Silly-
looking life-size cutouts, labeled in big letters, stand as visual aids to
the corny, melodramatic patter.

I noticed someone erecting an antique facade of thin, nasty synthetic fiber with fake aging smeared over it. Inside, in a forgotten
old saloon, developers had set up a historic diorama that would make
a Savannah huckster blush. Wax dummies wore period costumes
from places that Tombstone pioneers never knew existed. One was
a woman in a Mexican charro outfit, the Saturday night regalia from
faraway Jalisco, with wide embroidered hat, fancy pinched pants
and silver-trimmed boots. She was, future American generations were
informed, a "Mexican peasant working the fields."

A lot of Tombstone was carefully restored. Shieffelin Hall, brought
back from near death, was a vast adobe social center, one of the
finest western buildings of its time. For a while it was a museum,
plastered with Visit Me signs. It was quietly returned to its original
purpose, a town gathering spot, and struck from the tourist map.
There was nothing exciting about a social center.

Before moving north, I took a side trip to New Mexico. Santa Fe,
more than anywhere else I saw, had held the line. Its tile and mud
downtown was lovingly preserved. Even a huge new hotel, built to
look old, managed to fit in smoothly. The leafy plaza exuded its rich
past. Up on Canyon Road, artists and artisans hung out in lively
cantinas. Old adobe homes meandered up the hills. Santa Fe had
some of the world's best opera and music festivals. The catch was

you had to be a retired movie mogul to buy anything substantial.

I discovered the other catch attempting to find dinner with friends at 9:00 P.M. At a classy little bistro downtown, the maître d' was tucking into a rare tournedo. They were done serving, he said. With a snide smile, he added, "It's that kind of town." No, it isn't. The people who built it, and gave it their spirit, ate dinner at midnight. The restaurateur, who had probably come a year earlier from Greenwich Village, was part of an alien overlay I noticed elsewhere. But you can't have everything. Santa Fe felt great.

Then I went to Corrales. Years back I'd bought an acre among ten other homesites on the Rio Grande, just outside Albuquerque. If Tucson went the way I feared, it was my backup. I hadn't been there in a decade. But whenever a drunken soldier stuck a gun in my gut in some unruly part of the world, I'd think of my cotton-woods securely protected in America. That is why I was flabber-gasted to find on my land that an S. Rosenblum had nailed a notice to a tree, duly signed and stamped by authorities, announcing his imminent pig farm.

I ripped off the sign, the way it was done in the old westerns, and strode quickly to the Corrales Town Hall. No one seemed to know much. The clerk had no record, but the zoning officer would. He was out, but someone else had the key to his office. But she was out. Meantime, I talked to a cop. "Gee," he reflected, sympathetically, "that's kind of too bad. Here you go away a long time to come home to find some guy putting up a pig farm. Yeah, gee." He shook his head and advised me where to find a judge in a nearby muncipality. Was I certain I didn't know any S. Rosenblum from Illinois?

Meantime, I am getting excited and thrusting the sign at every-one in sight. I closed my eyes and imagined a truckload of squealing sows hurtling down the Oklahoma Turnpike toward my retirement home. Clearly someone had noticed my long absence and found another Rosenblum. Signatures had been faked; now my time to challenge this outrage had expired. But a Rosenblum raising pork in Corrales?

The lady with the key arrived, but she needed another key for the files. She found it. The files, about to be moved, looked as if they'd been rearranged by an air strike. Nothing could be found, anywhere. The cop returned. "Say, man, you'd better get over and find the judge before he starts drinking."

Then someone remembered they had read about it in the town paper. It was an April Fool's joke on the neighbors.

CHAPTER

9

Rockies:
To Hell You Ride

On a Rocky Mountain morning in July, crisp and blue and scented, I went riding with friends up above Telluride, Colorado. From the trail we looked down at the old mining town, brought back from the edge of ghosthood by dedicated people who liked its freedom. A grizzled wrangler name of Monty, in homemade chaps, kept half an eye on our rented horses. But like us, he was back a century, when Butch Cassidy had raided a bank on the Victorian main street we could see far below. The dirt trail suddenly opened onto a flat, broad meadow. This was the wide open West. My friend Gretchen, a rider almost from birth, let her horse break into a light trot. Monty sniffed and bellowed: "Walk yer horse!"

Monty was a nice guy; he was simply scared. "People are so damn quick to sue, even if it's their fault," he said. "You wouldn't believe what we get hit with." I'd believe it. From the time I first thought of reporting on America, I'd heard lawsuit stories. My files bulged with them. But somehow I thought this little town up a box canyon might still settle its problems in the normal way, with Colt .44's at twenty paces. If any place could escape modern times, it would be this crevice on the back side of the Rockies' southern slopes. Though the town was likely named for a type of gold ore, a lot of locals prefer to believe it is a contraction of "To Hell You Ride." Time, however, has caught up with the romantics.

Merry-go-round horses are the least of it. Dogs must be leashed. Fireplace permits are traded like late Van Goghs, and stacks must be fitted with high tech smoke condoms. Cars are ticketed for contravening parking laws only slightly less complex than the INF Treaty. Smoking, I think, is allowed only in groups of two or less, at the bottom of abandoned mine shafts. With all of this, people love Telluride, and it is the closest thing I have to an American home. But like almost everywhere else in the Rockies, it is a bizarre mix of time and space.

At breakfast, in the window of the Excelsior Café, I put myself back again in the last century. Colorado Street out front was still wide enough for a full team of oxen to make a U-turn without tipping over their ore wagons. No one had torn down the big stone bank or the little clapboard brothel warrens around the corner. At the next table sat a couple of rough-looking guys in battered hats and bushy ginger mustaches. Then the waitress handed me a menu and announced, "Our special quiche this morning is artichoke."

The bank, after a time as the Elks' Club, had become a T-shirt shoppe, run by a defrocked lawyer from North Carolina. It was one of six shoppes on Colorado Street offering souvenir shirts bearing out-of-place legends. Some identified the wearer as a hero who got down Telluride's Plunge, a precipitous ski slope, but none said how. One shirt fitted fine; it read, "Shit Happens."

The Elks, meantime, had built a hideous modern structure on the main street. Directly across, yet another monstrosity was thrown up hurriedly in 1986 before people could come to their senses. It masks the old courthouse bell tower, thus destroying the town's trademark skyline from the only road in. A few years earlier, some moron had converted the fabled brick Opera House wall into something that looks like a Reform Jewish temple in the Midwest. A few other landmarks were allowed to decay and crumble or were refashioned for the yup class.

There is easily enough left to satisfy anyone but us troglodyte absentee landlords and the diehards who won't realize that towns do not change only when inhabitants are too poor to replace their shutters. But far more than physical, the conflict is spiritual.

More than anywhere else I had yet seen, the setting of Telluride brought home America's imperiled middle distance between our free-spirited self-image and the Orwellian pall that is descending fast upon us. Local history explains why.

Telluride dates back to a maverick rock breaker of the old order. He found enough gold, silver and other metals to dig in hard. When it turned out his mine was too far from a power plant to use direct current, he invented the world's first alternating current. The remote little settlement was, for a time, the best-lit town in America. When Cassidy robbed his bank and fled, Nunn got himself captured by the bandits because he charged too far ahead of his posse. L. L. Nunn was that kind of guy.

Men anchored machinery above town on cliffs a mule wouldn't go near, and they laid tracks through impossible high country. Women set up schools and hospitals in pioneer fashion. By the turn of the century Telluride was on the map. Among others, William Jennings Bryan dropped in to speak of his Cross of Gold.

When union organizers arrived, mineowners packed dissidents in railcars and ran them out of town. Slag was left where it lay. Telluride was not Dodge City, but neither was this Amish country. Patrons got rowdy at Big Billie's bar, but if anyone outraged decency, she bounced him out without reference to local police.

By the 1960's Telluride's first incarnation was over. Mines were closing, and there was nothing else. Fewer than a thousand people stuck around, too attached to the place to leave. Then the new pioneers moved in: floaters; professionals ready to drop out; artisans; adventurers on trust funds and dirtbags in search of somewhere peaceful to crash. Drugs and assorted looseness followed, and a group of townsfolk responded in the old way. They hired Sheriff Everett Morrow.

With a scarlet neck, a mean Oklahoma drawl and an enormous six-shooter strapped to his thigh, Morrow might have been a Hollywood spoof. His foul-tempered dog slept under the county's patrol car, snarling at anyone who approached. Morrow's favorite line was "There's one road in, and one road out," usually delivered with the follow-up "Now, you got one hour to git outa town." But the winds began to shift when he used his line once too often. He ordered out of town a young man who, in no condition to drive, ran off the road and sued.

About then the Slate, a coalition of newcomers, won the municipal elections. First off, a mild-mannered new mayor from back East went to fire Morrow. He would not give up his gun. Finally, he went to work in the mines, and for more than a year afterward deputies would have to go find him to call off his dog so they could get to the sheriff's car. The Slate combined the freedom of a hippie commune with the services of a real city.

About the same time the ski developers came in. With a little thought and some money, it was clear, Telluride could be a world-class ski resort. The idea appealed to townsfolk, as much for access to fresh powder as for the capital tourism would bring. But what was the price? How many condos and vacationing yahoos could the town take? Would Telluride, gasp, go the way of Aspen?

For a classical, sword-banging morality play, the stage was immaculately set. The main characters, Greed and Purity, were pacing the wings, mumbling their lines.

At first, it was the kind of comic opera stuff that drew people to Telluride. The new sheriff, Bill Masters, was a lovable sort of hard-ass who believed laws must be enforced. The town marshal, Hank Smith, respected order but felt people ought to live and let live. Then a bunch of seized cocaine, state's evidence, disappeared, and the sheriff suspected it was up the marshal's nose. Masters and a team of undercover state narcs arrested Smith. Townsfolk amassed at the Roma for a rowdy party to raise a Hank Smith Defense Fund. Smith pleaded nolo contendere and never had to turn in his badge.

I once saw an official letter to some taxpayer from a councilman, on town letterhead, that began, "Dear——, I always knew you were an asshole, but . . ."

No one put on airs. If the dirtbag in line at Rose's Food Market looked like Elliott Gould, it probably was. If you saw a friend heading into the Senate, you left your car in the middle of the street and joined him for a quick belt. Feminists did not seem to notice the wet T-shirt contests at the Sheridan.

Then it got serious. The Telluride Company bought the ski resort operations and laid plans for a vast residential site atop the mountain. That would require an airport, expanded services and more lifts. People fought bitterly, for and against. Real estate prices multiplied fast as people from all over the place wanted a condo with a fireplace. The Film Festival, and festivals for everything from bluegrass to mushrooms, became world events.

Local government had real problems: When heavy air settled over the box canyon, the sky suggested Santa Monica on a bad day. There were sometimes more cars than parking spaces, and snow plows could not get to the curbs. After each thaw people remembered the streets weren't paved. Dust blew off the huge tailings pile at the edge of town, and pickier residents suspected the particles glowed in the dark. Laws would have to be passed; measures needed to be taken. Mayors, town councilmen and county supervisors would come and go, according to the changing will of the people.

With this background in mind, I came back as a reporter in 1987 and again in 1988. Telluride was struggling to hold on to its character, its status as a free-form asylum for loonballs and cowboys who take their white powder on the slopes or from spoons. But it was modern America, with its rage to make rules. Decent parents were raising good kids. Neither Greed nor Purity had stolen the show. My question was simple and painful: Was there any safe middle ground?

A few months before the horse ride, I skied over the same ground with Lito Tejada-Flores, a Bolivian-born gentleman of all talents who, among other things, was a recognized authority on winter bush beating. He was pissed because Sheriff Masters was trying to prohibit skiing outside of clearly marked boundaries. In fact, a lot of people denounced the hectoring signs forbidding Americans to roam their own land.

One could sympathize with Masters. People had been killed in avalanches recently. Each time the sheriff had to risk lives, his included, and blow his tight budget on rescue operations. But that was a worrisome philosophy: If you can't do anything, nothing can happen to you. If you can cross public land in boots, why not in boots with boards attached? When people challenged Masters, he found a modern answer. He said that if another skiing accident occurred, he would testify that the Telluride Company was negligent. In a land of lawyers, that was threat enough.

Lito had just came back from New Zealand, where he had hung out with the local ski patrol. Lito told me: "We got to one rope tow, and there was an innocuous little sign that said, 'Wait until skier ahead of you is past the pulley before clicking on.' The ski patrol guy grabbed the sign and flung it behind the lift shack. He muttered, 'I can't stand fucking signs that tell you what not to do.'"

As he did on most social phenomena, Lito had thoughts on the subject. People who grow used to such artificial protection, to warning signs at every hint of danger, lose their natural ability to look out for themselves. "If you treat people like imbeciles, they'll behave like imbeciles," he observed. "We live in a terminally irresponsible society."

Most likely. I keep a few of Garry Trudeau's strips pinned to the wall, to keep me in focus, but I've also got one by Charlie Schultz. Linus is warning Lucy, or someone, about overeating french fries;

nonsense, she replies, if it were dangerous, there would be a warning carved on the side of each french fry.

Signposts proclaiming rules and the American urge to standard-
ize, to code, dim the town's aura. Past Society Turn, up the narrow
blacktop stretch into town, a sign declares Telluride a national historical preserve. A joy-killing, freeway-size marker, it conveys none
of the charm that caused it to be erected. Farther along, the county
"improved" some land for residential lots. The lots were too low,
along a drainage channel, and did not sell. But they met American-
sized specifications. Wide paved streets separated useless sidewalks.
Streetlights glared at regular intervals. Lovely old willows were cut
away. It all looks like the set for a suburban sitcom mysteriously
dropped into a nineteenth-century mining town.

In Telluride little things added up. There was, in 1988, the Great
Hook Incident. John Micetic, a realtor who was replaced as mayor
by a developer, had ignored two parking tickets. One, he said, was
because he was in a rush on volunteer fire department business and
misread a parking sign. But he did not dispute the tickets; he was
going to pay them, Telluride style. He paid no attention to a bench
warrant, waiting for the phone call that said, "Okay, John, it's time
to pay." Instead, two marshal's Jeeps hemmed in his car.

Micetic tried to pay up. It was too late, the cops said. A tow truck
was on the way. Tow truck? Telluride has no tow truck. Ah, it was
driving the thirty-five miles from Norwood. But, Micetic argued, he
was a volunteer rescue officer. He did not want to walk to the ambulance if his beeper sounded. Then he should not have flouted the
No Parking sign. The truck arrived for the first towaway in Telluride history.

There was also the Hot Tub Gestapo. I had lured friends to Telluride by extolling its exuberant spirit and broad mind. The condo
unit we selected advertised an outdoor hot tub, but at 10:30 P.M. a
steel curtain covered it. It closed at 10:00. The caretaker agreed to
leave it open until 11:00 the next night, but he lied. We survived,
but the question remained: Why does a Telluride hot tub close at
an hour when much of the civilized world is just sitting down to
dinner? The answer was that freedom to use a tub is lost to the right
to silence for someone who, if he leans out his window and carefully
aims an ear trumpet, might hear water gurgling.

To be fair, it was still America. I was free to go to a convenience
store and, with no questions asked, buy enough cartridges to eliminate the caretaker and fifty of his friends. In any case, the man was

right. A large sign stated clearly that the tub closed at ten. It was
written.

Outsiders fall on this sign business immediately, but most Americans dismiss it as pointless trivia. After a while, I suppose, signs and
railings and curbs become invisible. In fact, it is big business. In
Louisiana I talked to a man who ran a large sign company. His bible
was an inch-thick federal code book, with details on sizes, shapes,
colors, thickness, reflectability and resistance for any marker that
might be seen by the public. States add their own specifications,
sometimes far more stringent than the federal codes. This, he asserted, allows officials to exact payoffs and kickbacks. On one particular monthlong Louisiana road repair job, he said, a quarter of
the total cost was for temporary signs.

Our national passion for great Day-Glo Warning signs is not widely
shared. At Victoria Falls in Zimbabwe, just out of the unguarded
back gate of the national park, a clearing leads to the muddy riverbank. A few slippery rocks are swept by a torrent of water heading
into some of the world's most treacherous falls. Only the crocodiles
that swarm around can swim hard enough to resist the current. Far
out into the water, someone painted on a log in faded little letters,
"Do not go beyond this point." At the lip of the falls, where a single
false step would send you skidding down the slime into a bottomless
caldron, there are no signs at all. The people in charge figured if
you had to be warned in such a case, there wasn't much hope for
you anyway.

By the time I reached Colorado, I realized all this solicitousness
was not merely because authorities were worried about our health.
Like Monty, the nervous wrangler, anyone could get sued. Americans these days seem to trade tales of legal horror the way kids do
ghost stories around the campfire, and I heard about another, just
up the Rockies. Two brothers borrowed money to buy a ranch in
Montana. They went broke and sued the bank for making a risky
loan. And they won, getting the ranch for free along with a hefty
cash surplus on top of it.

One of my favorites is the Albany man who sued New York State
for one million dollars for breaking his ankle in strawberry Jell-O.
At a charity fund raiser he had paid five dollars for the right to
jump into a swimming pool filled with Jell-O and hunt for hidden
prizes.

The problem, of course, was that you could no longer assess risk.

Whatever the circumstances, was a broken ankle worth one million dollars? It was all relative. A Washington, D.C., jury awarded a young boy ninety-five million dollars because his hand was deformed by a morning sickness drug taken by his mother. Of that, seventy-five million was for punitive damages. By comparison, a youngster in France received twelve thousand dollars when he lost most of his face because of negligence.

Lee Iacocca hammered at this theme, addressing the American Bar Association. Individuals and companies were afraid to take risks anymore. Ninety percent of civil actions in the world were initiated in the United States, he noted, and Americans spent thirty billion dollars suing each other. "In the old days," Iacocca said, "if a neighbor's apples fell into your yard, you worked it out over the back fence, or you picked them up and made pies. Today, you sue."

One result was that lawyering was good business. Students could make $30,000 a year, as clerks, before the last year of law school. I clipped a piece about a Florida family that had to beg charity after receiving a $3.5 million malpractice settlement. Some money went for hospital bills; the rest went to lawyers.

Another, of course, was that insurance companies insulated themselves from risk by refusing policies. Small pleasures, like diving boards, were excised from American life.

Telluride learned this the hard way. After some debate Telluride booked a Grateful Dead concert. Whatever else might befall the town, it would build a day-care center with proceeds from the beer concession. But no one would insure a town that sold beer around the Grateful Dead. The concert was dry.

Lack of insurance, I learned later than most Americans, forced a lot of towns to cancel fireworks celebrating our birth as a devil-may-care free nation. Telluride is not among them. The volunteer fire department's annual pyrotechnics, set against glittering snow on a steep canyon, is one of the world's more thrilling sights.

I had started this reporting job at the fireworks over the Statue of Liberty. A year later I went to Telluride for the Fourth of July picnic. No American cliché is more durable than a small-town Independence Day picnic, and it is easy to see why. Few French dishes approach Telluride barbecued beef and watermelon eaten on a blanket in the town park. Coleslaw seems to taste better when the neighbor's kid drops a softball in it.

Hanging out with friends on the freshly cut grass, I sensed the depth of America's relaxed confidence. It was deep-rooted, beyond the worn-down formulas of ritual speeches. Only a few flags were out. One was on a pole at the baseball diamond. Another was knotted around the neck of a golden retriever. Talk was of town politics and hang gliding and more beer. A foreign issue came up once: Someone was going sailing in Mexico. For a warm and happy afternoon I put aside my mantle as globalist kvetch, seeking to shed light in the darkness. Screw the world; I was back home in America.

The best part came at sundown. We were on Nancy Pitt's deck overlooking the town, eating chicken and drinking too much. With great merriment, we blasted illegal bottle rockets over the heads of a couple of fire wardens, who were busy with their own illegal Roman candles. Then the real stuff started. Fiery salvos and spurts of dazzling color lit the entire valley. Telluride might have been built as a stadium for fireworks. Parallel streets stepped up the sunnyside slope, like giant bleachers. In the park below, huge crowds gathered directly under the rockets set off from Firecracker Hill. At each spray of rockets, the town reverberated with kids' squeals. We elders bellowed in appreciation.

And then a miracle worthy of Lourdes occurred. To judge from the antismoking hearings, a majority of citizens were afflicted with violent allergies triggered by the whiff of a distant cigarette. But for a half hour without letup, the searing phosphorus pumped acrid smoke until the valley was almost obliterated in a blue cloud. Hardly anyone seemed to notice.

Every holiday is big in Telluride, which manages to put a twist on each. On St. Patrick's Day, when the rest of the country drinks green beer, local brew stays its normal color; the people who drink it turn green. Once I managed to be there for the Halloween dance, compared with which the Rio carnival is a come-as-you-are party. I saw two stacks of cardboard boxes dancing with amazing grace. A stick of dynamite waltzed gracefully, clutching his detonator. Five giant fish swam erect, with satiny tails brushing the floor. A guy in a motorized wheelchair directed them with a fly rod. The Twins, two beautiful sisters, wore old-style dance hall gear, with sparkle, frilly fetched-up hems and enough perfume to settle the West. A political candidate, in cutaway tux and eye makeup, was disguised as a horse's ass.

The raw energy transformed costumed characters into life. Magpies and Madonnas spun in couples, assuming poses reserved else-where in the world for serious mental deviates. One guy danced alone in old wool mountain pants, a stove-in hat and a druid's beard to the knees; his was no costume. He whirled with abandon, stomped heavy boots on the high school gym floor and flung his legs far over his head. Onstage a town clerk in a zebra-striped cat suit was bellow-ing into a mike: "I'm so glad I'm a-living in the U.S.A." Bet your ass.

About the last thing I remember is my pal Gene presenting me to a friend. I had thought he said, "Mort, this is Sally Sick." But before I could say, "Hello, Ms. Sick," she was barfing all over the floor. By then no one had the guts to look below his knees anywhere in the gym. Mavis Bennett, for example, dropped her car keys and decided to walk home.

In balance, the picture is clear. Telluride has changed from a state of mind to a real place. But still, a pretty good place.

Take, for example, Steve Estes's attempt to tunnel into the Bank of Telluride. He and his associate got a little lost underground. They kept banging the concrete floor from underneath, setting off a vi-bration-sensitive alarm. After a while the newly muscled forces of order found his trapdoor. In the city that might have been a pretty big deal. Steve got a month in the jail down in Montrose for tres-passing the hard way. He might have gotten a longer sentence if Telluride had had its own jail and he could have worked during the day, Masters explained, but the court figured he had to feed his family.

Or take Rudy Eisner, who lived alone in the woods. The cops suspected he poached the odd deer for food. He was what some people would call strange. "Once I saw him eat a ten-pound bag of potatoes, raw," a rare visitor told me later. "After a while he says, 'I don't feel too good.'" But the sheriff liked him and left him alone. "If he is capable of living outside all winter under conditions that would kill a normal person, is he endangering himself?" Masters asked, rhetorically. "No," he answered himself, pragmatically.

Or Billy Jo Moffatt, who gave up a three-hundred-thousand-dol-lar-a-year job on Wall Street to find happiness selling his photo-graphs from an isolated ranch down the Dolores River. "I just decided there was more to life than following someone's lights through the Holland Tunnel," he said. "You never make enough. There is always another fifty thousand dollars to spend on another membership, or something, and you're in the hole again. Who needs it?"

Some old-timers moved away after the Slate took over, and others have died. Maybe twenty are left from Telluride's earlier days. Two of them are sisters, born in the town and lifelong residents. I called on Elvira Wunderlich, in fine shape at seventy-four, to see what she thought about things.

Telluride needed the new blood, and the money, she said, and she has nothing against skiers. But she was outraged at the new buildings downtown that dampen the old charm. She was saddened that so many young people treated the old with disrespect, even scorn, elbowing them aside at the bank and post office.

Mrs. Wunderlich was amazed that hardly anyone wanted to know about the past. Her own memory was sharp as a scalpel, down to conversations a half century ago. As town clerk she arranged the various skeletons in the closet. As a hairdresser she did up the hookers before big Saturday nights. But no one has any questions. Overall, I asked, what did she think about Telluride?

"It was such a pretty little town," she said, with a sad shake of the head. She thought a minute and smiled. "It is such a pretty little town."

On a Sunday afternoon I went to Jim Davidson's school reunion at the tiny town of Rico, down the road. It was not a high school reunion. It was for everyone who had ever been to the Rico school, since 1902. Howard Ramsey, for example, went to first grade there in 1904. I expected him to be frozen in time, a living relic from the time when the crumbling little settlement throbbed with mining. Howard, however, was having none of that.

"We travel all the time, seeing the world," he said. "Just came back from Australia. G'day, mate." He was off soon for South America, he said, adding: "Both sides." Ramsey had left Rico for a forty-year career in Bell maintenance. Then he had retired in Portland, Oregon. But he remembered a few changes around Rico. "When I was in school, all the kids had burros," he said. "Now no one knows what a burro is." He remembered the first phone, with its hand crank and cranky operator. He'd had Rico's first radio, a little crystal set.

"When I got some scratchy sounds—KGW, the only broadcaster in the state—I let out a holler," Ramsey recalled, the seventy-year-old details fresh in his mind. In 1918 he went to France for his first big geography lesson. He survived the war but picked up wanderlust. Nearly ninety, he still pored over his maps. "Next, I don't know. We might go to China."

The photo album given to Ramsey showed a much different town from the needlepoint bedcover someone had done of Rico's present skyline: a few little buildings and a lot of mountain. Back in 1892, Rico had seventy-eight businesses, fourteen hotels and fifty-nine mines. It shipped up to ten railway cars a day of ore. At the turn of the century Rico's population was four thousand. Today it is a few hundred. About the only business was Ron's Galloping Goose, which served Telluride Beer, brewed in Monroe, Wisconsin. The abandoned church announced, "Carl Dixon preaches from Revelations, Sunday at 3 P.M.," but it did not specify which decade. The only hotel was closed down, its sole inhabitant the mysterious ghost of a miner who slams doors on the third floor.

Four passenger trains came through town in the heyday. Now there was just the road, and you missed Rico if you blinked twice.

But the people who stayed love it. You don't get much farther below the Key Line than Rico, where strangers are not for fleecing. As an outsider I did not know to bring a plate to the picnic. But Ila Stark, the schoolteacher at the food table, took care of that. I bought three dollars' worth of chicken—eight fat pieces—and she wrapped them in paper. Then I asked about the coleslaw. She ladled two huge dollops into an electric blue trash bag. "It's on sale today," she said, with a merry laugh. "You can have it."

Chickenshit Bingo takes place in Norwood. It is the periodic feature of a cowboy bar in which a chicken is released over a large bingolike card, and you can figure out the rest. I did not get there. But I got to Denver.

Denver is fine, if you can avoid Stapleton Airport. The city's tidy skyline, when not obscured by pollution, is stirring against the mountains. Rolling green suburbs shelter comfortable western houses. But I am no neutral source.

By pure coincidence, Denver loomed in my life as a faceless computer zapping volts to my software. In a series of incidents I found myself as much a source as an observer in what was happening to our society.

First, I learned my Telluride house had gone uninsured all winter because I hadn't got the bill. The company had abbreviated my Paris address to meaningless letters. It was too long, a person told me over the phone. I shortened it. "The computer won't accept it," the person said. I explained that the language was funny where I lived. Did the computer want me to move? "That might be better," the person said, dead serious.

Then my Diners Club card initiation fee was not paid; it was another mail mixup. A person left me a message in Telluride, and I returned the call within the hour. But she had canceled my card. A second person promised to fix it. Two months and several people later, with my credit microchip stained, I asked the first person for a letter to clear up my credit. She refused. I insisted. Dropping her phoneside manner, she laid down the law: "You want to be treated different from everybody else."

I wondered how everyone else was treated.

Next, I applied for an equity loan on my house. There would be just a few formalities. Nine months later we were still at it. The company demanded to know why I had more money in the bank than I had claimed. Finally, the loan was denied. My credit was fine, and the appraisal I paid for checked out. But by some mathematical gibberish, the company could lend only X percent of the something over the value of the something. I think.

But I could have the maximum allowed, for a price. There would be just a few formalities. Four months later I was told if I submitted an application with supporting documents—that is, if I started again— by a deadline that had passed two days earlier, I'd get the money. A lawyer got me an extension. But yet another person wanted photos of the already appraised house.

These were pretty paltry hard-luck stories. People in a computer age hardly noticed such contretemps. And I thought about that for a while.

The Constitution guarantees inalienable rights, but the average citizen seldom deals with the courts. What matters are the day-to-day dealings: credit cards; insurance; banking. Mostly we face trial by computer. You are guilty until proved innocent. You cannot face your accuser. Appeal is limited. And punishment is cruel and unusual. If you are declared uninsurable or uncreditworthy, your life as a functional citizen is over.

In broad areas we seem to be falling under a creeping corporate martial law. You can choose to flout it, but that might mean dropping out of systems vital to the good old American way.

This is not so farfetched. My own computer thinks it's Dirty Harry. If I punch the wrong buttons, the screen admonishes: "Illegal Command." How many days of our lives, and chunks of our treasure, have gone into correcting the havoc caused by some person's clumsy fingers on a keyboard?

Few Americans challenged corporate martial law, it appeared, because of an admirable faith in the system. Eventually things turned out all right. If not, hey, what can you do? That applied also to checking bags on airplanes. But I'd been gone too long; I trusted baggage handlers even less than computers.

On a flight from Denver to Telluride my plane stopped in Gunnison. To be safe, I watched from the foot of the steps. Sure enough, the guy hauled my bag off the plane. I started to tell him, and he screamed at me. Again I tried. Outraged, he twisted his face to a snarl and jabbed a finger at me. "Get back on board!" I outdecibeled him: *"Put my bag back on the fucking airplane!"* He checked the tag and tossed it back, without a glance in my direction.

Leaving Telluride, I had less success. My bag got on the commuter plane to Farmington, New Mexico, but I did not see it transferred to the Phoenix flight. The agent dismissed my concern. But it wasn't in the hold. A baggageman told me it had gone to Albuquerque, but the agent refused to report it; she shrieked at me for delaying the flight. Since no one messaged Albuquerque, the bag returned to Farmington, missing three flights to Phoenix. I had to go to Tucson. When the bag reached Phoenix and got lost, I phoned the airline president. Magically it arrived a half hour before my New York flight the next day.

This might be mere kvetching but for what it suggested. On a dozen consecutive flights in America, my bag was lost four times. I began to suspect that everyone lost his suitcase on every flight and just figured he was among the unlucky few.

Corporate marshals have worked out devices to calm down excitable misfits like myself. The trick is never leave a victim dangling in silence. I happened to call the Tampa *Tribune* and took a tour of hold lines. First, a recorded voice asked me to wait and added: "You will soon be given the attention you deserve." I got the person I wanted, but he had to take another call. Every few moments a voice said

something like "Your correspondent will be right back to help you.
. . ." For all the electronic imposter knew, my guy could have been
carried off by crazed weasels, or he might have left for a month in
the Turks and Caicos. Meant as a courtesy, it amounted to an insult.

You can tell what concerns the modern Rocky Mountain free-
thinker by paging through the classified in *Westword,* Denver's icon-
oclastic weekly: "Need 89 overweight people to try new herbal-based
weight control program . . . Antique French doors . . . Crystal
healing and chakra balancing . . . Genital warts . . . Insomnia
Anxiety . . . Achieve with Hypnosis . . . Alcohol & Drug, a meta-
physical view . . . Bulimia recovery . . . Disillusioned? Lonely? . . .
Discover your own power and uniqueness. NLP therapist . . . Men
Affected by Sexual Assault (MASA) . . . Women's Issues."

Massage ads stress the word "legitimate." A few novenas recruit
candidates. One entry offered "Free Goldfish with this ad" from a
person seeking someone with whom to "tiptoe through the carna-
tions," who promised, nonetheless, a good sense of humor. A guy
wanted a "crazy (no pros) woman-child for purposes of co-creation.
. . . Must be open to wonder, cherry floats, sardine bouquets and
ruthless mariachis."

There was "Tall Galahad looking for tall (5'10") fair maiden appreciating differences between cognac and brandy, eating and dining. . . . Beachcombing, tasty jazz, wailin' blues and dressy evenings
as important as morning espresso with oranges, afternoon thunder-
storms with Mersault and evening candlelight with precarious
conversation. Timid, vestal, clingy? Beware! Articulate, witty, mid-
evil? Sally forth and contact this knight." I was curious about the
difference between brandy and cognac, but as a SWM, I didn't
write him.

Up in Boulder, I went to visit the magazine for real SWMs, *Soldier
of Fortune.* Publisher Bob Brown, lovable in his hardass way, was
having his troubles. The magazine had run classified ads for people
who sounded a lot like contract assassins. It was being sued by people who said family members were murdered as a result. *SOF* was
appealing a $9.4 million judgment. Editor Jimmy Graves was scorn-
ful. "The Great American Dream is no longer to start a business
and strike it rich, but to make a killing from a jury," he said. "These
people in the juries, they're thinking ahead."

I looked around Brown's office. A zebra skin and trophies dominated one wall. There was some bizarre machine for hanging upside down. Weird shapes of steel were laid out on a conference table.
A tripod weapon sat in the corner. Open packs spilled Levi's and
camouflage gear across the carpet. Boots, combat and cowboy, lined
a wall. Brown's cap urged "A Bolder Boulder."

So how did they like the town?

"Not much tolerance for eccentrics." Jimmy shrugged.

Right. But eccentrics far short of the *SOF* crowd had mentioned
that everywhere I went. Since my conversation with Dick Eder, about
the censoriousness of antismokers, I'd been collecting other kinds
of examples. In a country espousing free choice, people could be
shockingly intolerant of what did not suit them.

Sex was the major field. In Fort Worth a Mrs. S. C. Layton wrote
to the paper: "Why is it against the law to have nudity in bars, yet
the nudists are allowed to have their camps in the country? How
can any sane, normal family go to one of these? Nudity is a sin, no
matter if it's overseas or here. Let's get rid of nudist colonies." It
was easy to see why someone would not enter the closed precincts
of a nudist camp. But how could they feel justified denying freedom
to those who did?

In Chicago a technology nerd figured out how to piggyback on a
cable television channel, and for a split second he revealed his scan-
tily clothed ass on screen. It was funny; it was no more prurient
than anything seen routinely on any beach. But some vulgar-look-
ing man interviewed about it said, "I was so mad I felt like throwing
something through the TV set." He sounded unconvinced, like a
bad actor saying what he was supposed to.

What was it about us? On European television naked people do
things they'd be arrested for in many U.S. states. Nearly every country on the northern rim of the Mediterranean has nude beaches.
Catholic Frenchwomen sunbathe naked in the middle of Paris. AIDS
notwithstanding, on-premises orgy clubs operate in much of Europe. It made sense that America was not ready for all that. But we
were still trying to revive Cotton Mather.

In London and Berlin free expression is the custom. Hair, in spikes
and patches, comes in every shade a buzzed-out mind might imagine. Clothing does not necessarily include cloth. But in California a
teenager sued Disneyland for not letting her in with pink and purple hair. "They don't know what the person is like," argued Tonya
Slobod. "It's just not fair." Disneyland's defense was that it was greed,
not discrimination. Garish "guests" detracted from its own perform-

ers. But I had seen mildly unusual people on the loose who were snickered and stared at like mandrills escaped from the zoo.

Our intolerance went a lot farther. In Denver a man grumbled in a bar about wetbacks and illegal aliens until the waitress threw him out. He then tried to run down four Latino teenagers. Finally, from a distance, he shot a twelve-year-old boy skateboarding in front of his home.

Later *Newsweek* ran some inspiring Fourth of July sketches of extraordinary Americans, including Susan Loomis, who shared her modest Connecticut apartment with four abandoned kids who had AIDS. But her real name was not Susan Loomis. The magazine explained, "The neighbors don't sympathize with what she is doing."

And that carried over into our actions as a nation. How else would we explain hiring thugs to sabotage, secretly or overtly, people whose ideology differed from others'? This was something to pursue in Washington. It was plain enough but hardly simple. The guys at *Soldier of Fortune* who got me reflecting on intolerance produced a magazine destined for those thugs we hired.

At the least, I thought on leaving the magazine, these guys will tell you what's on their minds. Later I spoke to a man about a news story with Jimmy's help. He was a travel agent who knocked off occasionally to fight the odd war. "My goal is killing Communists," he said. "If I can look back and think Castro has one less Commie because of me, my year is made."

I had gone to Colorado because I knew the place. I went to Idaho because I had never been there.

Boise takes a lot of gas from people who don't know it. Possibly that is because it is a small city lost in the great stretch of Transhudson that didn't make it into Steinberg's celebrated view of the world from New York. It is, in fact, a pleasant little town, beautiful in a few places, and most of its two hundred thousand inhabitants are deeply attached to it.

Once its name was pronounced Bwa-SAY, meaning "a wooded area." But the city has long since lost its final accent, if not its trees, and the French mock it by calling it Bwaz. Not that Boiseans think much about France. The morning after I arrived, I was driving 47 miles an hour in a 35 mph zone. A cop stopped me, and I handed him my well-fingered French license.

It was cold out, and the cop invited me to sit in his cruiser. In the back seat. As soon as the door slammed, I noticed an absence of handles. A thick shield separated me from the police officer and the enormous riot gun clamped to his dashboard. I get tense in custody. He asked a lot of questions, and I answered them crisply. Finally, he repeated, "You from France?" Yes, I replied. "You speak English awful clear," he said. I was about to say it was a nice language and suggest that he learn it, too. But more than a smart ass, I'm a coward.

In Boise, Diane and Judd DeBoer took me in hand. It was cold and soggy at night, so we did the logical thing. We went to a high school football game. Among fuzzy memories of the past, few come through as clearly as watching the Tucson Badgers, in shiny red and white, pound away at the Amphi Hamsters, or whatever they were called. Cheerleaders were enthusiastic, but their movements were calculated not to incite frosty Monday morning comments from Miss Thistlebottom. And there was always the Tucson High School Marching Band, pumping out John Philip Sousa in creased trousers with little peaked policemen's caps. This game was different.

To start with, the grass was blue. My understanding of football was that you had to be muddy, with green streaks on your white uniform pants, so the cheerleaders knew whom to go home with after the game. Sports, I thought, was a noble extension of conflict with nature. Somewhere along the way, grounds keepers must have decided nasty plastic grass, in designer colors, was easier to cut.

The scoreboard flashed advertising; was there anyplace left in America without a commercial message attached? It also blinked cheers indiscriminately for both teams. Now here is a lesson in insincere blather. Hey, ball, have a nice day. How can the scoreboard want both sides to win? It might, like a good sport, back the visitors. Or it could be honest and support the home team. Then again, it might just stay the hell out of it and tell us who is winning.

But mainly I noticed the band. Half time was a Vegas-style reggae carnival. Seventy-six trombones were the least of it. There were kettledrums and marimbas and electric strings. Legions of young women marched in gold lamé tops and navy blue spandex, twirling silver-sequined rifles instead of batons. The décolletages would have had the Tucson school board in emergency session. Then the game started again, and a nine-year-old yelled, "The referee sucks." Kids get an early start in Boise.

The next night we went to *Camelot,* a local production put on with great skill and enthusiasm. It was a major event. The Blimpie nearby

advertised a new flavor in honor of the show "Carmelot." We didn't
have time to try it since one is not fashionably late in Boise. Seats
not filled by five minutes to curtain are given to someone else.

Driving out of the lot afterward, cars formed in two straight, im-
mobile lines. No one wanted to plunge into the light traffic on the
road. Everyone else waited with unnerving patience. If I'd swung
out of line across the wide expanse of empty asphalt, the way I
would anywhere but in America, I'd have been home before the
next two cars left the lot. In Idaho, however, that would be a hostile
act. Instead, I talked back to the car.

I was in a friend's new Chrysler, and it kept bitching at me. When
I first got in, a disembodied voice intoned, "Please fasten your seat
belt." I nearly jumped through the roof. Later it observed, "A door
is a jar," and I had to ponder the logic until I realized someone had
left a door open. When it nagged at my speeding, I thought fondly
of those junkyard crushing machines.

On the way home from *Camelot,* I noticed an American flag the size
of a schooner sail. It belonged, I was told, to J. R. Simplot. I went
to see him.

Simplot, at seventy-eight, was a ruddy Daddy Warbucks in a
checked suit. He sat behind a huge desk dominated by an ashtray
in the shape of the item that had made him a billionaire: a potato.
As a kid, dirt poor with only a sixth-grade education, Simplot
scrounged potato scraps to feed to his pigs. He put together a little
money and started growing potatoes. With his earnings, he bought
a potato sorter to expand his operation. He took on a partner and
then bought him out. After a while there was nothing he didn't
know about the magical little tubers.

He figured out how to dry potatoes about the time we went to
war against Germany, and he landed a hefty military contract. More
recently, when a slick outfit named McDonald's worked out how to
market fast-food hamburgers, Simplot came along behind with frozen french fries. He sold a hundred million dollars' worth of potatoes a year to the chain and rapidly branched into fertilizers,
phosphates and cattle.

Even during the Depression, he had been packing away land. As
luck would have it, some of it had gold on it. He shifted quickly to
the modern world. While still fascinated with potato chips, he
branched into microchips, dabbling in computers. People estimate
his fortune at somewhere over a billion, and he suggests that is a

reasonable, perhaps paltry, guess. What difference does it make? He is a long way from feeding scraps to pigs.

"I didn't get much education," Simplot told me. "I beat 'er all the way. Nobody got a penny in my rig. I'm not Houdini. If you ask me how I got here, there's only one answer: I hung on. Only smart thing I did was hang on in there, and I didn't stop when I had enough."

I asked him if a young J. R. Simplot could start today with potato scraps. "It's a different atmosphere," he said. "Everything costs so much now. Nobody can accumulate enough money for the long pull, to start from scratch and to build up to a billion and a half. The laws are the same. You can still go out and bet your judgment. You can build a better mousetrap. But it'll be a damn complicated mousetrap. It's all so damn complicated now."

But, he said, it is still America. "It's been awful good to me."

Simplot was worried about foreign encroachment. "We're not in good shape. We're losing too many jobs to competitors. I don't like it. We want to let in anything anyone makes in the world, but we have to protect ourselves. By God, I don't want to go backwards."

He was especially worried about Communists. "There's a billion of 'em, and they're dumping goddamned things in for one fifth of the cost. If we let the Commies in . . . We're lettin' 'em in with these Yugos." He paused to snort. "Ruples!" he said. "Who wants a ruple? I never saw anyone scramble for a ruple."

He was equally concerned about immigrants. "This immigration, we'd better cut it out. If somebody said everybody who wants to can come in, we'd get a billion people. That fence, we've got to hold on and keep 'em out. We've got something here: freedom and buying power."

Simplot works full days and plays hard. And he is still making plans. "Basically," he said, "we're in the food bidness. But the potential is far greater. We're looking at cloning and genes. Genetic engineering. Man, you start fooling with that stuff . . ." His eyes gleamed. I thought of him in the genes bidness and got a slight chill.

He is looking for more land. "I own a lot of land, and I love it. We're running out." He has some of the richest mines in the West, but he is feeling pressure. "You go to Japan, you never see the sun set. They don't have all these ecology kicks. Here there's no place to smelter your ore. We could have a utopia."

But he returns to his theme.

"I just love America, love America. See what we produce with her system? What we've got? Nobody is even close to it. I been every-where in the world. You name it, I been there. South America, that's a great country. It could produce enough stuff to provide for a billion people, but . . ."

Simplot was just getting warmed up, but I had taken enough of his time. He spread his hands reflectively and summed up his phi-losophy, in case I'd missed it: "I've had a good life. My only worry is how long I can stay and how much fun I can have. I've seen [our system] come a long way, and I like it. Hell, there's nothing close to it in the world. But if we can't compete on this dog-eat-dog basis, we'll get eaten up."

Later I met the flip side of J. R. Simplot. Carl Yanick loves Amer-ica just as much, but he sees it from another angle.

When Simplot was amassing money, Yanick was riding trains, dashing across freight yards a half step ahead of the cops. "Those old railroad bulls . . ." He chuckles, launching into a harrowing tale of the Laramie depot. He punched cows for a while in the Boise Valley. Then he ended up in Salt Lake City, a chef and caterer. He never made much money and never worried about it. Now, a year or two older than Simplot, he lives in a comfortable house and makes what may be the best breakfasts in America.

He was worried about Reagan. "He's an actor," Yanick said, with a wave of dismissal. "I think he's a warmonger. And he is creating a debt that's going to ruin the country." He was clear on Central America. "We've got no business there. If they've got a better way, they can go kosher, for all I care."

I mentioned that I had seen no blacks in Idaho. That didn't bother Yanick. "I don't think it will be fifty years before they take over the country, but by then maybe they'll be pretty good people." Yanick, meantime, had ceded the floor to Ethel. They'd been together a long time.

Ethel was national secretary-treasurer of the Cowbelles, the wom-en's auxiliary of the Cattlemen's Association. A charter member for forty years, she had gone through six ribbons on her old typewriter putting out a newsletter. And she was not happy at pressure that forced the Cowbelles to call themselves the Cattlewomen. "They think it carries more clout in Washington," she said. "We should have kept the name, not because it's cute but because of tradition. But the world is changing, and we've got to change with it."

*

My last stop in Boise was a pre-Christmas cocktail party and sale at the community-supported crafts gallery. A choir in plaid dinner jackets sang carols, with sweet grins frozen on their faces. I longed for someone poisoning himself with cheap black tobacco. A man of about thirty-five walked by, clutching a stuffed moose head with long black eyelashes and a silly grin. The man was also grinning. He was the mayor. In a brief, friendly chat, he explained why he liked the city. People seemed to like him, too. He gave my hand a hearty shake and said: "Enjoy Boise." I did.

I drove up to McCall with Gretchen, who was reared there. She was Miss Wool, a Job's Daughter and a demon on the slopes. For seven years I'd had McCall up to my eyeballs. Soon enough, I could see why its devotees were so fanatic.

Physically the place has been overrun. No one has managed to foul up Payette Lakes and the magnificent mountains around them, but plastic and sheet metal have crowded out old wood buildings. Someone put up a movie-set western town center; buildings marked "Hotel," "Post Office," and "Old Town Market" are only facades. Despite the modern blight, however, people were as easygoing and friendly as a community might be. Spiritually, McCall was doing fine.

We headed off to a llama farm, run by a friend of Gretchen's, and got lost. I stopped to ask directions. A gentleman named Robert Fisher, in a Dayton Tires baseball cap, put aside whatever he was doing. He carefully explained about fences and culverts and twists in the road. He would have spent all day helping out a couple of foreigners he would never see again.

In fact, I saw Fisher again within the hour. Coming back, I decided to play around with my rented four-wheel-drive Jeep and got stuck on the muddy shoulder. The more I tried to move, the more the Jeep tipped toward the deep drainage ditch. As I sat there rehearsing my speech to Mr. Hertz—I know it was a dry road, sir, but . . .—Fisher drove by in his pickup. He looked a little puzzled. "Don't ask," I said. Without a trace of a smirk, he dug out a length of rope. With a sharp yank I was back on the road.

Mostly we saw the Browns. Gretchen's grandfather, Theodore Hoff, was a pioneer logger in northern Idaho along with Carl Brown. The Hoffs moved on, but the Browns stayed. Warren Brown, nearing eighty, pilots his own plane over his beloved Salmon River and all the forests around it. He took us for a ride.

Idaho's vast wilderness area is closed to vehicles and the trappings of modern America. You pack in, and you pack out. Hunters have to do it the old way, on foot, giving game a chance. More or less. When the season opens, pilots scout the forests to spot herds of deer from the air, thus saving a lot of needless walking.

"As far as you can see is wilderness, and you can only see a small part of it," Brown yelled over the engines. "See down there?" He pointed to a patch of what looked like virgin forest. "We've logged all of that. Doesn't look so bad." He indicated another thick stand of trees. "That was a big burn. Fire, about twenty years ago. It's all grown back."

He showed us Roosevelt Lake, a town of two thousand until a slide dammed up the river and drowned it. We looked at abandoned mines, and a mine that was working. Mostly he showed us rich, empty land. It was clear enough that however crowded the country was getting elsewhere, a whole lot of it was left.

Later we saw his son, Frank, still a logger at heart. Among other projects, like ice sculptures, Frank has developed a little machine with straps and dials that diagnoses ailments by reading electrical impulses. People swear by it, but the American Medical Association wants to hear no such quackery. Frank just shrugs. "Legal fees and ridicule, who needs it? I'd have to go to Mexico or Africa to test it out, and I'm not ready to go." My own suspicion is that his contraption works wonders, and the world is losing out on some extremely low-cost, effective apparatus. But who am I?

Ketchum had intrigued me ever since Hemingway ended his life there. The old wanderer could have settled anywhere. Why Ketchum? We drove down to find out.

The ride was amazing for anyone who loves the West, which is not necessarily everyone. At Smith's Ferry we found a great old roadhouse: cougar skin on the wall, carved Indian at the bar; knotty pine planks and nicked old tables. Suddenly a woman swept in, followed by a small retinue. She wore plastic green sunglasses, colorful summer tights and strong perfume. She sniffed loudly and announced, in a petulant whine: "I wanted to stop at a restaurant, not a place like this."

Heading south, we drove from Fourth of July Creek to Champion Creek, across a wide open valley under the Sawtooth Mountains. There were broken grassy plains, worm fences and jagged peaks on the horizon in every direction. This was where to wax eloquent about the United States. It was this limitless expanse of pure freedom that had lured Hemingway home. A flat blacktop road stretched forever, straight as a shotgun barrel and smooth as its bore. You could spin out of control and still not hurt yourself; about the only danger was delirium from the joy of freewheeling through a free land. I unleashed a "YA-HOOO" and jammed my foot to the floor. Suddenly I remembered where I was.

At any moment the mirage on the horizon could produce the man with the radar gun, the hassle, the points against the license, the entry into the insurance company's computer, all threatening temporary banishment from the brave new world. I could just hear Clark: "Slow the wagons, Lewis, the marshal's got a radar trap behind that rise."

More slowly we rolled into Ketchum.

Mary and Ernest Hemingway left Cuba for Ketchum in 1958. They paid fifty thousand dollars for the Robert Topping chalet, an ugly two-story concrete structure with a lovely view. "You'd have to come from a test tube and think like a machine not to engrave all this in your heart so that you'd never lose it," Hemingway wrote. But a lot of it can be found today only engraved in old-timers' hearts.

A section of board sidewalk was preserved out front of Lane's Mercantile Building. Elsewhere Ketchum had gone the American way. Like Tucson on a smaller scale, it had started fresh. Residents cared mainly about the mountain; Ketchum was a base camp.

Buildings tended toward phony logs in the fireplaces and drywall that Hemingway could have put a fist through. If ol' Papa took one of his famed strolls up Highway 93 these days, he'd be ironed flat by an RV. The old house's four windows now gazed onto a subdivision of homes across from a giant Holiday Inn, a golf course and a mushroom patch of brown and gray condos. Nearby, Ketchum Trailer Park abutted the Tenth Street Light Industrial Center. The Heartache Café was for sale.

This was no great local tragedy. "Hemingway's house?" reflected a waitress named Joanie, a Ketchum resident. "I'm not even sure where it is."

Whiskey Jacques had a memento, a painting of Hemingway and Gary Cooper asleep at their rifles. Speakers the size of black rhinos blasted western swing onto a dance floor where the post office once stood. Chuck Wagon and the Wheels were a favorite attraction. A trapdoor behind the bar led to tunnels and forgotten rooms where patrons played poker and drank during Prohibition. Now booze was legal, and hardly anyone played poker. Papa's days were gone.

CHAPTER

═══ 10 ═══

All the Gold
in California

At lunchtime on Rodeo Drive a Beverly Hills cop who looked a lot like Eddie Murphy lounged on his motorcycle, smoking a cigarette. I snapped his picture, and he grinned, a sure bet for a colorful interview. But I moved too slowly. Suddenly his lap was full of giggling Japanese women posing for their friends. As a matter of fact, all of Beverly Hills was full of Japanese people doing one thing or another. Frequently it was buying three-million-dollar houses on time share.

"The Japanese, you wouldn't believe . . ." my friend Howard Ruby started out, but he was wrong. This was Los Angeles, and I would believe anything.

To begin with, anyone who expects "Los Angeles" to mean something precise knows less about the place than I do. The distance between Bel Air and South-Central Los Angeles, ten miles as the crow flies if the crow has oxygen, is roughly that between Pluto and Uranus. You can lose yourself in China, plot Central American counterrevolution or retire to a Buddhist monastery without leaving Los Angeles. And that is no reference to Hollywood, which adds the past and future to your possibilities.

It is knit together by a freeway system that works wonderfully when not crowded, between 2:00 A.M. and dawn on Wednesdays. There is a certain unifying air about what locals call the Southland. But after that you've got to get specific. To say you love it, or hate it, is like declaring yourself on the subject of food. It is a matter of taste and appetite. Whatever you might like, there is a lot of it.

Altogether, metropolitan Los Angeles takes in 12.6 million people, spread over forty-one hundred square miles, with a gross national product bigger than Australia's or India's. It has passed Chicago as America's second city and is gunning hard for New York. Since 1975, 1.5 million immigrants have moved in, mostly from Asia and Latin America, to replace the 1.3 million citizens who have moved somewhere else. Where New York stagnates, L.A. burgeons.

My initial views were highly colored. Surely L.A. had gotten a bad rap. I'd been there before, in no particular hurry on sunny days, and thought it was great. All of that highway-mayhem, let's-do-lunch, gang-war, pet-cemetery, litchi-flavored-douche stuff was surely so much ignorant slander. Surely.

Under the slightest scrutiny, the whole place breathes *reductio ad absurdum*. It works hard at being Los Angeles. It is as if people were consciously parodying themselves. Not everyone, obviously. A whole lot of perfectly ordinary people inhabit the region. Now, if they would just make themselves known.

My first encounter set the tone: At a three-hour cleaners in Sherman Oaks, I watched a woman carefully lock the doors of her Alfa convertible, leaving the top down. Her white tights were lacquered over legs far too skinny for such flaunting, and they were crisscrossed to the knee by leather straps attached to towering spike heels. Her electric green blouse billowed like a spinnaker. The woman strode purposefully inside and emerged less than a minute later, at the same pace. With a toss of her hair, an unlikely shade of auburn, she leaped into the car and squealed out, music blaring. Dodging the gravel she sprayed at me, I noticed her license plate: "DYNAMIK." Oh, please.

In New York the disparate sectors live tumbled atop one another, and most have worked out a begrudging coexistence. In Los Angeles, with insulation of space and sunlight, most circles touch only at intersections. I had a strong taste of this even before I got there. At a fancy tourist bush camp in Botswana, I came across a pleasant L.A. public relations woman. She was thickly powdered and perfumed, had affected a funny voice, wore heels with her khakis and said, "EEEK!" at anything louder than a mosquito buzz. I liked her. Around the bar that night she talked about remodeling her office: "First they sent three enormous Mexicans who couldn't speak a word of any language. . . . And then they sent over two sand monkeys.

. . . I can't stand anyone who doesn't speak Engl—"

I broke in. Sand monkeys?

"Arabs," she explained.

The owner, a charming hostess and also from Los Angeles, did not want me to get the wrong idea. She told a story about Nat King Cole's moving into Bel Air. "He said to his new neighbors, 'I hear there are some undesirables who want to move in. I worked all my life to afford this, and I don't want any undesirables moving in.' " Message received: We were discriminating about class, not race.

To see Southern California best, I looked for guides who laughed off the circles but moved easily within most of them. The Rubys, for example. Howard is one of those generous-spirited rich people you've got to love. Since he started as a poor kid in Cleveland, and he is an honest developer-entrepreneur, he qualifies as breaking the bank in the American Dream department. His Bel Air house is worth more than Chad earns in a year, but he put it together himself with exquisite taste.

Mrs. Ruby is Yvette Mimieux, the actress, but someone else besides her would have to tell you that. She grew up as your typical Hollywood kid, with a Mexican mother and a bunch of guys killing themselves to get her attention, and now she reads a lot and has loyal friends who would eat worms for her.

The Rubys are about as far as you get from food stamps without being hounded by Robin Leaches and assorted other leeches. They lose their bags only if the whole plane goes astray. They know where to eat well, but it is hard to beat Luigi's meals in their own *orangerie*. When Howard remarks that he has closed a $150 million deal on a simple handshake, he is not boasting; he is merely make conversation about the American way. "It is a great country," he says. Who could argue?

We drove around Beverly Hills to see how it was changing. Block after block, we saw the same thing. "That one, look," he said, indicating a hideous new construction that sprawled to its lot lines. "And that," he added, pointing to one that was even uglier. In each case, he mentioned a price. It was never under $3 million.

Speculators had found a gold mine. They bought up graceful old houses on landscaped lawns, usually in the $1.5 million range, and tore them down. Then they put up bigger places, which immediately doubled their investment. Among the best customers were Japanese syndicates that sold time shares in Tokyo. There was also most of the upper class of Iran, which had cut out during the Islamic Revolution, not to speak of the Saudis and Lebanese, or the Latin Americans who did their deals in cash. "This stuff is all dirt cheap for most foreigners, with the dollar the way it is," Howard explained.

Not long before, Sultan Bolkiah of Brunei had bought the Beverly Hills Hotel for $300 million. He was astonished when the Rubys refused his open-ended offer to buy their Bel Air house as a place to camp out when paying an occasional visit. If the price is right these days, few resist the wheel of fortune. The sultan settled for another tent for something near $35 million.

The Japanese especially like Beverly Hills, but according to L.A.-based Kenneth Leventhal & Company, they bought at least $13 billion worth of American real estate in 1988. That compares to $1.86 billion in 1985. Tokyo moguls are especially famous for cruising down Honolulu streets and pointing out the windows at houses to close a deal. One network reporter interviewed a Honolulu real estate agent who, in her Maserati convertible, warned against criticizing the Japanese. "They won't come where they are not wanted," she said. That seemed a curious remark for someone who was a ten-minute drive from Pearl Harbor.

One could hardly fault Japan, sated with excess yen because of a devalued dollar. Americans bombarded Japanese investors with offers. If working families were priced out of the market, those were the breaks. The war was over. But it was not as though it had never happened or as though U.S. hysteria had not condemned Japanese Americans to concentration camps within the lifetimes of people who aren't that old. Either we all healed very quickly or anxious sellers forgot what the whole Palestine problem is about. Arabs did not lose their land; they sold it, piece by piece.

In Southern California real estate is leitmotif to everything. "I'll be a little late," I heard a Malibu broker say into the phone. "I just closed a deal for six-point-six million dollars, and . . ." She gave me a little wink, my share of her triumph. On the wrong side of Santa Monica, crummy old places that went for fifty thousand dollars not long ago now bring three hundred thousand dollars.

Whatever people say about California, they are not flocking out of it.

∗

With space at such a premium, the wreckers never sleep. Every building is under scrutiny. If the ground under it might be better used—that is, might return a greater profit—its days are numbered. On Ventura Boulevard one evening I came upon a lovely little green patch among the Cadillac dealers, the Oriental rug emporiums and the fast-food and fern joints. Cowering behind a chain-link enclosure labeled "Rent-a-Fence," back in a glade of banana trees and palms, was a 1950's-style motor court. Its little one-story bungalows around a puddle of a pool made no economic sense in an age when hotels were mammoth and all had the same names. Tony Perkins would have to find somewhere else to stab women in the shower; this place would be gone as soon as busy wrecking crews got around to it.

Nearby a two-story apartment building was torn down to make way for a three-story apartment building. There was no time for an A. Schwab, Optometrist, to forge a clientele. Names like The Eyes Have It had to turn heads. The trick was to suggest status, as in Designer Travel. Sometimes wonderful things popped up overnight. New restaurants and shops put ideas into practice, and pressure remained to keep them up to their promise. But the overall effect was cultural turmoil, with little chance for character to settle over any particular neighborhood.

In Santa Monica new land use has brought the waterfront atrocious gray multistory condos. Century City is a gleaming stand of glass and steel towers full of lawyers, agents and various other 15 percenters. Orange County, which is not Los Angeles but assuredly the Southland, is one vast field of building materials temporarily in use.

None of this explains why Hollywood and Vine is such a dump. No American intersection is more redolent of glamour and glitter. It is the heart of Tinseltown, where America's dreams come true. So why is it occupied by a tawdry loan shop, an ersatz Brown Derby that might be a Denny's in Denver and some nondescript structures? Why are the starry-eyed young women on its fabled sidewalks wearing leather skirts and low-cut tight sweaters with sleeves long enough to cover their forearms?

They promised me movie moguls in Bentleys, and I got greasy punks on Yamahas. Up Hollywood Boulevard, I saw an interesting old building that surely was something significant; it turned out to be the Church of Scientology. I looked for the Grauman's Chinese Theater I had always heard about; the Chinesey facade was there, with all the handprints and footprints, but it had been renamed Irving's or Mann's or something. The old trappings of glory lay behind chicken wire in pawnshops. Mainly, downtown Hollywood was fast food and fast fixes, joints pushing booze and boozers pushing joints. Jesus Christ, Toto, this isn't Hollywood. Who was safeguarding our dreams anyway?

To find today's Hollywood, you go to the Universal Studios in Burbank. For a mere $16.95, you can join the twenty-five thousand people a day who are bused around the back lots. But most of the tour is not even a real look at the unreality of moviemaking.

Directors are too busy to mess with an unending stream of tourists, so special displays are set up at strategic points along the way. You can see the A-Team's black van and the hopped-up sports car that took Michael J. Fox *Back to the Future*. Sound stages and sets show how it would be done if anyone were there doing it. Universal had even opened up a branch office real studio in Florida to save East Coast people the trip.

At one point the guide recounted past sightings. Weeks earlier a small crowd had chased Robert Redford into the men's room. Someone had once spotted Raymond Burr. Meantime, Yvette stood unnoticed in the middle of the crowd, which was not prepared to find a real movie star in their midst.

To amuse people awaiting their tour, Universal has built a village with displays on the theme of successful films. I went into the Temple of Conan the Barbarian. A huge wooden sword was embedded in a papier-mâché stone, and I asked a guide about it. "That's from *Conan*," he said, suspicious I might be putting him on. "What else?" King Arthur was someone else's story.

Afterward we had lunch with Stanley Donen, a grand old veteran whose movies include *Singin' in the Rain* and *Charade*. He was confident the Hollywood environs were turning out fine new stuff. The mood was high among young filmmakers, with more ideas and energy than money. That made sense. Actors like Robert Redford and Clint Eastwood settled comfortably into director chairs and channeled earlier profits into other people's work.

The movie business was healthy, adding to income with advertising spin-offs. Carolco Pictures authorized a $2,250 "special edition" Rambo knife but drew the line at Rambo rubbers.

But when I asked Donen about the trend to colorize black-and-white films, his face colorized dangerously. "We've already lost that one," he muttered, and we went on to something else.

Before arriving, I had assembled a fat file on the practice of defacing black-and-white films with color; I'd hoped someone would have found a way to block it. Ted Turner, who had bought MGM's film collection, had settled the argument the American way: "I can do whatever I want with them." He could also paint a bra on a Rubens if he owned it. In fact, that was probably next.

For those to whom art still mattered, Woody Allen testified to Congress about the vast shifts in mood and impact that colorizing can bring. In any case, he said, it was sinful to alter a director's work. In a hypothetical conversation he has a colorizer declaring: "The American public is very stupid, very infantile. In fact they're idiots. They can't enjoy a film unless it's full of bright colors and rock music. The story means nothing—the plot, the acting—just give the fools reds and yellows and they'll smile."

In *The Maltese Falcon,* he said, a colorized Bogart is not tough but silly-looking. But then, why not? If the health fascists won one more victory, the cigarette dangling from Bogart's lip would be replaced by a spoon of yogurt.

S. J. Perelman defined Hollywood as having the ethical sense of a pack of jackals, which I always thought was a little hard on jackals. But sometimes you had to sympathize. Months after I left Universal Studios, a crowd of twenty-five thousand howling fundamentalists was out front waving signs. Martin Scorsese had directed *The Last Temptation of Christ* about a sexually tormented Jesus. Critics pronounced it a serious, important work, but hard-line Christians called it blasphemous, likely to shake people's faith. We shouldn't be allowed to see it.

One had to wonder if someone's faith could not endure ninety minutes of celluloid. Even more, where were they when George Burns played God? But Universal loved it. One executive chortled into a TV camera: "You couldn't buy better publicity."

One afternoon Yvette came back a little shaken. She had driven by LeConte Junior High in Hollywood, where she had gone to school. "Class gets out at three o'clock, and at three-ten, you can see the crack dealers lined up in their cars, wearing two-hundred-and-fifty-dollar Fila track suits," she said. Apparently Beverly Hills cornballs and successful drug dealers favored Italian velour warm-up gear. The drug dealers also liked all white BMWs, with white bumpers. But that was not what worried her. "It is anarchy in the schools now," she said. "Gangs are completely out of control. Police can't deal with them. They all have guns. Schoolkids, in junior high, keep guns in their lockers."

Hispanic and Asian families had emigrated to California. Blacks moved to Hollywood from somewhere. And as in the South, white parents were putting their kids in private academies. "I didn't see one blond head in the whole school," Yvette said. "There are a lot of Asians and Latinos, mostly blacks. When I went there, we didn't have any blacks. You could see a whole sociological upheaval, like a wide fast-moving river."

Yvette thought Americans were getting so violent because they faced no discipline as children. "When you've been in Asia, you notice how fat and sloppy everyone is," she said. "In India you might see a family group sitting on the floor in chaos, but there is an integrity at the core, from within."

Whatever the reason, 387 gang killings during 1987 qualified as violent. Victims included a little black girl playing on swings, a few grandmothers and others caught in crossfires. Something like six hundred gangs, with seventy thousand members, accounts for a lot of craziness. Profits from crack and cocaine, marketed not only in L.A. but also at major crossroads in the West and Alaska, buy heavy weaponry.

When the city sent a thousand cops into the streets on a sweep against gangs in early 1988, it made headlines in Paris's conservative daily *Le Figaro*. The French reporter described the "Crisps," meaning Crips, and the Bloods in lurid terms. She underscored her story with a quote from the police chief: "This is Beirut here."

Such metaphors are tricky. Any number of outraged citizens can point out that they live normal lives in South-Central and East Los Angeles. But then again, so can a lot of Lebanese who survive in Beirut. Urban war zones are perfectly normal until the shooting starts.

I took an evening drive among neighborhoods decorated in stripped cars and barred windows, and nothing untoward happened. But if anyone needs it, I can provide a long list of people who were not so lucky. L.A. police already were taking it seriously when Dennis Hopper's film *Colors* focused national attention on them.

Then they took it really seriously. A woman I know called police to report that some kids were hanging around her house. Rather than "bunch" or "group," she used the word "gang." In minutes a fleet of police cars had squealed up the street.

Time and again, people warned me not to take Los Angeles at face value. I should look under the surface. So I went to see Barry Groveman.

"When Mayor Bradley flushes his toilet, it takes eight hours for the stuff to get to treatment," said Groveman, a lawyer who specializes in below-the-surface L.A. "Where does it go? Does it take a train? The average toilet is flushed eight times a day. Where is it all going? We've got a real crisis here."

As county attorney Groveman was the one who made companies caught dumping hazardous wastes take out newspaper ads admitting their guilt. He sent polluters to jail. Now, in private practice, he is doing battle against sewage, which he does not think is funny.

So much has been dumped in the ocean, he said, that the water off Santa Monica is flavored with exactly what it tastes like. Local fishing is dangerously contaminated. The only other options are burning waste, which pollutes the air, or dumping it onto landfills. "There should not be any more building beyond which we have the ability to provide sewage," Groveman insisted, but no one seemed to be listening.

Volume of sewage is only part of it. So many pipes are leaking, Groveman said, that 20 percent of California's water supply is already tainted. Dangerous chemicals dumped down drains mix into explosives. In places, deadly cyanide gas seeps up to the surface. "This is already happening, every minute of the day," Groveman said, warming up to his bigger message. "The wonderful technologies that made us all so lethargic are now exacting their price."

National studies suggest that every single underground storage tank in the United States is leaking or will leak. At the time West Virginia and Pennsylvania were struggling against oil spilled from a million-gallon Ashland Oil tank, but that, Groveman said, was a mere foretaste. "Wherever you are, there is one in your neighborhood. If you marked each underground tank with a red dot, the map of the country would be a solid red mass. And every one of them is s ticking time bomb."

Since New Jersey, the topic seldom arose in my travels. *USA Today* ran an opinion page on waste, and one man remarked that he was too busy to think about garbage; it was the business of those responsible for disposing of it. An occasional story told about a load of waste in search of an unused corner of the rung under which to hide. A ship from Philadelphia spent eighteen months trying to dump toxic ash in someone else's backyard. When it finally came home, pier workers wouldn't touch it. Neiman Marcus caused a stir by marketing red bags as "the neat, convenient and fun way to dispose of trash." Garbagemen who confused them with infectious hospital waste, always kept in coded red sacks, were not amused.

But signs of imminent crisis were all around. At McDonald's a sign boasted OVER 65 BILLION SOLD. I could only think of sixty-five billion chunks of Styrofoam boxes choking us to death.

In *The Graduate*, the film of the 1960's, an importuning friend of the family throws his arm around Dustin Hoffman and confides, "The future is plastics." In the 1980's, Groveman said, the future is waste.

People talked about the smog being "less," but if true, that was relative. Far from the city, sometimes, you couldn't see the forest for the air. Pollution was killing hardy old trees and seedlings, causing needles to yellow and drop off. At the Giant Forest of Sequoia National Park, six thousand feet up and fifty miles from the nearest city, summertime ozone levels were often higher than federal health standards. Human lungs suffered more than trees. Unlike cigarette smoke damage, the scientists said, ozone scars were permanent.

In L.A. you are likely to find something interesting up every street you pass. There is one in Sherman Oaks, for example, where a couple of beefy guys sat all day long guarding the modest little home of Michael Reagan, the President's son. But that's only the sidelight. Better yet is Robert Feiner, around the corner. Back in 1968, when federal authorities decided people could own their own telephone equipment, Feiner started a company called Phonetele. He developed a system for companies to limit employees' long-distance calls, and he started to make a whole lot of money.

American Telephone and Telegraph, however, insisted on a device called a protective connecting arrangement. That's where the trouble started. Feiner says AT&T did not provide the necessary equipment. Complex maneuvers took place involving the Federal Communications Commission, California authorities and judges. It was not until 1977 that Phonetele equipment could be used, and by then, of course, its function had been built into AT&T equipment. The market was gone.

Feiner filed an antitrust suit in 1974. When I saw him in mid-1988, he was still fighting it. For fourteen years his sole occupation had been suing AT&T. Briefs and files filled a large garage. Two lawyers carried his spear. He has long since spent the hundred thousand dollars he raised to file his suit, but he suspects AT&T still has money to spend. He can talk about his phone wars from breakfast to midnight snack without repeating himself, but his friends tend to leave the room well before then. His favorite theme is what he calls AT&T's "studied contempt" of his claim.

He is not particularly paranoid. But then he carries a .357 magnum wherever he goes. If he ever wins, he could collect three hundred million dollars; related suits from other companies could cost AT&T more than a billion. "It is not that I think they would do anything to me," he said. "It is just that I am not sure they would not." One morning, when he went to his car to drive to a crucial deposition, he found disemboweled fish entrails neatly placed on his windshield. He is making no accusations. But he is taking no chances.

AT&T is one thing. The other is the courts. It was not until 1981 that the Ninth Circuit Court ruled Feiner could sue. He had to file a writ to get a decision. The discovery phase ended in June 1984, and the case went to a judge for a decision. Feiner was still waiting.

"Can you imagine what it is like for a small businessman to be left twisting in the wind for four years?" he said. In fact, he had been jousting with a giant for eighteen years by then. He detailed cases of judicial incompetence, gross hypocrisy and questionable practices. "Justice delayed is justice denied," Feiner concluded. "Even if you eventually win, there is no joy to it. You are so beaten down you're a loser. This is cruelty."

Before completing this manuscript, I called Feiner for the latest word. Three weeks short of four years the district court judge ruled against him. His lawyers appealed, confident they could drive trucks through the decision. But Feiner had to start again, this time in the circuit court.

When I listened to Feiner, it was hard not to sympathize. The facts were plain enough: He had a marketable device—his first few customers loved it—and suddenly he was up against big business and the courts. I was in no position to declare a winner, but I wondered about AT&T. What was this Goliath that would brook no Davids in its monopoly position? What kinds of human beings were behind it? Suddenly I realized: I was. I owned some AT&T stock.

That was how corporate martial law worked in America. AT&T was only an example. A bunch of pissant little investors like me were the citizens, and we elected people none of us ever saw to make decisions that shaped lives, without the hindrance of checks and balances.

Feiner's real passion is history, and his shelves are lined with fat volumes on obscure subjects. I asked how Americans today compared with those who fought World War II. Though an energetic patriot, he was worried by what he called a flabbiness and weakness of will. "If the Russians walked in and talked about who would collaborate," he said, "this would be a collaborating society. Anything to make a buck and get along. I guess I'm a little old-fashioned: Take the flag and charge up the hill. But to survive long enough to go to the mat, you know what that takes these days?"

He had shifted the metaphor back to his business at hand, but that seemed reasonable. "You can't really touch 'em," he said, laughing at himself. "Excuse me, I'm going to stick my thumb in the water and make a hole. I'd go back to the law of the gun, but I don't even know who to shoot. You can imagine the boardroom: 'Before you shoot us, could you tell us what it's about?' You can't even indulge in a good fantasy."

Feiner gave a final shrug and said, only half-jokingly: "Next time I'm gonna use the Mafia. It's quick, clean and probably just as fair."

I had planned to visit Sandstone, the pleasure ranch—or fuck farm, as some devotees preferred it—immortalized in Gay Talese's *Thy Neighbor's Wife*. I'd been there some years ago and found it active. It was a members-and-guests weekend club, with a hot tub, massage tables and large spaces known as ballrooms. Couples swore they had found the only way: openness; trust; an absence of jealousy. People switched partners, or shared them, with varying degrees of psychological ease. Variety and lack of restraints, according to the philosophy, reinforced strong relationships and cut the losses on phony ones. Some people believed it deeply; a lot of others liked the naked bodies and willing genitals.

Friends who had been energetic members told me they would check. They had dropped out of the philosophy themselves. Sandstone was operating only every other weekend, they told me later, and activity was limited mostly to conversation. Private clubs dealt in orgies, they added, but they had nothing firsthand to report. Fear of AIDS had reached the swinger set.

Soon enough I gave up the idea of applying pop psychology to the Southland. About all I could do was collect vignettes. When first tempted, I questioned a Los Angeles psychiatrist named Shelley I met on the way to Telluride. First, I wanted to know if it was stress that pushed people to gunfire on the freeways. She laughed at me. "That happens everywhere," she said. I wondered if she had heard about the pilot who pointed a gun at the pilot of the plane next to him in traffic *over* L.A.

Later I saw an item in the Santa Ana *Register* she might have missed. A guy in a pickup tried to pass two women hemmed into the fast lane by merging traffic. When a space cleared, he forced their car off the road and repeatedly smashed into it. One of the women jumped out and screamed that there was an infant in the car. The guy pulled the driver out by her hair, threw her on the road and kicked her. Then he tried to push her off the overpass on which they had stopped. Passing motorists finally restrained him. I was doubtful I'd find a similar case in Nebraska.

The woman who called this to my attention was an accountant who had just moved home to Los Angeles from Paris. We'll call her Rona. She was so mild-mannered that her boss lectured her severely; American business is aggressive, he said, and she should forget everything she had learned abroad.

After a brief report on what she had determined about life in Los Angeles, Rona announced: "I'm going to learn how to shoot a gun." It was like Sister Mary Elizabeth declaring she was going on the pill.

"You can't imagine it," she told me. "There is no loyalty, no friendship. Anyone will step over you to get to the top. When people see you headed toward a mistake, they will let you make it so they can benefit."

She was miserable. No one cared about food or culture. People talked only of work and money. There was no courage, moral or otherwise. They washed their oysters, for God's sake. "There are two white lines you are supposed to live between here, and if you go outside those lines, there is something wrong with you," she concluded. "Adventure is gone."

Rona had gone to Europe to broaden herself but found it was smarter to disguise that fact. Whenever she suggested a new approach, supervisors pointedly remarked that she was no longer in France. Once she called the Hotel Ibis in Anaheim and pronounced it as the French owners would: ee-BEES. "The operator laughed at me and said, 'You mean, EYE-bis.' "

A few months later I phoned for an update. Rona had quit her job. She didn't know what she would do. But she wanted no part of L.A. Accounting.

Rona had bought a condo in Orange, one of those tastefully tacky developments where everyone has to wear white to go outside for the paper. She had just attended a violent all-evening homeowners' meeting. A crisis had arisen. Who says people don't get involved anymore?

It seems the water in the decorative little moat was turning green, making it look like a real stream, and residents along it wanted to run the filter longer. The residents who lived too far back to see it did not want to share the electricity cost. But the first group argued they had paid a premium for their moat-front view. It went on until someone changed the subject: Unknown residents had not properly sealed a trash bag, creating unsightly messiness in the commune garbage hut.

Finally, the meeting ended with a bombshell. A woman had discovered a dog turd at the edge of her property line. The whiff of one hound attracted others. And everyone in the room knew that every dog in Central America was just two days' drive away.

Rona's distress echoed that of a writer friend who had also moved back to Los Angeles. "It is the violence, the aggressivity, the crassness," she said. "You don't push a button, you hit it. There is no gentleness here."

But a third friend found humor in it all. A professional New Yorker, she moved to Los Angeles for a job in the garment trade. I visited her temporary quarters in Venice. "You want a La La fireplace?" she asked, flicking a wall switch that sent gas flames leaping over a plastic log.

"The good news is they smile a lot," she said. "The bad news is they are airheads. The new rules are: Don't get excited. Don't push anyone. This place is crazy; all the nuts are shaking loose and landing out here. The first guy I met tried to get me in a three-way with his girlfriend."

She liked parts of it. "The driving is not so bad. You're enclosed in a space by yourself, with your music, without the ickies of New York, the people breathing on you in the subway." She liked the art museums, the theater and the music that long ago spiked L.A.'s reputation as a cultural wasteland for anyone who took the trouble to look around.

Some parts she didn't like at all. She told realtors that AIDS came from gold shag rugs in Los Angeles, and none of them laughed.

That's what I noticed. People didn't laugh much. Los Angeles had been the capital of wit to me ever since a jerk I knew in high school went to Newport for a holiday and told some thirteen-year-old girl he would like to get into her pants. "Why?" she asked. "There's already one asshole in there." Not elegant, but L.A. The funniest thing I saw was a sign in a radio station control room which, over a smiling yellow face, read, TOUCH THIS AND DIE IN A POOL OF BLOOD.

Humor was often a plaintive gibe at the new human condition. Somebody sent out a card reading, "I buy things I don't need with money I don't have to impress people I don't like." And some funny things were not supposed to be laughed at. Like the state panel for self-esteem. Or the plan to spend forty million dollars on an arch honoring immigrants while homeless immigrants fought off starvation.

But things are always lively. People, for example, tend to have unusual problems. An advertising executive named Bob Rosenberg spent a harrowing afternoon late in 1987 looking for a pug dog named Paddington. Wearing a twenty-thousand-dollar diamond necklace, it had trotted out of a film studio, while creative types and crews laid out the television commercial it was to star in.

A thirteen-year-old girl in Orange County had just gotten a "substantial" scholarship for turning in her parents to face drug charges. "I'd do it again," she said. The money was for European rights to the story from the *Mail on Sunday* in London, which, having contributed further to it, would doubtless editorialize on American greed.

An older Californian was struggling to keep her twenty-seven-inch-high horse, named Ragtime. Neighbors complained it was a farm animal, although it was smaller, and quieter, than a lot of dogs.

She expected to lose; people got the creeps from miniature animals.

Aaron Spelling was taking flak from people who thought a fifty-six-thousand-square-foot house was obscene in a world where people slept under sheets of cardboard. Others' worries were closer to home; the new lavish mansion would block their views. But this was L.A., where flak bounced off the rich and successful.

For ten thousand dollars, you can hire a contract killer. For less, Ed Lewis in Orange County, naturally, will make you artificial boulders or even fake *Tyrannosaurus rex* footprints. As one customer put it, "People like to see nature rather than flat concrete." If you can't afford a cellular phone, you can buy just the antenna and a phony casing. Lewis would probably make one out of fake marble if you paid for it.

On a Sunday I went to the Rose Bowl in Pasadena. There was no football; it was a flea market. In one corner I saw a woman holding a book entitled *The Road Less Traveled.* No, the man was explaining, it was not a travel guide. It was a spiritual experience. The woman put it down quickly, holding it by the edges as she might an avocado peel. Nearby a guy selling Peruvian hats was showing off a small terra-cotta object, also for sale. "That's eight-hundred thousand years old," he said, with a self-satisfied smirk. "I was in jail seven days in Peru for smuggling it out."

Some clown named Wally on Great American Radio was ranting on about "the hate-filled vultures in the left-wing news media." His theme was pornography, which, he said, "unlocks the zippers of Americans' minds." It interested only a minority, so the majority should crush it. With censorship, he argued, we could restore the Ozzie and Harriet days when you turned on your TV with safety.

He badgered some guest, who struck back. Why should America wear blinders? Did we want an empty TV screen, a blank newspaper? Why didn't Wally take on drug abuse and alcoholism? "You gotta turn on the light, Wally," he said. "No one ever died from an overdose of pornography."

Wally, of course, had the last word: "Well, your days are numbered, pal. This is a moral country, a religious country." Great American Radio would be on guard.

I leafed through a little book called *L.A. Superlatives* by Roy Kammerman. A grizzly rented for a thousand dollars a day. Mae West lived in her apartment forty-eight years, and Judy Garland switched homes twenty-five times in forty years. Paul Bern, who reportedly tried to consummate his marriage to Jean Harlow with a dildo strapped to his waist, once attempted suicide by flushing his head down the toilet. John Barrymore helped rescue him. But the ghost most often seen is Lionel Barrymore's.

Finally, I had lunch on the water with Ed Dearborn, that travel agent who liked to get involved. He defined his politics simply: "I believe in killing Communists." Dearborn had flown for CIA-owned airlines since the Congo and Laos in the early 1960's. In the 1980's he was air adviser to General Singlaub's supply operation to the Nicaraguan contras. He knew his Commies. He was the sort who got described as a male chauvinist pig and laughed it off. In fact, he was courtly and generous, with a rich, easy laugh. In his own way he was a fierce patriot, rigid in his code.

He hated drugs, for example, and he did not like the way American secret operations in Central America made it so easy for them to enter the country. He described a hardy bunch of mercenaries, dope pilots and amoral killers who found contract labor with the CIA. "We have such a shallow network of people that we are desperate for allies," he said. "There is no way to run an investigation on these people. You take who you can get."

The conversation recalled a talk I had near Austin with John Stockwell, a CIA spook turned author who had skulked around in Vietnam and Angola. CIA recruits, he explained, are taught that intelligence is amoral, that right and wrong do not enter the picture. "If this is the first commandment, that you are amoral, and you're dealing with people who kill, who run wars, you've got no problem with drug dealers," he said.

Stockwell saw it in Indochina. "You didn't have to look very far to know that helicopters were flying chickens, goats and, God knows, heroin." He caught his office manager running heroin to Saigon in a CIA Jeep, but a superior officer told him to forget it. They had other priorities. The difference, he noted, was that back then the drugs' destination was some Asian base. Now it was the United States.

"In the contra network," he said, "you've got planes flying around with mercenary pilots, who by their own ethic are amoral. That's the irony of justice in the Third World. They've finally found something more valuable than bananas and foreign aid, and they get to mess up U.S. values in the process." At one level, he said, drug money had corrupted the culture: sheriff's departments in border counties; judges; bank officers; military people. At another, there was a hundred billion dollars a year in drug money that the banks were not about to let go to Switzerland or the Soviet Union.

Smugglers with important telephone numbers in their pocket had enormous clout. "Some civil servant worried about sending his kid to college will grumble and bitch and tell his wife, but he is not going to let the guy go," Stockwell said. In sum, while Nancy Reagan was just saying no, a lot of people on her husband's payroll were just saying fuck it.

The facts never really came out, he concluded, for a simple reason: "Our society, the media, cannot deal with it. It is too cruel, too hideous."

By Los Angeles I had found a pattern emerging. At each stop I focused on things going wrong; I was reporting. But I was also sketching portraits, and I looked for things going right. A picture is seldom good or bad. The danger, of course, was winding up with one of those *USA Today* opinion polls: three yes and three no. In the end, I found, a single strong image stuck with me at each place, tinting the picture around it. Here it was making a right-hand turn from the left lane on a street in Venice.

The street came up fast, and I had to cut across a lane of traffic. I signaled and looked back with that universal helpless shrug which prompts even Parisians to elementary courtesy. The first guy scowled and sped up in case I tried to sneak in. One after the other, drivers refused to pause. Some smirked; others tossed their heads arrogantly. But the last, a swarthy little person in a white Mercedes, stared straight at me. He slowed just a little and then stomped on the gas when I started to cut in. I had not realized he'd been merely savoring the moment. With nothing more than his eyes, he delivered his clear message: "FUCK YOU."

Welcome to L.A.

When I was growing up, San Diego was always the forgotten bottom corner of America, an underdeveloped but pleasant little outpost on the other side of Tijuana. It was where rich old people retired when they weren't Jewish. I knew about it because my dad liked deep-sea fishing. We'd go to Point Loma and hang around the docks, the way captains used to find crews in Shanghai, until we found a

Bogart with a boat to charter. Later it came up only when I made a wrong turn on a freeway in Los Angeles.

But suddenly it was on everyone's lips. The Super Bowl was in San Diego, and sports reporters turned travel writers. It was the seventh-largest city, fastest-growing, with a perfect climate, friendly people and on and on. I put it on my list.

The place had a certain charm, decidedly America. Along the water I stopped at the *Star of India,* a fine old iron-hulled merchantman of the past century with the sort of magnificent woodwork that no one will ever do again. The ticket seller was perfect, a nasty old salt who snapped orders like a short-tempered mate on the haul up from Mozambique. In the forepeak I imagined the men who sailed such a ship and packed it with enough Birmingham cloth, nails, gunpowder and ideas to implant a small nation's ways on an empire over which the sun never set.

A voice like fingernails on a mirror cut into my thoughts. "Look at that, Ernie. Look." A woman with blue hair and fuchsia pants pointed up at two people climbing in the rigging.

"How can they let them do that?" Ernie wanted to know.

Soon a cluster of people stared up at the couple. One man shook his head in disbelief. "But there is a sign that says you can't go up there."

His wife added, "It's so *dang*erous."

The day was dead calm, the ship sat upright at the wharf, and the couple was only a short way up a thick rope ladder amid a comfortable nest of spars and sheets. I wondered if Ernie and his pals, inured to their cocoons of No Breathing signs and insurance policies and law officers, could even imagine how the *Star of India*'s crew untangled its topsails when the ship lay over at forty-five degrees during a screaming typhoon in the dead of night.

Nearby a bustling place called Anthony's Fish Grotto hung out over the water. You could almost reach over and scoop fish out of the surf. But the menu looked suspicious; it referred to a "fresh worldwide catch." The trout was "flown from Idaho." The halibut was from "icy Alaskan waters." And so on: Australian lobster; Hawaiian tuna; Norwegian salmon; Long Island oysters.

I asked the waitress if anything came from close by. She looked dubious. The red snapper? "I don't know where it's from; it just comes to us." The shrimp? "It's from the Gulf, but it's fresh." In American restaurants, it seemed, the definition of "fresh" was "not spoiled."

You could not even smell the fish. Though on pilings over the water, Anthony's was encased in glass, sealed in all seasons. Presumably, it was for safety. What if, God forbid, a sea gull splashed soup on someone's polo shirt, inviting legal action?

Farther down, I explored a highly touted waterside mall. Pleasant enough, it was one of those complexes where people spend money on things no one could possibly need: funny hats; bears with clocks in their stomachs; ice cream cones the size of medieval torches; T-shirts boasting of sexual prowess or the fact that the wearer had been to San Diego. People had fun, just hanging out. Some college kids danced nonstop to raise money for Easter Seals. I was mostly struck by the parking lot.

A vast apron of asphalt was choked with large cars full of people anxious to alight. I wondered how much of America's productive and intellectual capacity was given over to sitting idly staring at an inert bumper up ahead. Every so often a departing car would vacate a space, and someone would say, "Yuk, yuk, how much can we sell this for?" Or someone would tell a harried pretender, praying he could edge his nose in ahead of three others cars: "Har, har, two dollars!" At least you knew what everyone was thinking.

At Balboa Park I circled twenty-five minutes until a Pontiac backed out of a space. "Hey," the driver shouted. "How much will you give us?" Set among fake but impressive old Spanish buildings, the park is great on a sunny afternoon. The zoo is at hand, and there is every manner of street performer. A stocky man in peacock feathers, silver glitter, Plains beadwork, purple ribbons, furs, bird headdress and dime-store bric-a-brac worked hard at an Indian dance, sweating rivulets in the sun.

"Thank you," he said afterward, passing around a clay spirit pot. "If you have any questions, feel free to ask." I asked where he was from.

"New Mexico."

What pueblo?

"Farmington."

This was confusing. Farmington, a small city not known for fondness of Indians, seemed an unlikely base. I asked his tribe.

"Aztec."

But, I persevered, Aztec country was much farther south, and in any case, hadn't the tribe died out under the Spanish?

"There are millions of us," he said, shifting uncomfortably and turning back to his drum. I tried a half dozen other questions, to all of which he replied, "Aztec."

Just then another inquisitor arrived, an eight-year-old boy, who asked, "Are you a real Indian?"

The man took the kid's hand and said, "Shake hands with a real Indian." The boy was satisfied.

The man had the kinds of chest scar left by the Sioux sun dance, but he was not from the northern plains. He was probably part of a California sect I'd heard about, big on bears and sun dances, that regarded all Indians as Aztecs. I seemed to be the only person around who cared, so I left him in peace.

On the way out, I cruised La Jolla, land of Cadillacs, cardiacs and cataracts. People love to dump on the place as a self-indulgent bubble where the loudest sound is the slap of suntan lotion on shoulders and those without visible means of support are ground into dogmeat. But not me. As a comfortable haven for people who've put energy into doing well, it is great. It is landscaped well, built solidly and heavily taxed; who are we to throw stones?

Driving back to Newport, I found the lower reaches of the dream still alive and well. I craved pizza, but I wanted some authenticity. At the first joint that looked as if it were chained to no other— Agostino's—I asked the friendly young guy at the counter, Agostino: Was your father born in Italy? "Yup. He's right over there." Luigi Di Fante, born in Formia, was dribbling mozzarella onto dough with the care of a concert pianist checking out the keys. A sign in his kitchen read SKINNY COOKS CAN'T BE TRUSTED, and he qualified for full confidence.

The place had just opened, but it already had a faithful California clientele: women in black silk stockings and track suits; men in black silk stockings and track suits; Afghan hounds fresh from the dog grooming salon next door.

Luigi's was one of the stories your friends' grandfathers used to tell. He came looking for the golden streets. He worked hard in someone else's restaurant and then ran his own. With his earnings, he moved to Laguna and opened a pizzeria and deli, which stocked those esoteric olive oils and hard biscuits you can find sometimes only in Salerno. The place did not just deliver; Luigi's son, Ray, left half the profits in tire rubber squealing down Highway 1 to get orders off while the sausage was still hot.

＊

Still warm from Luigi's pepperoni, I picked my way among freeway signs and ended up in Anaheim. Next up was Disneyland, and I needed a motel. On a brilliantly lit strip I chose the Sir Ru Dimar Motel at random. What difference would it make? In America you could always count on a clean room, a television set and an ice bucket. At a front office a young man emerged, adjusting his dhoti; the room reeked of mutton biryani and mango pickles. The last two motels I had stayed in were also run by Indians, including Howard's Inn in Eunice, Louisiana. Both were spotless but exuded that sickly sweet scent so beloved by Bombay housewives. I got a key and prepared my nostrils.

Not well enough. No Indian housewife had been near room 27. It stank of last year's mushrooms, the result of semitropical air and filth trapped too long in the barf-green drapes. Three fingers of liquid sat in a Colt .45 bottle left by the bed. Someone had lost a free-for-all on the chairs and table. The motel had thoughtfully left some travel brochures, for San Francisco. I had refused better rooms in Guinea.

It was late; I went to sleep on top of the bedspread. At 9:00 A.M. the desk clerk could not check me out. He did not know what to charge me for the "direct-dial" telephone advertised on the marquee. I was to wait until noon. I tried reason. Then firmness. Finally, I shouted. He called his boss. "No problem," the man said. "Leave your credit card form blank, and we will fill it in." Life had taught me not to do that in places that require a two-dollar deposit on the room key. After fifteen minutes of debate he named an arbitrary amount. It was too little. I left a little more and drove around the corner to the Magic Kingdom.

A giant sign over the gates of Disneyland proclaims it THE HAPPIEST PLACE ON EARTH. Underneath, the sign notes POPULATION 263,000,000, suggesting that the entire United States is Mickey Mouse. It is true that the place has grown to be synonymous with everything tacky modern America has to offer the world. But Disneyland is not to be judged by us adult curmudgeons looking for trouble. You have to watch the face of a little girl in the full embrace of a larger-than-life Goofy waiting at the inner gates.

I stopped for breakfast, and a rosy-cheeked young man rushed up with a menu. His nametag said "Randy." He scribbled "Belgian waffles" on his pad and scurried off, returning almost seconds later with a warm plate. On it was that large grinning mouse face, complete with ears, made out of waffle batter. Randy's own grin never left his face, and he moved in those quick, jerky motions of early animated cartoons. I asked if some days he didn't feel like going home and strangling his hamster.

"No, it's just the way I am," he said, grinning. "I go home at the end of the day still in the same mood. You meet people from all over the world. Every day something happens."

But something bothered me. At the press office the woman's smile stretched to reveal the hard steel of the cashbox behind it. The whole idea of the place, that you could make up the past and the future, not to speak of the present, by shutting your eyes real right, seemed to be a questionable lesson for kids. Spelling it all out, complete with voices and colors, seemed to spoil the appetite for real knowledge and deaden the sparks of imagination.

Everything had a price. Under the little bridges, man-made creeks were full of coins, thrown by people hoping to bribe the spirits. Reviewing my notes later, I decided I had gone a little far here. Why can't happy generosity mix with profit? Then again, there was Mihail Chemiakin. An expelled Soviet artist, he celebrated his new home in America by painting the world's favorite rodent handing a can of Campbell's soup to a Russian count. Mickey sued him.

After an hour I went to where kids graduate when they are done with Disneyland. The South Coast Plaza is a mall with valet parking, two million square feet of shopping and eating space. Its more than two hundred businesses include three giant versions of what we used to call department stores.

A guy named Nick, who sells knives, thought it was great. "You see women coming with their families to spend the whole day here, just trying on dresses, visiting, having coffee," he said. "Kids love it. Teenagers hang out and pick up girls. No one gets too rowdy or out of hand. The security is tremendous. Cops are here in a shot if you push this security button. Every store has one."

It seemed as if every store also had a Help Wanted sign. Standing indoors behind a counter at five bucks an hour was not a popular pursuit in Southern California. As a result, the quality of service was mixed. This is not fortunate for the outsider who ventures foolishly into a mall without prior training.

At Brookstone I found a neat little tie rack and carried it to a young man at the cash register. He sniffed hard enough to ruffle papers and frowned mightily. He scooped up the item and propelled me back whence I came. As we traveled, he observed loudly, "We're going to be putting back the tie rack." Then he asked, "Have you ever been in Brookstone before?" as in, "Have they ever let you off the leash before?" In Atlanta, I replied, thinking that was the headquarters and this was merely the West Coast branch office. That really marked me as a rube, since there are apparently 85,680 of them, from Newport to Ulan Bator.

"Well," the young man explained, shaping his lips carefully around each syllable. "It is exactly like in Atlanta. First, we make up a sales slip and then . . ."

That was nothing compared with finding my car. I thought I'd remembered where I left it. Thirty minutes later I was not so sure. There were four lots on split levels, 10,804 spaces in all. Of course, the mall and American ingenuity had an answer to that problem as well. For a hundred dollars, you could buy a beeper to locate your car in a California parking lot.

From the Southland I drove north to San Francisco. In Santa Barbara an old friend showed me the new houses in the hills. "The problem is to get water meters, but some builder greases somebody, and that's it," he said. As we drove around, he named off prices as if they were addresses. "The Meisner house, fourteen million. The Smedleys, twenty-five million . . ." Real estate had quintupled in a decade, and it was still headed upward. People paid an extra million to live inside the country club, protected round-the-clock by a private army, so instead of bandits at the front door, you had golf balls at the back window.

The club, on an old lemon orchard, was not cheap. At the time you could lease a cottage for six months a year, for thirty years, for four hundred thousand dollars. But that was pin money for a lot of people. In Santa Barbara it is nothing for a high school kid to roll up in a new Mercedes convertible next to his teacher's battered old Volkswagen. The tough part about Santa Barbara is you can't find baby-sitters.

A short ride north is Solvang, started by Danes who built some of those comfortably quaint Scandinavian houses. At some point, present townsfolk realized they were on to a good thing; they did up Solvang with nauseating cuteness. With a thick layer of geegaws, they created Denmarkland. A huge Dutch windmill—what the hell, it's European and starts with D—rose over Normandy thatched roofs. A lady with no Danish blood, in a German dirndl, sold "Great Dane ice cream cones" and "Danish-style hot dogs," which looked suspiciously American. No one had the marinated salmon on which real Danes feed.

I overheard—all right, I eavesdropped on—a New York couple discussing where to eat. "But then you don't get nuttin' local," the man said.

The woman replied, "They got da Danish meatballs. It's all local."

The aebleskiver were local and good, even if you had to eat them at some place that advertises "Hans Christian Andersen Restaurant, Yummys for the tummy since 1946."

I asked a waiter why wienerschnitzel was listed as Danish. "You sound like you been to Europe," she said, a little miffed. "To us, it's just normal."

The only authentic thing was the Bethania Lutheran Church, built from the timbers of a ship settlers decided they would not need for a voyage home. But it was deserted. Everyone else was buying Dane Ties (get it, dainties?) at a lingerie shop or meandering around a robin's-egg blue windmill at Hamlet Square. Something was rotten in Solvang.

But up the road there is the Lompoc mission, a carefully preserved adobe complex built by Spanish Franciscans two centuries ago. A little sign noted the ranger was away; could visitors please put their fees in the box? New Deal workers had saved the mission from ruin between 1934 and 1942, and it remained a peaceful, fascinating reminder of the American heritage.

There was a brief disturbance. Some middle-aged men in identical scarlet baseball caps and shirts burst in and offered noisy impressions of the exhibits. "I'll tell you," one shouted, "back then men were men, and women were damned glad of it." But they washed along quickly, and I spent a few hours, grateful no one thought it profitable to create a Missionland out of Lompoc.

San Francisco has always felt as if it could be dropped without trauma into Europe, Asia or Latin America. I didn't plan to be there long, expecting only minimal culture shock. Wrong again. When I left the country, the hungry i featured the Kingston Trio. These days it is "Lolita Topless. Love Mates." The Purple Onion's sign was in Chinese.

Elsewhere in North Beach, a sign urged, HAVE A PRIVATE TALK WITH A LIVE NAKED GIRL. Haight-Ashbury is a couple of streets. La Victoria in the Mission, which once had food straight from the depths of Guadalajara, served processed corn tortillas that tasted like potato chips; "it just happened, I guess," my favorite old waitress said. "It's not so good, is it?"

Those were the minor disappointments of a time-warped traveler coming home. But casting a detached eye, I saw what looked like profound changes in mentality. Parts of San Francisco—the drugged up, the dropped out and the pissed off—were getting totally out of hand. And almost everyone else was working harder than ever to stay within those two white lines my accountant friend hated in Los Angeles.

I remembered no place in America weirder than Powell and Market, where the cable car swings around; its collection of druggies, thugs and assorted burnouts made the back lots of Berlin seem bourgeois. This time I found some clean-looking white guy singing "Rocky Raccoon" to indifferent passersby. A friendly cop in a small booth marked "S.F.P.D." suggested that her presence might have a certain dampening effect. "When we find the homeless still asleep at ten A.M. and tell them it is time to sit up, a lot of them mosey on down somewhere else."

Union Square, no longer a three-ring street circus, was all business. The odd mime still mugged in front of Macy's, but merchants had run off the musicians. Even the cable cars themselves seemed to be slipping away. Herb Caen noted in the *Chronicle* that forty of them had been given wheels as part of a private tourist fleet. The Muni operated only thirty-seven real ones. In the Castro, gay politics were complex. The financial district smelled more like Wall Street than I remembered. San Francisco seemed to be slipping into a mainstream.

At the other end, young blacks in Sunnydale called themselves the Don't Give a Fuck gang. Street gangs have been as American as the Shriners since well before *West Side Story*. In L.A. drug marketing gave many of them a specific purpose. But there was a nihilistic note to that name, a sign that we were bleeding away something important.

Ted Lempinen, a *Chronicle* reporter and novelist, was concerned about the extremes. He had made a study of grim quirks of the American society: child molestation, satanic cults and irrational murderous freak-outs. I've known him well for a long time, and I've learned to respect his reporting. He makes no reckless conclusions. That was why he scared the hell out of me.

A lot more goes on than we know about, Ted was convinced, because hardly anyone puts together the disparate pieces. Child molesters seldom reach the light since lawyers easily demolish young witnesses, especially those describing bloody occult rites. Sacrifices go undetected because police cannot read the signs. Secret societies fester in the military, shielded by authorities.

The Army closed its day-care center at San Francisco's Presidio after reports of widespread child abuse. Military authorities told the *Chronicle* that Lieutenant Colonel Michael Aquino, a "possible suspect," could keep his top security clearance. Aquino, a highly decorated Vietnam veteran, was founder and high priest of a satanic church called the Temple of Set. Religious freedom, guaranteed by the Constitution, covered the devil.

Multimillion-dollar complaints were filed against the Army in early 1988. More than sixty children were alleged to have been molested.

Specialists agreed the problem was serious. In mid-1987 San Francisco Police Officer Sandi Gallant, a recognized expert, said sixty to seventy solid cases had been investigated around the country in three years. By early 1988 she was averaging four calls a day on satanic outrages involving young children and teenagers.

In widely separated areas kids reported strikingly similar weird sexual acts, animal mutilation and drugging. Like Ted, Sandi Gallant suspected it was the tip of an iceberg. But, she said, the more bizarre the allegations, the harder it was for prosecutors to make them stick, particularly when witnesses were under five. Even with medical evidence, most cases are dropped as too weak.

A look at a computerized file of news reports offers clear evidence. If you know what you're looking for, patterns emerge. Some kids were fantasizing. But often a case dissolves with a child's echoing an eleven-year-old's remark in Pico Rivera, California: "They always said nobody would believe us if we told."

Subjects overlap, and data is impossible to gather. The federally funded American Humane Association in Denver noted 113,000 child molestation cases in 1985, a 13 percent rise from 1984. It had no information about Satanists. Mostly it was the kids' parents. In *By Silence Betrayed,* John Crewdson estimated that thirty-eight million American adults experienced some sexual abuse as children. He extrapolated the figure from a 1985 the Los Angeles *Times* poll.

"I think there is a massive social breakdown at a dozen different levels," Ted said. "When you put the pieces together, you start seeing a society that only looks nice on the surface but is secretly capable of unconscionable acts. Child molestation is epidemic, but it is only one aspect. . . . A lot of these secret societies are linked under the surface. Sex is right at the center, whether it is drinking baby's blood or other perversions."

Beyond organized cults and societies, he fears an atmosphere that nourishes them. Religious fanaticism adds to it. "These people are so perverted, so repressed they can't even dance. They imagine these orgies and have to work them out. . . . Suddenly, there is this invisible force which seeps out and takes a kid, and you suddenly find him slit open in a parking lot."

By 1988 reports of teenage Satanists were common, fueled by heavy metal music, twisted by drugs and guided by occult symbols. Three Missouri youths were charged with beating a nineteen-year-old companion fifty times with weighted baseball bats before flinging his body into a cistern, along with a flayed cat carcass. One defendant had fixated on the lyrics of Megadeath's "Black Friday":

> *My hammer's a cold piece of blood lethal steel*
> *I grin while you writhe with the pain that I deal. . . .*
> *Their bodies convulse in agony and pain*
> *I mangle their faces 'til no features remain.*

Lisa Levitt Ryckman, exploring the subject for the AP, found it to be a major national problem. Detective Bill Wickersham of the Denver police told her: "The kids will tell you themselves: 'What do we have to live for? You've crammed religion down our throats. You've destroyed everything. You've built bombs that can wipe out the world. So we live for today.' That's what Satanism says—'Do what thou wilt.' "

When you consult the computer on "teens" and "suicide," a lot appears unconnected with the devil. The American Academy of Pediatrics estimated four hundred thousand suicide attempts a year by teenagers; six thousand succeed. After four youths had gassed themselves in a Bergenfield, New Jersey, garage, Herbert Kohl noted in *The Nation* that too often people look for personal reasons. Mostly the problem is that teenagers reached out to be pushed away.

"What the schools and the media and the community never look at is the world these teenagers decided to abandon," he wrote.

The bizarre fringe was immeasurable. But some general trends unsettled me. For one, civility had taken its licks. Ted Lempinen, as civil a human as exists anywhere, told me about getting onto a jammed bus when a small woman slithered in ahead. He gave her a gentle hip check and asked, "Don't you think that's a little impudent?"

She replied: "It doesn't matter to me. You're stupid."

Compared with French crowds, San Franciscans in such situations seemed mannerly to me; compared with crazed cattle on stampede, they seemed a little pushy.

And then there was this alacrity with which some people thrust themselves into the lives of others.

The town that took such pride in open-mindedness is now a nonsmoking section. At an old tavern in the avenues I found an antique dark wood bar from the cheroot and embroidered-vest days. It had a brass cash register and what looked like the original glasses. Ahhh, I thought, feeling the old-boots atmosphere one was meant to feel. And I lit up a pipe. The bartender swirled up to me, glaring as if I had just relieved myself on the bar. His arms windmilled wildly and ended up akimbo on his tightly trousered hips. "You can't smoke that in here."

Just the day before, Harry Jupiter, a mild-mannered writer on the *Examiner*, lit up a cigarette on the sidewalk outside the St. Francis. It was a pleasant day, with a light breeze. A woman nearby stiffened and poked her husband. "Make him put it out. It's bothering me."

San Francisco epitomized the phenomenon I'd seen everywhere. American health fascists seemed unable to abstract their personal feelings and see the larger questions. This is largely a freedom issue: one person's right to produce an annoying substance versus another's right to clean air. Fairness involves principle, not preference. It is all individual. Cigarette smoke does not bother my asthma, but screaming kids stress my nerves.

What amazes the outsider is the lack of compromise. Obviously too many smokers ignored polite requests not to pollute the immediate atmosphere. Nonsmokers refuse to distinguish between the odd puff of smoke and a spurt of cyanide gas. So we legislate, prohibit and moralize. What should be a simple societal adjustment becomes all-out war, in which the victors take no prisoners. On one flight a woman was outraged when the stewardess could not find room for her coat in the nonsmoking section. Okay, secondary smoke. But lapel cancer?

It was not just smoking. In a crowd at San Francisco airport I cut my finger on a luggage cart and dripped blood on the floor. The man next to me looked far more horrified than such a minor wound warranted. Then I realized where I was. If I could not find a handkerchief fast, I would start a riot. AIDS is nothing funny, and certainly not in the Bay Area. But I suddenly knew how lepers felt. I was a large rat in a fearful city waging war against the bubonic plague.

The time had come for a serious talk with a professional. I sat down with my old pal Barry Goodfield, a psychotherapist who commuted between San Francisco and Europe. He specialized in stuff like sex and aggression, repressed hostility, birth traumas and the ways societies affect individual behavior.

He had just had a brush with the hardening society. His father had died at Sequoia Hospital in Redwood City. During the final days he slipped an heirloom ring back on his father's finger, a important gesture between them. After Barry's father died, the ring was stolen. "When I spoke to the director about it," Barry told me, "he looked at me like I was an idiot and said, 'I can't imagine why somebody would put an obviously valuable ring on an obviously terminal person. I can't imagine it.' " He had no apologies, Barry said. Only contempt.

Before talking, we watched a Geraldo Rivera report on violence against homosexuals. A gay woman had been raped repeatedly by someone who said he was doing it for God, making a real woman out of her. A paramilitary group had brutalized a young boy, and when arrested later, one snarled, "We were just giving the faggots what they deserve." Someone asserted that one in four gay men, and one in ten women, had been physically assaulted. Rivera also talked about violence against Jews, referring to the "Semantic race."

It was sensationalism, a reflection of some reality but without much context. But it was about what I wanted to know from Barry. Why did so many citizens of the world's most favored nation spend their energy kicking the shit out of each other? Were we weird, or what?

Partly, he said, it was a lack of anything substantial in Americans' lives. Culture, for many, was reduced to thin whiffs of nostalgia and kitsch. A kid across the street, for example, was getting rich cutting up 1959 Cadillacs for wall decoration.

"People have a deep longing for individual meaning," Barry said. "Don't think of America as losing its power but rather as Americans losing some of their individual identity. When governments are bailed out by corporations, and corporations by governments, how are you going to be an individual? Who are the heroes? Could you imagine twenty years ago our heroes would be corporate executives, guys who've never done anything more heroic than manage a company? That is not enough.

"How many *Death Wishes* do we need before we get the message that people are hung up about violence and want some individual action?"

The antismoking militia was only a symptom, he said. "People's territory is being imposed upon, and they have a sense of how little space they have. Now we have sanctioned a way to do this. Powerless little people have found a way to express their aggression with collective sanctions."

But that was nothing. "We haven't seen the yuppy backlash yet. Just watch in ten years. These people are still climbing the ladder. Wait until they get to the top and see how much nothing they see. When they realize the goal is the process, not the result. All of these people who have been playing by the rules are going to feel betrayed. When they get there, there won't be enough money and cocaine to blow them away."

Already people were accepting what used to be unacceptable behavior. "You're talking frustration, pressure. The movie industry is showing that people have to release pressure from their systems. But unless you have a formula to decrease pressure, anything you do is only throwing water out of a boat that is sinking. When these people who've played by the rules find themselves betrayed, God knows what will happen. You think the 1960's were something? You're not going to see people making love in the parks. They're going to be killing people."

Ultimately, Barry said, "The message is 'I need to be an individual,' and that means a lot of silent depression." Meantime, more drug use is making it all go faster. "We don't need to go faster," he concluded. "We need to find the fucking steering wheel."

*

I also asked Barry about Willard Scott. Along with the Key Line, I had been applying the Willard Scott Index on my travels across America. The *Today* show weatherman had always fascinated me on short trips back. The yuk-yuk, look-at-me stuff was at least distinctive, and a lot of people obviously liked him. Was this America?

Everywhere I went, I posed the question. At one extreme, there was Jane Ariosa, a Baltimore woman with a sense of humor and a good heart: "I love him. He makes me laugh. I think he's a riot." At the other, there was Peter Dykstra, a press officer in Washington: "I think he's a moron. Actually he's a pretty inoffensive moron, but he encourages other would-be Willard Scotts who leave him far behind in moronness."

Barry nailed it down: "He is straightforward, unsophisticated and speaks to Americans with his sense of humor. Basically he reflects the positive, simple attitudes which Americans want to hear, especially in the morning. He is proof that the Rotarian lives. He can say 'tornado,' 'hurricane' in ten different ways and make you laugh and put on a short-sleeved shirt and go to work."

Was Willard Scott America? "Well," Barry concluded, "this is the guy we send to Europe every summer in polyester, who the Europeans talk about."

Having heard a psychologist, I went back to a sociologist. Gary Marx was in town. Remember him from Boston? "Be leery of wise people bearing generalizations." We sat down for one of those fascinating, frustrating chats we normally have.

The setting was not conducive to silent depression. We were lunching splendidly, deep in the stunning California wine country, having just browsed at a general store offering Tuscan mushrooms and sixty-one kinds of mustard. It was one of those bright blue days about which Willard Scott waxes poetic. We had just toured vineyards that had resisted a Florida developer's great idea: He wanted to launch a Great Elephant Safari so visitors could check out wines "perched high atop gigantic pachyderms."

Gary warned me not to go overboard on the problem of drugs. "Crack is a trivial issue compared to poverty and malnutrition in this country," he said. Combating drugs was far less a police problem than one of adjusting grave imbalances.

The reporter in me pressed hard for some guidelines and formulas. I would even settle for a few broad trends. Gary wasn't having any of that.

"How can you expect consistency in anything as diverse and complex as a society?" he asked. But so many things seemed to be falling apart, I said. What about corruption, violence? Even littering had once again reared its ugly head. Gary shrugged, the dispassionate scientist. "There are so many conflicting values and so many legitimate definitions of morality you can't expect it to work very well."

By the time I drove over the mountain in Marin County, things were looking pretty good. Happy kids bounded out of station wagons; Samoyeds nosed into their designer dog food; hot tubs burbled away. Mainly I was headed for Bolinas.

Once, when I lived in Singapore, a friend named Sally Slaughter gave me a John Stewart record. Whenever I got exasperated by Singaporean automatons scrambling for money, I'd play a song that went: "The mayor of Bolinas is digging for clams. The folks of Bolinas, they don't give a damn." This would be my kind of place.

Stewart at least had the spirit right. Bolinas has no mayor. The closest thing is the water commissioner, who grants permission for water meters. Or rather, doesn't grant permission; that is probably the only thing stopping Bolinas from being McCalled into modern America. If you don't have a water meter, you can't build a house. The town is frozen in time, a haphazard settlement of shambling houses hanging over the water, wood bungalows, geodesic domes and a funky old downtown.

Bolinas is on a spit of land just forty-five minutes north of San Francisco, but you have to know how to get there. Townsfolk, not fond of tourists, tear down the road sign pointing the way. Most real Bolinas people are pretty friendly, in fact, but the little town attracts some strange visitors.

One morning I drove to a friend's place along a narrow dirt lane, which is a street in Bolinas. A woman in satin shorts, jogging ahead of me, glanced back briefly. I slowed to a crawl. At the first cross street, where she might have given me room to pass, she kept to the center. I inched along another quarter mile to the next street. She did not move over. I gave the horn a gentle tap, and she whirled around with a withering stare.

I recounted this on arrival, and someone observed she was from San Francisco. "Bolinas people don't jog," he explained.

I was with my trusted sidekick Gretchen, who was having a breathing problem. We communicated this to a resident artist we knew, and she was thrilled. "Oh, good," she said, "I can help." She would expand Gretchen's mind with a little therapy. Contemplating the prospect, she extended her index finger and wiggled it happily. "I love to get in there and tinker."

People in Bolinas are convinced it is the safest place in America. As an old Indian energizing ground it has an aura from the gods; you just can't stay too long, legend warns, or you'll get very strange. The Rainbow Rabbi (not to be confused with Dr. Rainbow) and assorted gurus with vast reserves of spiritual/chemical wisdom can reorder minds in danger of wandering. Also, there is Mad Jane, who walks around with strips of tinfoil to deflect radiation from the vicinity. And Ponderosa Pine, who protects trees by lying down in front of bulldozers. Besides, who would want to hassle a place like Bolinas?

Then again, it is not so safe. Ortega occasionally terrorizes the beach in his ATV. You never know who might be tampering with your waves. But worse, just beyond the brackish lagoon is the rest of America. Taking down road signs is not enough to protect an anarchical little town.

Among the first things to go was the local Fourth of July picnic on the beach. It was a high point of the year for parents, who tend to be deeply committed to raising happy kids. Just another American insurance casualty.

But Bolinas will not change fast. On a Sunday morning I watched someone pick up the *Chronicle-Examiner* and extract the Help Wanted section. He carefully spread it out on a rain-moistened bench, as a cushion. That was when I met Perry, fiddler and general craftsman who had just restored a Vincent Black Shadow motorcycle and was building a boat. I asked what made the town so different. He did not hesitate. "It is where people who aren't related to you hear you have the flu and send over a pot of soup."

On the flip side of Bolinas is Dublin, to the east of San Francisco. The community outlawed ugly houses, imposing five-hundred-dollar fines for crimes ranging from failing to mow the grass or paint the shingles to leaving a nonfunctioning appliance in view. The city investigated every complaint, and enthusiastic vigilantes kept the beauty cops busy.

I had run into this tyranny in Tucson. When my mother fell terminally ill, my sisters and I took turns staying at her little town house in a modest project called Desert Glenn. Occupied with other worries, we let the yard light go out. An anonymous printed note slipped under the door reminded us to replace it. Several notes later the Committee's tone grew abusive. Didn't we realize, it implied, how vulnerable our neighbors were to the desperate wetbacks kept away only by our seventy-five-watt yellow bulb? Not once, on the other hand, did the Committee inquire about our mother.

North of Cloverdale, Highway 101 crosses the Russian River and peters out into a battered two-lane blacktop through gorgeous forestland. Telltale concrete pillars warn that the modern world is not far away, but the interstate is not in yet. For a short stretch, however, the road climbs a hill and widens to a six-lane divided runway. It is beautiful open road, through redwoods. I stepped on the gas and, almost immediately, noticed that the scenery included a black-and-white California Highway Patrol car.

Ol' Jim Strong couldn't have been nicer, for someone who just snapped a speed trap. No nonsense with the computer or lectures on how to drive. He was reasonable on the speed he wrote on my ticket, although I suspected he was guessing. He helpfully advised me that there was a traffic court just beyond a clump of trees over there, and he let me make an illegal U-turn to make sure I got there. He said good-bye and added, with a wink, "By the way, fasten your seat belt. It's required."

A small hexagonal building marked "Leggett Valley Community Center" was empty but for a loft accommodating the "Long Valley Justice Court." A cheery woman sat inside, sorting through a fat stack of tickets. I mentioned my pleasant experience.

"Oh, Strong," she said. "He's a sweetie."

The experience would cost me seventy dollars, which I would have to mail in. I considered ducking it, but then sometime, probably when I was about to enter an emergency room in Maine fifteen years later, the computer would find me and reveal me to be a dead beat.

"Bye," she called as I walked out. "Sorry you got popped."

Not far away I stopped for breakfast at Hopland, in a little café run by three aging women. At opposite ends of the counter two customers discussed their ailments with the waitress. They imitated coughs, wheezes and seizures with stunning accuracy and suggested remedies. "Not that stuff," one said. "It makes me vomit; gets me nauseated all over." I studied my eggs.

Invited to join the conversation, I mentioned the speed trap. One man told me about his twenty-three-year-old son who was about to be a societal vegetable: He got two tickets, neither for over sixty-five and his insurance rates rose by a thousand dollars. Now companies are threatening to cut him off entirely, meaning he couldn't drive. The other man told me why my radar detector didn't work; the California Highway Patrol does not use radar.

You had to sympathize with the cops somehow. Except perhaps for Indonesia, I have never seen worse drivers than in the United States. It's not so much lack of skill as a dangerous blend of timidity and hostility. Since I had listened to Barry, it made sense. People drove 53 mph in the fast lane like unconscious molecules in a group. If you made any gesture to pass them or persuade them to move over as road engineers intended them to, you invaded their territory, and may God help you. Driving is obviously a way for people to drop pressure; the problem is that it floats over the road, and everyone else picks up. But then, having listened to Gary Marx, I fear I generalize.

Up around Garberville, farmers glance nervously at the sky when their crops start to ripen, just like farmers everywhere. But they are looking for helicopters, not storm clouds. Marijuana growing is a billion-dollar industry in northern California, but it is easy to lose a lot of money fast.

"It's pretty intimidating when one of those things swoops down and a bunch of guys jump out and start ripping up your plants and all," allowed one young farmer named Alan, who had lost half his 1987 harvest to CAMP, the Campaign Against Marijuana Planting. He was thinking of doing something safer, maybe even legal, on a quiet island somewhere. Still, the half that survived was some of the finest Humboldt Gold on the market, and at three thousand dollars a pound, it was better than picking cantaloupes.

I spent two days touring pot farms around Garberville, courtesy of a few trusting friends. Although the quotes and facts are accurate, I've scrambled a few details to confound the narcs. Not that many people seemed worried. Dope has gotten to be as natural to northern California as the redwoods and salmon streams.

Pot farming is an overwhelming example of flexible morality in America. "Everything in this town is linked to it," said Hank, a successful and sneaky operator who has yet to lose a plant to CAMP. "Everyone: the realtors; grocers; shopkeepers. Grandmothers who were horrified when people first started planting here are now making extra money trimming the buds at harvest. Fathers who were dead set against it now raise a few plants of their own. Local cops mostly just shrug."

A glance around backs him up. Hardware stores offer four-foot-high racks of the sort of scissors favored for trimming buds. Nurseries sell mounds of specialized fertilizer. Townsfolk are not particularly reticent about the subject. It is their industry. Short of a few weirdos around town and a lot of stoned deer lurching about the forests, there is not much cause for complaint.

I met one guy who was busted not far away with three pounds of marijuana. No evidence was presented against him, however. Soon afterward the cop's wife was driving a new sports car.

Contrary to popular belief, few dope growers are entrenched behind machine-gun nests and packs of crazed wolves. Some farmers have booby-trapped their fields, and Uzis are not unknown in the back hills. It is wise not to ignore No Trespassing signs. But most of the thousands of producers are placid souls just trying to make a dishonest dollar.

"Do I look like a mercenary?" asked Alan, who does not.

Hank has a lot of guns, but he is a hunter. "People aren't going to go around killing for their crop," he snorted. "The idea is to hide it and not call attention to yourself."

In fact, few enterprises show more good old American ingenuity and perseverance than farming marijuana.

When CAMP was first formed, enforcement was easy enough. Large clumps of marijuana plants grew as tall as small palms. The same giant Huey helicopters used in Vietnam made lazy circles, like buzzards, and closed in for the cleanup. But a lot of growers had been in Nam, too, and they knew why we lost the war. The Hueys won some battles but could not turn the tide.

The next season plants were dispersed in little bunches, connected by buried PVC tubing for watering them. But CAMP officers located the pipes with infrared photography, thus equipping themselves with detailed maps to hidden plants. Using small, agile choppers, CAMP ran the ridges and ravines of Humboldt's wildest backcountry. So farmers grew pot in trees.

Today pot is farmed in large plastic grow bags tied up in trees and scattered widely over vast areas of rolling land. On one three-hundred-acre spread I stood on a hill with a successful farmer who hedged his bets by raising some cattle. He stabbed his finger in various directions. "I've got three plants over there, a few back in there, some down there," he said. "We had to bring in soil anyway. If the stuff is in the ground or in a bag, what's the difference? But the real problem is watering."

Afraid to use pipe, farmers carry water by hand. The strong ones carry seven-gallon buckets, fifty-six pounds in each hand, for a mile over the ridges and gullies. In hot weather, plants need water every day.

As authorities poured on the pressure, the war got nastier. The state confiscated land on which marijuana was grown. And more people were leaving their pit bulls unchained to discourage uninvited visitors. In schools kids were taught to turn in their parents, along the lines of "If you really love your mommy and daddy . . ." Some parents kept their children home.

A lot of growers lived in oblivious squalor. Garberville schoolchildren were checked for head lice once a week. Hank's hired hand made nearly forty thousand dollars a year and had no expenses. But he was always broke, looking for money to pay his cocaine dealer. For others, it was the sort of hard, simple life of the old frontier. A rancher-grower I met had just lost three calves in one morning to his neighbor's dog. That evening he rode over and found the neighbor's family on the porch, with the dog sleeping it off nearby. He shot the dog and rode off without a word.

Garberville had calmed down a lot from the heyday. When buyers rolled up from San Francisco in big cars with bored girlfriends, the town's little boutiques stocked French lingerie at Rodeo Drive prices. Travel agents sent planeloads of people off to Bali. But it was back to Oshkosh B'Gosh overalls and only an occasional ruckus at the Brass Rail. But no one is seeing lights at the end of tunnels.

Overall, the Drug Enforcement Administration estimated, domestic marijuana production might have been as much as 7.7 million pounds in 1987, three times the 1981 figure. That was a quarter of the market.

In Brussels later I ran into Secretary of Agriculture Richard Lyng. When he suggested I look at farming in his home state, California, I told him I had. As I recounted the foregoing, his eyes widened. Finally, he said, "If you could go around and see all that, why couldn't a narcotics agent?" For that matter, why couldn't we beat the Vietcong?

Standing in a primeval northern California forest, you feel as though the giant redwoods could shield you from anything. What are the passing modes of men to a thousand-year-old tree? Less noble timber might be felled for paper to record the day's events; redwoods are forever. Unless, of course, someone gets greedy. As I left California, the Pacific Lumber Company was preparing to cut down thousand-year-old redwoods to pay off debts incurred in a Texas tycoon's hostile takeover, financed by junk bonds.

Pacific Lumber was described as "Paradise with a waiting list" in a 1951 profile by the *Saturday Evening Post,* not only for its treatment of employees but also for the slow pace at which it harvested redwoods. Charles Hurwitz decided to double the rate of cutting, however, to pay the $795 million debt his Maxxam Group incurred to buy Pacific in 1985. Even millers and loggers who once scorned the "tree huggers" had closed ranks, fearful for their future.

State authorities issued permits, on the ground that three-quarters of all redwoods were still safe on public lands. That was the same argument oil companies used in pushing for permission to drill off the coast near Garberville; California had a lot of coastline. In fact, loggers and environmentalists said, Maxxam was clear-cutting wide areas. A *New York Times* piece on the conflict quoted several as predicting another Appalachia.

Funny how it was unconscionable, or at least foolishly shortsighted, when the Ivory Coast cut down its irreplaceable tropical hardwoods. For California to sell off the oldest living things in America, it is private enterprise at work. Or maybe I'm missing something.

CHAPTER

══ 11 ══

Okie from
Muskogee

After poking around America's extremities, it was time for me to get into heartland. And I knew where I wanted to start.

Back in the days of drugs, sex and rock 'n' roll, Merle Haggard put the other extreme on record. "Ah'm proud to be an Okie from Muskogee," he sang, describing a decent, God-fearing community which flew the flag, wore bras and kept uncharred draft cards safely tucked in hip pockets. Simple pleasures, he suggested, ran to getting blasted on white lightnin'. Jerry Jeff Walker's version of "Up Against the Wall, Redneck Motha," ended with a rousing "kickin' hippies' asses and raisin' hell . . . Muskogee, Oklahoma, U.S.A." If today's hippie class was mainlining Filofax, I wondered, what about the guys who added three syllables to the word "shit"?

A question burned from even farther back: Was Oklahoma corn really as high as an elephant's eye? I noticed somewhere the International Rodeo Finals were about to start in Tulsa. A phone call ascertained that Wilma P. Mankiller, chief of the Cherokees, was at home in Tahlequah. With no further ado, I hurried off to eastern Oklahoma.

At Tulsa Airport the man at the car rental gate boomed, "How ya doin'?" and then waited, interested, for me actually to tell him. With a warm glow I set out to discover Oklahoma. I started by switching on the radio.

Flat, hard words tumbled out in a rush: "Jesus Christ warns you against sin! . . . Pluck out the eye. . . . It's better to live life blind, maimed and crippled than to go to hell. Jesus Christ says sin is serious."

By the time I reached the hotel I had learned that the AIDS virus did not come from the green monkey in Africa but rather from Russian and Chinese Communist scientists working at a lab in Maryland. The entire population of the United States would be infected by 1992. However, Jesus Christ would intervene in time. For details, I only had to send ten dollars to a post office box in Broken Arrow, Oklahoma.

At the hotel a mimeographed sheet listing events for the rodeo started out: "8 A.M. Cowboys for Christ Bible Study." God was a majority priority, it seemed clear, so I drove out to Oral Roberts University. ORU, in Tulsa's Southern Hills, is a handsome example of Sun Belt Modern, with gold glass and futuristic shapes. Parking lots full of sensible sedans and COME TO JESUS bumper stickers sprawl among buildings radiating from the prayer needle. Properly called the Tower of Prayer, the building looks like a gilt sliver thrust upward through a flying saucer. It contains a visitors' center which features a thirty-six-minute audiovisual trip through Oral Roberts's life.

When Roberts was a child suffering from tuberculosis, God nearly called him home. He recovered and devoted his life to spreading the Word. More recently, when Roberts ran low of cash, he warned that God would make the call for real unless he came up with eight million dollars by a fixed date. A Florida dog track owner came through, but the mission was not necessarily saved. Roberts, one critic put it, had turned God into an extortionist. The incident happened shortly after the Bakker scandal. Roberts's "Expect a Miracle" television program lost a fifth of its audience.

The cash flow problem hit hard. Along with the university, Roberts had built the City of Faith, a sixty-story hospital. It towers above a set of praying bronze hands, the tallest building in Oklahoma. Also, the largest hands. The lobby's soaring ceiling is hung with glitzy chandeliers that reflect a golden glow. High–tech equipment trundles down spotless corridors. All that is missing are customers. The City of Faith has the slightly forlorn feeling of a toned-down Trump Tower on a day off.

But problems did not drive off the faithful. In the Journalism Department I met Julie Ann Hall, managing editor of the *Oracle*. "I wanted to come to a school where you're fed spiritually as well as academically," she said. "I didn't want a party school. I'm happy I came." I asked her if friends teased her about Roberts's call-me-home episode. She stiffened a little. "People make remarks. I don't let it get to me."

In the prayer needle I met Wayne Bateman. He was going around for a second look at the Oral Roberts diorama; he and I were the only ones there. Afterward we sat down to talk. Wayne had graduated from John Brown University and, after working awhile at an accounting job, decided to give his life to the Word. "I searched the scriptures," Wayne told me. "God showed me who I am. He didn't want me there, and he said, 'Go.' " I asked how he would live and how he would accomplish his mission, and he smiled. "The Lord will take care of it," he said. Meanwhile, he was an itinerant Bible bum.

"God is pouring out his spirit, these are the last days," Wayne informed me. "Men are neglecting his will. They hate each other, and they are killing each other and working their will against each other." Suddenly Wayne asked if he could pray for me. I said sure. He asked the Lord to provide his brother Mort with all the sources and safe roads necessary to complete his task, to show him the way and watch over him. Who could argue with that? We said good-bye with a very warm handshake.

Evangelism, Michael Wallis insisted on the phone, is a small part of Tulsa. True enough. Tulsa is one of those places that score high on the New York eyebrow meter. That is, tell some New Yorker you are going there, and his eyebrow will scuttle upward. "Why?" he will ask, thus identifying himself as someone who has never been there. Chicken-fried steak and homemade pie at Norman's Buffeteria is reason enough, but Wallis can go on all weekend without repeating himself.

Tulsa, Wallis wrote in a magazine piece, "is a thriving metropolis which combines the hospitality of the South and the charm of the Southwest with Eastern sophistication and Midwestern values." He also wrote a book about Frank Phillips and the oil people who made vast fortunes and then plowed them back into lovely "Okie deco" buildings, art museums and, for the most part, their employees' well-being.

The place had a good claim in its nickname, the Oil Capital of the World, until the patch started running low. It went through some tough times. Today it is a tight community, proud of its past glories and hung up about its rawboned image. There are plenty of rednecks in Tulsa, but that large sector of people who cover their necks in Italian silks is not real wild about that. And in truth, Dodge City it is not.

Wallis tried gamely to get us in trouble one night. We drove by Cain's Ballroom, original base of Bob Wills and the Texas Playboys and birthplace of western swing; since it was only Thursday, it was closed. We cruised the hooker district beyond the tracks and spotted only a very few tidy-looking workingwomen. I settled instead for a midnight tour of the skyline, a handsome little knot of buildings from the 1920's to 1930's, when Tulsa couldn't spend its oil earnings fast enough. Most Tulsans were home watching reruns of *Cheers*, pressing their slacks and resting their lungs to be able to say, "How you doing?" with force and sincerity all day long.

The next day, at the Tulsa *Tribune*, editor Jenk Jones, Jr., chuckled at my quest for redneckery. "Yes," he said, "unfortunately that element exists, but it is not the whole picture." He showed me a world map covering his father's office wall. It looked as if a large plate of spaghetti bolognese had been dumped on it. Colored strands reached from Tulsa to every place Jenkin Lloyd Jones had traveled, following a policy of connecting the community to the outside world. "I get around a little myself," Jenk Junior added, with more modesty than his tattered passport required.

He introduced me around the newsroom. One reporter's European immigrant parents gave her a new name: Anna America. As I hung around later chatting with people, every few minutes Jones leaped up from his desk to come over with another fact. Tulsa, for example, was a seaport; canals linked it to the rivers into the Gulf of Mexico. He knew freight tonnage figures. And I shouldn't miss Guthrie, above Oklahoma City with a Scottish Rite Masonic Temple that makes the Trianon look like a Holiday Inn. Isaac Stern and Itzhak Perlman played there, he observed, "not a bad pair of fiddlers for a small town."

The *Tribune*'s subscribers include the Atwoods, who also get *The New York Times*, the *Wall Street Journal* and the *Washington Post*. But he's a doctor, and they're not average; I called the house and got one of those recorded please-hold-on and mausoleum-music tapes. I warmed to the family instantly. They were passing around a book I had just written, and I decided Tulsa clearly was mainstream. For the Atwoods, Tulsa was a pleasant mix between big-city culture and piece of the country big enough for a decent golf course.

At Waite Phillips's old house, now an impressive art museum, people take hampers of Moët et Chandon to sit by Italianate fountains in the vast gardens and listen to chamber music. Walking around, appreciating the Phillipses' taste in art treasures, and the access to them, I thought about the opening line of Donald Trump's *The Art of the Deal:* "I don't do it for the money." Neither did the Phillipses, but then they gave most of it back.

In Tulsa there are more rednecks than black ones. Back in the 1920's, so many wealthy black businessmen had set up enterprises that one thriving strip was known as America's "Black Wall Street." And then, one afternoon, a black deliveryman allegedly made an untoward remark to a white woman elevator operator, and confusion ensued. Spurred on by inflammatory editorials in the paper, it came down to shotguns and torches. Whole city blocks were razed in the pogroms that followed.

Today, however, no one is trying to burn down Elmer's. Every day but Sunday, Elmer turns out mounds of ribs, spicy sausage and bologna barbecued in a pit that may be declared a national monument.

I also had a fine meal at a place called Kentucky Fried Chicken. It was the old familiar colonel, all right, but this was not junk food. In Tulsa all the franchise rules went out the window. The grease seemed fresh. Counter attendants were the sort of motherly ladies who belonged in real restaurants. Customers wore shirts and ties and freshly laundered pantsuits. The potted plants were so glossy I had to snap off a small leaf to be certain they were real. The bathroom was gleaming and free of graffiti except for one discreet entry over the urinal. A gentleman had left his name and number but had the delicacy not to describe what he had in mind.

After so long in America, I was immune to the plastic silverwear and paper plates. In these pleasant surroundings I enjoyed lunch and tried to ignore the fact that it, like most of the meals I had eaten in the United States, was an adventure in modern chemistry.

In the course of a day, I knew, the little chicken shop would see everything from black tie to shoeless shitkicker. The city was like that. And overall, Tulsa's identity crisis has a certain pathetic quality to it. The Gilcrease Museum has much of the country's finest western art. Frederic Remington's "Coming Through the Rye" is practically the city's trademark. It is a bronze of four cowboys on a toot, riding hell-for-leather into town with guns blazing. These days, however, people would take them for Texans.

The cowboys over at the Double Tree were quite a shock. As a kid in Tucson I loved the rodeo. Great clouds of dust, scented in sweat and horse droppings rose into the clear blue air. Rodeo hands, in greasy chaps and Levi's jackets, always seemed as if they had left the herd at Ajo Road and, if they didn't end up in one of those long white ambulances, would be back at the campfire that evening. In Tulsa the rodeo was held on a basketball court, under a concrete roof. Contestants favored bright red stenciled jackets of a Taiwanese synthetic, like roadies for a rock group.

These days rodeo cowboys might live on a ranch, but they were too busy to mess around punching cattle. They are professional athletes, like football players with a year-round season, and they spend their time on training and technology. "Yeah, we don't yahoo around like we used to," Mike Swearinton told me. "It's business." Swearinton, the only rider to qualify in every event but roping and women's barrel racing, was second-place all-around champion for 1987. He made it to 125 rodeos and earned just under forty thousand dollars. "All the new equipment and techniques available have cut the times. . . . [B]efore, if you could throw a steer in twelve seconds, you were doing good. Now, if you can't do it in seven, eight seconds, you're out of luck." Urbane and well scrubbed, he seemed more like a narcotics agent than a rodeo hand. I asked him where he was from, and he chuckled. "Near Buffalo, New York."

Back in Tucson, the Lord's name came up only casually, as when someone sang a little ditty that went: "Ah don't care if it rains or freezes, long as ah got mah plastic Jesus, sittin' on the dashboard of mah car. . . ." But Ray Hood, from around Stillwater, Oklahoma, was not only a leather craftsman but also a free-lance evangelist. It made perfect sense to him that each day's schedule at the Tulsa rodeo started with Bible study. "You can't be a cowboy and be an atheist," he said. "You can't crawl over the bucking chute onto that nervous animal and not believe. Every cowboy I know has professed that there was someone out there bigger than him." I met him the second day out, and he was on crutches. A bronc threw him, and he broke a leg. "My first finals, first event," Hood said, shrugging philosophically. "There'll be more rodeos."

The Christian idea pervades the rodeo. Dan Dailey of Peaster, Texas, scored seventy-five points atop the Tulsa Twister, a saddle bronc of some repute, to win his tenth all-around world championship. He was thirty-six and still riding hard. Afterward he did not thank Wheaties, his mother or a close shave with Gillette. "I'm thankful that I'm still strong and doing as well as I am. I believe Jesus has got everything planned out for us, and I'm following his plan."

The Lord, not the devil, seemed to be running things a lot more than I had remembered was the case at rodeo time. Each night at the dance enough beer got drunk so that people were none too steady for the "Cotton-Eyed Joe." The odd, mean glare suggested old times. But no one brawled; I detected no use of recreational chemistry; nobody yelled, "You stole mah wife, you horse thief." For better or worse, another American edge seemed to have been blunted. But still.

The elevator doors opened on the eleventh floor at the Double Tree Hotel, and I was nearly blinded. Light flashed off a contoured wall of silver sequins, up to the shoulders of a very beautiful dark-haired woman. More sequins, on her black cowboy hat, spelled out "Miss Rodeo USA 1987." I wrestled my tongue for a few floors and came up with a lame "Are you losing your crown tonight?"

The woman flicked on a dazzling smile and said, "Sunday. I'm almost a has-been."

She was, I learned later, Paige Hoffmann, an international business student at Auburn University, from a little plantation near Montgomery. When she arrived at the dance, I told her I was a reporter from Paris and interviewed her. After about ten minutes she glanced down at the business card I had given. "Oh," she said. "Paris, France."

There was none of that Miss America protocol nonsense. "Hey, you gonna dance with me tonight?" one cowboy asked. "You gonna ask me?" Paige's chaperone was her mother, a lovely woman named Martha Sanders.

The next night I watched Paige bring in the colors. Cowboy pageantry is always something to see. To open the rodeo, a hard rider from each contingent circled the ring with a flag. There were a lot of state flags and a lone red maple leaf. Of the 101 contestants in the International Rodeo Finals, 100 were Americans. But no matter.

The lights dimmed, and a spot picked out Paige's gleaming sequins as she sat erect on a dappled gray, Old Glory resting on her shoulder. The horse picked up speed, wheeled around an imaginary barrel and broke into a blurred run. The flag snapped and popped, louder than the pounding hooves.

I later saw Martha and remarked that she must have been proud. She beamed: "Isn't it a great country?"

At the *Tribune* I had met Jim East, who filled me in on Muskogee. His lip curled when I mentioned the song. "That damn thing made our lives miserable in high school," he said. "Guys used to cut the cord on the jukebox whenever someone played it. Finally, they had to take it off. At first the business community liked it because it brought attention to the town. Then reporters started writing about Muskogee, and they got mad." Apparently Muskogee people were upset at suggestions that they were too backward to be druggies and perverts like everyone else.

"Oh, Muskogee's not so bad," East said, and he ran down a list of places to check out. There was the Brass Rail, on Broadway and Main. "That might be closed," he said. "They've been having some serious drug and knifing problems." He thought a minute about some others. "I don't want to get you killed. They don't like outsiders too much." He wasn't sure which one had the pool tables with a sign saying COME ON IN AND LET US RACK YOUR BALLS.

The Brass Rail was bolted up tight, but I found Toby's down the street, next to Suzy's. It had been the Round House, established by ol' Kenny, who now ran a tastefully raucous bar at the Holiday Inn up on Highway 69.

Toby's was right out of Merle Haggard. It had some fancy bottles, but Ron, the bartender, spent most of his time tugging at the beer taps. SHIRTS AND SHOES REQUIRED, a sign ordered, with a smaller BRAS AND PANTIES OPTIONAL.

Occasionally the assembled crowd would sing along with a rousing ditty on the jukebox that goes: "Got some gas in the truck, and I don't give a fuck, 'cause I'm off to the rod-e-ooo. . . . Piss me off, fuckin' jerk." I saw a lot of cowboy hats but even more calf-roper caps, those fit-all-heads baseball caps in which you can lean back in your pickup without crushing a hatbrim against your rack of guns. Any one of them might have been the guy who shot Dennis Hopper from the truck window in *Easy Rider*.

Soon enough I found myself wedged in between Wayne and J.W. Wayne's corduroy cap read, "I'm a Wild and Crazy Guy." He looked Muskogee, rawboned, rough-edged, with a lot of Oklahoma topsoil under his fingernails. He grinned a lot, revealing a gap in his front teeth wide enough to fishtail through in a pickup. J.W. was burly, with a bushy gray beard and cowboy leathers. I couldn't see much of ol' J.W. His left eye, set in a crag of sunburned wrinkles, alternately gleamed and twinkled. But the other eye was masked by the downturned brim of a black mountain man hat around which was wrapped a large rattlesnake with its jaws wide open. I think it was dead.

After a while J.W. wanted to know where I was from. His eye narrowed suspiciously as he tried to work out what a writer from Paris was doing in Muskogee. But I had bought the beer, and he wanted to unload. Snatches of J.W.'s discourse were clear enough. The snake, for example, was a zebra rattler from somewhere exotic in Montana. "This is the only one like it anywhere," J.W. said. "If it wasn't, I'd blow the shit out of it. I'm like that." I assured him I was one of a kind.

Without subtitles, it took some time to work out the problem at hand. As near as I could make it out, J.W. had invited Wayne to crash in his small home but remembered, too late, that he was a loner. "Don't get me wrong, I just don't want no one living with me," he repeated, with rising heat. At each repetition Wayne sank deeper into his glass of Bud.

Part of the friction was Sue. She had gotten the bartender's attention for me by yelling, "HEYYY, GODDAMMIT!" at a pitch that endangered the brandy glasses, and she introduced me to the two guys. Sue was unofficially with Wayne, but I suspect they had made it in J.W.'s precincts, triggering some volcanic movement in his loner's soul.

It was getting late, and J.W.'s snake was starting to twitch in a lifelike manner. Wayne had slipped from morose to comatose. Sue asked if I would take her home. We made it outside with no bowie knives thudding into the doorjamb. I suspected the situation qualified as getting lucky, but I was happy enough to be breathing out of both nostrils. I dropped off Sue and went to heaven.

I'm dead meat is eastern Oklahoma for letting this out, but heaven is Slick's Barbecue. Better even than Elmer's. The attentive reader may have detected a certain bias toward food in these pages. There are two reasons. One, the way a culture feeds itself and takes time to enjoy meals—or not—reveals a great deal. Also, I love to eat.

The barbecue lover's rule of thumb is, The cruddier the place, the better the food. By that measure, Slick is Escoffier himself. His place is off the main highway into town, bearing some name, not Slick's, in faded paint. The walls are decorated in assorted memorabilia and inadvertent kitsch. What matters, however, is what is on the tables. The barbecue comes chopped, sliced or sandwiched, and sauces in color-coded squeeze bottles range from nippy to Holy Shit.

Heaping plates are cheerfully served by waitresses, but ol' Slick doesn't trust anyone with the money. Each time a check is to be paid, he drops his backed-up orders and comes out to the cash register. Sometimes he remembers to wipe the grease off his fingers. Usually he hands back wads of bills so pungent that everyone in town knows where you've been until you spend the last one.

As Slick counted out my change, I expressed admiration for his art. "It oughta be good," he grumbled as he shambled back to the kitchen. "Been doing it forty years." Before he got away, I shook his hand. As a result, Slick lingered with me for a week.

In the little town of Tahlequah, just up the road from Muskogee, I followed signs to the Tahlequah Gun and Knife Show in the Community Building. I bought a two-dollar ticket from two cheery young women and walked onto the Iran-Iraq front. Thousands of rifles lay spread out on camouflage bunting, stacked in rows and piled in corners. Pistols ranged from Buntline specials to miniderringers the size of a Mars bar. Parents with fascinated kids on their shoulders strolled down rows, inspecting the latest in murder weapons.

Most shoppers were hunters, a class of people I would rank with cigarette smokers. I am not a partisan, but as long as they don't blow their bullets in my face, I will live with their choice. But down every aisle, characters in tiger camouflage and combat boots slung around semiautomatic weapons with a familiarity that chilled me. I wondered what a white-tailed deer tasted like with seventeen slugs from an Uzi.

As a kid I always wanted a .22. A man named Terry, of Murdow, Oklahoma, had an interesting variation. For a thousand dollars he would sell me a tripod-mounted automatic-fire .22 with a laser-ray scope that projected a small red dot on whatever was about to be wasted. After I asked a few stupid questions about the gun, Terry began looking at me funny, and I moved along.

Don Alberty offered a splendid array of handcuffs, daggers, throwing stars, noxious chemicals and mounds of guns. The centerpiece was a black semiautomatic 9 mm rifle, capable of bursting thirty-two shots in the space of a few heartbeats. It was the sort of personal machine gun guys had wet dreams about in Beirut. What does one use this for in Oklahoma? I asked. Don shrugged. "Oh, home protection. Playin' around. My old lady uses it to meet people halfway up the driveway."

Anxious to avoid his driveway, I asked Don where he was from. "Muskogee," he said. I mentioned Merle Haggard. He was highly amused at the song's assertion that people did not do dope in Muskogee. I also mentioned gun control. "People can believe what they want, but they can't stop others from using guns." He had two hundred in his personal collection, not to mention the stock he offered for sale. "Just look around this room. Americans don't want gun control."

On the way out I talked to a sheriff's deputy in chin whiskers, who puffed comfortably on a pipe and kept a benevolent eye on the proceedings. Do you need a permit for any of this stuff? I asked. Just days before, an Oklahoman had become the latest in the series of Americans who periodically blow their fuses and gun down everyone in sight. "Naw, we pretty much ignore it as long as you don't display it too much or carry a loaded gun in a vehicle. You don't need any papers."

This gun stuff I never managed to understand. The right to bear arms is a basic American guarantee, and presumably that extends to keeping a tank in your driveway. But it did not seem to fit with a society that arrested its litterbugs. It also seemed at odds with Americans' concern for strangers' health. You would think lead in the lungs was a more immediate danger than secondary smoke.

Even anarchies like Italy, which ignore seat belts and speed limits, want to know what people have in mind when they apply for gun permits. In the United States any psychopath can buy a Saturday night special; he breaks the law only if he drops the sales slip on the ground. There is no litter lobby. The National Rifle Association, however, has 2.7 million members, and it does not give an inch. The NRA ceaselessly points out that people, not guns, kill people. Guns,

however, help out a lot. I just didn't hear about many armed rob-
beries with crossbows or vials of hemlock.

On average, there is only slightly fewer than one firearm for every
man, woman and infant in America. A lot are hunting rifles, but
forty million people own sixty million handguns that police know
about. In Florida anyone could carry a pistol as long as he kept it
in view. Almost anyone could get a concealed weapon permit. "Victims of crimes must also have rights," said the legislator behind it,
suggesting that increasing use of guns was bound to multiply.

Whatever the legalities, outsiders can hardly believe where the
fascination with guns has taken Americans. Down the road in Oklahoma, a man named Patrick Sherrill, who had come home from the
military addicted to guns, walked up to the Edmond Post Office one
day and started firing. Emptying three weapons, he killed fifteen
people in a quarter of an hour. In Miami and elsewhere police lagged
behind in an arms race with drug syndicates. The unlikeliest people
were learning to shoot. And there were groups of weirdos like the
sort just up the road from Tahlequah.

A colony of maybe fifty survivalists lived up the hills above Still-
well, near the Arkansas border. I met a Cherokee who knew them.
"They're always walking around with guns, training and like that,"
the Indian told me. "One time I was walking in the forest and saw
this guy way up in the top of a tree. I hollered up, 'What are you
doing in that tree?' He got real mad. 'How could you see me?' Man,
these guys are crazy."

Some of these groups are committed to the cause, followers of
The Turner Dairies, who can't wait for the promised Armageddon
when they get to shoot the shit out of all sorts of black, Jewish,
Communist, faggot, Mexican enemies. Others are mercenaries-in-
training, the kinds of guys who answer *Soldier of Fortune* magazine
ads looking for mean guys.

Many more of them are weekend warriors at play, people who
are able to channel their lethal impulses into simulations. In Tucson
a guy I know told about his splatball club. Teams stalk each other
over rough terrain. When someone gets the drop on an enemy, he
shoots him with a pellet of paint to mark the kill. Later I saw a *New
York Times* article on the growing sport.

"It is everybody's fantasy to sneak up behind a guy and blow him
away," the reporter quoted a New Jersey elevator operator as saying. Maybe. More likely that guy was sick, and so was a lot of the
society that produced him.

*

Chief Wilma P. Mankiller was worried about the gun crazies in Cherokee country, but she had bigger things to worry about. One of them was how to take a people from spirit worship to the space age without losing at both ends.

It has been awhile since Cherokee chiefs wore feathers to work. Ross Swimmer, who abdicated to head the U.S. Bureau of Indian Affairs (BIA), favored three-piece gray suits and Republican ties. His well-starched predecessor, who had governed the tribe for decades, also ran Phillips Petroleum from Tulsa.

Chief Mankiller sat behind her substantial desk, wearing a silk blouse and scarf, hair styled and makeup carefully applied. She answered each question in a precise, thoughtful monotone. Behind her a Harvard certificate exuded solemnity. The carved seal of the Cherokees looked like a corporate logo. I was talking to a deputy assistant secretary of health, education and welfare on a busy morning. But her eyes twinkled. When I asked if I could take a snapshot, she said, "Sure." Then she added: "But I can't stand up. I've got on jogging pants."

Not bad, for symbolism. The chief, half Cherokee and half Irish-German, was leading her tribe along the edge of two worlds. What you saw on the surface was not always what burned beneath. But Wilma was not one to dwell on abstract symbols. She had work to do.

"We're successful because we're very sure of ourselves; we know who we are," she said. "We have a strong sense of culture, of mixing old culture with modern ways. . . . First we send in the medicine men. Then we send in the lawyers." The day before, she had turned down a proposed casino on Cherokee land. "When we look at business development, we look at income generation as a way of creating jobs. We're trying to build an economic base in the community," she explained, adding: "We're trying to find new ways of using the land. Most of it is very poor, but we are willing to work very hard."

The Cherokees have not had a lot of luck with white men and their land. Southern settlers found the Cherokees doing well in the Carolinas. Under army guns, the Indians were dispatched to Oklahoma along the "Trail of Tears," a romantic euphemism for a death march. Oklahoma land was parceled out among the Five Civilized Tribes. When the Osages came along later, the Cherokees sold them some of their worthless ground as a homeland. That particular parcel remained worthless, but underneath were some of the world's richest oil fields.

Today there are probably a hundred thousand Cherokees, of whom eighty-one thousand are registered. They are the second-largest tribe, after the Navajos. To qualify as a tribal member, a Cherokee must trace back to a family recorded in 1906, when the rolls were established. Mixed blood counts; some Cherokees are only one thirty-second Indian.

Cherokees have no reservation. Their rural houses are often indistinguishable from those of their non-Indian neighbors. They wear the same Levi's and patterned shirts as everyone else in eastern Oklahoma. That is what throws a lot of people off.

"A lot of our rural communities are very distinct, homogeneous with similar cultural backgrounds, and the language is Cherokee," Wilma explained. "At the other end of the spectrum there are people with a nominal portion of blood who are several generations away from people who can speak Cherokee." What they have in common is a state of mind that non-Indians have trouble understanding.

The chief had just returned from Austin, Texas, and in a polite, controlled way, she was livid. She wanted U.S. Department of Commerce support for a plan to revive dying skills. The Cherokees wanted to create an institute to examine herbal healing, natural sciences, tribal traditions and the old ways. "This would give tourists a legitimate look at Indian lore instead of the silly things," she explained. She saw a man from the Economic Development Administration.

"He could barely keep from laughing," Wilma recounted. "When we finished, he said, 'If I made that proposal, I'd be laughed out of the office.' We were stunned. This was really racist. It makes your whole history and culture seem subject to ridicule. We were very upset. We run serious, successful businesses . . . and we want responsible tourism with a better look at our heritage. I spend days and years trying to teach our people to be proud of our culture and who we are, and here this guy comes along."

The chief hardly rose above her monotone. "I have trained myself not to respond in anger to anyone," she explained. It was clear, however, she would have loved to have scalped him with a made-in-Taiwan rubber tomahawk.

Charley Soap, Wilma's husband, joined in the discussion. He is full-blooded Cherokee, strikingly handsome, lanky with a princely nose and piercing dark eyes. He wore a cowboy hat, boots and the ubiquitous Levi's. His grandfather, at ninety-two, had just decided to pass along his medicine man skills to Charley.

"People think a medicine man is some guy in horns dancing around a fire," Charley said, distressed at Wilma's Austin experience. "He is a professional. How do they think we healed ourselves all those centuries before they came around?"

The chief summed it up: "It is an inability to accept the fact that we can be equal and different. A lot of people want to deal with us as if we were in a history book or a nice painting. They like us because we wear business suits. But they don't want to hear that we have our own religion, our own ways. The BIA is not helping. It is like a parent who never lets the child grow up."

Before leaving Oklahoma, I went up in the hills to see Thomas Muskrat. Still young, Thomas is a patriarch in the old manner. He has an important forestry job, and he also spends much of each day making jewelry, knives and moccasins. He had revived some dying Cherokee artisan techniques, using animal bones, feathers and old pieces of metal. "I used to go to the craft fairs," he said, "but I don't think too much of them. I'd rather have my things so poor people can afford them."

Most of his time is for the tribe. He drives sick old women to the doctor. He teaches kids the old crafts. He organizes community activities. Wilma recommended me to him, and he gave up an afternoon to show me around.

As we drove up Oak Ridge, a Toyota pickup rattled on past us. A kid in the back grinned at Thomas and raised a triumphant fist. Thomas grinned back. It was Billy Jack Sanders. At the top of the hill, Billy Jack eyed me nervously. He approached slowly. With a sly grin, he took a chaw from Thomas's can of Bull Durham and then shuffled off, avoiding my eyes.

"Take that kid," Thomas said. "He is twelve, and he is having real problems with English. He speaks Cherokee. The school is in English. He'll be too old for his class pretty soon, then probably get discouraged and drop out. That is just what happens."

We had gone to meet Anawake Soap, as old as this century, who had raised Billy Jack along with more kids than anyone could count up. We talked at each other for fifteen minutes, but neither of us spoke a word of the other's language. Afterward Thomas Muskrat translated the essential part. "It is good to know other people," Anawake Soap had said, "but people should speak their own tongues."

CHAPTER

=== 12 ===

Indian Country

Wilma Mankiller chortled when I asked if sometimes she felt like the prime minister of a Third World nation. "Yes, once in a while I do," she said. "I could talk to someone in Nicaragua and have the same problems, trying to get plumbing to houses, economic development to villages." She was speaking figuratively. In fact, I found, a lot of Indian reservations were underdeveloped microstates in the strictest sense, with governments steeped in corruption, nepotism and civil rights abuse.

Indians had always been important to me. As a kid I went to school with Navajos, camped on old Apache outposts and rode my motorcycle around Papago lands. Abroad, a Navajo turquoise bracelet went with me everywhere, an undefined talisman against whatever. Every time some South African wanted to shift the topic from apartheid, he'd say, "And what about your Indians?" The truth was, short of forked tongues and broken arrows, I knew very little about my Indians. This would be the time to find out.

Of the 1.37 million American Indians counted in 1980, 332,000 lived on 260 reservations. The biggest was the Navajo Nation; half of its 200,000 members were on or around its sprawling reservation in Arizona and New Mexico. But tiny patches of Indian land were scattered across the country. Each tribe chose its own leaders and, under broad Interior Department guidelines, ran its own affairs. For many Indians that was a mixed blessing.

After several trips to Navajo country and stops at little reservations elsewhere, I looked at the Indian situation where many of the worst problems arose. In Washington.

*

Indians, I learned, had been another one of my blind spots. As with
black-white relations, I had assumed we had worked out past wrongs,
and time was at work toward a better future. In some ways that was
true. Some Indian sovereignty had been restored, and federal officials tried to help tribes without suppressing them. But to an aston-
ishing degree, the practical result was that Indian affairs were handled
like our aid to Africa.

The problem was what civil rights lawyers, and a lot of Indians,
called the Iron Triangle. Tribal governments kept peace at home,
allowing the Senate Committee on Indian Affairs to take comfort
that Indians' lives were in their own hands. And at the Bureau of
Indian Affairs, legions of red and white jobholders dispersed a billion dollars a year through the tribal leaders.

Foreign aid works like that. Stable African governments leave busy
senators in peace. The Agency for International Development doles
out the reward. The wrinkle is that stable often means oppressive. In
Africa that can be safely ignored. But Indians are American citizens.

Take Carolyn Benally, who was a Navajo employment officer at
Shiprock, New Mexico. She wrote to Peter MacDonald, the tribal
chairman, that too many officials were insisting on jobs for relatives
and cronies. The tribe had a civil service code and a backlog of
qualified applicants. When no answer came, she wrote to a local
paper and got some action. She was fired.

Ms. Benally hired John Chapela, a lawyer in the tribal capital of
Window Rock, Arizona. But he did not offer her much hope. He
had lost his own job as head of the Navajo Housing Authority because he was linked to the wrong party. Whatever the U.S. Constitution said about due process, she had no appeal.

The 1968 Indian Civil Rights Act put all cases not involving ha-
beas corpus and felonies under tribal court jurisdiction. The question immediately arose: What happens when judges are under the
thumb of tribal government? The answer came ten years later from
the U.S. Supreme Court: nothing.

An Indian named Julia Martinez sued the Santa Clara Pueblo in
New Mexico for refusing to allow her children tribal membership
because she had married outside the tribe. Men who marry outside
could enroll their children with no problem. The Supreme Court
ruled that Congress did not provide specifically for federal review.
The "tribal forum" was the last word.

The decision meant that Indians, though citizens, had limited recourse to the Constitution while on the reservation. If they were fired without due process, or denied federally funded housing, or stripped of their businesses without compensation, they were in the hands of the guys who did it. If they were lucky, honest and independent judges ordered redress. But only if they were lucky.

On northern Plains reservations, Indians complained of police brutality, of property seizures, of banishment from tribal lands. Election fraud was often blatant, and public funds were squandered with scant accountability.

"There have been and are many ethical, competent and responsible elected Indian officials, but we have had more than our share of Ferdinands and Imeldas," Trudell Guerue, former chief justice of the Rosebud Sioux, wrote to the U.S. Commission on Civil Rights. The Martinez decision removed accountability and allowed tribes to use their courts as political weapons, he said.

Charley John was one of two Navajo judges removed after ruling against Peter MacDonald's use of seventy thousand dollars in tribal funds to pay F. Lee Bailey to defend him in a tax case. John, with degrees in philosophy and political science, stuck to local affairs in Shiprock, New Mexico. "This is analogous to a Mexican general-type mentality," he told me. "Leaders want absolute power." He thought a single good case in a federal court would put back the fear of accountability.

Among the little Red Lake Band of Chippewas, in northern Minnesota, lawyers could plead only if they spoke Ojibwa, had lived on the reservation for a year and were Chippewa. That let out just about everyone. Tribal affairs are directed by Roger Jourdain, chairman for nearly two generations. Once, when press coverage irked him, he banned reporters from the reservation.

One Interior Department lawyer I knew well, with long experience on a range of reservations, told me such absolute control allowed leaders to indulge in "gross criminal corruption."

The U.S. Civil Rights Commission and lawyers in the Justice Department tried to persuade Congress to amend the 1968 act. I put the question to a range of Indian law experts; nearly all called federal review painful but essential. Steven Pevar, in Denver, put it this way: "The situation on reservations is an abomination." Dennis Ickes, a former deputy undersecretary of the interior, called the reservations "our Gaza Strip."

But it is a delicate question. If a lot of Indians want judicial review, some others do not. They point out that ever since white men abused Squanto's hospitality, Indians have been screwed. After Little Bighorn, there was Wounded Knee, and Washington gave the orders. The BIA was such a mess that even its director, a former Cherokee chief, argued it should be dismembered. If Indians had legal problems, Indians should work them out.

John Chapela felt that way. "I would benefit personally from federal review," he told me, "but Indians would be the losers." He was collecting signatures to recall MacDonald. "His goal is to bankrupt the Navajo Nation to pay for his gold-plated retirement," he charged.

Impeachment was not likely. The Navajos had a supreme court and a justice department under the Tribal Council. They spent two million dollars a year on public relations and lobbying to be sure people got the right image. But in the end, MacDonald amounted to president, chief justice and speaker of the house. Not to put too fine a point on it, an American dictator.

Window Rock is so small most people leave town for their morning cup of coffee. Except for the handsome old complex of natural stone buildings where tribal business takes place, there is a Fed Mart and the tribe's Navajo Nation Motor Lodge. Two powerful men cohabit the place: MacDonald, who was elected chairman, defeated and then returned to office; and Peterson Zah, who replaced MacDonald for one term, to be voted out later in an election he still contests. Window Rock is not big enough for both of them.

Just before Zah left office, he made a private foundation of a tribal entity to raise money for scholarships. It was more effective that way, his proponents argue. MacDonald, however, claims it was a ploy to give Zah a job in Window Rock. The tribal chairman did not add the logical conclusion: Zah could not expect any other kind of job in town. After a brief period the tribe reclaimed the foundation and dissolved Zah's board.

Then the lawyers went to war. MacDonald sent officers out to change the locks on Zah's door. Zah obtained a temporary restraining order from the tribal judge at Window Rock banning anyone from interfering with his work. The tribe sent a lawyer to Chinle, a hard night's drive away in New Mexico, to get a different order. Police shut down the whole building, locking out not only Zah but also eighty people in the Education Department and other tribal offices. A group of employees went to MacDonald's office, looking for alternate work space, and two were fired.

Duane Beyal, a colleague of Zah's, remarked, "The integrity of the Navajo Nation is reduced to this game of musical doorknobs."

That was one scandal. The other was "Bogate." MacDonald's government had found a ranch near Tuba City, the Big Boquillas. The Big Bo was short on water but had passable grazing land. It had been on the market for twenty years, but in 1987 it was sold twice at the same time. Middlemen bought the ranch for $26.2 million and sold it to the Navajos five minutes later—for $33.4 million.

Federal investigators had a few questions. Wasn't that a little steep for appreciation? Wasn't it strange that a principal middleman was a golf crony of MacDonald's who raised funds for MacDonald's campaign? And what about the Coconino County record that showed MacDonald had paid off the mortgage on his retirement home shortly after the deal was approved?

Zah had a fat file on the operation and was happy to share it. "I am against the idea of federal court appeal because it diminishes the sovereignty of Indians," he said. "But this government's actions have made it necessary. We will suffer, but we have no choice."

Zah, a tall, burly man with graying hair, tended to boots and turquoise jewelry. MacDonald favored nicely cut three-piece suits. Both made their points with articulate outrage.

I asked MacDonald if he felt a heavy weight, with such power over people. "It is an awful responsibility for one man," he said, "but it is in our customs and traditions."

It wasn't exactly. Tribal governments were yet another federal idea to make it easier to govern reservations. A hodgepodge of systems evolved. In 1934 the Indian Reorganization Act helped a lot of tribes write constitutions. The Navajos declined. Its chairman is not even bound by a basic charter.

MacDonald received me in his nicely appointed, no-nonsense office, a dignified leader anxious to talk about his people. His main goal was to draw development to the reservation: small industries, businesses, tourist facilities and "vendor villages" for selling handicrafts. He had talked to Oleg Cassini about a designer resort at Canyon de Chelly. As on other reservations, underemployment approached 80 percent. Sheepherders were overgrazing the land, and oil revenues were not nearly enough.

He defended the Big Boquillas deal. The Navajos had not been advised of the markup. Some profit is normal, in any case; it is the American way. He was not being unreasonable toward Zah; when he lost the last election, he said, Zah ran him out of his quarters with unseemly haste. "I suppose that sort of thing is inevitable with tribal governments," MacDonald said.

I mentioned MacDonald's shutting down of the *Navajo Times* in 1987; police locked out the staff before they could finish the day's edition. The publisher said it was because the paper criticized the chairman. "It looks pretty bad," he said, chuckling. "If we had thought about how it was perceived, we would have done things a little differently." Actually, he said, the paper was losing money.

Every article I had seen about the chairman mentioned Gucci shoes. I mentioned that. MacDonald stepped from around his desk, and we both peered at his feet. "No," he said, "just regular J. C. Penney's, I think."

He nearly convinced me. But then I wasn't too surprised when the Senate finally dug into tribal corruption, in early 1989. A Bogate middleman testified that MacDonald had already received $125,000 for the deal when congressional investigators moved in; he was to have been paid up to $750,000, the witness said. MacDonald's son, Peter Jr., volunteered that routine $1,000 payments from contractors and businessmen were referred to as "golf balls."

MacDonald declined to appear in Washington, but he said over the Navajo radio station: "Yes, I have accepted gifts, but that is not a crime." Through a spokesman, he added: "These kinds of acts of appreciation are part of Navajo culture." It was simple racism that motivated senators to challenge tradition, he said.

Tribal council members disagreed. In stormy sessions, several demanded that MacDonald resign. Instead, mysterious "hate sheets" appeared accusing dissenters of various crimes from attempted murder and rape to drug abuse. A Phoenix reporter saw tribal employees stapling them together in MacDonald's lobby. Eventually, the chairman agreed to an indefinite leave. With pay.

But all that was later. In MacDonald's office, we talked a lot about Indians in general. Whatever his personal appetites, the chairman had given thought to the wider issues. He beat up on the BIA for a while and delved into the attitude behind it. He remembered, word for word, a hectoring lecture Navajo leaders had received in 1964 from a white Indian agent. The Navajos were debating some issue when the man stood up. "Until you learn to behave like adults," he told them, "I'm going to throw you out and padlock the chamber. . . ."

The encounter did not seem about to slip from his memory.

"People don't take the time to understand what Native Americans are all about, where they want to go, how they want to get there," he said. Mostly, he said, he worried about energizing the young, breaking out of a cycle that had crippled Indians for generations. "That is what bureaucracy generates. You give up. You lose hope. It is a poverty of the soul."

The latest plan was a computerized system for locating Indians on the reservation. Remote hogans would have standardized signposts so emergency vehicles could find them. In case of a ruptured soul, an ambulance, or a taxman, could respond.

I discussed impoverished souls with Barry Goodfield, my psychotherapist friend. He had been involved in child custody cases and spent time on reservations. "This poor self-concept is the same thing you see in colonial Africa," he said. "They get a bigger piece of pie, but nobody gives them a fork. We talk about the old genocide. It is the creeping white-Anglo value system. That's the genocide."

Spiritual, emotional confusion had created a generation of reservation yuppies and Market Street burnouts, Barry said. Their religion and traditional legal systems were undermined. Children grew up unable to take pride in their own culture and unwilling to accept another. They lost dignity. "We have absolutely crippled them psychologically," Barry said. "We didn't wound them in the knee. We wounded them in the ego."

Over at Crownpoint, I found plenty of dignity. Butch and Mary Ann O'Neal fed me enchilada pie and chili that could blister enamel. Butch is a consultant, although the term awkwardly fits a guy with a glossy black horsetail of hair, only slightly smaller than Michael Spinks, with a shuffling gait and a deep, merry giggle. He advises tribes on development. Butch is half Cheyenne River Sioux, with a European blend on the other side. Mary Ann is pure Navajo, of the beautiful maiden variety, and smart as hell.

Moments after I sat down, she mentioned MacDonald, "Big Mac" she called him, and a thunderclap shook the house. We laughed pretty hard, but Mary Ann, a Zah supporter, knows you don't mess around in Navajoland. Butch had directed the Crownpoint Institute of Technology, a training school for advanced skills, but had to leave when MacDonald took office. Mary Ann is a nurse, and they stayed in the pleasant little housing project behind the new Indian Health Service hospital.

"It's normal for a new president to put in his own people," Butch said, "but not down to the secretaries and janitors." The problem was not just among the Navajo, he added. On most reservations, if an Indian crosses the people in power, he can waste away in squalor. He might lose not only his job but also government-funded housing and other benefits.

"You can have free speech," he said. "But you pay for it." I asked about police brutality. "It happens, but people don't say anything, because where do you go?" Mostly Indians live their lives and avoid official encounters as best they can. Young Navajos had shot two tribal policemen and burned them in their Jeep at Monument Valley. A whole clan knew who did it, but it took the FBI six months to get anyone to talk.

Later someone else made this point: "Look, it's perfectly straightforward. If you work for the wrong side, you're going to get nailed, and your kids are going to get nailed. They don't have to use violence when there is no protection against retribution. There are no other resources but what they control. When you have that, you have absolute tyranny."

It was a paradox, all right. On one hand, it was America. On the other, it was Haiti with housebroken Tontons Macoute.

Crownpoint, in northern New Mexico, is a settlement of prefab buildings and shacks. There is a Mobil station, a Chevron and a Circle K. The grimy little Cozy Corner serves fried chicken, but the nearest drink is a long drive away, off the reservation. In shopwindows, signs warn, NO JOB OPENINGS. NO APPLICATIONS. Men of all ages relax in the shade, apparently unperturbed by the message. At the Fed Mart, families in rattling pickups pull up from distant homes, stick-walled hovels or geodesic hogans. A lot of them are there to exchange movies at the video counter.

Dotted with satellite dishes, it is as good a place as any to watch the world. I told Butch I was about to go to Central America to look into government involvement in drug trafficking. "I saw that on television, but then it was dropped," Butch said. "You watch these things, and then you wait for a reaction. You think, 'Oh, boy, is there going to be an uproar!' And then it doesn't come. It's scary. People just don't give a shit. You're disturbing their comfortable ignorance."

Butch shook out his thick rope of hair and boomed a laugh at the absurdity of it. "Do people really want to be free?"

We wandered over to see Glenn Rodriquez, a doctor from Oregon who had been at Crownpoint a long time and had just volunteered to stay longer. He ran the new hospital. The Indian Health Service, he explained, had been a handy spot for young doctors seeking an alternative to Vietnam. It had gotten to be more stable, but it had its weak spots. Later other doctors expounded on that theme: Some incompetent people ended up in places no one else would go. Good doctors worked with short supplies in crude conditions. On some reservations medical care was better than anywhere else in rural America. On others it was awful.

A physician who had been to the Pine Ridge Reservation, in South Dakota, had seen a fifteen-doctor hospital run by seven people. "It was a war zone," he said. One pediatrician was nearly killed by parents who blamed a complication on him. On another reservation, he said, "It scared me to be there; the people running the hospital were kids, the dregs of the medical profession."

Alcoholism was a crippling problem on almost all reservations. Indians died of cirrhosis and from being smashed up on the roads. Mean drunks kept the emergency rooms busy. Liquor is banned, but that just means a longer drunken drive. Some Indians cut Lysol half and half with water. Listerine sales go up at holiday time. Occasionally someone tries antifreeze.

No one was sure why so many Indians abused alcohol, Rodriquez said. There was certainly a genetic element. But there was also the constant problem of life on the "res." What else is there to do? Opinions ranged widely. Georgianne Tiger, a Blackfeet friend of mine, had offered: "I think it's social. My mother was taken to a fancy bar, with ice cubes and little umbrellas in the glasses, and she was amazed. She had never seen Indians drink out of anything but a bottle inside a paper bag. You grow up seeing your uncle lying drunk on the ground because he can't get up and everyone else just steps over him. It's perfectly acceptable."

Some Indian Health Service doctors try to work with traditional medicine men. They learn what fits in and what must be avoided as dangerous. Sometimes they steer a patient away from Western medicine, reinforcing their belief in more easily available remedies.

I talked about this with Frank James, one of those fresh-faced Renaissance men in running shoes whom only the United States seems to produce. It took me a day to fathom the range of his various interests, but one of them was native medicine. He was disturbed that overprotection had deprived Americans of simple, effective drugs.

"You can't patent a plant," he said. "Garlic reduces cholesterol, but you can't patent garlic." The American encyclopedia of pharmacology was twice as fat in 1950 as it is now, he said. Herbs and natural medicines that could not be commercialized had been expunged. To be accepted as safe and effective, a product needs certification from the Food and Drug Administration. "That costs around fifty million dollars," Frank said. "Who in their right mind is going to spend that on something you can't get a patent on?"

In medical school, he said, no one wanted to hear about healing herbs. On the res, he could study what the Indians know. He estimates about a third of the common natural medicines show good results. Not enough is known about another third. The last third, he added, can be dangerous as hell.

Frank, the Indian enthusiast, was also a cowboy. He took Butch and me riding up on the dramatic ridge south of town. We drove to the corral in his utility wagon, *Peer Gynt* spilling from the speakers. He knew about rugs and architecture, and he had picked up Chinese on a Ford Foundation grant. Oh, and Russian. He was deep into politics, trying to mobilize support against messing around with Central America. Even more, he went to conferences around the world for the International Physicians for the Prevention of Nuclear War.

He looked about twenty-seven, and this was starting to amaze me. He knew about grizzlies and Yellowstone. At the moment his passion was DNA. Think about it, he said, we could split eggs and maybe trace mankind back to the same person in China. Butch ended that line of thought: "I don't want no one splitting my eggs and finding out I came from the same place as that fucking Ronald Reagan."

We talked about Frank's wife, who was a clown. She learned clowning from priests in Central America. "The only weird thing she's into is angora rabbits," he observed.

I asked Frank where he'd been born, and he looked puzzled. "Well, I started to be born in—" We settled on Butte, Montana, but his parents had moved a lot.

Frank's sturdy desert horses picked their way up the rocks until we got off and scrambled on without them. He also knew about geology and suggested we look for shark's teeth. And snakes. One seemed more urgent than the other. The higher we got up the mountain, the deeper we got into Indians.

Butch worried about the old people who vanished, uninterviewed, taking libraries of lore with them. There was Yellow Indian, named by federal agents with limited imagination. His wife, a relative of Mary Ann's, had died at one hundred and seven. Her great-grandmother's mother had been captured by Spaniards. She escaped and made her way alone across Mexico. Latest in her line was Joe Indian, who came home from Vietnam and drank himself to death.

Frank told me about a Blackfeet drifter from Montana who had found himself a quiet spot near Tucson. He made people nervous. One day when he was in town, feds killed his dogs and ran him off. Bigotry and misunderstanding were deep-seated. Both showed up at odd times, in different ways.

We climbed and hiked. After a while we reached a high meadow of waving purple flax. Sharp cliffs dropped away, and you could see halfway to Canada. The air, with nothing in it but hawks and butterflies, was warm but fresh. It happened to be my birthday, and I felt pretty good. In fact, I was beginning to see what this Indian business was all about.

Melvin Pahe knew what had gone wrong. His job, until he lost it in the Zah showdown, had been to discourage youngsters from starting alcohol and drugs. It was a big job.

In his grandparents' day, he said, people shaped their lives by the four cardinal points. The east was white, and it meant self-discipline: running in the morning; rolling in the snow. The south, turquoise, symbolized self-reliance and dependability. The west, yellow, was family and friends, teaching and learning. And the north, black, was rest. A rich spiritual framework rested on those points, and each Navajo knew who he was.

"With my parents, everything was education," Pahe said. "They were removed from that traditional learning, and they had no access to the old teachings." Government schools had no room in the curriculum for cultural frivolities. "My generation followed along in that direction, and the old teachings were dormant. My kids don't know a thing about them."

Today, he said, where do they get their values? "There is no self-esteem. Their reality is hitting people, drinking. That is a lack of self-discipline."

*

The Indian wars against encroaching white men ended in 1890 at Wounded Knee, in South Dakota. They started up again in 1973, at the same little creek on the Pine Ridge Reservation. Even more than in the past, fighting was among the Indians. "White people are always asking why Indians can't agree among themselves," Butch had mentioned. "When did they ever?" His point was, Why should they? Could white people?

The new uprising was led by the American Indian Movement. Its leaders argued that activist politics were the only way to make their point. They wanted to dissolve the BIA and reclaim rights lost by their fathers. They wanted a spiritual and cultural revival. More moderate Indians scorned the movement. They felt the threat of violence, the occupation of buildings, would only worsen a delicate situation. For some, AIM stood for Assholes in Moccasins.

In Telluride I met David Dunbar, former counsel to the National Congress of American Indians and a veteran of the last wars. His mother was half Sioux, with some French, German and Chippewa; his father was mostly Blackfeet. David Dunbar lived on a reservation until his father died of alcoholism. Traveling around with his mother, he dropped out of nine different schools. He went to Vietnam as a marine and came home to study law. A specialist in Indian affairs, Dunbar settled down to pragmatism.

"It's the Indians, not the whites, who drive up your blood pressure," he said. "There is so much politics, infighting, you can't believe it. There is such miscommunication, you can never satisfy everyone." He has a story about a man walking along with two buckets of crabs, the white men's and the Indians'. Someone asks the man why the Indians' bucket had no cover. It doesn't need one, the man replies. Every time one crab starts to get out, the others pull him back.

"In most cases negotiated settlements are the best solutions," he told me. "Five to six people a day would call me to say, 'What the hell are you doing, negotiating with white people? It's never done us any good.' But if you don't negotiate, it's a judge who decides. I was surprised at the ignorance of some Indians, perpetuating hatred and mistrust. I would say we are into a new era. Still, hating the white man is a popular political theme."

Tribes should defend their languages and cultures, he said, but that is not the issue. "The thing to remember about Indians," Dunbar said, "is that they see this conflict as political, not racial or spiritual."

About the only thing Indians agreed on was the BIA. Ross Swimmer, head of the BIA, was one of its harsher critics. "Tribes have to have the responsibility in determining what is best for their own people," Wilma Mankiller had said. "It is extremely paternalistic, terribly bureaucratic. It's not the people in it, but the system. Swimmer is a conservative Republican. I'm a liberal Democrat. We end up saying the same thing. His agenda is reducing federal spending. Mine is to build responsibility and self-reliance."

But, she added, "the obstacle is Indian people. They gripe about the bureau, but if you say to someone, 'Why don't we change it?' they don't want to. But it's got to be changed. They could just write a check and audit us."

Dunbar felt that ironically, Reagan's austerity worked out as a benefit. "Tribal governments have been so dependent on the government dole, and other money they qualify for, that they did nothing," he said. "They've been made to realize that it is not a bottomless source. It is starting to run out. Economic development is the new catchword."

Indians discovered leveraged buyouts. "They are getting smart," he said. "Instead of going on a two-week drunk, they are starting to use the money against government, using Arab bankers and leverage to acquire power." They buy out successful businesses close to reservations and let former owners stay behind until Indians take over gradually. "Before," Dunbar said, "when tribes bought something, they threw everyone out and replaced them with Indians. That was the kiss of death."

Inevitably Indians and whites face problems rooted in history. Federal and state authorities tried for four years to prosecute James Billie, chief of the Seminoles, for shooting a rare Florida panther. Billie argued the animal was essential to healing and religious ritual. The case was finally dropped.

In Palm Springs, California, Indian land alternates with non-Indian parcels, and the tribes make large amounts by leasing it. Developers who built a resort and golf course there have tried hard to strike a deal with the Tohono O'odham (Papago) near Tucson. In Montana bitter disputes surrounded fishing rights on the Flathead Reservation, a patchwork of Indian and leased land. "This is supposed to be a reservation, and I cannot even walk across it without getting shot at," Ron Weaselhead, a young Flathead, told me. Bumper stickers read, SPEAR AN INDIAN, SAVE A SALMON in Washington State.

Once, when I was talking to a California businessman, the subject of Chippewas arose. "Yes," he said, with a smile of satisfaction, "we used to steal their wild rice." He explained that Chippewas spent long days in the marshes, thrashing the rice into canoes. They were extremely hard workers but naive about business, he said. As a result, he got a great price.

Bigotry makes it harder for Indians, Dunbar said. It is most obvious near the reservations. For a long time no Navajo would be seen at night in Farmington, New Mexico. It just was not safe. In Page, Arizona, an Indian woman and her daughter were roughed up. The circumstances were not clear, but tribal authorities made allegations against the sheriff.

"As you go west, you feel it: animosity, racism," Dunbar told me. "White people just don't like Indians. I can understand it. We're dealing with people without much education, people who resent our land. A lot see Indians as having dual nationality and special privileges. I remember one rancher saying, 'Why the hell should we pay for the sins of our fathers?' "

The worse thing, some Indians say, is that people don't even hear their own slurs. Suzan Shown Harjo, executive director of the National Congress of American Indians, brought this up in testimony before the U.S. Civil Rights Commission. She was a Washington Redskins fan, she said, "but I don't think it would be tolerated if there were in the nation's capital . . . a team called the Blackskins, if I got out on a football field and dressed in an Aunt Jemima outfit, and this good gentleman got out in a Stepin Fetchit outfit for the Blackskins." She nodded toward Chairman Clarence Pendleton, Jr., who was black.

"There would be a race riot if we had a team called the Jew Boys . . . or the Black Chicks," she went on. The problem, Harjo said, was that people still had the same cowboy movie running in their heads. "Indians are identified as an era, not as a people."

Marley Shebala understood the bigotry, and she didn't like it. A Navajo who covers the reservation for the Farmington paper, she is one of those universal woman reporters with glasses halfway down the nose. Like my sister Jane. They walk in smiling and half distracted, but something makes you quietly lock your files. Essentially Marley does not take shit. One day she threw a fit in an Albuquerque music store when she asked for Indian music and the clerk directed her to the "Foreign" section.

"You wish they would be blatant about it," she said. "They smash you in the face, and you can smash them back. Now they smash you, and you don't even know it. It hurts when you see people treated disrespectfully, laughed at when they don't deserve it, or pushed around, or told to stand in certain lines and have other people served in front of them."

Marley laughed when she told me about Albuquerque, but she had stopped smiling. "It just really hurts. You are angry, and you don't know what to do. What we do is we say our prayers. We pray for patience. We have medicine to comfort us. And we endure."

In April 1988 the Supreme Court upheld, 4–3, a Forest Service decision to build a road of dubious need through the Chimney Rock area in northern California, the sacred sites of Yurok, Karok and Tolowa Indians. Their religion was based upon the privacy, silence and undisturbed natural setting of the small section of ground. Dissenting, Justice Brennan wrote:

> Today, the Court holds that a federal land-use decision that promises to destroy an entire religion does not burden the practice of that faith in a manner recognized by the Free Exercise Clause. Having thus stripped respondents and all other Native Americans of any constitutional protection against perhaps the most serious threat of their age-old religious practices, and indeed to their entire way of life, the Court assures us that nothing in its decision "should be read to encourage governmental insensitivity to the religious needs of any citizen."

He said the Indians were told they could practice their religion, but "a marginally useful road" destroyed the basis of it. "The safeguarding of such a hollow freedom not only makes a mockery of the 'policy of the United States to protect and preserve for American Indians their inherent right of freedom to believe, express, and exercise their traditional religions,' it fails utterly to accord with the dictates of the First Amendment."

After all these generations young Indians stay on the reservation. If they go somewhere else, most float back and then move on again. I talked about this in Crownpoint with Roberta Lewis, a teacher whose father was governor of Zuñi Pueblo. She blamed entrenched discrimination, which has shaped Indians' lives.

Outside, she said, Indians find scarcely veiled hostility. At home they have to rely on largess from Washington the way a Third World nation depends on foreign aid. "We get either not enough or too much," she said. "There is too little of what you really need, and the things that they give you don't make any sense. It is a hard thing, but we are caught in a catch-22 situation. When they want to be grandiose, they call us the first Americans. But that is the closest we come to being considered part of the human race."

Even when given a chance, she said, Indians don't take it. "What holds us back? There is a lot of passivity, pacificism. People like to say it's stoicism. I don't know if it's an inherent quality, genetic, but it is a philosophy of accepting, of just saying, 'That's the way it is. . . .'"

This, reinforced with subtle discrimination, keeps Indians in their place, Roberta said. "It's in the human nature. When I appear in person after talking to someone on the phone, and they see I'm an Indian, they'll say, 'How come you talk just like an American?' Unless you want something very badly and are adamant about it, you don't get it."

For Roberta, comparisons with Africa are no rhetorical exaggerations. "If you look at the Third World," she said, "you find the same issues here, in the land of the free. What does that say about the Constitution?" She talked without heat, and I mentioned that. "You know, we're more frustrated than pissed off. We're beyond pissed."

A look around the school made her point. The building was sinking into the sand. It would cost $1.5 million to fix it, but the Navajos didn't have the money. The Commerce Department had built the school but budgeted nothing for maintenance. It was designed for air conditioning, but no one had installed it. Windows were sealed in the ninety-five-degree heat. Sound-operated outside lights had been put in for security; it cost $70,000 to repair them.

Someone had sold the school a lease contract for an IBM copier. Photocopies cost eighteen cents each. The whole operation looked like those white-elephant foreign aid projects I had seen all over Africa. Instead of USAID, however, the initials were different.

The school represents someone's willingness to help Navajos learn the skills they need to make it in the modern world. But what about the ones who want to be left alone? The government built an airstrip on grazing land near Crownpoint. Before the first five planes landed, a sheepherder had shot out the lights.

CHAPTER

=== **13** ===

Heartland:
The Kansas City
Milkman

You've got to be pretty weird not to love Kansas City. It may be the most livable city in the country, especially if your priorities run to grease. "I mean, serious grease," asserts Larry "Fats" Goldberg, who should know. "This is the best eating town in America. And it's a pretty good town anyway." Kansas City's main drawback, coastal dwellers say, is that it is smack in the heart of the Midwest. At which midwesterners chuckle politely while waiting for them to go back to the coast.

Midwest is not so bad, I discovered, whatever it is. No one yet has been able to define the term or draw lines around the place. Kansas City definitely qualifies. And Omaha, Nebraska. But what else? This question is an obsession with an upbeat new magazine called *Midwest Living*, published in Des Moines. It glorifies cooking with raspberries and following Abe Lincoln's footprints around Illinois. "To most people," it quoted an expert as saying, "the Midwest represents all the pastoral, wholesome, corny things in an urban age. It's very consistent that people think of us as hardworking, yet friendly and easygoing."

Yup. The Heartland. *Midwest Living* defines its territory as twelve states: Iowa, Nebraska, Missouri, Kansas, Indiana, Illinois, Ohio, the Dakotas, Minnesota, Wisconsin and Michigan. That sneaks in the Great Plains and the Great Lakes, the prairie and the Badlands, but why quibble? By that description, 5 percent of midwesterners live on farms. Nearly a third of America's Fortune 500 companies are based within those borders.

I focused on Kansas City for several reasons. One was Fats Goldberg. Fats is a pretty silly nickname for such a mere slip of a man, but once he was a blimp. He lost 135 pounds in a year, and even as proprietor of perhaps the best pizzeria in New York, he did not gain it back. The secret is in his *Controlled Cheating*: "Strict dieting with nutritious foods for six days, with one day off for gluttonous behavior." The book is hard to find, and he may have given me his last copy. He's that type of guy.

Calvin Trillin, who loves Kansas City as much as anyone, sent me to Goldberg, to whom he is friend and Boswell. To widespread grief, Goldberg had closed his pizza place and moved back to Missouri. He was mysterious about the reason, but it appears to involve being close to Lamar's crullers.

"People are so nice here it fakes you out," he said. "Great-looking women. They smile, and I think, 'That's for me,' but they're just being friendly. No one honks. You could be eating meals at the light, and no one would honk." But, he said, outsiders could fit right in. "If you talk fast, you're all right. I send back Cokes if there's not enough fizz or syrup. You could give these people dog doo-doo, and they won't say anything. If you call your lawyer, he rings you back."

Goldberg has not given up on New York. "It's a lot harder there, but people are wonderful. On every block you find nine different stories. Kansas City has no action. Action is going to a movie. Still, this place is an undiscovered jewel."

That was the main reason I was there. Everywhere I went, people asked if I was "probing the Heartland." That medical metaphor seemed to be America's favorite figure of speech. Hey, what the hell: Just about every Heartland specialist pointed to the two halves of Kansas City as the semilunar valves, the underappreciated little conduits through which the nation's lifeblood pulsed on its way to be cleansed.

In fact, there is something to that. The Midwest is a clear vantage point for examining where America is headed. People there take time to reflect on what is important to their lives. Old values and customs seem to dissipate first from the coasts and the big cities. New ideas don't take hold unless they settle into the Heartland.

For all the surface good cheer at the heart of America, there was widespread, deeply rooted fear and loathing. Take the Memorial Day Beer Ball Tournament, an annual classic in the backyard of a nice guy named Dan. Beer ball, Dan explained, is a lot like softball except there is only one rule: You must have a beer in your hand at all times. Even at bat. He had printed scorecards for the foreign beers to be tasted. Months went into finding the ugliest shorts in Kansas City, given away as uniforms. Dan was enthusiastic about his little invitational: "When you have doctors throwing up, tenured professors hanging from their knees in a tree trying to drink upside down, lawyers saying they won't sue under any circumstance, you know you're reaching the right level."

We found such a good level we never got around to playing. A dozen professionals of various sorts decided to unload. All said they wanted me to get America right.

Dan, a political scientist and international consultant, started by explaining that he was moving to Scotland. "I can't wait to get away from this place. It is fucked. When we were a functioning economic unit, everyone had a specialty. Now we're all making Wendys. I think everybody in this country is pissed, if he is really honest. If you ask anybody here what we do best, nobody can name anything, except be opinionated assholes. We do that better than anyone, except maybe the French."

An accountant picked up from there: "Everything is so corrupt, complicated. I won't even begin to tell you things we do to get through an audit. They force us to do it, with the system."

A travel executive added, "Americans don't know how much of a police state we have become. And all the hypocrisy. I'm so sick of it. It's so sad that people can't open up their eyes and live with people."

It went around like that. Finally, a history professor summed it up: "It is our arrogance and nationalism. Things are going to get worse before it gets better. We don't learn from anybody. What kills me are the blinders. There are such obvious examples of injustice that people close their eyes to. We have such faith in progress, and we learn nothing. Americans have lost their souls."

*

I sought a more sober reading from Don Hall, chairman of Hallmark Cards, whose family for years has cared enough to want the best for Kansas City. The Halls contribute heavily to civic causes and the arts. Hallmark's whole operation, down to cutting and shipping, fits into the glassy Crown Center, an office and hotel complex that brought some new life into the central city. I asked Hall what he thought of the shape big business was taking elsewhere.

"Corporations are getting faceless, losing traditions and even losing their names," he said. "Companies are tossed around like pawns. In that world there is no consideration of the individual, of the community." He acknowledged Hallmark was easier to handle; it was family-owned. But he said the problem was that few executives were good corporate citizens.

"These old companies have survived, they have a heritage and tradition, but nobody seems to care anymore," he went on. "These people will just kill off an old company. This trend is idiocy."

The problem, Hall said, was that short-term gains were too easy. Unless executives understood ethics and basic human values, it could only get worse. He hoped people were getting fed up. More corporate leaders might change their thinking. "I don't think you can legislate that," he concluded. "But the responsibility is immense, for every individual. If you lose that, you will lose that element that made this country great."

For him, it was part of a bigger problem. I had heard people evoke it over and over. "The new kids coming up have not been given any briefing on ethics," he said. "That should come from the schools or the family, or both. But nobody knows how to teach it. And the parents are so darn busy. Thirty years ago I would have never thought about how to do business in an ethical way. It would never have occurred to me."

In the end, Hall said, it was dangerous and distressing. "The takeover mentality is abominable. A lot of people are making vast amounts of money by hurting people. This creates a pressure. Companies are judged on how they perform each month, not even every year. It is not fair."

Worse, that made it impossible for even generous executives to think about long-term planning, let alone any form of largess not immediately connected to improving their corporate image. The bottom line has no asterisk explaining profit reduced by civil responsibility.

But the Halls were rare even among private companies. Andrew Carnegie wrote that a rich man should live modestly and "consider

all surplus revenues which come to him simply as trust funds, which
he is called upon to administer in the manner . . . best calculated
to produce the most beneficial results for the community." But that
was 1889, when the score was kept in other ways.

This America-in-Decline stuff was on a lot of lips, all across the
country, and there was no consensus. Some people threw up their
hands in the face of the inevitable. Others dismissed it as so much
negative nonsense; things change. The answer was clearly somewhere in between. I was still gathering evidence, but early returns
were unsettling. Ever onward, I went to the reporter's source of
sources: the Kansas City milkman.

Decades ago Reynolds Packard, an old UPI hand, wrote a novel
called *The Kansas City Milkman*. It is even harder to find than Fats's
diet book. Its message was that if a foreign correspondent's dispatch
was clear to a milkman in Kansas City, it was well written. He was
your average reader. That was no longer true, I learned. There
were no more milkmen in Kansas City. But I tracked down the last
guy to quit.

Ben Zarda's Bavarian grandfather, Frank, came to Kansas City in
1910 with two brothers and some sisters. After three years at odd
jobs the Zardas bought a few milk cows. They pioneered home delivery by trundling milk cans down the street on a pushcart three
times a day. By the 1950's the thriving company owned 160 cows.
Drought crippled the herd, and the family held a brief board meeting during the ritual 8:00 P.M. dinner. They sold the herd and went
full bore into processing and distribution. No longer dairymen, they
were just milkmen.

It was a noble business. During the war, when women were off
working in bomber plants, Ben carried 120 keys to let himself in for
deliveries. "Sometimes the old grandma was living there, and you'd
see if she was all right," Zarda remembered. "You'd let the dog out
for a minute. At the end of the route you'd chop up the ice for the
kids who swarmed around."

Milkmen were part of everyone's family. "Sometimes he was the
only friend lonely people had," Zarda explained. "People would leave
notes for him to run errands. He would be invited to meals and
family parties." I mentioned all the jokes about babies who look like
the milkman. Zarda's mouth wiggled in happy recall. "Let me tell
you, they weren't all jokes."

Holidays got raucous. "Everyone handed you a drink," he said. "If you weren't careful finishing your route, you were in trouble. But you knew the policeman, and he knew who to call to come get your truck."

By the 1960's supermarkets and paper cartons were taking a toll. By 1973 home delivery was history. It should not have surprised me. About the only regular deliveries left are the postman, bringing junk mail, and the garbageman, who carts it away. If the iceman no longer cometh, why should Ben Zarda? But there was something tragic about it all.

"We probably stayed with it ten years longer than we should have," Zarda said. "I wrote personal letters to customers going back three generations, and I still feel bad about it today. For shut-ins, old people, that was the high point of their day."

Meanwhile, there were the milk wars. Big national dairies came in during the 1950's and fought bitterly for the supermarket ac-counts. Antitrust suits over pricing took thirteen years to resolve. In that time, Kansas City's 120 independent dairies dwindled to a half dozen. The Zardas were the biggest. They opened thirty of the country's first convenience outlets and pioneered a national trend by adding gasoline pumps to milk bars. But they weren't big enough.

In the mid-1980's they teamed up with Mid-America Dairymen, a Fortune 500 megamilkery from Springfield, Missouri. Then they sold out entirely.

We were eating breakfast at the Plaza. The little containers of half-and-half said Zarda Dairies. We both knew there was no such thing. Ah, but did the customers know? Did they care? On the one hand, big deal: A name is a name. You sell goodwill; it's the Amer-ican way. But then there was no Frank Mid-America pushing his cart down Broadway eighty-five years ago. Didn't anything mean anything anymore? This brought up America-in-Decline, and by now we were past milk.

"There is no more commitment to quality," Zarda said. "The per-sonal pride in your product is falling away. Consumers catch on. There's no faith in a name anymore. Before, you wouldn't let that happen. It used to be that a guy who drove a Chevy could get in a fistfight with a guy who liked Fords. No one will speak up for a brand today." I wanted to tell him about the New York advertising man I met who told me how copywriters extol products with no basis in fact—"It's mostly the same shit, anyway" was how he put it—but the valet brought his Jaguar, and we said good-bye.

*

Sitting at the Plaza, I had a sense of what is no longer in a name. The Plaza suggests heavily that some Spaniards settled in sometime since Coronado. It is more a small section of town than a mall, with an imposing hotel, shops, Spanish-style streets and fountains. In fact, it is the result of some Kansas City moguls' trip to Seville. They felt the place needed a touch of Iberian flair, so they created it. To be honest, it works fine. It was built with quality a half century ago, and its aging trees and worn sidewalks fit well with new glitz. Besides, growing Spain in a cornfield is pure Kansas City style.

You have to drive around to appreciate the city. Planners seem to have figured out proportions. Parking is simple, and traffic flows. There is a rush minute when lots of people are hurrying to work. But most have figured out the timed traffic lights, and they hurtle down major arteries in tightly bunched packs. The stately old downtown is backed up by the Crown Center, not far away.

A large park abuts the imposing Nelson-Atkins Museum of Art, a rich art museum with even more Chinese tomb figures than in Albany, Texas. Laurence Sickman spent a lifetime collecting rare Asian art, which competes with floors of old and new masterworks. There is far more theater, jazz and general entertainment than the average New Yorker would believe.

As in most American cities, there is a black section, and it is poor. That's where you find Arthur Bryant's, where the counterman says, "What's happenin'?" and hands you a plate of barbecue for which some people would desert New York. A lively Mexican barrio could be South-Central L.A., where the food gets no better than the California Taqueria. Kansas City, Kansas, is smaller and less lively. A river separates the two cities in places. Elsewhere they meld without a crease.

In a few Kansas City houses Los Angeles drug gangs had found surprising harmony. Away from their disputed turf, police said, they worked together to control the local drug trade. As Larry Goldberg noted, local people usually stepped aside for pushy types from the coast.

Before leaving town, I found a spot on a bluff that, if pressed, I might describe as the heart of America. On Quality Hill, a block from the huge cow on a pedestal at the American Hereford Association, two old cut stone archways looked out to the occupied prairie. Down below, broad lanes of a freeway traffic emitted the pollution that increased Kansas City's ozone level by 42 percent from 1987 to 1988. Behind, intricate tracks carried freight trains in every direction. And in the middle distance, barges moved downriver. Grain silos, smokestacks and tin towers stretched far beyond, industrial forest.

Fading paint of factory walls spelled things like "Superior Toy & Novelty Co." and "Standard Seed Company." The archway itself, none too pleasant-smelling, was scrawled with dirty words and ethnic epithets. "Fag's Lookout Point" someone had written. A swastika was painted by somebody too stupid to get it right. A later artist wrote, "Support your local KKK," to which someone had retorted, "Die Facsit."

Esthetically the view was hardly beautiful. But there was something about where it was, what it meant and what I knew was just over the horizon. I felt good, even proud, but also let down by a promise that went wrong. From that spot on the hill I got a strong sense of America and how to appreciate it. Either you had to get up very close. Or you had to stand a long way back.

North of Kansas City, at a place called Turney near the Kansas border, I visited Peaches Dixon and his wife, Dee. I'd met a lot of farmers, but the Dixons were blue-chip Americana. The farm, bought, sold and inherited within the family for 102 years, started at 120 acres. Peaches came home from killing Japanese in 1945 and worked for a quarter a day, lunch not included. He scrounged enough to buy some of the land. Over the years he parlayed it into 720 acres. He raised wheat, corn, soybeans and, all going well, three thousand hogs a year. No fruit trees. His nickname came from Elbert, his real name; Elbertas are peaches.

Some years Peaches and Dee cruised the Orient after harvest. Others, they wrote off sixty-five thousand dollars on their taxes and wondered at which of their well-painted doors the wolf would appear.

"I love farming, but no matter how much you like something, you've got to pay your bills," Dixon said. "I sell seed corn and insurance just to support my habit." Like farmers across the country, he knew the best cash crop was a job in town. He worked seven-day weeks, farming his land and another 250 acres leased from neighbors who commuted to Kansas City. He rented out his spare house. With extra income, he hired men to help him.

Every year was different. During the bust after the 1970's boom
he nearly lost his farm. "I had debts from fencerow to fencerow,"
Dixon said. "We didn't know whether we were going to last or not.
Loan officers, presidents of banks made some bad judgments. New
people were brought in, hatchet men, and you didn't know what
your banker would do. We farmers made mistakes. Maybe we bought
some things we shouldn't have. Maybe we didn't live exactly the
Spartan life. But there's no point in blaming anyone. We're all in it
together. They almost forced money on us. Money was so available
it was pathetic."

When debts came due, he said, inexperienced bankers were telling farmers what to do. "That's the golden rule: The fellow that has
the gold makes the rule."

After scrimping during good years, the Dixons got back into the
black. Grain prices dropped, but pork rose. "There's an old saying,
if you hold on to a pig's tail, he'll pull you out of a mudhole," Dixon
said. "By God, that's what happened."

Then, after they had managed to get in a crop before a dry spell,
a freak hailstorm destroyed 70 percent of it. Federal insurance saved
him from disaster, but he went two years without a harvest. "You
talk about gambling," he said. "A businessman can just shut down.
But the hogs got to eat."

When I talked to the Dixons, things were fine. Afterward drought
set in. As I traveled, I watched it spread until half the counties in
the nation were declared disaster areas. As I sat down to write at
the end of the summer of '88, I phoned the Dixons to check up on
their news.

"Well," Dee said, "the corn crop is thirty-five to forty percent gone.
My husband took out federal crop insurance, so I guess he is sleeping at night when some others aren't. A young man down the road
who'd pulled himself up was doing real good. I hear he's being
foreclosed."

The Dixons hauled a lot of water. Hogs don't sweat, and if you
don't wet them down, they die in the heat. "We're not complaining,"
Dee said. "But I don't think we'll make much money this year. We
thought maybe in two more years we'd sell and get off the farm.
But the way it is, you just can't sell. These are bad times." Her flat
Midwest monotone faltered here. She hit the word "bad" unchar-
acteristically hard.

*

To beat back the vicissitudes of agriculture, the federal government was spending twenty-five billion dollars a year, on one thing or another, which worked out to about sixty-thousand dollars per subsidized farmer.

Peaches thought that was pretty stupid. "The government doesn't know much about what it is doing in a lot of things, and farming is one of them," he said. Farmers have grown addicted to support. "It would be better if the government was completely out of it. Whoever does a good job survives. Those who can't make it don't. A farm is a business and has to be run that way."

But farmers would have to get a fair price. "The farmer has subsidized the consumer," he said. "In the United States about fifteen to sixteen cents of every dollar earned goes to food. In some countries it is eighty to ninety cents." Dixon would not want to live in those particular countries, I was sure, but he had a point.

All professionals could use a little backup. Writers, for example. But one must accept a difference. The only person who can eat words is the guy who wrote them. I'll admit that the tomato is mightier than the pen. Farmers need a safety net against the weather and world price fluctuations beyond their control. Loans and erosion control aid are essential. But when you consider where else public funds are needed, it seems criminal to underwrite inept, lazy or larcenous farmers.

The vast dole network was too complicated even for an efficient bureaucracy, let alone ours. When too much food was produced, the government decided to pay farmers handsomely to leave their land in grass. People nearing retirement stayed around to collect the money, hoping land values would rise in the meantime. Some younger ones took the money, bought more fertilizer and planted closer. Overall, stocks were drawn down, and when drought struck, there were serious imbalances.

Zarda had mentioned the dairy scam. Because so much butter and milk had been produced, the government bought up herds for hamburger. But large companies simply sold off their driest cows and kept the best ones. Subsidies spurred production.

Commodity support systems involve credits and delayed deliveries, which big companies can manipulate for major gains at the expense of taxpayers and small farmers. With lobbyists, lawyers and operating capital, major producers somehow manage to fatten themselves up in lean times.

It was this last point—big companies—that set off Dixon like a firecracker. He said he had seen grain companies pour dirt and impurities into export grain shipments, right up to the allowed limit, to make an extra buck. "People overseas take us at our word, and they see they can't trust us," he said. Worse, he saw big companies taking over the farms.

"The family farm is in jeopardy," he said. "I feel very strongly about that. These are America's roots. With a family farm, if it does its business right, it does its job right. If these corporations get hold, I guarantee that'll change. It's like Russia and collective farms. There is no real incentive. It is just a job. I hope we never see that here. It won't work."

We were out by his pigpens. "Now, you take these hogs. You got to love these animals. You got to be here all the time. Yesterday I took a load of them to St. Joe and brought back five thousand dollars. They been with us six months, and I don't know if they are alive today. You know what I'm saying? It will destroy the backbone of the country when it gets down to dollars and cents."

By then, I had learned, getting off the farm was the American way. Devastated little communities tried everything to keep themselves going. Rolfe, Iowa, offered twelve hundred dollars cash, a free lot and a year's swimming and golf privileges to anyone who built a thirty-thousand-dollar house. Since 1980 its 1,122 people had dwindled to below 1,000. William Winkleblack, of Rolfe Betterment Inc., told a reporter: "We don't want to be a big city. We just want the school to survive. We want the grocery store to make it."

The congressional Office of Technology Assessment estimated that by the year 2000 three quarters of America's grain, fibers, fruits and vegetables would be grown on 50,000 farms, huge open-air food factories. In 1988 there were 650,000. Between 1981 and 1986, 300,000 farms were lost. Farm population had dipped below 5 million. A century earlier it was estimated at 21.9 million, and then it had peaked at 32.5 million in 1916. It stabilized, and after World War II it began to slip.

Kenneth Bean, in *The Harmonist,* wrote that a family farm failed every eight minutes in 1986. Massive combines harvested a crop that took an eighty-man crew. Chemicals altered the natural balance. "This depiction of giantism in American agribusiness is supposed to impress us. Yet, if we are indeed progressing, why must we invest eight times as much capital as we did thirty years ago? As more small farmers are squeezed out, it becomes easier to see the land as a factory, not as a living thing."

Since 1950, he wrote, potato beetles have been treated with fifteen insecticides and now enjoy a blanket immunity.

In These Times mentioned Herbert Jones's 762 acres in Hamilton, Missouri, lost by foreclosure to Mutual Benefit Life Insurance. Bulldozers pushed out the antierosion terraces, uprooted 150-year-old trees and shoved debris into the ponds. The idea was to turn a patchwork of fields, pasture and woodland into a single tract to interest an investor after cash crops. Hired tenants plowed up and down hills, eroding the soil. "They've grown lots of cockleburrs since they took over," Jones said.

Not everyone was so worried. Often bigger small farms, not corporations, did the taking over. Agribusiness had its limits. But unquestionably, part of the culture was dying.

Farmers like Dixon know about the rest of the world. They can't afford apathy. Most have clear ideas about foreign competition. For all the bedrock anticommunism, not many will argue for starving out the Russians. Dixon, for one, can tell you what he thinks of President Carter's grain embargo over Afghanistan and using commodities as a political weapon. That comes as little surprise from people in the food business.

But Dixon takes his worldview seriously. He has put out a lot in the name of the flag.

"In this country we don't have any idea what war is," he told me. "On Memorial Day I'll be in the color guard. I'll put on my uniform and fire my rifle and look out at the people. It doesn't mean a shit to them. I want to walk over and kick 'em in the ass and make 'em realize what freedom means. We'll drink more than we should; we'll have a hell of a time. But damn few will understand that it is a day set aside to contemplate that." We had been at it all morning. He glanced at his pigs and relaxed. "That's another part of life."

I drove off thinking about farming. Years of covering African hunger had turned me into something of an agriculture freak. And for all the technology and wealth, I was amazed at how little difference there was between us and them. In the end it comes down to two basic functions: striking a deal with the government and praying for rain.

On the way to Kansas City's fine airport I dropped in at Leavenworth. I was not planning to stay long, but I wanted to see the potential home for too many of our new class of leaders. It was worse than I had pictured. Its forbidding concrete mass, trimmed in iron bars and heavy coils of barbed wire, sat off in a field. I could almost hear machine guns chatter. With some trepidation, I drove up to the front gate and saw an imposing sign: WELCOME. U.S.P.

At night it probably showed colorized Edward G. Robinson films reedited for modern America: "Back in your cells, you filthy maggots. Have a nice day."

Indianapolis is another kind of city—India-Noplace, they used to call it, and some still do—but it has its charm. It is one of those midwestern places where you understand how television sitcoms can blithely declare, "To be continued," without a shimmer of protest. Unless someone repossesses the couch or Russians invade, that's where people will be next Tuesday.

Actually I spent more time in Bloomington, at the University of Indiana, than in Indianapolis. I drove to Bloomington over what the weatherman called "slick spots." Even for snowy roads, the phrase seemed a little misplaced. "Slick" is not an Indiana adjective. The place is goodhearted and good-natured. It is hardworking, God-fearing, decent, honest, brave, clean, cheerful, thrifty and reverent. Slick it is not.

Bloomington is the home of Willis Barnstone, whom I met in Argentina when he came down to translate Jorge Luis Borges. By the time I caught up with him again in Indiana, his list of published books had climbed to thirty-nine, on everything from obscure bits of yesterday's Greece to tomorrow's China. Willis is a poet and professor of comparative literature. He is also an artist and operawright, a linguist and translator, a serious scholar of the old sort, a gentle thinker and a friend of great generosity.

He is also a little loopy about day-to-day trivia. Once in Chile, he wrote to the editors of a sophisticated travel magazine, who knew him well. Since he was an expert on Christmas Island, and it was so close, why didn't he do a piece? Back came the reply: We assume you mean Easter Island, and go ahead.

On a snowy morning in Bloomington, we raced around the campus in his battered Toyota, and he shouted over the weather coming in the door he had never got around to fixing: "Let me just show you this library." Great, I thought, still somewhat misguided on midwestern institutions; I steeled myself for shelves full of *Catcher in the Rye* and *Tractor Illustrated*. Moments later an urbane—okay,

slick—curator was showing me ink sketches of my Paris neighborhood in a 1739 Plan Turgot, part of a fabulous collection of rare
French works.

That was nothing. The Eli Lilly Library contained 360,000 old
books, 100,000 pieces of music and 6 million manuscripts. It had
2,200 letters between Ezra and Dorothy Pound and Keats's last notes
to Fanny Brown. On the sumptuous walls Sully's portrait of George
Washington gazed around at famed paintings of his successors. A
comely George Sand hung next to a pouting Samuel Pepys. Molière
bordered Lope de Vega, among dozens of originals I had admired
as prints.

We stuck our heads in the I. M. Pei Art Museum, just long enough
to see a Picasso and a Pollock among a stirring collection of modern
sculpture. Then we toured the vast opera house, with a stage larger
than that of New York's Met. IU has four symphony orchestras, all
good, and offers a thousand concerts a year. At the Indiana Memorial Union, Willis remarked, "I had lunch here with the Dalai
Lama a few months ago." Fearing immodesty, he added quickly: "A
lot of other people were there, too." En route to class, we cut through
an Oriental languages center offering courses in Mongolian, Uzbek,
Uighur and Manchurian.

Then he took me to his comparative literature class. Twenty un-
dergraduates, waiting for a lecture on the mystics, instead got an
itinerant reporter who grilled them on what American students knew
about the world. The question had hardly left my lips when Alexina
Hutchins, a freshman from Philadelphia, waved her hand. It was a
subject to which she had given some thought.

"I don't see how they can know what goes on in other countries
when they don't even know where they are," she said. The day before, her geography professor had asked a class of seventy-five students to locate Vietnam on a map of the world. Three could do it.
"People put it in Africa. They put Africa in South America. No one
knew anything," she said. "It was frightening."

I asked the class why this was.

"Students are more worried about being successful, preparing for
a good job, making money," another freshman answered. "They don't
care about things that don't touch them. The whole focus is on Bobby
Knight, basketball, things like that." The others nodded in agreement.

One young man raised his hand. He knew where Vietnam was,
and he wanted to talk about it. He was distressed that the United

States had gone home and callously left behind all those prisoners of war in Vietnamese camps. He seemed to have elaborate details about Americans cast aside by officers too gutless to save them. I knew men were missing, and there were unresolved questions over bodies; but he was talking about abandoned POWs. Had I missed something? Suddenly I recognized his source. It was the plot of *Rambo II, First Blood.*

At the time Ethiopians were starving in what promised to be as bad a famine as the 1984 calamity that had caused such a stir. Did anyone know that? Did anyone care? There were a few embarrassed shrugs. "It just seems so far away," Julie Fisher said. "It doesn't affect me personally."

Another student added, "My friends wonder why we should do something for another country when they owe us so much already." That is, everyone else was beholden to the United States and, by and large, ungrateful for our largess. We were clean, off the hook. What I didn't understand was what five-year-old Ethiopians a few days from death were supposed to give us in return.

This was a disturbing echo of a call-in talk show I had done in Los Angeles. I had written a book on Africa that argued the meager cost of a sensible foreign aid policy was nothing compared with the price of Third World turmoil; that we were shockingly selfish was beside the point. A young woman who called in had not read it. "Um, this may sound cruel and everything," she began, "but why should we help those starving Africans? What have they ever done for us?"

I suggested to Willis's class that students might care more about the world if someone could help whet their appetites.

Leo Cook from East Berlin, the one in Pennsylvania, did not agree: "I think you give us too much credit. A whole bunch of us are very secure. We don't want to sacrifice any money out of our pockets to help anyone else."

Someone else continued "Most of our friends are concerned with *Days of Our Lives.* It's just easier to sit in front of the boob tube and eat ice cream and talk on the phone."

Michelle Martin, a freshman from nearby Lowell, rose to that remark. "I have a friend who refuses to watch the news or read a paper. She says that we are in a nuclear age, and it is too much for her to deal with. She would rather escape. Instead, she knows every rock group, every video." Michelle feared that students were hardly more interested in American matters than they were about foreign affairs. In her constitutional law class the professor had mentioned someone named Burger, and she wanted to know who he was. "I asked four people, and no one knew. One said to me, 'What does he sing?' Finally, I found out from a book." He was the chief justice.

At the end I asked the class if they thought their younger brothers and sisters would care more or less about the outside world when they entered college. All twenty agreed: less.

But afterward a handful of students stayed behind to discuss the question. They agreed we were ignoring our responsibilities. We talked about Central America, Afghanistan, the Middle East and, mainly, Africa. Someone suggested the class do something. In a flash, each pledged five dollars, and all were laying plans to raise cash from every student in the country.

This was America at its best. These students saw a problem and instantly banded together to attack it. But this was also America's weakness, the automatic assumption that the solution was money. More, we needed a policy to help eliminate the causes of famine. That required understanding and sustained interest.

I looked at Alexina Hutchins, who had explained that her parents had taught her as a child why the world was important. What advice could she give reporters and writers to make foreign news more appealing, to attract the interest of young people? She thought a minute and gave a hopeless shrug. "Put it in soaps."

Luis Beltran, a Spanish colleague of Willis's, was not surprised by my experience. "At first, Americans didn't talk about Spain," he said with a chuckle. "Now they don't talk about anywhere. They are more involved in their careers. Students want to go to other countries to have fun, to travel, but to learn the language, understand the people, follow events, no."

Almost everything I had seen suggested that conclusion. In Arizona I spoke to a large journalism class about what it was like to be a foreign correspondent. After a few war stories a young woman raised her hand and asked, "Aren't you glad when it's all over you can come home to America where it's safe and free?"

I was, of course. But her manner left no doubt that she was certain America was the only island of democracy left in a hostile world. She seemed unaware that in sixteen healthy democracies in Europe, you don't have to turn around when you hear footsteps behind you. Australia, New Zealand and Japan, among others, had slipped her mind. Canada? Comparative freedom and personal security are tricky concepts to qualify, but a dozen countries could match us, if not comfortably leave us behind.

Instead of answering her, I asked a question: "How many of you think the United States is the freest and most democratic country in the world?" Every hand shot up; no one paused first to think about it.

That night in Bloomington, however, Willis and I went to a funky coffeehouse called the Runcible Spoon. At every table someone was sketching, or diagramming a circuit, or editing a manuscript, or playing chess. We thrashed out the Gaza Strip and then touched on a few other places. After a while a graduate student in geology got up and introduced himself. His name was Myron. "I don't mean to interrupt," he said, "but it is so good to hear people talking about things that are important." With a little encouragement, he went on: "People don't seem to care about anything. They talk about the Broncos or the 'Skins. You just don't hear about what is essential in the world. Sometimes I wonder if there is anyone who cares." For one, there was Myron.

There was also Willis. A culture that can produce a man like him is doing something right. But he was worried about the future. "Raising your voice is a bad thing now," he said. "Confrontation is a bad thing in America. I hate the word 'confrontation.' It only means that you're thinking."

I brought up something I had noticed all over. In a lot of languages you vary the tone and pitch of your voice to make a point. In the United States people tend to snap back, "Don't raise your voice at me."

Willis nodded. "They are so interested in seeing people treated fairly that if they detect one transgression, they've got to get even," he said. "That is how it is. Anytime you mention something twice, they think you're a fanatic. You're not supposed to be involved or passionate. Instead, there is all that suppressed heat, anger."

We were having breakfast with two friends of his, a sculptor and a political scientist. By the time we finished the grapefruit, thoughts were flying so fast I did not manage to put names to the quotes I copied down. It didn't matter. Both said the same thing in different ways. Each was delighted to rail and rant for a change. I just nodded and wrote.

"Everything takes place with a small screen between you and reality. Everything is simplified and dramatized. We have become shockproof so that nothing really reaches us. There has been a devaluation of emotions."

"There is such a bombardment of information. Jerky stuff, in flashes, which causes a dulling of the senses. You stand in a grocery line [and see] all those magazines. Muzak is always going. All the colors and shapes. How much stuff do you have to decipher and knock out of the way?"

Kevin Collins, the political scientist, had a theory: "The problem is the Americans' suspicion of silence, the obsession to fill up every available space with noise. We have lost the empty spaces that are important for assimilation. You know how fruity department store music sounds. But people are comfortable with it. Father knows best. The result is everything remains on the surface. Something must be wonderful or horrible."

Americans make the constant flow of messages into a virtue, Kevin concluded. "You always must be busy. That is the work ethic."

Marc Robarge, the sculptor, picked it up from there. "Sometimes I realize how odd I must look when these people walk by and I'm sitting. I hear them thinking, 'What's this guy doing?' It's only the old people and the crazies who stop and sit. But I need the spaces, and I take them. It is easier in New York than here. With all the other crazies, I feel right at home."

New York was not a lot better. I remembered a remark by Jean-Jacques Sempé, the French cartoonist who often draws covers for *The New Yorker*. He did an occasional series for the magazine that reflected an amused Frenchman's view of America. Except that Sempé was no longer amused and he was not anxious to return.

"There is a certain drying out of America, a loss of the flavor of life, of the things that really matter," he said. "People see things in concrete, business terms, and they reject what has no obvious purpose. It is suspicious just to sit on a park bench and do nothing. For me, I have a great need of things that are useless."

Race came up. Bloomington was one of the many campuses reporting severe racial clashes among students. Berkeley was supposed to be the worst. At the placid University of Michigan at Ann Arbor, violent, hateful incidents had blacks bitter and defensive. It was a full generation since Martin Luther King and the others had broken so much ground. White kids, with no historical sense, couldn't understand why blacks needed a leg up. Blacks, equally removed, tended to take offense quickly.

Often enough, however, there was no subtlety about it. At Bloomington someone burned down a black student's dormitory door. I was surprised, but apparently blacks had caught on to Indiana. "When we try to recruit blacks from the South, we find their perception of Indiana is a rural, southern state, with the attitudes associated with it," a journalism professor told me. True, Martinsville, between Indianapolis and Bloomington, was a cradle of the Klan. For a long time some townsfolk bragged no nigger had ever dented a pillow there and of a black traveling book salesman who once disappeared mysteriously.

This was beginning to get me seriously pissed off. For all the people who weren't racist, of all the various colors, there seemed to be a whole lot of others. In the Midwest, without the basis of social history, prejudice against blacks seemed particularly stupid and selfish. I found black prejudice against whites insulting and narrow-minded. Then there were all the other directions and degrees. At the beginning I took it easy. As an outsider I was reluctant to exaggerate. But I had seen enough. Anyone who denied it couldn't see any better than a Klansman too dumb to cut holes in his sheet.

But this was good old elusive America. Sitting at Willis's breakfast table, I began to feel I was wrapping the ribbon neatly around the society, and the package was unsettling. Less than a day later Andy Lippman took me back half a century to another world entirely.

Andy is the American nice guy, one of those great people given the gift of beaming sunlight. You can dent his smile temporarily with some disturbing thought. Then all the positive mitigating forces rush in, and he is grinning again. He took me up to the rural North, where people are so nice it makes your teeth hurt.

Our headquarters was Jim and Blanche Pressler's bed-and-breakfast at White Pigeon, Michigan, a hard buggy ride from the Indiana Amish country. Three rooms in their home, River Haven, were available to guests. Walls are paneled with embroidered homilies and home truths and some photos of their son who did not make it back from Vietnam. Fluffy pillows and lace are piled on the beds. A No Puffin' sign hangs in the living room, and one assumes automatically that also means "No Cussin'."

"In six years we haven't had a single problem," Jim said. "Once some fellas asked if they could drink beer, and I said all right, but they'd better do it outside the house. So they sat down on the riverbank and had their beer. I offered to take away the empty cans, but they wouldn't hear of it. That's the closest thing to what you might call a problem."

He almost had a second problem with me. I ate so much breakfast—eggs and country meats, flapjacks, fresh and stewed fruits, biscuits, homemade jams and things I couldn't identify—I nearly exploded all over the needlepoint doilies.

River Haven is rich in paintings by Emma Schrock, an Old Order Mennonite who lives with her aged mother and sister near Goshen. Gnomelike, partly crippled, she scuttles about with vigor. At sixty-three she turned out a painting a day, not to speak of cards and prints. A book on Grandma Moses sat on her table. A friend thought it might apply. "I don't think of myself as any Grandma Moses," she said. "But I like her." I asked Emma where she was born. Her eyes narrowed, "Why do you want to know?" I told her. "Oh," she said, eyes now twinkling. "I thought you might be after a story."

Unlike Pennsylvania, Indiana's Amish farmland is wide open, with a minimum of tourists stopping to gawk. Families had made peace with the nuclear age, but they weren't having any of it. Craftsmen operate peacefully in the old way, making quilts and furniture to sell in town.

In a barn full of fine furniture I met a respected elder, a bishop, by the name of Erwin. He was curious about the outside world, although he made it plain he had no use for it. Erwin's English was accented by Amish Dutch, but Europe was a distant blur. "London"—he mused for a moment—"is that in France?" He knew about the Rhine but not the Seine. He listened with rapt attention as I talked about it all.

"What kind of government they got in France?" he asked. "They got a Congress that piddles around, like ours?" Then, on familiar ground, he held forth with an amused smile. "You know, if I wanted to run for President, I would know that every four years someone would stand up and say that everything I had done was no good. They would talk bad of you, no matter who you were or what you did. Who would put up with that?"

I asked him about all young Amish people who worked in nearby camper and trailer plants. Northern Indiana was the RV capital of the world. "Works the other way, too," Erwin said. "Amish boys get out and see how silly some people live. People just get divorced.

They start wondering, Did I marry the right person? Then they go looking. It makes me sick to hear about that kind of thing."

Finally, I asked him about buggies. Did non-Amish people give them trouble. "Why not?" he replied. "Lot of silly people around. Especially if your horse is sort of skittish. They'll just edge over and see if they can't make him a little more skittish. They think it's funny. It's not so funny if you're in the buggy."

Next, I met Annie. Into her nineties, alone in a clapboard shack with an old wood potbelly stove, she is stooped and tiny, a mouse in a nursery rhyme. But Annie was a terror. She arose at 5:00 A.M., stoked the stove and went to work at the massive loom she had bought for five dollars in 1928. She made rugs from old rags. For Annie, it was no hobby.

After her daughter died, Annie had sold the family farm. Her middle-aged son, disabled and disturbed, depended solely on her. Friends helped a little. But she took care of herself. With a strong but shaking hand, she cranked old cloth through a cutting wheel. Then she weaved strips into colorful runners, expertly bordered on her tired old pedal sewing machine. They cost ten dollars. She was just developing another specialty: bright market baskets woven from discarded plastic bread wrappers.

Before leaving, I asked her age. Annie gave me a sly grin. "I don't know," she said, "but my fingers are ninety-one."

Modern times pressed on the Amish, but not too fast. The Shipshewana State Bank had two drive-up windows. But most people preferred to tie up their horse-drawn buggies and walk in. Before leaving, I noticed a small story in a local paper. The Lancaster Amish had won their fight against the road.

I'm not sure that item made the *Budget,* a broadsheet paper published in Ohio to keep Amish and Mennonite communities up on important news. Its rows of unbroken type reported what kinds of pie was served, and what the weather was like, on routine family visits. "I understand Jonas is building kitchen cabinets for the new house at his parents," one item announced. The *Budget* covered farm collapses, too; there wasn't much to say about that. The Amish proved that big was not necessary for survival. My thesis that a democracy needed well-informed citizens seemed to fall apart with the Amish. But not really. A little wisdom wouldn't hurt either.

The Turnleys lived nearby, above Fort Wayne. Peter Turnley, a *Newsweek* photographer, was a friend in Paris, with the perfect attributes for his job: a sweet face and granite balls. Looking at that freckled visage under a halo of reddish curls, you knew nothing could happen to him. Also, you sensed, it if did, he was ready. Peter confirmed my theory that small-town people—whether Hoosiers or Tuaregs—do better in foreign climes because they are more flexible. Big-city street smarts apply mainly to the streets you learn them on.

"There is something about running into a real problem and calling your lawyer in Fort Wayne, and hearing him say, 'Okeydoke,'" Peter said. "You know you're going to be all right."

Peter's parents sold antiques from an overstuffed old house in the woods. Firmly liberal, uncomfortable with the present and worried about the future, they had a real good time anyway. Americans are starting to see the value in their heritage, in old things, both said. They were awaiting evidence. It was Peter, the eternal optimist, who was getting edgy.

He flew into O'Hare and, taking a wrong turn off the freeway, ended up driving ten miles up through South Chicago, probably the most desperate expanse of real estate in America. "I've never seen the poverty in the Soviet Union that I've seen on the South Side of Chicago," he said. "It was as dangerous as anywhere I'd ever been, and that's talking about Libya, Beirut and Iran. I felt more uncomfortable than any foreign danger zone. I was in a foreign country, a complete foreigner simply for being white. It was Sunday, and people were coming out of church; but I still felt the ominous threat."

A friend of ours, listening, told of once starting into South Chicago. He changed his mind when a bullet pierced his car door, just missing him. He called the police, who told him to go to the station if he wanted a report for his insurance. No, he said, there is a sniper shooting at cars. The reply seemed to be, he said, So?

I had been to Chicago a few times in recent years, and I knew my friends were right. Chicago was a city the way Texas was a state: Generalities fitted poorly, and the range was vast. It was no toddling town. Chicago was far more attractive and spacious than its image suggested. France's influential weekly Le Nouvel Observateur headlined an article on Chicago EVEN MORE BEAUTIFUL THAN NEW YORK. Then again, the following pages had a map that situated New Mexico in Arizona.

All in all, the place was great and a lot of fun if you could get the hang of it. The city had long ago outgrown the Al Capone cliché many foreigners still carried in their heads, but it was hard to know what had taken its place. An ominous feeling suggested how much went on below the surface that even a curious visitor would never know. Chicago was a speeded-up microcosm of the Midwest the way New York was of the whole country. It was the capital of a lot of sophisticated or funky things. It was probably the most segregated city in the country. And its politics were like nowhere else. "What is routine, everyday business in Chicago, people go to jail for elsewhere," wrote James Squires, editor of the Chicago *Tribune*.

It would be tough to cut into a few paragraphs. By the time I sat down to write, a fresh batch of Chicago clippings had joined the pile. It was discovered in April 1988 that Steve Cokely, an aide to Mayor Eugene Sawyer, had delivered two years of anti-Semitic lectures to the black Nation of Islam. A Jewish conspiracy planned to rule the world, he said. Particularly, he explained, the AIDS epidemic was the result of Jewish doctors' injecting the AIDS virus into black babies.

In *The New York Times*, a respected Loyola University psychology professor, Eugene Kennedy, observed, "Virulent anti-Semitism has gripped Chicago's black community." He quoted the Roman Catholic priest and writer Andrew Greeley as saying, "If I were Jewish, I would be terrified." He noted that a Holocaust monument and several synagogues in Skokie had been vandalized.

A Chicago *Tribune* poll suggested only 8 percent of the city's blacks thought Cokely should keep his job. But it took Sawyer nearly a week to fire him, and he made it plain he was acting under duress. Cokely linked up with black extremist Louis Farrakhan, who said Jews were upset because "the truth hurts."

To the clamor that he take up the issue, Jesse Jackson replied that he had already spoken out against anti-Semitism. "I don't see anyone holding a press conference condemning Koch," Jackson said. The anti-Semitism was scary enough. If there was little danger of a Nazi majority, it was sickening that a modern American had to fear the horrors he'd fled in a darker world. But here was more evidence of how yet another facet of racism, the multiple standard, was poisoning our society.

New York Mayor Edward Koch disliked Jesse Jackson, and said so, because of past links to Farrakhan, Yasir Arafat and Jackson's own crack about Hymietown. If Koch hated blacks, he did not let on. What connection did Jackson see between a personal opponent and a man who accused a people of murdering black babies? More, why was there no outrage? When Jimmy the Greek made a stupid physiological remark on CBS television about black athletes—one with which a lot of blacks agreed—he was flung off the air for racism. Cokely was nearly a martyr.

My last book was on Africa, and here, back home in America, I was facing the same phenomenon. A white majority was giving blacks an automatic benefit of any doubt, applying separate standards and thus implying they were inferior. That seemed as racist in America as it did to excuse African leaders of corruption and brutality because they were backward subhumans.

Generations of inequality demanded economic considerations, hiring priorities and quotas. But that was a technical adjustment of a socioeconomic balance. On moral and human grounds I had thought all men were created equal. As Sheriff Arnold said in Alabama, all you can do is ensure the opportunity; the rest is up to the individual.

From Fort Wayne I headed back toward Chicago but got only as far as Gary. I still had a lot of America left. Faced with a choice, I wanted to go somewhere I had never been. On Gary's main street, posters reading, "Gary, Something Special," over a rainbow were a tip-off. Some civic-minded people were trying to breathe in new life. But Gary was dying. About the only good news was that closed steel plants reduced the habitual awful stink.

The smell lingered, with enough pollution to discolor your car in minutes. But, as in Gary, West Virginia, things were rough in Gary, Indiana. Unemployment was 17.9 percent. U.S. Steel, which once had jobs for 29,000, was down to 5,000. The city lost a quarter of its population in a decade, dropping to 137,000 inhabitats, 85 percent of them blacks. The unions that had priced themselves into disaster still scared off investment. Not even drug dealers could make a decent living.

Mayor Richard Hatcher's twenty years of iron rule had ended, but no one had any ideas for what to do next. Everyone, on the other hand, knew what was wrong. Gary showed with brutal clarity the impotence of governments in the face of local economic crisis.

"Virtually every federal project that exists has failed in Gary," observed Rich Grey, city editor of the Gary daily, the *Post-Tribune*. "The government, Congress, has no central focus. It was designed for failure." In the booming 1970's, he said, federal money poured in and evaporated. He snorted. "They had job projects teaching people to rake leaves."

Rich, a young black with a master's degree and street smarts, found welfare a disaster. People who didn't need money got it. People who did need it got far too little. And it was set up to force little girls to have children. At last estimate, 60 percent of births in Gary were illegitimate, and 65 percent were to teenage mothers.

"These girls know the only way you're going to have anything for yourself is to have a baby," he said. "They think, 'The only way I can get away from the guy who beats me up every night because he wants my body, or he's frustrated because he can't do any better, is to have a baby.' "

A depressing thought was forming, and Rich read my mind. "These things I've explained to you, everybody understands them, and nobody cares."

Just like foreign aid. If you study it to death, send out the anthropologists, you are doing something. But things were easier to ignore overseas. Again, Rich was ahead of me. "If you don't educate, these people are going to be right next to you."

Schools were the only way to break the cycle. Kids had to learn to handle their own lives before thinking of birth control. They faced a future that looked bleaker by the year. Rich was one of the few young men in town with a job that did not involve fast food, at a minimum wage.

Indiana, he noted, was spending twenty-two hundred dollars a year to educate one child. One prisoner cost the state twenty-eight to thirty thousand dollars a year.

My family, which first settled in Milwaukee, had swallowed a lot of Lake Michigan. During the time I was abroad, that got to be a disgusting thought. Much of the Great Lakes had turned to cesspool. Over the last decade, I learned, the lakes looked and smelled a lot better. But only the marine life that tried to live in them knew what a lasting mess we were making.

Chemical pollution was harrowing, and scientists feared the lakes were merely a microcosm of what we were doing to the oceans. We banned DDT in 1972, and we continued to ship it south. Daily the winds blew back contamination from as far away as South America.

Only slowly were we realizing the earth was a single ecological unit. DDT and PCBs showed up in penguin livers deep in Antarctica. Mysterious fish kills left New Jersey beaches littered. Red tide baffled, and worried, biologists in Maine.

Experts in a dozen countries had warned me that ecological warnings were seldom steady hums that got gradually louder until someone decided to listen. More often you woke up one morning and half the seals in Scandinavia were gasping for life.

In the end, when you capsulize the Midwest, the word is "nice." The people are nice. Unless you're some kind of troublemaker, it is where you are likely to have that nice day.

At a Bob Evans in Indianapolis, a chain restaurant of the good kind, ordering catfish to go was a spiritual thrill. The waitress, named Dana Dobbins, cared about the order. I mean it. She raced around getting it together although no one else was waiting. She stuffed in double tartar sauce. She handed it over with a brilliant smile. Then, with sincerity no one can fake, she said she hoped I'd enjoy it. Hey, I live in France; this was an experience.

Dana, it turned out, had an infant son who stayed with her mother when she worked. They were saving money to start a typing service. Her father had come home from Vietnam on drugs and died when she was nine. Her mother raised five kids, a black family on the good side of town. She paid for food and rent on fifty dollars a week. Could she get help? I asked. "My mother has never been on welfare," she said. But what programs were available? Dana laughed. "I don't know nothin' about welfare." She'd raise her a kid on a salary and love. Nice.

The next time I went back, Bob Evans was jammed for breakfast. I got a table but decided not to wait. Before I could get up, a blinding flash paused long enough to say: "Be with you in a minute, hon. We're short this morning." It was Barbara Jordan, B.J., a grandmother in running shoes, hottest waitress in North Indianapolis.

"I love people," she told me when things calmed down. "This not only pays my bills, it makes my life. In nine years I could count on my hands people in here who could be considered nasty." She worried that people weren't instilling values in their kids. "I believe in correcting discipline, spanking," she said. "The Lord made a place for it, and it's padded. Now it's called child abuse, and I suppose they'd have got me for it; but my kids turned out all right." People thought a lot of B.J. "It's a privilege to come to work," she said, going back to it. Nice. Nice.

But figure out this one.

In Bloomington I went for a drink at Nick's at its craziest time, during a game, but I found a parking space. For Buenos Aires it was big enough for a beer wagon. For Bloomington it was tight. Trying my hand at nice, I gave it great thought. By backing up just to the edge of the depression, I would not block the drive. Or get a ticket. That left enough room for the car in front to get out, just in case the five feet in front of it weren't enough. I got out, surveyed the situation and decided to back up a few inches more. Feeling like a Hoosier, I went inside.

Twenty minutes later I emerged. Someone had scrawled in lipstick across the windshield, in huge, angry red letters, "THANKS!"

Life is like that these days, my psychotherapist friend Barry Goodfield explained later. Stress and frustration build, but it is not acceptable to let it out. Finally, the system has to unload. For that woman, I was the guy who had stood her up or cut her off at the light. Or I was her father. It was anonymity, no confrontation. Had I been there, she might even have been nice. But God help the next guy.

Oklahoma gentlemen check out the hardware at the Tahlequah Gun and Knife Show

Slick's Bar B-Q in Muskogee

Chief Wilma P. Mankiller and her husband, Charley Soap, with the great seal of the Cherokee Nation. Wilma asked to remain seated for the photo; she was in jogging pants.

Butch O'Neal (with all the hair) and Frank James, riding up ahead above Crownpoint on the Navajo Reservation

Peaches Dixon tends his hogs—and his insurance and feed business—on his 720-acre farm near Turney, Missouri. He's proud of the past, of two minds about the present, and uneasy about the future.

Amish farmers waste little gas on errands. This is a crowded parking lot at the Shipshewana, Indiana, bank.

Bobby Plump, who shot the basket heard around the world as depicted in the film *Hoosiers,* lets us know what a Hoosier is. His daughter did the needlepoint.

A small part of a large crowd at final time trials for the Indianapolis 500

In the lot outside Bobby's office, a bumper sticker made the point of Hoosier Hysteria.

Welcome to Detroit. An unidentified but cheerful man stops by the city's trademark monument: Joe Louis's right fist. It is downtown, across from the Renaissance Center.

Graceland, Tennessee. Nonstop visitors peer at the graves of Elvis and his parents in the backyard rotunda, the last stop after rooms full of trophies, jumpsuits, eccentric furnishings, and shag rugs on ceilings.

Paul Pryor, chief breeder at Calumet Farms, encourages Alydar to have a nice day. The horse lost the 1978 Derby to Affirmed, in the next paddock over. But he's worth $60 million anyway.

Some durable housing in Tunica. Sugar Ditch was just behind until it got razed after the glare of publicity.

Schwab in his store on Beale Street. You gotta meet this guy.

Whitefish, Montana: Willie Rice, ready to stop. After forty-three years on the railroad.

This is the bison that nearly ironed me flat. Most Yellowstone visitors have enough brains not to stand in front of him while looking the other way.

A Mainer, or Mainiac as some prefer, speaks his mind on the back of his Chevy.

Portland, Maine, makes room for dogs and travelers. I never figured out what this pleasant stranger planned to do with a million gallons of sesame tahini.

Portland, Oregon: Fenton Eulberg, ready to go. As usual.

Across from the White House, in "Peace Park," William Thomas keeps up his permanent anti-nuclear vigil, with full-time help from his wife, Ellen.

A merrymaker and a Washington, D.C., park police-woman discuss the Fourth of July.

CHAPTER

=== 14 ===

Hoosier Hysteria,
Bluegrass Fever

Back in Tucson, at one of those intellectual soirees where you want
to drown people in their Sancerre spritzers, I got caught between a
magazine subeditor from New York and a local creative writing
teacher. The hostess mentioned what I was doing, and both of them
brightened. "Oh"—one sneered happily—"yet another book about
the United States?" The other wanted specifics. I mentioned Indiana high school basketball. He asked: "What could you possibly write
about Indiana basketball that hasn't already been written?"

Nothing, of course. That was the point. Every American knows
Indiana doctors start newborn infants breathing by hitting them from
fifteen feet with a chest pass. Gene Hackman immortalized the state's
peculiar passion in *Hoosiers*. More recently a national best seller dis-
sected Bobby Knight, who someone had to tell me was the Indiana
University coach.

That was why I was interested. The heaviest missile Knight ever
launched was the chair, flung at a referee. Yet guys like Yegor Li-
gachev, who share in the ability to slam-dunk Indiana halfway to
China, are all but unknown.

At some point we had crossed the line from sports fans to fanat-
ics. Newspapers that carried a column or two of foreign news devoted a dozen pages to sports. I'd planned to weave in sports as I
went along, but I soon discovered the subject had its own language,
literature and lore. For an outsider, America's obsession with sports
was a separate chapter, and there was no better place to get at it
than Hoosier country.

*

The phrase "deafening roar" takes on new meaning in the Bloomington gym when the IU Hoosiers tear the limbs off visitors, five at a time. When the victims are the Purdue Boilermakers, deafening roar is a laughable understatement. As it happened, I was at floor level, just off midcourt, by what is regarded locally as a miracle outshining the Shroud of Turin.

When I landed at Indianapolis, my pal Andy Lippman had exulted into the phone: "Hey, I think I can get you a ticket to the Indiana-Purdue game." My reply, a noncomprehending "Huh?," will be talked about across the state for as long as hoops are nailed to the sides of barns. Within a day strangers would stop me on the street to ask, "Aren't you the guy who didn't want to see the Indiana-Purdue game?"

Among the things I didn't know was that it was the last scramble for the NCAA championships, and Purdue was nearly at the top. The other thing was that tickets to the game were being traded one for one with Gauguin originals.

During my absence abroad I had lost track of basketball. It had been my favorite sport. At the University of Arizona I sat almost alone in a smelly gym watching the Wildcats defeat the Hohum County College Gerbils. Like college baseball, it was just another pastime for the nerds until football season started. Suddenly the Wildcats were about to be national champions in play-offs drawing the kind of attention once reserved for the World Series. And I was catching up, right there in the heart of basketball heaven, within furniture range of Bobby Knight.

You could not miss the mood. Three steps away, a woman who ate sparingly and well did backflips from the shoulders of a muscled male cheerleader. At the first basket an ungodly scream filled the gym. Then it got noisy.

IU led, 33–12, in the first twelve minutes, playing very good ball. But Purdue caught up and, with five minutes left, was out front. IU sank a three-point goal and moved ahead, but then fouled. Purdue missed one shot, then made another. At four minutes it was Purdue, 74–72. IU hit for three to lead, 75–72. But Purdue scored twice and led by a point with less than three minutes to go. No one, I noticed, was leaving the gym.

At 2:04, IU's Dean Garret missed one free throw. Then he made the second: 76–76. Purdue scored three: 76–79. But Garrett went back to the free-throw line. He made one, 77–79. He made another, 78–79. The six-ten center had already scored twenty-nine points, but it was nearly over. With 1:03 left, Garrett missed a lay-up. After a vicious scramble for the rebound Garrett sank a ten-foot turnaround jump. 80–79. Talk about your pandemonium.

In fact, I missed the last four seconds. I had to beat the crowd onto the freeway back up north. Within a few hours Andy was taking me to an Anderson High School game. Indiana-Purdue is one thing. But even with basketballs, Anderson plays hardball.

Getting in was already a triumph. The Anderson Indians' gym, the Wigwam, could hold 8,996 hysterical Hoosiers, but tickets were scarce. Some rural high school gyms had more seats than their towns had people. Twenty-nine Anderson families had kept season tickets for at least fifty years. Louise Greve, in her eighties, was leaving hers to her grandson in her will.

Before the game and at half time the band's swirl of American flags and spray of glitz made that band back in Idaho look like amateurs. Someone read a credo: "I am proud of our past; I am proud of our heritage; I am proud to be an American." Old guys with gnarled faces ignored the cheerleaders' nubile breasts and the kid duded up in feathers. They wanted action.

The Indians came on the floor like an Iranian platoon prepared for martyrdom. Expertly linked plays, unspoken signals and chess-like anticipation of the other team suggested uncounted hours of practice. For someone who did it the old way, some decades ago, it was an amazing sight. I spent a lot of time trying to put it down on paper and finally gave up.

"You just can't get across the feeling to people who haven't grown up there," remarked Peter Turnley, who had. "But when my brother's school got to the state championships, I would get so excited in the end of the games that I couldn't breathe."

Peter had first told me about Hoosier Hysteria. His explanation was as good as any I heard in Indiana: On isolated rural farms, sports, like sex, is what you can do by yourself. It costs nothing to tack a bushel hoop to the barn, and you don't need anyone around to fling a ball at it. A few guys can play pickup basketball. A tiny high school needs only a half dozen kids who can walk and see straight to field a team.

Hoosiers don't compete over many things. The blood lust comes out in basketball. And everyone watches. California, a big basketball state, draws two hundred thousand fans to high school finals. In Indiana, with twenty million fewer people, the crowds topped a million. Cinderella, Indiana style, is an unknown hamlet from the dark side of the state facing the monsters of Muncie Central in the championships. Delirium is what happens when the little guys win. That's what happened with Milan, pronounced *MY-lun*, in 1954.

"Today it is thirty-four years later, and they're still talking about it," said Bobbie Plump, the shy, skinny kid in Gene Hackman's movie who made that last shot heard around the world. Some facts were blurred in *Hoosiers*. The coach was not a has-been making a comeback but a twenty-four-year-old, two years out of college; the town objected to his crazy plan to use a man-to-man defense. But the jump shot that had won the state championship with seconds on the clock, that had been Plump's.

Just as in the movie, Plump had stood with the ball, running out the time. Finally, the coach signaled. Plump made a jump shot from the edge of the free-throw circle. It hit the back of the rim and dropped in. "I knew when it left my hand we had won the game," he said.

"If it wasn't for that, I wouldn't be talking to you today," Plump told me in his insurance agency at the fashionable north end of Indianapolis. He has earned a comfortable living only partly because he is a good insurance man. The truth is, Plump is delighted to admit, people like to talk about that shot. "When I meet someone, they go, 'Plump? Plump? Hey, aren't you . . .' It is amazing, all this time, and people still remember the details of the game."

For Plump, Milan was the big city where you went for a bag of popcorn. It had a thousand inhabitants. He came from Pierceville, population forty-five, the first kid in town ever to play varsity. Plump remembered being too bashful to ask for a second piece of cake at a birthday party. He stammered and retreated from girls. "On the basketball court I wasn't shy," he said. "I could talk to the others as an equal. That's where I was comfortable."

After the historic game, Plump said, he had to give a speech to the Police Athletic League in Indianapolis. He was terrified. His first joke got a laugh, and he was home free. These days he talks a few miles a minute, and his arm shoots out like a striking cobra when there is a hand to shake.

A game ball sits in the corner of his office, along with his black and gold jersey, number 25. His scrapbook is discreetly put away, but he can find it, if asked. The Indianapolis *Star* carried the news in two-inch letters across the top of the front page. There is a photo of the Indianapolis motor cop who escorted the team back to the tiny town, tears streaming down his face. He was so excited he took the team the wrong way around a traffic circle, an unthinkable breach of Midwest order.

Cars parked in cornfields miles from Milan, and the victory party nearly leveled the place. A neighboring fire department had been baby-sitting Milan. Nearly every inhabitant in town had gone north for the championship.

The team has a yearly reunion. "The last few years have really been more enjoyable than when we actually did it," Plump said. "Not many people have the opportunity to relive the greatest moments of their lives."

On the way up, Milan defeated Crispus Attucks, containing a skinny sophomore named Oscar Robertson. Until 1947 Crispus Attucks could only play the state's two other black teams. But Robertson, who virtually defined the dribble, won the prized title of Mr. Basketball and was a three-time All-American at the University of Cincinnati. After him Hoosiers accepted blacks.

More or less. Not long before I got there, the mostly black Evansville Bosse team headed for Heritage Hills in Lincoln City. Just as their bus passed Abe Lincoln's childhood home, a cross burst into flames along the road.

Most blacks live in two of Indiana's ninety-two counties, and finals often start with no black players on the floor. Anderson's team was mixed, but hostility simmered over subtle racism at the school. It was triggered when a player charged that Coach Norm Held had made a racial slur. Nonsense, replied Held's backers. He did not abuse players. That was Bobby Knight.

But then, Plump had told me, basketball was where Indiana farm kids got to know blacks. On the general subject he spilled forth names and numbers, starting with that 1893 game at Crawfordsville, the first outside Massachusetts, where James Naismith had invented the game two years earlier. Naismith came to the Indiana finals in 1925 and couldn't believe where his game had gone. Plump told me about the team that won three championships in a row and ol' Big Shaw who played in the thirties.

I had planned to ask him more about Indiana, but I didn't have to. On his wall was a sign his daughter made, which said it all: HOOSIER. A PERSON BORN OR LIVING IN INDIANA, INDUSTRIOUS, HOSPITABLE,

DOWN-HOME FOLK WHO ENJOY POPCORN, INDIAN SUMMERS, RACE CARS AND BASKETBALL.

Race cars were where I was headed next. But I spent some time reflecting on Hoosier Hysteria. Having looked around the country, I could see that Indiana high school basketball was only an example of a nationwide mania. In Kentucky basketball was hardly less popular. Texas, Oklahoma and Ohio played football for keeps. And so on. It seemed evident that would mean a lot of pressure on coaches, parents and, even more, kids.

As it turns out, I had a high school basketball star in the family. Alec Kay, my sister Jane's son, played for Tucson High School. Since he was only six feet tall and a white guy, you know he had to love the game. That he was an Arizona all-star meant less to him than his reputation as a good sport.

Al was one of those American kids around whom team sports are supposed to be built. You could see it coming. When he was three, I'd toss him pomegranates from the backyard tree, and he would burn them back in a fast-breaking curve. If he dropped an easy one, he didn't whine the way I did. He stopped and puzzled over how he had been holding his fingers. When he played high school and college ball, Al would have rather broken a leg than a rule.

It was with some disgust, therefore, that I heard his briefing on what was going on in school sports in America. Practices varied widely. A lot of teams were scrupulously clean. But no one missed the pressure. If a kid did well in junior high school, the high schools wanted him badly. School district boundaries determined where students went, but flexibility is the American way. Failing all else, a family can always move. That, of course, was nothing compared with competition among universities for high school stars.

A quick glance around brings an uninformed outsider up-to-date. *Sports Illustrated* profiled some guy who bred his son from birth to be a football champion, never letting him near a Big Mac or anyone who might tempt him to waste his vital bodily fluids. There were all sorts of colorful mysteries: Did a thousand dollars in cash drop out of the express envelope from a University of Kentucky basketball coach to some California student who had sent a tryout videotape? Some massive scandals were proved and punished. What worried me most was the pervasive small stuff I heard about from Al and all of the sportswriters I trusted.

It was easy enough for alumni to arrange with a car dealer among their number to find a Corvette no one else was using. Part-time jobs could pay well with few demands. There was always Christmas or, what the hell, a well-placed envelope here and there. Teachers could be prevailed upon to understand priorities. Where there is a will, the list is endless. Obviously this is not universal. But from the evidence it is hardly uncommon.

The aboveboard stuff was bad enough. Someone told me about seeing a junior high football game in which one team seemed older and stronger than the other. Parents there had arranged for their sons to repeat eighth grade so they would reach high school as old pros. It happened at a lot of schools where coaches and principals were happy to go along.

"They're redshirting eighth graders," my informant had said. "Redshirt," I learned, was as American a term as Egg McMuffin. A player, allowed four college seasons, can sit out a year in a red jersey to defer his eligibility. If he sticks around a fifth year, no trick for many athletes, he is a wily veteran in his last season. Though common in college, the practice had found its way down to some junior high schools.

For a correspondent who is only a casual sports fan, there seemed to be some parallels here. In sports the test is supposed to be how you play the game. In the Wide World of Reality the score matters more. We hold an edge because we play a cleaner game. More people line up behind us. But a lot of spectators are beginning to lose their faith in America's fabled sense of fair play and sportsmanship.

When I first went abroad, Americans were widely seen as well-meaning people who learned to do the right thing by playing wholesome games after school. Our various assassination plots and covert meddling were overlooked as aberrations. Since Vietnam, and especially since Central America, that has changed.

You can't take this sort of pop analysis too far. But the lesson is plain. When other societies see American kids corrupted by beer-bellied old farts willing to do anything for a vicarious Friday night thrill, we pay a price.

I thought of this again later, in another way, as the Olympics opened in Seoul. The games had long since lost their ancient purity, but athletes devoted lives to them. One after the other, teams marched in somber decorum, holding their flags proudly aloft. Then the Americans boogied in like the E Street Band. Five athletes wore Mickey Mouse ears. Some held up signs reading, HI NBC, trying to

catch the spotlight. They spilled out of formation, masking the Van-
uatu team, attending its first Olympics.

I could just hear the reaction to criticism that followed. "Vanu-
what?" Alec Kay wouldn't have liked it.

Part of the problem in Seoul was that a lot of American kids grow
up thinking of the world as a huge theme park for their amusement. But then, who could blame anyone for forgetting that some
other cultures regard the Olympic Games with almost sacred rever-
ence? For us, they are a major commercial extravaganza. After the
winter games in Calgary someone complained to his newspaper that
ABC had messed up the "Adlympics" by throwing in all those snatches
of sporting events. I think he was being sarcastic.

I decided not to dig deeply into professional sports. The World Series is not so much different from World Cup soccer except that
only teams from North America get to play in it. As those guys in
Tucson wondered, what could I add to the general knowledge? But
I admired the passion with which other inside outsiders flung themselves into the sports they missed.

Charlie Campbell, the AP news editor in Paris, devoted his vaca-
tions to baseball. He seldom missed spring training in Florida. In
1988 he found a slight change. Harcourt Brace Jovanovich had
bought a faltering amusement park near Orlando. To add to its
allure, the new owners contracted the Kansas City Royals to train
there. But this was big business, and the lawyers stepped up to the
plate. Now large signs and frequent public announcements warn
people in stilted corporatespeak to beware of projectiles and various
objects of the game sailing over the left-field fence.

In Florida each big-league team has a farm team that bears its
name and the name of the town where it spends each spring. The
Montreal Expos, for example, have the West Palm Beach Expos.
There was an exception, Charlie reported. When the Houston Astros moved to Kissimmee, the owners decided to make it the Os-
ceola County Astros.

Technology had muscled in on every facet of sport. They even put
up lights at Wrigley Field, for God's sake. But the instant replay

rule was more than I'd expected even for the technoloonies. Cameras second-guessed the referees. The whole point of sports seemed to be human beings. They drop the ball. They make bad calls. It all works out in the end. If it doesn't, that's how it goes, sports fans. While I passed through, this was a matter of some debate. To an outsider it looked like yet another way to squeeze the juice out of life.

I could see why it was a big issue. It is impossible even for tepid sports fans not to get caught up in such matters, especially the big stuff like the Series, or the Super Bowl, or the Kentucky Derby. No one but Americans can crank up such hype. Every year there is "the game of the century." For weeks in advance, newspapers and newscasts are choked with trivia about players, teams and the cities where they compete. The 1988 Super Bowl, promising moderate excitement, was the "Ultimate Game," prompting former Dallas Cowboy Duane Thomas to ask: "If it's the Ultimate Game, how come they're playing it again next year?"

People talk about little else. Anyone can join with a few snatches of sports talk. Around Super Bowl time, a simple "How 'bout them 'Skins?" would fix me for the afternoon. The World Series is even easier: "Who's startin'?" The Olympics can be trickier, but simply muttering about one nationality or another usually does it.

Each big event is magnetic and addicting. At the Super Bowl there are more cameras than players. And one half of the nation sits in front of a television set. When the postgame flurry subsides, there is something else. All year long. It's enough to take your mind off what Vanna White is wearing.

One extravaganza I knew something about was the Indianapolis 500. My dad was an Indy freak, and so was I; but we never managed to get there. The closest we came was watching Roger McClusky, a Tucsonan like us, on Arizona dirt tracks. On a second brief trip to Indiana I went to the time trials.

The name I remembered most was Wild Bill Vukovich, who won back to back in 1953 and 1954. He was leading in 1955, but his racer cartwheeled over the backstretch wall, and he was decapitated. In 1988 there were two Bill Vukoviches around. I found Bill, Jr., who had retired. But his son had just qualified. I asked how the Indy 500 had changed since the old days.

"If you find a team that wants to hire you, you gotta bring your own money," said the middle Vukovich. Car owners once fought over drivers. Now, as contract employees in a big business, drivers have to hustle a ride. Owners balance their costs with sponsors who might pay $350,000 to stick their names on someone else's glory machine. And drivers break in by bringing along sponsors. "You got a million dollars? You might do it."

Also, Vukovich said, speeds were getting to the limits of human reaction. In his father's last year the record was 140 miles an hour. He broke the 180 mph barrier in 1972. And his son had to compete with speeds of more than 200. "Cars can go faster, maybe," he said, "but drivers can't."

The high costs and corporate overlay have turned racing car drivers into workaday businessmen. Bobby Rahal, who looks like a mild-mannered accountant, carries a briefcase and talks about golf. He just happens to get in a car and drive two hundred miles an hour.

It was something to see. The old wild men who closed the bars with a groupie on each knee were home in the right bed with Ovaltine. Guys tempted to cheat on the road never knew when some minicam might make them as famous as Gary Hart. Drinking was just not 1988 American. There were exceptions. But not many.

Crews are the same. Once four guys were a big team, and they knew about wrenches. Now yup-class engineers by the swarm watch pulsing electrons. Cars cost three hundred thousand dollars and a fragment of a fraction in time is vital. The Penske people can spend forty thousand dollars on uniforms alone.

The smart drivers worked their fame into fortune. A. J. Foyt was back again, at fifty-three with six grandchildren. During his ten thousand miles around the Indy track, he had competed against half the drivers who started in the race's seventy-two-year history. He had won four times in thirty tries. "I don't think the new generation understands how hard racing used to be," he told Steve Herman of the AP. "Now, money buys anything. It's so much easier. It used to be man and machine. If I wanted something, I had to build it."

But now he has the money to buy it. Foyt is a one-man conglomerate, with interests in the largest car dealership in Texas, racehorses, hotels, oil wells, the Houston Astros baseball team and even the largest chain of funeral homes in America.

I made a black-humor remark about that last activity, but Mike Harris, AP's racing maven, set me straight. The last bad year at Indy was 1973. After three days of accidents and death, all the rules changed. Engineers developed fuel cells and self-sealing lines. Drivers sit in space-age safety pods. Freak accidents had killed two drivers since 1973, but mostly, Harris said, "injuries are only crushed limbs."

The year before, Pancho Carter had hit the wall. The car flipped, and Carter slid six hundred feet on his head, with the car on top. No slow thinker, he moved his head from side to side to keep the helmet from wearing away in the same spot. Harris called him to check on his injuries. "Well," he said, "my neck's a little sore." Carter was nothing if not resilient. During the 1988 time trials he ran two cars into the wall, and not long before qualifications ended, he was looking around for another ride.

As I was leaving the track, some drunk kid slammed my car from behind. It was not too serious for me; but he had no driver's license, insurance or registration, and it happened under the nose of a handful of the same Indianapolis cops who had beaten up an AP reporter for sheer meanness in a previous season.

It suddenly occurred to me hardly anyone talked about alcohol. Surveys indicated one high school kid in four had gotten himself, or herself, properly pissed in the recent past. Peer pressure was enormous, kids reported. Drugs were a problem because of the corruption and violence surrounding them. But for sheer human damage, good old legal, plentiful alcohol was worse.

From Indiana I drove south to Kentucky, where I watched a $60 million horse roll in the mud. "He's a real pig," observed his breeder. It seemed a curious way to refer to an animal that earned $350,000 for a roll in the hay. Alydar is the prize stud of Calumet Farm, one of the best and probably the most beautiful racehorse factories in the world. Affirmed, in the next paddock, won the 1978 Kentucky Derby just ahead of Alydar and then took the Triple Crown. But he's not as good a stud.

There are a lot of horse farms around Lexington, in the stunning countryside where the blood is as blue as the grass. From a high knoll Calumet cuts the breath. Its red-trimmed white buildings stretch out of sight, over low hills. Shimmering white wood fences mark out lanes and separate paddocks.

High tech laboratories hide in old wood barns. Under one roof is a giant horse Jacuzzi.

The chief breeder, a young Kentuckian named Paul Pryor, explained how it all works. A mare that comes calling is showered and led into a teaser corral to exchange glances with the stallion. She is taken to a breeding barn where grooms strap a thick leather pad across her mane and back. Alydar is a rough breeder. Pryor let me figure out the rest. I didn't see any tapes of Ravel's *Bolero* lying around, but I think I got it.

In the barn next door I read the little brass plaques of horses that had waited their turn: Whirlaway, Citation, Forward Pass. The list went on.

At thirteen, Alydar might breed for another decade. That is a lot of costly horseflesh. In 1985 the Keeneland auction sold an untested yearling—Seattle Dancer, out of Nijinsky II and My Charmer—for $13.1 million. Calumet has six other studs. Altogether, fifty-five thousand foals a year are sired in North America.

The Lexington area is as rich and lush as America gets, with fine old traditions and white-bearded colonels who wouldn't be caught dead frying chicken. The land reminded me of the most beautiful parts of Europe. Feeling caught somewhere between outside and inside, I took a drive around the neighborhood, from Versailles to Paris.

Versailles, pronounced *Ver-SALES,* is a gleaming white relic of the Old South, complete with church steeples, a brick courthouse and storefronts built when people still believed in real wood. Flowering plants and weathered walls suggested a permanence that was rare in America. It was lunchtime, and I was sure I would find an old kitchen whose staff knew all about gravy.

I asked a young motel clerk where to eat. "You want to sit down?" she asked. It was true. Versailles, like the nation around it, ate junk on plastic. The drive to Paris involved a bit of freeway, as it did in France, but the farms and funky old villages were pure Kentucky. Midway is a double row of 1800's buildings along the tracks on Railroad Street, preserved by owners who treasure them. I felt a warm rush at finding such old-style beauty, so unlike any other part of the world. The scale seemed right in Kentucky.

At Paris I stopped for gas. I mentioned to the young man at the pump where I lived. He was polite but a little puzzled. Where? It was only natural. Not many Frenchmen knew about Paris, Kentucky, either.

But the world was moving in on rural Kentucky. Up a road called Cherry Blossom Lane, near where Americans made horses, the Japanese were making Toyotas. The name came from a local contest, and someone had suggested Oh, What a Feeling Road.

I was in a Ford, and in a hurry. On a four-lane rural road I got behind a woman going well under the limit. Her huge station wagon was full of kids climbing over the seats. She clung resolutely to the left-hand lane, and I didn't want to pass on the right. I beeped gently, afraid to frighten or infuriate her. I flashed my lights and pulled up close before dropping back. Finally, she moved to the right, glared at me and shot back to the fast lane ahead of the impatient guy behind me.

This stuff happened so often I got to dreading American roads. On freeways with four lanes going in the same direction, people moved slowly, side by side to the left, leaving the inside lanes empty. Faster drivers simply shot past on the right, endangering the lane blockers as much as themselves. I tried the European tricks—blinking to the left and flashing—but more often than not this prompted the guy ahead to punish me.

Eventually passing, I studied the drivers' faces. A few were obvious creeps, doing it on purpose. Mostly they seemed to be good old folks who had never been told anyone else used the road. Occasionally I thought about calling one of those 800 numbers that public relations people paint on trucks so you can hassle their drivers. But I wasn't interested in visiting on anyone the wrath of corporate martial law. I just wanted to know what people were thinking.

I had seen one driver headed to Chicago who left no doubt. His bumper sticker said, DON'T LIKE MY DRIVING? CALL 800-EAT-SHIT.

This was Kentucky, and I wanted to see more horses. At Keeneland, just outside Lexington, I talked about racing with the spokesman, Jim Williams. The game was changing fast, he said. For one thing, yearlings brought more realistic prices. Auction sales were $336.3 million at Keeneland in 1987, down 25 percent from 1984. "We're seeing some Japanese now," he added.

But racing has gone electronic. Keeneland ran 144 races a year, but intertrack racing beamed video relays from the "host plant." People somewhere else entirely could bet by computer.

The term "host plant" seemed jarring for Keeneland, a prewar track of surpassing elegance. Its clubhouse floor bore faint traces of all the bourbon sloshed over in high anxiety. Down below, ladies' rooms were marked in gallant gilt lettering. The snack bar, built in a time when food was a minor issue, was tucked discreetly out of the way. The deep green shrubs spelled "Keeneland" in well-clipped letters.

In the end, of course, it was horses, not moneymen, that decided. At Indianapolis, at the Olympics and in the big leagues of every other sport, men were finding ways to shave time. New techniques and training moved inexorably forward, and the record books were reedited at a steady pace. But not with horses.

Tracks could be made faster, Williams said, but not without risking injuries. But all the money at stake, and the hoo-ha and hype about the races of the century, did not translate to the animals. They ran by nature. It was exhilarating, and purebred racehorses loved it. Still, they had a limit. Winning could mean only so much. What would they do with more oats or a gold-plated stall?

That, I think, is what is meant by horse sense.

CHAPTER

═══ 15 ═══

Motown to Graceland

"Detroit is a great place to be from," said comedian Jango Edwards, in Europe at the time, when I asked about his hometown. "But not so great to be at." Never having been there, I suspected Detroit was the real heart of America. Or at least some vital organ farther down. It had gotten such a bad rap that it must have something. In any case, I had to go see it. Nothing has shaped America more than the automobile, unless maybe it was Gladys Knight and the Pips. That was all Motor City.

Once in Detroit, I couldn't leave. Clearly most of its reputation was well deserved. White and black people wantonly trashed one of the nation's finest old cities, by neglect, bad planning and violent upheaval, leaving much of it shards and moonscape. Human and material wreckage is staggering. But there are rich pockets of things that can only be Detroit. An indefinable spirit exudes. Detroit is as bad and as good as America gets.

I met a burly Irish priest named Bill Cunningham, a sort of Jimmy Breslin with good teeth, who runs a volunteer group called Focus:HOPE. His unruly gray mane and a booming laugh suggest a tinge of biblical blarney, but he looked hard at reality in Detroit.

"This is the stage, right here," he said, stabbing a meaty forefinger out the window. "We have the greatest confluence of conflicting forces outside the Middle East. If you can do something in Detroit, you can do it anywhere. If you can do it elsewhere and can't do it in Detroit, it doesn't matter anyway." Social upheaval and economic distress are what fire the blood, he said. "La Jolla is not the hotbed of cultural development; it's the graveyard. The cutting edge is not in Lakeland, Florida, sitting around the pool talking about laxatives. Here we've got a revolution."

The word "revolution" has taken on a moldy tinge, like "fantastic" or "special" or "wonderful" with a lingering accent on the "wonnn." But Father Cunningham was not messing with hyperbole. He meant revolution.

The line between the First and Third World, often subtle in America, is razor sharp in Motor City. If you go north along the Detroit River to where the city meets Grosse Pointe Park, you can stand with one foot in Swaziland and the other in Switzerland. To the north, lush lawns spread between fine old brick homes. Prowl cars cruise the clean streets; pink-cheeked mothers push prams down the sidewalks. To the south, garbage-strewn empty lots separate collapsing buildings bearing faded signs reading ALABAMA-STYLE CHICKEN and MISSION BAPTIST CHURCH. Abruptly people change color.

It is the same downtown. Renaissance Center, an ambitious piece of high tech urban architecture, soars over the Detroit River. Private investors built it as a means to pump new life into the city center. But it is an island of hotel rooms and offices, surrounded by a moat of approach ramps and parking lots. Across a wide street the real Detroit begins. The first thing a visitor notices is a mammoth black iron fist suspended on chains. Only later, if you stick around to find out, do you learn it is the city's monument to Joe Louis.

Downtown is a forbidding forest of largely abandoned buildings where few white folks venture after dark. Detroit's two lively newspapers have not abandoned their respective homes at the heart of the city. But for many people in the richer suburbs, even daylight is not enough safety. I heard people living only minutes away brag that they had not been to Detroit in years.

But that was the point. You could look at the deserted twenty-five-story building that housed the J. L. Hudson Company, once the world's tallest department store and the toniest emporium between the coasts. Or you could notice people's little gardens poking up colorfully among the rubble.

The night I arrived, I wanted to see *Colors,* Dennis Hopper's film on L. A. gangs. When I showed a white reporter friend the paper and asked where the theater was, he blanched. "You don't want to go there." A half dozen people had the same reaction. It is in Grand Circle Park, the Times Square of Detroit. It seemed an appropriate place to see *Colors*, I decided, so I went. How bad could it be?

Except for my own apprehension, it was not bad at all. Since I had been so assiduously warned, my antennae were bristling. But the audience, mostly young couples, seemed far less aware than I was that I was the sole white. No one mugged me or offered me drugs. The only rowdy person was a towering black cop who seemed to be staggering slightly as he made a few rounds of the darkened cinema. He paused a long while near a nice-looking woman. "What do you want to see this for?" he asked, in slurred words. His voice boomed across the theater louder than the actors' voices. "It's dumb. That guy gets killed, and . . ." In a tidy thirty-second review, he dissolved all suspense in the movie, which had just begun.

The next day I mentioned the experience to Bob McCabe, the charm-steeped director of Renaissance Center; he is a passionate booster of downtown Detroit. Of course, it wasn't bad, he said. I should have gone to On Stage, a hot new restaurant in the same building as the theater, run by a foresighted white guy with faith in the place. Let us be honest, however. There is crime in that area, and a guy could get hurt if he handled himself wrong.

That was a pattern I had seen often, if nowhere as bad as Detroit. We are talking class, not race. It is just that in America race and class are often the same thing. The more privileged levels decide an area of town is dangerous, and few dare go there. The area then loses whatever chance it had of recovering, and progressively, it gets much more dangerous than it was to begin with.

It is a serious problem. Except for guys writing books or retarded liberals, who wants to make the effort? We are not a particularly adventuresome people, whatever we like to think. Face it, a lot of us are chickenshit. The average young couple on a night out, given the choice between Grosse Pointe and Grand Circle Park, does not ponder long. If it is like that for a lousy movie, imagine buying a house, picking a school or opening a business.

But that is what is so singular about Detroit. Late one afternoon David Lawrence, Jr., publisher of the Detroit *Free Press*, piled me into a car and instructed me to keep my eyes open. In Palmer Woods we saw the handsome houses and sculpted hedges of wealthy blacks, indistinguishable from those of white neighbors. We made a three-minute raid into one of the world's more beautiful restaurant interiors, at the Whitney House, in a restored mansion not far from the riot debris. In that grim wasteland near Grosse Pointe Park, we passed Indian Village, an island of affluence inhabited jointly by blacks and whites. More precisely, relative affluence. A $65,000 Indian Village home might cost $350,000 a few blocks to the north, across the border.

The point was not that some blacks have money. It is that in Detroit you never know what is around the corner. A lot of wealthy blacks move away as fast as possible. On Elijah Muhammad Avenue, where the tanks rolled down to Central High School during the 1967 riots, I passed the church where Aretha Franklin's father preached. But Aretha lived in Bloomfield Hills, even farther out than Grosse Pointe.

The person who told me about the Franklins used a tone of voice I'd come to recognize. It said: And how much do blacks do for their brethren once they arrive? That always seemed to be odd reasoning. A lot of blacks did feel some social responsibility to their race. That struck me as a noble stance. But why should it be demanded? Skin color was a pretty weak affinity as a basis for blunting one's own aspirations. I did not notice many whites offering their guest rooms to homeless people of their race.

One curious juxtaposition is the funky little house on West Grand Boulevard near General Motors, across from Ford Hospital. A large sign out front reads HITSVILLE U.S.A. It symbolizes as vital a part of Detroit as the neighboring buildings. The house is where Berry Gordy started Motown Records.

Back in the early 1950's Detroit pulsed with the music that came North with the people who migrated up to make cars. Gordy fitted the old blues with V-8 Hydraglide and heavy-duty shocks. He borrowed eight hundred dollars from his family, and the rest is history.

Gordy had a good ear and an uncanny sense. One day some people brought in a ten-year-old blind piano player named Steve. The master listened a moment and exclaimed: "That kid's a wonder." Kevin Lowery, the manager, took me to Studio A, the tiny room where it all happened. From behind a Stone Age three-track mixing board, I looked through a window at a battery of boom mikes on floor stands. Then I walked into the Room.

In the corner some kid's playhouse partitions made an echo chamber near a little white piano. Cheap acoustical tile peeled off the ceiling. Mostly I looked at the floor. The wooden planks were scuffed from the shoes that had stomped and shuffled on them. I tried to picture the shoes' owners: the Temptations and the Jackson Five, Marvin Gaye, Martha and the Vandellas, Stevie Wonder, Smokey Robinson, the Supremes, Gladys Knight, the Four Tops.

My spine tingled, hard, as if I'd been shocked, and Kevin chuckled. "Everyone does that," he said. "People from everywhere. Europe, China. It gets 'em all."

By then Motown had long since taken its recording facilities out to Los Angeles. Afterward I heard Gordy sold the company to MCA. Detroit lagged far behind New York as a music center and competed with Minneapolis and even Muscle Shoals, Alabama. Of the old bunch, only the Four Tops were still around town, and they recorded elsewhere. But a stroll around the museum, with a look at the familiar album covers and the walls full of gold and platinum records, is balm to the believer. You can build all the churches you want. There is only one Jerusalem.

Over at United Sound Studios I just missed the Four Tops. We were supposed to meet, but they finished up early and blew town. It worked like that with new technology, explained Mike Iacopelle, the chief engineer. "At Motown everybody was in the room at the same time, and at the end of the day you had a record or you didn't," he said. "The vocalist had to be good enough to do it without any humongous mistakes. With multitracks, we can add it all later. Instead of the interaction of many, you have the interaction of one."

He said the Four Tops' recording sounded great, but it was headed back to Los Angeles to have the music stripped off and put back on. "People get in love with that," Iacopelle said. "Instead of being used for a guy who's good to touch up details, it's used for someone mediocre to get something acceptable." Electronic percussion replaces real people, and the result is nearly perfect technically. But that was the problem. "It's those minute little changes that make the feel," Mike said, snapping his fingers to initiate them. "Human imperfection."

The next day I met Cincinnati Milacron. Cincinnati made Cadillacs at General Motors' Orion plant. One hell of a worker: never missed a weld, never called in sick, had no union card, skipped lunch breaks and never, ever talked back to a foreman. About the only thing Cincinnati didn't do was join the bowling league. Robots can never get their fingers in the holes.

Every car off the Orion line had five thousand body welds, and robots were doing 87 percent of them. But there were other jobs for humans. The Orion plant, north of Detroit, covers 77 acres under a single roof. My directions to the public relations office began: "Go long that wall to column A-40 . . ." We are talking 3.9 million square feet, with 32 miles of overhead tracks for moving components and a 32-mile-long assembly line.

In just under a minute a new Cadillac Fleetwood or DeVille, or an Oldsmobile 98, rolls off the line. Each car has been thirty-eight hours in the making. And it is all American.

How long does it take to make a BMW? I asked my guide.

"Gee, I don't know," she said, genuinely puzzled. "That's not a GM product."

You couldn't blame her. Although General Motors makes five basic flavors of car, the combined options work out to one trillion different mutations. Detroit had come a long way since Henry Ford offered buyers any color they wanted as long as it was black.

When I visited, Orion employed sixty-one hundred people on two shifts, and they made $13 to $15 an hour. Benefits were calculated at another $10 an hour. Germans, Italians and Japanese made more, but Koreans earned $2.50 an hour. GM workers knocked off half an hour for lunch and got two weeks, or four weeks, of annual vacation. Otherwise, they went about their precise jobs with single-minded attention. The United Auto Workers union was not showing too much muscle. Most people seemed damned happy to have a job.

Afterward I went back down to West Grand and talked to George Eads, the company's chief economist. I asked if what was good for General Motors was still good for the country. Eads winced; it was a lower blow than I had meant. GM had just laid off forty thousand workers and was fighting hard. Other U.S. automakers were struggling, as well, for obvious reasons. Foreigners made good cars, well suited to the market.

Eads replied, "We must recognize that GM as a company is not automatically dominant in the American auto industry. We have to work for every sale and every part of the share. For us, that's a very big change." Basically, he said, U.S. automakers had realized that they had to provide quality. "The quality, reliability, of our cars has got to be as good as anybody else's. We can do better."

I appreciated his honesty. But that seemed like a curious admission for an industry that had been in business for most of the century. Out West I'd spoken to a GM dealer who grumbled: "They just get sloppier, with engineering faults our own shop could fix." A patriotic executive remarked: "You can say all you want about yuppies and status; I drive a BMW because we don't make anything near as good."

Over the course of my reporting, I'd rented every make of car Detroit produced. Most were comfortable enough. But except perhaps for the Thunderbird Turbo, I found nothing I wouldn't just as soon lose in quicksand. And the other Fords were the worst of the lot. Overseas hardly anyone wants a Detroit car, except for oil sheikhs, who favor Cadillacs. They are too big for most cities' streets. There is no service. And they just don't stand up to the competition. The Japanese, when rich enough for luxury cars, lean toward German sedans. Even in what ought to be preferential markets, Detroit lags behind. Later, during a ten-day trip to Central America, about the only American four-wheel-drive vehicle I noticed was a stalled Cherokee I had to help push up a hill. In El Salvador, American reporters favored Russian jeeps. Overall our deficit on cars and trucks was forty-five billion dollars, more than twice the amount of surplus for aircraft.

True, U.S. companies make cars abroad few Americans would recognize. Joint production and mixed management have befuddled the old lines. And foreign automakers have come to the United States. "It is hard to know whether Honda is American or Japanese," Eads said. "It is high-quality automobile. Its young, flexible, highly skilled labor force is managed extremely efficiently. The ticket of admission is to do as well as a firm like Honda."

He explained the background: "Exporting abroad is a fairly new phenomenon for Americans. During the thirties, forties and fifties our cars in assembly plants abroad were simple knockdowns. The notion of designing for export, of tailoring for export, is not something U.S. producers thought about. This country absorbed the production. I think the industry should have paid more attention to the world."

The western General Motors dealer had said, "Detroit couldn't make a good car, that's all. For a while they were playing the shirt label game, taking Japanese cars and putting their name on it. And I had to sell those turds. Maybe now they'll catch on."

*

In Japan, where leaders have paid attention to the world since Admiral Perry kicked in their door, they know whether Honda is American or Japanese. The issue is not emotional, nationalistic or racial. It is a matter of payment balances, economic wherewithal and, eventually, security. Free trade works fine when everyone's rules are the same. But the disadvantage is that the guy with the inferior product loses.

Department of Defense figures for 1987 showed Japanese plants could get hold of new machine tools up to five times faster than U.S. plants. In the United States ten times as many electronic components had to be sent back on production lines.

And in our obsession with Japan, we had hardly noticed that Western Europe had agreed to abolish all internal economic barriers, forming a bloc even more substantial than the United States or Japan.

The Honda solution, bringing production to America, addresses only part of the problem. Maybe, as Isuzu advertises, its cars are domestic if the jobs are held by Americans. But what is good for Isuzu is not necessarily good for America.

Washington, Eads noted, shot Detroit in the kneecaps. About the time Japan started to expand, federal authorities decided to regulate the automobile. Japan could start from scratch, while Detroit engineers were tied up redesigning cars to tight specifications for fuel economy, emissions and safety. Consumer advocates had a reply: Why wasn't that already done? The arguments were endless. But what it all meant to the worker was clear. Complexity edged out unskilled labor.

"If you consider what each company is expecting in a new worker," Eads said, "that rules out the notion that you go up to the factory gate and say, 'Do you have a job?' We are treating people like college applicants, putting them through a battery of tests. This must be quite a shock for out-of-work Detroit autoworkers. There is tremendous pressure on this country's educational system in all areas. If you want to pay these kinds of wages, you want to have an output that can pay for these kinds of skills."

Even more, he concluded, that is what all American manufacturers face. They will have to rethink and retool. "We've got to develop the techniques that allow us to afford to pay the kinds of wages that our workers expect."

*

And this is where Father Cunningham comes in. He has watched industry around Detroit roll over people, and he is worried about the bigger picture.

Focus:HOPE's volunteer work in the inner city was linked tightly to the auto industry and foreign trade. For Cunningham and everyone else I talked to on the subject, the key was jobs. Welfare, if a last-ditch safety net, did nothing for anyone's dignity. Nor did it fill up anyone's day or offer challenges or a fresh set of friends and role models. People needed jobs.

Under the new rules, however, job candidates not only had to read and think but also had to have enough discipline and self-esteem to show up on time. In vast tracts of America's cities young people did not qualify. It didn't matter whose fault it was; eventually everyone in the nation would feel a piece of their frustration.

After decades of experience Cunningham saw an infernal cycle. Kids born to mothers who could not start them out right were sent to schools that could not handle them. "If there was ever a desultory, despondent group, it is Detroit's teachers," he said. "A survey I saw found thirty-eight percent of them would leave their jobs tomorrow if they could get another job somewhere else. Thirty-eight percent! That is burnout." And then, if students manage to emerge educated and free from drugs, they face the real problems.

"There are tremendous inequalities that are part of a racist society that is fundamentally hypocritical," Cunningham said. "America's ideals are unimpeachable, but the performance is a violation. America doesn't really do what it says it is going to. The woman in the harbor, and all that. Our goal is to take those broken promises and convert them into honest aspirations, to find out where the promises were broken and assume the goodwill of people to make good on it."

Cunningham believes in the classic Greek sense of discipline. You have to perceive what is needed and then set about doing it. Hope is in the biblical sense, a contract, not a wish: You do this; I'll do that. No exceptions, nothing for free. In job training sessions there are no excuses for absence, not even nuclear attack. "We work among high school graduates who are seventy percent on the street, no college, no jobs. We take four hundred and fifty people who have only the whisper of a possibility of a Wendy's job. We get them, for example, jobs in banks. The banks know we are going to give them workers who can shake hands, look people in the eye, can spell, show up on time, drug-free. They're happy to pay six dollars and ten cents an hour."

At the machinists' training center I met Gino Highsmith, the director, a black engineer who had given up a job paying far more. He was turning out skilled people and getting them jobs. But he agreed that the only real solution was for authorities to get the basic problems in hand, starting with drugs. "When I was a kid, we had parks and schools had evening hours for recreation," he said. "Now everything is locked up. You get these kids with nothing to do, watching guys make two hundred dollars a day. You think they're going to join the labor force?"

Kids need values, he said. "It's got to be the parents who teach them, but what do you do with kids from broken homes?" This was getting to be a depressing nationwide chorus. "You've got babies having babies. How do you give them values? If not the home, school or church, they pick them up from the streets. We've let the street replace the school."

I was beginning to get the message about the underclass in America. Rich Grey from Gary came to mind. The point was not whether we richer people wanted to come up with solutions. It was when we would realize there was no choice. One way or the other, it seemed plain as glass, we'd be hearing more on this subject.

Back at the center Cunningham laughed at the turbulence around him. "This is like Creation. It is Genesis revisited. The process is as important as the schedule and outline. This isn't hope, like I hope the Tigers are gonna win next week. The alchemy of it is that Focus:HOPE means a contract to work toward something."

In the end he gets back to jobs. Cincinnati Milacron is not the threat, he insists. He boomed with laughter about a robotics demonstration he had just seen. In the first room the tip dropped off a robot's arm before it got to work. "Oh, shit," the engineer said; no one could fix it. Some foul-up forced cancellation of the second display. The group moved on to the last room, and a guy met them at the door, stammering: "Ah, I don't think you should go in there."

What lacks is quality and flexibility. "Our stuff doesn't have to be proven. We just make more firecrackers in the closet that never have to work," he said. "Reagan represents an attitude of defensiveness. Of holding on. I saw this picture of an Oriental kid who had just gotten beat in a fight. He had a big smile on his face. 'Ahh, someone has a better way.' Why don't we get excited that there's a better way? This new fear of risk? That's what life is all about. If you're not taking a risk, you're not alive."

From the city that put the world on wheels, this was tough stuff. In my mind, the word "ingenuity" had always been prefaced by "American." Risk was the American way. But this silver-tongued Irish priest was on the button. What I had seen abroad, he had seen at home. "We either come to grips with our dishonesty and mediocrity," he concluded, "or we're out of business. Everyone will be making Wendys in the year 2000."

This, I knew, was sensitive ground. Every time I turned on the television set, Bob Hope was pointing to a "Made in U.S.A." label in his shirt, reminding people that we still manufactured things. If that helped the balance of payments, it was probably money well spent. But it was some spectacle for outsiders. It always made me think of those small African embassies with dusty glass display cases of corned beef and matches, evidence of their national production.

Father Cunningham's partner is Eleanor Josaitis, a mother and comfortable housewife who twenty years earlier decided someone had to help. She organized a vast feeding program. It was limited to pregnant women until a woman on the phone, after listening to the rules, said: "I'm seventy-two years old. Do I have to be pregnant to get food?" Eleanor added 29,000 old people to the list. She set up Focus:HOPE's day-care center, among other projects, and supervises 450 volunteers. She knows what she is up against. "I'm about as close to Mary Poppins as you will ever see in your life," she said. "But this is a burden."

Before accomplishing anything, Eleanor said, people had to break the pattern of fear. "If a twenty-two-year-old woman in the suburbs picks up the paper and sees seven more teenagers killed, you can talk until you are blue in the face," she said. "To her, the whole world is coming to an end. She would no more go down there than . . ." She didn't have to finish. "Gangs are real in this town, and they're drug-related."

A person a day is killed in Detroit. A lot of murders are among friends, Detroit boosters point out, but dead is dead. Most kids who have a choice can't wait to get away. Those who stay figure things out fast.

"I can sit in front of a TV set and, in a few minutes, see the answer to any problem is a handgun," Eleanor said. "You, Mr. Electronic Media, are establishing my honor system for me. A little old lady doesn't mean a thing to me. I'll hit her upside the head same as anyone else. I can flip around and get all the blood, guts, sex and gore I want. In an hour's time I can be MacGyver and solve all the world's problems with a little glue. Why should I have to sit in a classroom?"

Her fight is to break fixed ideas. "If I don't know anything about you, I'm going to carry my preconceived notions," she said. "But take that twenty-two-year-old girl. What's in it for her? She has no stake in understanding anyone else's culture."

I had heard something similar in almost every city I had visited, but this time it sank in. Detroit was the big league. I hoped like hell it wasn't a glimpse of the future.

Focus: HOPE's logo is two interwined hands, one black and one white. "They are reaching to each other," Eleanor told me. "I am not naive enough to think they clasp."

In *Beverly Hills Cop* the writer who had Eddie Murphy's Axel Foley come from Detroit knew what he was writing about. Detroit cops are a breed apart. In a year four officers were murdered while doing their jobs. And as with any other collection of humans, the pressure produces extreme—and vastly varied—responses.

One morning I heard some great Motown sounds echoing up the atrium of a new midtown mall. Blue lights flashed on the glass. The Detroit cops were out recruiting. A happy crowd had gathered to watch. A Lionel Ritchie sound-alike, in official blue, sang with the Police Band. Smiling cops sat kids down in the front seats of cruisers parked on the tiled mall. An officer next to me, with a Polish name on his tag, grinned at the spectacle. Are you happy in the force? I asked.

"Sure," he said, "why not?" He clearly meant it; his was an elite fraternity, like the French Foreign Legion.

But cops around Detroit ought to be reminding us all of how far we have come from that friendly old patrolman twirling a nightstick on a neighborhood beat. The Turnleys know.

Peter Turnley's twin brother, David, had spent two and a half years as a photographer in South Africa for the Detroit *Free Press*. Among blacks especially, he was a local hero. I was with him during some of his reportages. We watched South African cops grab people arbitrarily and fling them against cars. We saw police pin back arms and jam metal cuffs on twisted wrists. Finally, he was thrown out, and he went back to Detroit.

David and Peter were driving through Grosse Pointe when a police car skidded around them and forced them to the curb. Cops raced to the car, hands on guns, and pulled David to the street. Exactly as in South Africa, his arms were wrenched up behind him and clapped in irons. David was taken to the station, and Peter followed in their car. During booking, a black cop noticed David's name. "Hey, I liked your pictures," he said, apparently missing the irony in the painful handcuffs he made no move to release.

David Turnley, police revealed, had an eighteen-month-old unpaid parking ticket. He had forgotten about it while working abroad. The story might have gotten even worse. But Peter noticed the arresting officers had neglected to read David his rights. Both went home. It wasn't South Africa after all. Only close.

Everything about Detroit seems to offer extremes, spiritual highs and stabs of anguish. For all the urban squalor, there are art museums to rival any city. Concerts and festivals draw huge happy crowds to the center of town. Nearly everyone, rich and poor, loves the Tigers.

At Dearborn, south of Detroit, Henry Ford's old estate is a terrific museum. Apart from antique vehicles and contraptions, fine glass and objets d'art and transplanted structures such as Thomas Edison's home workshop, there is an exhibit on the automobile and American culture.

I watched a film of people trying out their first cars. Excited couples in motoring clothes loaded hampers into rumble seats and headed out for adventure. In those days anything might lie ahead. A bridge might wash out. A wheel might fall off. Or they might have the time of their lives. I could feel their exhilaration. The thrill of it all was the surprise they knew lay ahead.

Afterward I saw the motel exhibit. There was a perfect replica of a room in the first Holiday Inn, from the 1950's. It was a breakthrough, the chain motel. American travelers could know in advance exactly what awaited them at the end of the day. The chain's slogan: "The Best Surprise Is No Surprise."

The exhibit also duplicated an early Texaco gas station from the days when new companies struggled to create images instantly recognizable to fast-moving motorists. There was that classic streamlined red Texaco tanker, with the funny finned tail. When I was a kid, one of those stations sat in the corner of Broadway and Alvernon. Ads said, "You can trust your car to the man who wears the star," and I'd think of John and A.J. I could picture Irving Texaco sitting somewhere at the end of the day, counting his money, and I was happy he had a few bucks of mine.

Ah, life was so simple then. Ben Zarda in Kansas City was right about brands. Corporate raids, sell-offs and buy-outs, multibillion-dollar lawsuits left the consumer in impotent puzzlement. You could no longer be sure if it was Westinghouse; you couldn't even be sure what Westinghouse was. But the new plunderers bought up the old familiarity.

The Texaco wars made less sense than the Iran-Iraq conflict. Texaco took over Getty. As a result, it paid three billion dollars, more than the gross national product of Nicaragua, to settle a lawsuit by Pennzoil. Then it really got confusing. They still try to tell me to trust my car to the man who wears the star. And I think, Horseshit. It could be Carl Icahn.

More competition for good jobs, and the threat of layoffs, had given executives enormous power over workers. Such invasions of privacy as drug tests, computer monitoring, lie detector examinations and even genetic screening for susceptibility to illness were hard to refuse.

About now I was feeling like Dr. Doom. Were so many things wrong at home? I'd seen a lot of good things I wasn't mentioning. There was Baltimore: The whole clapped-out downtown district of a moldering city had been brought back to vibrant life. I would not make it to Pittsburgh, but everything I read suggested rebirth. From a smelling, gray city where the river caught fire, it had moved to the top of Rand McNally's most livable cities list. Every society had inequities and iniquities, unemployment, poverty and racism.

But some things were different in America. Our crime was worse than anyone's. We did a lot less than most for the underclass. Employers were allowed more liberties with workers' lives than in almost any other industrialized country.

And a few basics stood out. I had seen most of the world. Nowhere, in the First, Second or Third World, were there so many kids who would sooner go to school without their shoes than their knives. Nowhere did I see so many preteens who knew more about small automatic weapons than I did, and I was a war correspondent. And nowhere, except possibly in South Africa, did I find so many members of the privileged classes unaware of the realities of poorer ones. This was not naysaying. It was only reporting.

I gave the last word in Detroit to Mell Ackerman, whose husband, Hank, had worked with me in Argentina. Hank had since been AP bureau chief in Cleveland and New Orleans. Now, in Detroit, Mell and Hank and their son and daughter were just emerging from culture shock. Mell is solid upper-end America. Educated and concerned, she grew up in northern Florida but had seen the world. A good mother and friend, she worried about what was ahead for everyone. She saw what I did and was deeply troubled by it. I asked if she was able to stay close enough to events to try to influence them. Mell glanced around the kitchen and gave a helpless shrug. "I can't even keep up with the laundry."

But then Mell was doing better than the woman I saw quoted in a local inquiring reporter column. She was asked, "What do you think of Manuel Noriega?" Her reply: "I don't think much of it."

The Tennessee Mission Baptist Church fits right into the slums of North Detroit. The sounds that Berry Gordy packaged had been the marching music of generations of poor southerners who drifted north back in the days when people still hired them to make cars. Having seen Detroit, I went to Memphis.

There are those who would argue that Memphis is the capital of the United States. What is a capital, after all, but the place where the King lives? The King is dead, of course. But there are also those who would argue with that. In the curious currents of celebrity in America, the handsome and thriving old Mississippi River port of Memphis has become an insignificant suburb of a place known as Graceland, Tennessee.

I've got to admit, before digging into Memphis, I followed the crowds up Elvis Presley Boulevard to Graceland. As might be expected, it is a hallowed shrine only on those few days a year when the faithful make their pilgrimage to commemorate the King's death. The rest of the year people in funny clothes come to gawk and giggle because it is a famous place.

On my tour of Elvis's home, studio and grave, I met an Australian lawyer. She was already a little shell-shocked from her American visit. On her first day, in California, she told a man she was a solicitor. He leered happily and reached for his wallet. "What incredibly bad taste," she said, louder at every room. By the time we got to the jungle salon, all animal skins and shiny wood carvings with greenish shag on the ceiling, all she could say was "Coorrr."

I wanted to agree with her, but I felt a little dirty. Elvis definitely would not have wanted me there snickering at his stuff. I sure as hell wouldn't if I were Elvis. The question arose, of course: Who was selling those double-digit tickets and running six hundred thousand people a year across the road in shuttle buses? Elvis had died with scarcely more than two million dollars in the bank. In death, he was a fifty-million-dollar corporation.

Smart businessmen had come in and junked those tinny dangling Elvis earrings. Souvenirs were the finest in Taiwanese class: baked ceramic tiles, with Elvis's signature under a red rose; mugs that said, "Graceland: Been there, Seen that." There was a twenty-minute video, for a slight supplement. You could walk through TCB, the velvet plush little airliner that bore the initials of the King's words to live by: taking care of business.

We walked among the gold records and sparkling jump suits. And walked, and walked. There were a lot of both. Above all, the Elvis corporation offered the grave, an impressive slab of concrete in a little shrine-courtyard at the end of the Graceland tour. It was all the more impressive when I picked up a weekly paper that assured me he wasn't in it. Elvis had been sighted peeling grapes in a Turkish seraglio or some such.

"The Elvis industry," observed a *Wall Street Journal* feature on it, "is like the universe: large, not fully understood, and expanding." The occasion was about a lawsuit over panties with Elvis's face painted on them. A British entrepreneur, who had run for Parliament as a member of the Elvis Presley party, felt the King belonged to his people. Jack Soden, who ran Elvis Presley Enterprises, Inc., argued that a dead celebrity's "right of publicity" came with the estate.

The corporation sued a best man at Elvis's wedding who wanted to sell some home movies. An Arkansas restaurateur, member of twenty-three Elvis fan clubs, was threatened over a collection of videotapes he sold on the side. "You don't sue fans for selling and trading," he told the *Journal*. Soden argued that most fans understood; it was all for Elvis's daughter, Lisa Marie, who would inherit the estate when she turned twenty-five in 1993.

By the time I reached Graceland, I had assembled enough background to write the four millionth Elvis book. Michael Jackson would have to duplicate the sales of *Thriller* every year for three decades to match the King's 1.2 billion record sales. But, as with Indiana basketball, what could I add? There was that gushing five-part series in France's hot daily *Libération*. A *USA Today* poll sometime back found nearly three times more people answered "Elvis" than "Bruce Springsteen" to the question "Who's the greatest rocker of all time?"

But a dip into Graceland, a visit to the steakhouse with grimy vinyl booths where Elvis was at home, a look at the three single-spaced legal-size pages of drugs he was taking when he died were enough to convince me. I liked his music. But where do we ever stop? Mike Zwerin, the master of music who writes from Paris, struck the note in the *International Herald Tribune:* "Put me in the arena with hungry lions if you wish, but Elvis is—along with stretched Cadillacs, daytime quiz shows and the Beatles' song 'Revolution' advertising sneakers—a key symbol of sleaze."

In downtown Memphis, Jacqueline Smith was afraid the same thing was going to happen to the Lorraine Motel, where Martin Luther King was assassinated in 1968. She was evicted from the closed-down motel in early 1988. When I met her, she was camped on the street outside. The state of Tennessee planned to convert the motel into a $8.8 million civil rights museum, which she thought would exploit King's memory.

"They've just taken the Lorraine from the people," she said, charging that black middlemen had made a deal with state authorities without consulting the community. "People raised a hundred forty-four thousand dollars to save the motel," she said, "and those lawyers have no more right to it than the little girl who gave three pennies from her piggy bank."

According to Smith, the motel would be turned into "a high tech tourist trap" that concentrated on the murder, complete with a laser beam to track the path of the fatal bullet. Instead, she said, the aging motel should be listed on the National Register of Historic Places, preserved as it is with federal funds. The state's $8.8 million could help the poor, whom Dr. King championed.

"You look at Graceland," she said, volunteering a comparison. "Elvis was a very private person. All those people coming in and making fun of his stuff, his furniture. But that was his taste. Onstage he belonged to us. But he deserved his own privacy."

*

Beale Street, in the heart of real Memphis, has been plasticized and sanitized for tourists. The city put forty million dollars into reviving the old back street where W. C. Handy played the blues that found their way to Detroit. The B. B. in B. B. King came from Beale Street Blues Boy; nobody coming to Memphis missed the place. It edged toward dereliction, however, and town fathers thought they'd spruce up their golden goose. It didn't work. Some flashy bars were fun, and the music could be good, but it was not Beale Street. There was only A. Schwab.

I walked into the seventy-seven-year-old building, past the tables of union suits with buttoned flaps and enameled chamber pots, to an ancient cash register in the back. A beaming, balding grandfather came forward and seized my hand. "Are you related to me?" he asked. I said I didn't think so, but we checked. Abe Schwab pulled down two enormous, heavy ledgers, and we poured over the three thousand names, mine not included, carefully entered in his own hand.

Schwab's business was preserving his family's 112-year-old tradition of supplying Beale Street with whatever it needed. His life centered on trying to find out who was in that family. The combination was about as heartwarming an experience as a returning lost American might encounter.

From the dingy basement full of antique scales and displays, to the top floor, with buttonhooks and buckles and bolts of cloth no one has seen in years, it is a working museum. In modern America the idea of merchandising is turnover; if something doesn't move, get rid of it. "We don't see it that way," Abe said, chuckling. "If we don't sell it, it ain't goin' nowhere. It's not hurting anybody. We work against the computer."

It takes three weeks to do the inventory. On the various creaking wooden floors, they've got sixty kinds of suspenders, not counting different colors. There is Leatherette at $2.49 a yard, 89-cent Lover's Moon perfume, and size 74 overalls. The "voodoo section" has herbs and magic creams.

Abe's father, to his last days, stood by the door to make sure every customer who went in came out with what he wanted. The family's reputation is such that not many people walk out with things no one noticed they took.

Still more fascinating were his lost scrolls of Israel, great tables and trees reaching from not too long after Adam to his own name and that of his wife, whom he called Dirty Gertie. His son, Elliott, was on the page and also standing by the cash register. He often slept in the attic, with his snake.

"It's a detective story, and you're the main character," Abe said, explaining why he spends three to four hours a day at it. "And it's fun. You find out things you're not supposed to know."

. Just then Jacob Goldsmith came in. The Goldsmiths had been friendly competitors with the Schwabs for a century but had finally sold out to a chain. Jacob had brought in his great-grandfather's naturalization papers, signed by Hamilton Fish back before photographs. Instead, it noted: "Nose: Rather pointed. Mouth: Small. Chin: Oval."

A lot of Memphis history was lost last century when doctors traced a yellow fever epidemic to paper. Almost everything written was burned. But some of it was found in Schwab's junk downstairs. "I'll bet I'm the only Jew in town with a Catholic baptismal font." Likely.

Abe was nearing sixty-five, and I asked if he planned to retire. He seemed shocked. "You don't retire," he said.

And I asked him about Graceland. Elvis had been a regular on Beale Street, Abe said. That was where he got his early music. Sometimes he came in the store, but Abe did not pretend to remember much about him. Graceland, he acknowledged, was not part of Memphis. "We have people come in and ask what sort of Elvis souvenirs we have," he said. "We say we don't have any, and they'll just turn and walk out."

I made another inspiring stop, farther into the rough part of Memphis. Alma Lovett had set up a volunteer day-care center, not only to baby-sit for working mothers but also to help them equip their kids for a better life. Her theme was restoring pride. If women could work, they could regain control of their lives.

"You're on your own with a job," she said. "You don't have to spill out your guts for your $121, $159 welfare check. I was a mother at fourteen, on welfare, and I'm bitterly against young mothers getting welfare checks."

Better housing was essential, she added. "Once you move into this public housing, you lose all self-respect. If you cannot live in dignity, you will not make it."

I was not surprised to learn her nemesis was drugs. "You lose kids between the ages of nine and ten if you're not real careful," she said. "You have to keep talking, keep them interested in something besides the street. By stealing from stores, robbing pocketbooks, they graduate."

Alma dropped out of ninth grade, and she struggled until age forty-three to get her graduate degree in business administration. Rather than take a job, she decided to help the community. I detected the note of rue I had heard in Detroit, from Eleanor Josaitis. She was nearly alone, with limited support and few volunteers. Public money was scarce. Many black leaders forgot the community once they left it. Alma gave me a variation on the bucket of crabs that David Dunbar had used to describe Indian bickering. "These leaders, they're just like a bunch of crawfish in a bucket," she said. "It's hard to get anything done."

In Memphis, Woody Baird showed me a pre-Christmas piece he had written for the AP about a family in the poorest county in the United States. They lived in Sugar Ditch, in Tunica, Mississippi.

Sugar Ditch was a disgusting little slum. It was named for an open sewer that carried a dark sludge that was not sugar. Woody had found Jearleen Simmons and interviewed one of her daughters. She badly wanted a doll. He asked what kind. She carefully unfolded a tattered advertisement and pointed to a Cabbage Patch. Woody wrote it, and two things happened: Jearleen's daughter received offers of Cabbage Patch dolls from twenty-three people, including a Texan who volunteered to fly one in by helicopter; and Tunica razed Sugar Ditch, moving a handful of families to a row of trailers at the edge of town. That's about it.

Tunica is a small town at the top of Mississippi, somewhere between Memphis and the Middle Ages. Poverty is hard to measure, but the figures put it right down at the bottom. Except for some temporary field work and the odd salaried job, there's not much but retail business and welfare. If blacks had achieved equality, no one had told Tunica.

Jearleen helped lead a struggle to call national attention to the town. She focused on housing but also on the daily discrimination that made black lives' miserable. Cameras came down, along with Jesse Jackson, and the point was made. But her kids were hungry as ever. Having won her battle, she was a refugee of the war. The day I met her, she was packed to follow the well-posted trail up north.

"The whole nation knows what we're going through," she said. "But if you can't defeat these white people, you better just shoot your brains out, cuz they got you."

Jearleen got a trailer with the others, but it burned down in an electrical storm. She rented a room downtown, but she said the owner evicted her as a troublemaker. He peeked out the door as I interviewed her, and his truck was parked out front. When I went to talk with him, his assistant told me he had left town. Jearleen moved in with friends, but everyone knew her. With a family to feed, she thought she would try Milwaukee. She was leaving that night at nine-fifteen. "I don't want to live in hell and go die and live in hell," she said. "I'm not going to let them downgrade me."

She hoped she could find a neighborhood free of drugs. "There's so much drugs here, you see 'em selling on the street corners," she said. "Wide open. There's no police, just men in uniform."

This was likely my last hard look at poverty in America, and Jearleen was an enthusiastic guide. An unlikely firebrand, she tended to roly-poly, with a merry laugh. She was smart as hell, without much education, and articulate once you got your Mississippi down. She had nothing against whites in general or even the men in Tunica who wore bed linen on dark nights. She just wanted a break.

Why, I asked her, did she have nine kids? Jearleen giggled, a little embarrassed. A few were accidents. But she had tried all sorts of birth control. Her last child was born in spite of a loop. I had wondered about that in other places. For some reason, birth control works better for rich folks. She had the kids, for whatever reason, and she was going to see they grew up as free, functioning Americans.

Two sons were with her husband, who was in college in Cleveland. She thought they'd do well.

We went down to the vast empty lot that had been Sugar Ditch. Just off the canal, now covered over, was where her house stood.

"We had so many cockroaches I had to put cotton in my kids' ears to keep them out," she said. "If I bought a bag of potatoes, I'd have to throw most of it out because of the cockroaches. Some man sprayed, and we took out a ten pound bucket of cockroaches. They came right back. We had wasps, snakes. The smell of that ditch, I had nightmares. I came close to committing suicide."

A high fence masked Sugar Ditch, and residents of the former slum gave it symbolism. "I heard some white man say they put it up so they didn't have to see those nigger faces," Jearleen said. "I'm telling you, there is slavery, right here in Tunica today."

There is not slavery, one can argue firmly, and Jearleen likely would admit to speaking figuratively. But that's what she meant, and many blacks agreed. A lot of Tunica blacks were former laborers turned out of nearby farms, too old or sick to work. What they saw related closely to how they imagined life was like before the Civil War. Never mind the facts. That was chilling.

With the publicity, people offered to take care of her children. "No matter how bad," she said, "I'm never giving up a child of mine."

That struck me as something the social analyses tend to leave out. Babies were having babies. A lot of young women couldn't take care of their kids. A few didn't want them. But what about the rest? If you strip away class and color and circumstance, what is really the difference between a hungry little Mississippi girl and a Texas girl who falls down a well?

The question is rhetorical; I know the answers. Whenever I asked, people would give me a hundred reasons invoking sociology, economics and psychology. At the very bottom I wondered what really was the difference. Maybe she shouldn't have been born, just as Jessica McClure wasn't supposed to fall into a pipe. But both circumstances happened. Is it the immediacy of danger and the drama? A whole childhood of desperation seemed dangerous and dramatic enough to me.

A review of Jonathan Kozol's *Rachel and Her Children,* about poor children in America, criticized a lecturing tone. "Self-righteous" is not an attractive adjective. But again I thought of Rich Grey. If we all knew about these problems, why weren't we doing something more? There are a lot of reasons. And most of them tend to dim the glow of the image we hold of ourselves.

There was a happier side. Downtown a young white store clerk exemplified a hopeful kind of southerner. You could tell by the way he handled himself that equality was not an issue. His first friends were black, and he saw faces rather than colors. He did not dispute Jearleen's view of Tunica, but he saw it as a part of vanishing mentality.

He worked with a young black woman of immaculate manner, the sort of polished person who, if Tunica bigots used the language of the old Congo Belgians, would be considered "evolved." She was great, directing ironic barbs at issues Jearleen hammered with a skillet. She fitted right in, clearly no one's slave, and looked every customer of any color straight in the eye.

I asked if things were changing for her generation, with new opportunities for education, different attitudes. I laid it on, expecting an answer to balance what I had heard in Jearleen's circle. She laughed a little, none too gaily, and shrugged. "No. Not really."

CHAPTER

═ 16 ═

Portland to Portland: Last Frontiers

In most outsiders' picture of the United States, the top part sort of peters out somewhere above a line between San Francisco and Boston. It is all mainly rainfall and Canada. I puzzled over a northern itinerary on a map in Paris when my pal Ed Cody walked in. My finger was in Oregon, and I asked him if he knew anything about the place. "Sure do," Cody said. "In fact, my uncle just shot my mother's washing machine in Portland." I put Cody's uncle on my schedule.

Except for my being born there, my contact with the northern reaches was rather thin. I left Milwaukee at the age of three and only went back for a few visits, all a long time ago. I'd spent a day in Seattle, long enough to see there was more than rain. But Montana, the Dakotas and Minnesota, not to speak of Maine, were all virgin ground to me.

The northern route was Jim Landis's idea. He had a theory: People along the top tend to feel forgotten, unappreciated and out of the main current. He's from Massachusetts and, worse, my editor; what did he know? Then I watched news film of Minnesota Twins fans celebrating the World Series victory.

Even allowing a certain leeway for American exuberance, it was an amazing sight. Great geysers of joy surpassed anything related to baseball. One ecstatic young man yelled into the camera: "After all those years of coming in behind, Humphrey, Mondale, we're on top." I got out the atlas.

Cody's uncle is Fenton Eulberg. At eighty, he wore his long snowy hair in a frontier flip. Trim and lithe, in faded Levi's, he looked as if he spent each winter on a trail bike looking for minerals in the Arizona desert, which was what he did. In Portland, when he was not off hunting deer or messing with his cabin on the coast, he split logs for exercise. They are probably not making any more Fenton Eulbergs.

"There ain't too much adventure left in the States," he said. "You think you find a new place, and then there's gum wrappers. The country's getting old." Was he getting old?

"Naw, I'm not slowing down any," he said, showing me the battered red Volkswagen camper he was outfitting for his next expedition. "Well, sometimes I get a little tired, walking." I asked if it was tough to be a Fenton Eulberg in modern America. "Not really," he said. "But you gotta watch them prospectors that live alone up in the hills. They get loony, start imagining things. You gotta yell a little before you come up on 'em."

Fenton never did much school, and he flipped through the newspaper only occasionally. But he knew all politicians were a bunch of conniving scoundrels. "I guess us and the country got to learn things the hard way every time," he said. "But I can't change things." He took a little TV hunting to watch the news, but not much else. "The best program, it's one word," he said. "Can you figure it out?" *Cheers?* "That's it. She was good."

Fenton never married. "When I found a woman I thought I could live with, she didn't want to live with me." He laughed. "I could still fool with a woman, but I wouldn't want to with one my age."

He rousted around at different things, usually around timber camps. He tried driving a truck. "I didn't know one end from the other," Fenton said. "When I backed it up into a building, they handed me a shovel."

For a while he raised dogs. His prize, a German shepherd bitch named Tanya, got loose one night and mated with a boxer. Cody got the result, Chinook, which looked like a bear and dented up the three cars that subsequently ran into him. Finally, ol' Chinook chased some farmer's sheep for evening sport. The sheep dropped dead of a heart attack, and the farmer shot the dog. Cody became a foreign correspondent. Fenton, meanwhile, had bought a boat he called the *Red Herring* and had gone off salmon fishing for twenty years.

That was Fenton's last career, fishing. He lived alone on the boat and supported himself well enough. During occasional hard times he came ashore and worked as a millwright, fixing saw equipment. Then he got sick at sea. "I just cracked up," he said. "Pushed myself too hard. You know how the nerves bunch up here?" He patted his solar plexus. "They just let go." He lay two days on the deck until he gathered enough strength to crawl to the radio. He retired and moved in with his sister, Cody's mom.

Fenton treasures his old stuff, steering clear of flashy new gear. But he had 1988 down pat. When he offered me coffee, I expected boiled grounds in a blackened pot. I got instant crystals in a microwave. Once Cody's wife made a sauce, and he complimented her on it: "This is as good as those fancy sauces your professional chefs make for the frozen dinners."

Sometimes he misses the old days. He has outlived most of his friends. He told me about two huge, husky guys who had once gotten him out of trouble. "I saw one awhile back, and he was this shriveled-up old man," Fenton said. "Kind of send shivers down your spine. Some were hard drinkers; some didn't drink. They still died."

He misses the old values. "We're born honest and taught deceit," he said. "I never locked my car or the door to my house. Now, God almighty." When he was fishing, buyers would just hand over cash at the beginning of the season. "They don't do that anymore." And generally, things are getting complicated. "I never get lost out in the desert, the mountains. Can't get lost. But I get myself lost in one of these supermarkets."

Still, he has his pleasures. An agnostic, he likes baiting the proselytizers. "You kind of egg 'em on, and then, when they get that fire in their eye, you back off a little." And he loves heading down the highway, sleeping wherever he cares to stop.

His winter trips are plotted like military campaigns. He haunts the libraries in search of old maps or other clues to lost mines. Fenton's trail bike is fitted with a special scabbard for his trusty 30.06. That was the rifle that bagged the washer, by accident. It was a gut shot, however, and damage was slight.

Portland was one of those fabulous stops. I'd seen enough elsewhere to make me apprehensive about where we all were headed.

What I hoped for, at the end, was more signs of strength. Surely, little clusters of people were generating warmth to keep the pot boiling until American society listed back toward a more generous spirit. I'd found some. But where else? In the Rimsky-Korsakov, for one.

The R-K was where I found John Nance, a long-lost friend and colleague from Asia. John was the first reporter to visit that tiny Stone Age tribe in the Philippines, and he wrote about them in *The Gentle Tasaday.* He messed around with television and other such craziness. Then he settled comfortably into Portland. I hadn't visited him in seven years, and I wondered, vaguely, if I'd find another couch rutabaga. Not hardly.

John was making a low-pitched living by helping people see around problems. He was steeped in friends who loved him, and he found some time to write. He had the intelligent traveler's ability to fit geopolitical problems into a human context. We stayed up most of one night reviewing the world's existential crises, especially those to which Americans contributed most heavily.

We started talking at the R-K, an old-shoe coffeehouse with a table that revolves sneakily on unsuspecting patrons and a life-size Erik Satie passed out in the bathroom, *Vanity Fair,* in his lap. The owner is Goodie Cable, who also runs the Sylvia Beach Hotel on the coast for people who never want to leave.

"I thought my whole generation had sold out until I opened the hotel," Goodie said. "Then all these people came out of nowhere. We talk all night, about ideas, art, music. Finally, I'm not alone in the world. It's the sort of building where when you walk in the door, it throws its arms around you." She was leaning toward purple and knew it. Goodie loved the role: Auntie Mame, by Proust.

A 1:00 A.M. river cruise did not materialize, so we moved to John's kitchen. "What the Tasaday do is show us ourselves, stripped of all the things we take for granted," he said. "What if you had never seen your own hairdo? How many months does someone spend looking in a mirror?"

Sometimes John took his Tasaday pictures to inner-city schools. The kids inspired and scared him. "They're just doing what was done to them," he said. "Once I asked, 'How many of you girls worry about rape?' All but one raised their hands. Three kids had their heads down. I questioned one. Some men had picked up her grandmother and raped her. The next day they found her in the trunk of a car, stripped."

I told John what Father Cunningham had said in Detroit: A poll found 38 percent of urban schoolteachers there would quit the next day if they could find other jobs. "Talk about a group of dispirited, disheartened people," he had said. I filled him in on Rich Grey in Gary and Jearleen Simmons in Tunica. None of it surprised him. He had been an inside outsider for a decade now.

By 4:00 A.M. we had finished the chunky-style peanut butter and the last of America's problems. It seemed pretty dark to me. John got that look, the kind that makes you understand how we all manage to keep moving forward. "All you can do," he said, "is look at the hope." Words to live by, if I ever heard any.

The next day we went to Powell's, a bookstore that covers an entire block. Its million volumes occupied the old premises of a car dealership. There were books on damn near every subject in the world, and *somebody* was reading them.

John had a lunch date, and I went off on the great salmon adventure. It was Sunday in Portland, and most restaurants were closed. I craved fresh salmon. I tried the dark wood dining room of the Benson Hotel, the nicely kept landmark of a city that cares about itself. It was late, and the menu was all sandwiches. The maître d' took one look at my crushed expression and left me no time to plead or bribe. "I'll see what I can do, sir," he said. Shortly thereafter I dived into the poached salmon filet of a lifetime.

From Portland I took the Empire Builder east to Montana. Few enough trains were left in America, and I'd whooped with joy at discovering it. It was one of those double-deckers, like a London bus with beds. The old brick station had been left intact. The tracks would follow the Columbia River all the way up into Washington, and I'd wake up in the foothills west of Glacier National Park. My childhood came rushing back: The porter was black; the conductor, with a spade beard and suspenders, yelled, "All aboooooard!"; the woman in the next compartment was older than I was.

I had bought my ticket from a tight-lipped young man whose fingers danced deftly over the computer keyboard. European sleeping arrangements vary widely, and I had a question: Was my two-berth compartment single occupancy? "You mean, are we going to put anyone else in?" He looked stunned. "Heavens!" His face rippled with distaste. "Oh, right," he went on. "We're going to throw a three-hundred-fifty pound fat lady at you. Don't make me shudder!"

For a few hours I clacked along in luxuriant splendor, not anxious to leave the cocoon of my compartment, which I had puffed happily full of pipe smoke. A vague discomfort nagged at me. This was a train. Paul Theroux owned trains. Screw it, this was America. Let him sue me.

Back in the bar car, alone at a large table, I found a graying black porter gazing into a Styrofoam coffee cup, oblivious of the beautiful scene outside. "Some river," I observed, sitting down. That was hardly a cut above "Hot enough for you?," but it got us started.

"Huh? What?" replied Willie Rice, looking up. "Oh, I wouldn't even have noticed if you hadn't said anything. Seen it so many times." He had been making the run from Portland to his home in St. Paul for forty-three years. He was planning to retire just as soon as he won a lottery big enough to land him in the luxury to which he was ready to become accustomed.

"I think I'll get me a Rolls-Royce," Willie said. "What do you think?" Definitely, a Rolls-Royce, I said. And a driver. "Oh, yeah," he said. "A driver, for sure."

Willie was not greedy, but he was no fool. He had paid his dues, and he knew it. These days his train is labeled Amtrak, but he has lugged trunks and folded linen for a string of proprietors. "A little while back we went to this three-day meeting to teach us how to do our jobs," he said, with a snort of mild contempt. "This executive tells us that we have the most important job on the railroad because we're the ones who meet the people. So I said, 'If we're the most important ones, how come we're the lowest paid?'" He slapped his knee and chuckled.

Not that Willie didn't like his work. "I seen it all," he agreed, prompted slightly. "Whoo-ee, the stories I could tell! Like about the Vice President and the prostitute. [He did not say which of either.] This certain Vice President picked himself up a prostitute and kept her in his compartment. But she didn't know who it was. Too bad, cuz she could've made some real money."

He has changed sheets for damn near every great person of his time, he figured, but the most impressive was Elvis. "The word went on down the line, and every place we stopped, the people mobbed the train," Willie said, beaming with pleasure at old memories. "Them girls threw themselves at the cars, tried to break the windows to get at him. I've never seen anything like it. It ain't like that anymore. No one has time for the train."

*

The nation's 233,000-mile rail network is only two thirds of what it was when Willie first went to work. Fast trains link Washington to New York and Boston. A few old long lines are maintained, along with a grid of intercity connections. Those still in use are in shaky condition. "Some are all right, and some are terrible," observed a salty old trainman aboard the Empire Builder. The old Soo Line between Chicago and Milwaukee is a mess. On another stretch, trains have to slow down twenty-six times between a couple of points that are not very far apart.

But a lot of the roadbeds that had tamed America were turning into jogging paths and hiking trails. The old train depots, stately temples of transportation, were being cleared away for parking space or converted into restaurants with fancy gold lettering on the windows. In places like Kansas City and Minneapolis, proud trains now skulked into town and stopped at nasty little mobile-home stations.

Food service was usually cold cuts and plywood bread on a squeaky plastic tray wrapped in cellophane. You stood in line to get it unless, in first class, someone slung it at you on the fly. Nicer trains do better than that. But Willie knew what it could be like. So did I. "In the old days you ate off a plate. The pies and bread were baked on board. Tablecloth, fresh peaches, demitasse, cut flowers on the table." His eyes misted at the flowers. "It ain't near the same. But you take these youngsters that grow up today. The only thing they know is this." Back then, Willie said, the railroad had a waiter for every six people. In modern dining cars, it is at best one per twenty.

For someone coming from Europe, all this was a shock. There dependable, frequent service links the smallest of cities, with every class of service from cheap to wildly extravagant. Our excuse, that America is too big for trains, falls away with a simple glance. France's TGV gets you from Paris to Marseilles in five hours. That is as far as from Washington to Boston. If you add up the time lost waiting for delayed planes and lost bags, railroads start to look better. But time is not necessarily of the essence. Do you really have to be there for a hamburger lunch? Wouldn't you rather sip champagne on a Chopin Express from Warsaw to Vienna?

The real problem seems to be that we are too self-indulgent for mass transportation. Worse, we are too ethnocentric to realize how much better Europeans are at self-indulgence.

*

Besides Willie, I met a riveter named Saundra on her way home to Montana. Sometime back, Saundra had settled into a well-paying job as a lab technician in California. But it was California. She moved to Kalispell, Montana, to work a shift, making metal boxes. When the train reached Whitefish, I saw why. If you've got the bent for Montana, there's no place like it. In Texas, Molly Ivins had observed: "People here are always talking about our big sky. They don't stop to think that is because there are no trees." Montana has trees with its big sky.

Infused with the spirit, I imagined myself a gentleman from Kalispell. Resourceful and tough, but chivalrous. Picture my delight at spotting a frail frontier lady in obvious distress, struggling with the hood of her Toyota pickup. Can I help? I asked. "It's all right," she said. She had just freed the catch and raised the hood with one arm while fishing for the supporting rod with the other. I started to hold the hood for her, but her hand snaked out to replace mine. "Excuse me!" she said, in a tone as close to "Fuck off!" as a frail frontier lady gets.

It had been awhile since I had thought of Henry James, but that encounter brought back a passage I had copied down:

> No impression so promptly assaults the arriving visitor of the United States as that of the overwhelming preponderance, wherever he turns and twists, of the unmitigated "business man" face ranging through its various possibilities, its extraordinary actualities, of intensity. And I speak of facial cast and expression alone, leaving out of account the questions of voice, tone, utterance and attitude.
>
> Nothing, meanwhile, is more concomitantly striking than the fact that the women, over the land—allowing for every element of exception—appear to be of a markedly finer texture than the men, and that one of the livelier signs of this difference is precisely in their less narrowly specialized, their less commercialized, distinctly more generalized, physiognomic character.

For the first part, ol' Henry was never closer to the mark. He wrote that on his day's equivalent to the shuttle flight from New York to Washington; he likely would have seen something different in Big Sky country. But today, even up North, the male visage was shaped largely by unmitigated business.

The female physiognomy, however, had split sharply in several directions since James's time. A wide segment had taken that "business person" face to chilling extremes. These women, dressed for success, emerged purposefully from power coffee breaks and strode off to fire the packaging department. Another group shunned the trappings of ladyhood and stood squarely on an equal footing with men. They celebrated womanhood, enjoying the odd girlish whimsy (not sexist: as in boyish grin). But you had to keep it straight, or you'd get brained with a tire iron.

This is not, one hastens to add, an exhaustive description of the modern American woman. Nor is it an invidious comparison with European women. But a strange trait marbles sectors of female society. Some permit themselves to address perfect strangers in a manner that invites a fat lip in the courtly Old World.

On a recent flight my assigned seat put me on the aisle; an empty space separated me from the woman at the window. She had stuffed the vicinity with a knapsack, two book bags, a large purse and an awkward object that Austrian security agents would have exploded on sight. She wore tightly laced sneakers, and her hair was pulled back tightly in a bun. Her lips were drawn. Tight. She withdrew her nose from a summer thriller, glanced at my carry-on bag and snapped: "They're not going to let you leave that there." I slipped the bag overhead, as I'd planned to do without counseling, and dropped some papers on the empty seat. She sniffed, tightly, and asked: "Why don't you find a seat where there is more room?"

In Bigfork, however, I was home. I had seen a clipping in Paris about Marc Wilson, who had left the AP to buy a newspaper. The Chicago *Tribune* wasn't for sale, he told a French reporter, so he bought the Bigfork *Eagle*. He also bought a large, beautiful house in the woods and never asked for the key. When I told him about my Key Line index, he laughed.

"The neighbors mentioned they'd seen some bears around, so my wife, Ginny, got all excited and thought we should get a key," he said. "She wanted to lock out the bears. I thought that was so funny I wrote a column about it. I not only don't lock my doors, I publish it in the paper." Ginny's parents still have trouble with the idea. In Detroit, with dead bolt locks, they need a key to get *out* of the house.

Marc found small-town journalism a new challenge. "One day a town elder came into my office, sat down and said, 'Marc, that story was too accurate.' "

Counting summer people's, Bigfork has 3,400 post office boxes. There are 510 kids in the elementary school. I was surprised, therefore, to find a huge theater and a resident company that put on

Broadway-quality shows. I watched *A Funny Thing Happened on the Way to the Forum* in some amazement. The 435-seat house had sold out for the weekend, and I barely got a seat Monday night.

The theater was a community effort. For fifty bucks, your name was engraved on your own brick out front. For more, the butcher thanks you when he sees you in the street. Bigfork is that kind of town. It is unincorporated, with no government at all. That explains why everyone respects the zoning, character and good taste of the place. Library books come back on time because they are library books. Hey, this is America.

After *Forum,* I hung out with the cast. Allan Chambers, the star, was a twenty-seven-year-old pro from Los Angeles. He was born with Zero Mostel eyes, but the rest came with work. A few locals took part, but mostly the cast was summer stock. Laurie Wilson, a drama student from Old Miss, was in pain. She broke a toe onstage and didn't notice it until the curtain. I sat in on the Ernie Awards, given weekly to the person who had screwed up worst. The winner had to wear a silly hat all week. If he did not, as is usually the case, the cast called an ITL meeting: in the lake.

Eden Atwood, a University of Montana student, believed people should draw their own borders. Especially theater people. "I don't want to know, to pick up a paper and read what someone said about something I can't do a goddamned thing about," she said. "I've got my world, my gods, what I'm studying for. . . . Come to my world, and you don't worry about the baby-sitter or nuclear war or whether you left the iron on. You leave all that at the door. We are always in the Twilight Zone."

Mostly I talked to a bass player named Michael Engberg. He wrote the kinds of protest songs I hadn't heard in twenty years. They were better, in fact. He had a lot of talent. Also, there seemed to be more to protest these days. His favorite was about an old man peering through a magnifying glass at ants on a sidewalk so he could stomp on all the red ones.

We were in a funky old bar which sometimes got raucous. When the summer stock people first arrived, some local kids hassled them. In a showdown a town bully picked a fight. But a stagehand grabbed his arm and threatened to deck him. "Go ahead," the bully said, in the tradition of the old West. "I'll sue."

Bigfork doesn't brawl much. It is essentially a short street of nicely aged wooden buildings and flower-fringed cottages dropping down to a vast blue lake. Barb Grinde Anderson, basket weaver and massage oil maiden, reckons it is paradise. "Can you believe it?" she reflected. "I've only lived in two houses in my entire life." She pointed to both of them in a single gesture. "People are so friendly here, so thoughtful of one another, it's hard to think about going anywhere else. It feels like a really safe, wonderful place to raise a family. We don't hear of rape. We don't hear of heroin. I know a few people who needled out, but not anymore. Some people started drugs, but they're not welcome."

The huckleberry jam lady said the same thing. So does Trish, keeper of a pleasant little bookstore, but she knew their paradise was on a knife-edge. "Each year we notice slight changes, and it starts to put a fear in us," she said. "All we can do is keep moving north, praying it doesn't get to us."

For real perspective, I talked to Molly, the Roofer.

I noticed Molly early in the day, painting a barn. She looked like a Lily Tomlin bag lady in funny pants, a floppy hat and feathers. She talked like a trucker. Later on Molly wandered into Trish's book-shop, and we were introduced. "That's Bigfork," she said, with a rolling thunder laugh. "The rest of the country is caught up in money, and we're trying to dump the stuff overboard." The only thing that scared Molly was that the yup class had discovered fly fishing.

Up close, I saw Molly Strong had delicate features that hard weather had not managed to affect. Her eyes were beautiful and sparked intelligence. She was pretty articulate for a Big Sky mountain bum.

"Yeah," she said, "I got a master's degree in English literature. I taught Latin and French, all that stuff. But I'm a runaway, just like the rest of 'em up here." She had lived in Florida, in big-city ghettos and various other places, all of which she dismissed with a toss of her short black hair. "It's crazy down there."

Molly grinned easily and spoke with a throaty rasp. "My only act of violence was to throw the TV out the window. Just flung it over-board. It does terrible things, ruins kids. Lots of kids don't want to experience life. They just watch it. They take somebody else's word for it, and that guy is trying to sell them something."

Just then one of her two daughters whirled in and curled around her waist. Molly smoothed the girl's hair and went on. "She's doing all right. Doesn't believe in drugs. Runs around, sees friends. Looks pretty healthy, no? We've got everything we need. You see my truck?" She paused for a laugh at the smashed metal relic. "At least everyone can recognize it. Don't need insurance, don't believe in it. I don't work for anyone I don't like. Got more work than I can handle."

Molly painted, roofed and raised Christmas trees, among other things. She donated a lot of time to the community. Mainly she fishes. Objective sources placed her among the best guides and fisherpeople in Montana, which was saying a lot.

"Everybody seems to be worried about job security," she concluded. "People will stab you in the back for jobs. Could slavery be any worse?" In Bigfork she confiscates friends' watches and suggests a different—as hardly anyone ever says in Montana—agenda.

"Up here we don't care what you have. Hell, anything I ever had has been taken away by lawyers, and bankers and ugly people." At that, Molly the Roofer gave a very loud laugh.

Bigfork had a different notion about the necessities of life. I wondered later what Molly the Roofer would think about a three-page ad Barney's ran in *The New York Times Magazine.* It showed a plucked and powdered model in black leather hot pants and a half mile of jeweled necklaces under the caption "All I want for Christmas is what nobody else has." The space alone cost a hundred thousand dollars. Some people up North call that as obscene as *Hustler.*

The simple act of spending seemed to offer comfort to a lot of people. I had met an English medical supplier who told me his company had to charge ten times more than the British price for a hospital bed to be able to sell it in the United States. "You Americans don't appreciate anything unless you spend too much," he said, with a happy laugh.

Also, I began to notice people were speaking English in Montana. They called a garbageman a garbageman, not a mobile sanitation engineer. An undertaker was not a terminal operator. I had been having trouble with new American dialects. Computerese leaned heavily on "interface" and "access," and those who spoke it processed their words like Velveeta cheese. Haigueranto was simple: You just added *ize* to every noun of more than three syllables. La La lingo was frustrating. I said, "Let's have lunch," to a Los Angeles person, meaning I was inviting him to lunch, and he laughed.

Some dialects got me mad, like Journocute, which made wordplays on things like foreign currencies. If one more headline writer mentioned Japan's yen to buy, I was going to pound him until he was a mark on the wall. The next Airplanistani-speaking person who told me to extinguish my smoking materials was going to get belted into a full and upright position.

Some of the Nurse Ratchet test tube talk was disconcerting. I never could hear "male bonding" without thinking of Elmer's glue. And who was the one poor bastard in the country who *wasn't* special?

But the worst was Corporate Smarm. People, I noticed, no longer reported to a personnel director but to a director of human resources. That was one for the Department of Animal Waste.

The language was laced with colorful figures of speech, but they mostly came out of the same box. If some guy says something funny at Adair's Saloon in Dallas, it has a decent shelf life until the last guy in Maine groans when he hears it. If Dan Rather says it on network television, it is dead by morning. But people gamely roll out the clichés: That fat lady won't hunt; it's not over until the bear shits in the woods, or whatever.

By the time I reached Livingston I was feeling real good about the Northwest. Missoula was crowded and tended toward pollution. But fewer than a million people in a state the size of California was not such a big deal. Bozeman was a sprawl of chain motels and crap-food joints. Still, its setting was beautiful.

I had stopped in Philipsburg, a living ghost town of magnificent dilapidation. The White Front Tavern was frozen in time, and I wasn't sure which. It had a carved dark wood bar, supported by grizzled young men in calf ropers' caps. On one wall was a very early photograph of John F. Kennedy, tenderly nuzzling a young and innocent Jacqueline.

One White Front regular was Henry Hull, ninety, who had not slowed down despite his damaged miner's lungs. I asked him when he had stopped mining, and he looked at me funny. "Haven't stopped," he said. An older customer is James Patten, who walked down each day for a snort. On his hundredth birthday, on May 25, 1988, the local weekly wrote an article now stuck to the bar's wall. Patten advised: "If you got something good, you'd better keep with it."

Dan Black, the young local editor, had a harsher lesson than Marc Wilson about the First Amendment at a local level. He wrote the first editorials the town had ever seen and nearly got run out of town. "I had my house egged, my car scratched," he said. "They can ostracize you till your life is not worth living."

In Livingston, that night, I found Tim Cahill of the little band of writers and movie people who'd moved there. I asked about the Church of Universal Truth, run by Elizabeth Clare Prophet, which had moved into a sprawling ranch near Yellowstone. I'd heard about some weird practices, like coffee enemas for the soul. Tim had joined a cult for *Rolling Stone* and knew about such things. CUT, he said, was basically a New Age overlay on the old Christian cast of characters, with some new rules to live by. "Protein deficiency and sleep deprivation tend to make you tractable," he said. "That's what I worry about."

No one had any real complaints against CUT, but it was the second-biggest landowner in the county; local folks were uneasy. Yellowstone scientists worried that a large ranch at the edge of the national park endangered wildlife and the natural thermal system. But that was an administrative, possibly legal, fight. "The thing is," Cahill said, "you don't want to be able to do anything about them."

When I explained my project, Cahill laughed. "You sound like you're looking for a place to settle, boy," he said. "Sounds like you're checking out the States to see if you can come back here." If he was right, Montana was it. Then again, it was summertime.

Yellowstone is not the largest national park and not strictly the oldest. Nor is it the most visited. It's probably not the most beautiful. But it is the granddaddy. It has everything: spectacular vistas and leafy trails; bears and buffalo; geysers and lakes and mysterious holes in the ground.

I added a park to my route with some trepidation. An honest look at America demanded I visit Yellowstone in summer. But traffic jams in the wilderness? With a job to do, I clenched my teeth and drove to the North Gate.

At first, it was as feared. Caught in a Winnebago sandwich, I inched toward Old Faithful. Then I discovered that great American secret, the wrong turn. You only have to turn left when everyone heads right. With some effort and imagination, you are alone. The figures said that 2.5 million people would visit Yellowstone in 1988, but they didn't find me.

Of course, campgrounds were overrun by lunchtime. Hotels booked up a year in advance. Pressure mounted on the Park Service to make things easier for windshield travelers, expected to double over the next decade; it would mean turning much of the untouched country into something similar to a city park. Old Faithful was already a zoo.

Perhaps someone can explain the world's rapture at an hourly gush of vapor. Old Faithful is impressive, no question. But really, it is a larger version of steaming manholes on Madison Avenue, which are easier to get to. The regularity is fascinating, but we ought to be used to it by now. Still, people hurry past the ten thousand other thermal wonders of Yellowstone to sit in a crowd around the one they know about.

Two jokes limp through the crowd, as regularly as the geyser itself. When eruption takes even a moment of the five-minute grace period after the posted time, someone yells, "Well, it's not faithful anymore." Then, with the first small spurt of foreplay, some jerk hollers: "That was it." The great ejaculation always thrills, however, and then people filter away, strangely sad.

The Old Faithful Inn is a mammoth four-story lodge, built entirely of logs in a time when we cherished craftsmanship. Each log fits its purpose. Heavy gnarled branches frame fireplaces and form window seats. It is the best of what you see in the old British Empire, but with American exuberance. The crowning touch is a log catwalk around the upper two floors allowing guests to find a private aerie for gazing at the majesty below. That, of course, is chained off.

"It's a liability problem," a staff member told me, somewhat sharply. "We get a million visitors a year here. You can imagine . . ." She did not finish the sentence but seemed about to say: "What boobs they all are." I never did work out whether we really are all boobs or if we are simply treated that way by authorities. Unquestionably, if some clown turned himself into a dark spot on the floor, his family would sue.

With liability and boobiness in mind, there are fourteen thousand signs in Yellowstone National Park. We are told again and again not to feed ourselves, or anything else, to the grizzly bears. We are advised not to stand in boiling water and reminded not to fall over cliffs.

I thought again about the back gate at Victoria Falls in Zimbabwe. If you couldn't work out that crocodiles were best avoided or that it was dangerous around a booming, bottomless cascade, there wasn't much hope for you anyway. You were allowed to enjoy wilderness the way explorers first found it, well before Walt Disney and Smokey the Bear.

It is not our rangers' fault. People who devote their lives to trees and otters tend to be pretty sensible. Most admit to exasperation with people who make rules necessary. I asked one if she could remember the silliest question she'd been asked. "People always ask where the bears are," she said. "I tell them, 'Why don't you ask about the otters? They're more interesting.' They say, 'Okay, where are the otters?' And I tell them they are in the same place as the bears. They have to look for them."

Fortunately for the bears, they are no longer easy to find. Until the early 1970's rangers fed them garbage so visitors could watch them up close. Maybe three hundred ranged the nine million acres of the greater Yellowstone ecosystem. When bears began confusing garbage with Uncle Ernie from Winnetka, problems ensued. Park officials hid the garbage, and the grizzly population crashed. They had forgotten about roots and elk. Now that grizzlies have had bear lessons, they are coming back. But at a distance.

Rangers also want to bring back the wolves, but the ranchers don't. Wolves might leave Yellowstone for lunch on calves or sheep. Since ranchers donate more to political campaigns than wolves do, Wyoming legislators stand firm. This touches an unsettling theme.

We used to think about the infinite American West, but those days are gone. There is only so much land, and somebody owns all of it. We own the most, and the Bureau of Land Management manages it for us. When ranchers pay BLM only ten dollars for a cow and calf to graze all summer, that's our grass. When ranchers get touchy and fence off public land, that might be thought an outrage. But we eat a lot of beef. Ranchers can be pretty good guys. The key is balance, and it's amazing what little attention we give to it.

Tad Bartimus, who covers the West for AP, talked to a Wyoming rancher about bears. "What purpose does a grizzly serve?" he asked her. "What does it contribute to society?" If the question has to be asked, it can't be answered. Except to ask, in turn, what purpose ranchers serve.

These days the big beef states are in the South. Feedlots are fine for cattle, but not wolves or freedom. A lot of taxpayers prefer watching wildlife to eating livestock. But ranching is part of America's heritage. No cowboys? Some suggest paying ranchers for their losses. But people who raise animals do not want to find them disemboweled on the back forty.

Edward Abbey brought howls with a piece in *Harper's* entitled "Even the Bad Guys Wear White Hats." Our public range was "cowburnt" for no reason, he said, dangerously eroded and taken away from people and wildlife "by hordes of these ugly, clumsy, stupid, bawling, stinking, fly-covered, shit-smeared, disease-spreading brutes." Ralph Beer, a *Harper's* editor and a Montana rancher, wrote to excoriate Abbey for neglecting to mention how hard some cattlemen worked to protect wildlife—and used no public range.

He agreed with Abbey that public lands were overgrazed for the benefit of a few, but he added: "The problem isn't cows, but the ridiculously overpaid and underworked 'managers' employed by the Forest Service, BLM, and various state fish and game departments. . . ." To which Abbey replied, yes, but they do a poor job because of pressure from the livestock lobby. To which . . .

These issues, vital to us now, will be critical to our kids. Maybe things are now the way most people want them. Probably not. What should be a matter of national choice is settled mainly by default in the ranchers' favor.

Personally, I draw the line at wild horses.

At the turn of the century two million mustangs ran free in the West, descendants of sturdy ponies the Indians stole from Spanish conquistadors. In 1971 Congress passed the Wild Free-Roaming Horse and Burro Act to stop mustangers from killing off the last 17,000 horses left on open range. By 1980 their numbers approached 60,000, which seemed a reasonable number for forty million acres in ten states. But they got in the way of ranchers who leased public land for their 4.3 million cattle and sheep.

Between 1985 and 1987, at the BLM's recommendation, Congress appropriated fifty-one million dollars to cut the herds in half. By 1988 fewer than 40,000 were left. Ranchers were allowed to "adopt" the horses, and not many questions were asked. Near Minnewaukan Flats an adopted herd of 400 was left to starve in winter. At least 110 died and many more were missing. The BLM suspended its program, but pressure remained to reduce the numbers. Evidence was clear enough. Captured horses were being sent for slaughter.

Was this where Manifest Destiny had taken us? Had we grown so blind to our real world, so obsessed with the small gain of the moment that we could turn our wild horses, the free-running, fire-breathing symbols of our old dreams, into dog food and glue?

*

Leaving Yellowstone, I got an unexpected dose of perspective. A fat, handsome buffalo grazed by the side of the road, and I wanted a picture. I stalked him quietly, keeping a respectful distance, and busied myself with F stops. I framed my picture and waited for him to lift his head. Without warning, an earthquake struck. I heard it and felt it at the same time, and I could only freeze and hope for the best. From behind me, the buffalo's pal was thundering up to join him. He passed close enough to fan me with dusty fur. It was some rush, well worth the price of admission. By God, you could still get yourself in trouble in a national park. Had I been trampled, I promise, I'd have blamed no one but myself.

Weeks after I left Yellowstone, the park caught fire. Flames, lashed by high winds, covered nine hundred thousand acres of forest, charring the edges of the buildings around Old Faithful. And then, just as everyone promised, it was over. Green shoots of grass and tiny lodgepole pine seedlings poked through the ash. Sun reaching the cleared forest floor brought new wildflowers. A lot was left un- scathed, in any case. "It will be different, that's all," Bruce Blair, a ranger, told Jay Mathews of The Washington *Post.* "There is no better or worse in this park. There is just change."

My plan was to fly from Billings to Rapid City, South Dakota, on my way to Minneapolis. It made perfect sense on the map. In real life, it meant flying to Salt Lake City or Denver first, and it would cost more than a ticket from New York to Paris. "They have little men in straitjackets figuring out these fares in padded rooms," ex- plained Christy Wistey, the Livingston travel agent. "Don't try to make sense of it." I had reserved a flight to Minneapolis after spending forty-five minutes on the phone with airlines. Christy quickly added 150 miles to my itinerary and reduced the fare by fifty dol- lars. "Just throw away that other flight coupon," she said.

I was not surprised. When I wanted to go from Kansas City to Denver once, eighty-one different fares flashed down the travel agent's screen. She routinely sold round trips to San Francisco from Kansas City. People just got off in Denver; it was cheaper that way. In fact, it cost less to fly to San Francisco from Kansas City than to St. Louis, a four-hour drive away.

A New York–California flight could cost four times as much if you left on Sunday instead of Saturday. Airlines worked out that businesspeople, on expense accounts, like to spend their weekends at home. "For international flights they go by linear miles," said my travel agent. "Domestically it is whatever the market will bear. They go for the businessman. If you follow your whim or want to go at a specific time, you'd better be rich."

Whatever the fare, flights up North were jammed, and I was running late. At Bozeman I was mashed in next to a 280-pound Baptist teenager in a yellow T-shirt, black bow tie and cap reading, "Jesus Rules," and I was grateful for the seat. That was nothing, in fact. On the previous flight I got stuck in the middle of Olympic tryouts for infant yodeling.

Air travel in America was a lottery in which you dreaded hearing the results. Accidents aside, you or at least your bags were likely to end up anywhere. At Kennedy Airport it could take ninety minutes in a cab to inch from the entrance to the terminal you needed. La Guardia was gridlocked half the afternoon. Airlines had redrawn the maps with their hubs and spokes, rolling passengers under the wheel. Overall, 450 million people traveled a half trillion miles a year in America, sometimes all at once.

On a TWA flight from New York to Tucson I checked with three different clerks to make sure I didn't have to change planes. At the Ambassador Club I checked yet again. "No, sir," the woman said. "It's a direct flight to Tucson." Once in the air, and they had my ticket, TWA told me the truth. My plane was going to San Diego. I would change in St. Louis yet again. But the flight was late, and the Tucson plane went on. The details would curl one's hair. But I got to Tucson—eighteen hours later, at 4:30 A.M., having driven from Phoenix. My bag made it two days later.

At St. Louis a man from India, Gandhi-like but with a prim tie and blazer, sat stoically next to me. When another delay was announced, he said, simply: "Shit!" He turned to me and added, "You realize, Americans are not more efficient than other people. They think they are. They live in their own world. It's really rather sad." He was right. I never thought I'd be nostalgic for Indian Airlines.

The hard part is getting straight answers to make alternate plans. No one listens. The staff adopts that patronizing tone and refer, by rote, to paragraph 4.B on page 49 on "How to Deal with Excitable, Deviant but Full-Fare Customers." In Phoenix I found a baggage clerk with a potbelly and a cowboy hat. When I asked about my suitcase, he shook with laughter. "Hell, there's so many things that happen to these bags, who can tell?"

Minnesota was yet another nice surprise. I was beginning to catch on that America's last frontier was not the West but the North. It took a hardy character to make it from October to May. But there was room to swing an ax and time to cut wood for your neighbor. The Far North attracted some real nice folks.

In Minneapolis I found Paul Linnee. His sister, Susan, also a correspondent rooted abroad, had known what I needed. "See Paul," she'd said. Paul described himself as a lunatic on the subject of Minneapolis and St. Paul, and he set about generously proving it. He knew about every ferryman who had ever plied the Mississippi. He had memorized the sock size of every third baseman in the history of the Twins. He knew every grain silo and railway freight depot that was now a yup-class condo and every elegant mansion along the cities' lakes. More, as head of 911 emergency communications he knew what people worried about late at night.

"I love this place," he said, clearly enjoying my appreciative noises. "They are good people here." About the only thing Minnesotans hate, he said, is the state of Iowa.

First, I seized an opportunity: Did the keeper of the Key Line lock his doors in Minneapolis? He didn't. Mainly, he added, it was because he figured a burglar would get in anyway. And his kids tended to lose keys.

A fair man, Paul had some reservations. He had seen too much human nature. For one thing, he worried about people's spines. "Most nine-one-one calls are for things people could take care of themselves," he said. "Snow blowers. They want an officer to go stop a neighbor from blowing snow in their driveway. Or about loud music. What happened to going over and asking directly?"

I mentioned the stewardess who had told me how Americans wanted her to stop people from doing things. Paul slapped his leg. "That's it, exactly. We have become so fearful of less than pleasant contact. We're afraid of confrontation."

At busy times, Paul said, it can take two hours for a cop to respond to a low-priority call. He was hurt by the criticism that brought. "Figure it out. To have one police shift, twenty-four hours a day, seven days, you need five officers. It costs thirty-five thousand dollars a year to maintain one officer. For us to cut that response time to twenty minutes, we would have to hire two hundred additional people." He snorted. "Who's going to pay for that?"

Jails were another problem. "People always want to put criminals in prison," he said. "It is a matter of pigeonholes, bed space." In Minnesota, he noted, a burglar had to be convicted four times before he did any hard time. "It is the same everywhere," Paul concluded. "People have a very wide gulf between what they want and what they are willing to pay for."

We cruised the poor inner city, black and Indian, and discussed the underclass. Minneapolis had 370,000 inhabitants, but its metropolitan area totaled 2.1 million; Edina, with 45,000 people, had an average family income of one hundred thousand dollars. Neighborhoods had to be kept livable, he said, to keep good families from fleeing to the suburbs.

"Population," he concluded. "There is an absolute dissolution of the family as we know it. We have to find a way to stop so many babies from being born without anyone to take care of them." He paused a minute, glanced at me and shrugged.

"Look, I've got this idea," he said. "Maybe we ought to think about giving a license to have a baby. You have to have a certain amount of money, not be a drug user. Only then will the state give you the pill to counter the pill you took two years ago to make you sterile. It's not practical and probably won't pass. But somebody has to kick this society upside its collective head. When will it pass? When murders are forty-eight hundred a year instead of forty-eight?"

Later on, alone, I went to Moby Dick's on the short downtown strip that harbored a few porno merchants, a gay club and a sedate topless bar. I'd been warned, but this being Minneapolis, I didn't believe it. Music thumped and thrashed in the barnlike room, pumping jolts of energy into the press of bodies. It was just a down-and-dirty bar, although drug and body sales on the periphery would not have surprised me. Couples of assorted colors, dressed in flimsy fabrics and clanking hardware, laughed, bickered, yelled, preened and played pool. It struck me that every city ought to have one Moby Dick, particularly Minneapolis; not everyone is a Lutheran minister.

After several decades, however, it was the death knell for Moby's. City fathers, or mothers, had decided that the sleazy block did not fit the downtown image. Property had been duly purchased, and the forces of right won another one.

*

Minneapolis, casting about for a city slogan, came up with "We Like It Here." It seemed the perfect sort of assertive, defensive, aw-shucks, stick-in-your-ear motto for the place. An outsider could see why people liked it. You could park near the Guthrie Theater and not worry about your car radio. People still reminded you Minneapolis was where the *Mary Tyler Moore Show* had been set. But something about the smugness wore on the nerves.

I had gotten used to Americans obsessed with themselves. For days I'd find no foreign story on the front pages of major newspapers. But in Minneapolis, Lou Grant's first stomping ground, a television newscast devoted forty seconds to its "Around the World" segment, three items including one about a U.S. warship limping home. Then the anchorgigglers spent a full minute chatting inanely about some barbecue one had attended.

This weighed on my mind when a news agency reporter took me to a food fair on the Capitol lawn in St. Paul. She was a thoughtful and generous person who made a living relaying news to others. We strolled among heavy people shoving food into their mouths with both hands. Garbage cans were spilling over with uneaten pizza and half-empty cans. It was getting me down. I brought up the outside world, and she changed the subject. I tried again. Somehow it seemed appropriate.

At the time drought had dried up half the counties in America. Minnesota was starting to look like West Texas. Its beloved lakes were dropping fast, and barges were stalled all down the Mississippi. We had warned of the greenhouse effect for years; had no one paid attention? She shrugged. There would be an impact on world food supply, I went on. In Africa . . .

A sort of smirk made me pause. I was amusing her. Look, I started to explain. She cut me off. "It's all so complicated people can't deal with it." But you can't ignore it, I pressed on. "You do what you can," she replied, suggesting that was nothing. "This is all too esoteric. Forget it."

Wait, I said, suppose someone was getting attacked over there, and you had a gun and could use it. What would you do? "I'd stop it. That's something I can do something about." But what's the difference, except for line of sight? It just takes more effort to deal with a problem you can't see. "If you can't see it, then it's not a problem."

This was my worst kind of nightmare, and I was getting passionate: Of course, these are problems, and someone has to pay attention to them. "You act like you've got to solve them all yourself." But . . . Suddenly she stopped smirking. "Look," she snapped. "I'm tired. Leave me alone."

True enough, I was an importuning boor from the outside. There was no cause for concern. Even if the scientists were right about the greenhouse effect, a lot of world would be submerged before the water got to Minneapolis.

But then there was Eric Utne. An incurable magazine junkie, he decided like-minded people needed a little help. He launched the *Utne Reader*. A small staff mines a weekly ore pile of a thousand alternative periodicals and publishes the nuggets in a lively little magazine with seventy-five thousand subscribers. It leans to the left, but editors throw in stuff from the far right to keep liberal readers on their toes. Utne fills in the spaces for interested people across the country who are fed up with barbecue gossip on the local evening news.

Sometimes he is accused of acting as if he had to solve the world's problems by himself. "But it really comes down to a simple enough philosophy," he told me. "About all you can hope to do is to make the world a little greener and a little kinder."

One faraway story concerned the Twin Cities. In early 1988 the St. Paul *Pioneer Press Dispatch* ran a ten-page special report on how duck hunters in Louisiana were decimating North America's ducks, a quarter of which had the bad sense to winter down there. Over forty years, the report said, duck populations had declined 60 percent. It quoted one unnamed hunter saying, "Nobody left me any buffalo to shoot. Why should I leave anyone any ducks?" It was a vital service to North American ducks. And to Minnesota hunters.

I moved eastward, running out of time faster than I was running out of America. Some things would get cut. Up north in Minnesota, the Mayo Clinic was adding years to people's lives. Doctors everywhere admired American medicine, and I had wanted to take a look. But the list was long.

In Paris, a French photographer back from discovering America had exalted to me: "Trucks! You must do trucks!" I wrote down, "Trucks!" All along, I'd watched the big rigs that laced the country together. They were why the railroads suffered; we had different needs in a wide-open land. Soon truckers symbolized for me what was left of our independent spirit, loners willing and able to flip the bird at overweaning authority.

I had talked to truckers but only in passing. Instead, I had a *New Yorker* piece by Bryan Di Salvatore. He predicted that trucks would soon carry those little black boxes that spy on airplanes, logging every yawn and quick detour of America's last kings of the road.

Also, I would not poke at the radioactive mess we had swept under the rug for decades. I'd watched in disbelief at the estimates—ranging up to nearly $200 billion—for cleaning up past nuclear folly and gearing for the future. It was a chilling example of what happens when governments live for the moment: We spend trillions for defense and risk having to beg for plutonium so the Soviets don't laugh at our deterrent.

I'd miss the twenty-year-old Massachusetts woman who still got hate mail for declining to stand for the Pledge of Allegiance in high school, three years earlier. And also the guy in New Jersey who organizes major events around wallowing in gooey food.

What the hell.

I booked a 6:59 A.M. flight to Portland, Maine, from New York, and my travel agent wrote the ticket. I had a mountain of luggage. At La Guardia the cabby asked what airline. The ticket said only Business Express. But I had talked to Eastern. Let's try Eastern Express, I said. The little terminal was locked. In the adjoining shuttle terminal, I asked the security lady if Eastern flights to Portland left next door. "Yes," she said. I unloaded my bags and waited. But a red light flashed in my uncoffeed brain.

A janitor led me into the terminal. I found no Portland tags at the counter. No one knew anything. Finally, I studied my boarding pass. It said Delta. No problem, the janitor said, Delta is just over there about two hundred yards. It was farther, but that was academic. It could have been in Sag Harbor; I needed wheels. Scooping up the computer and leaving the rest, I raced to Delta. No porter. A taxi line snaked from the shuttle terminal. I explained my plight to the first guy in line. He burst out laughing.

Flight time was approaching. Something about La Guardia choked off my thinking. Had someone stolen my bags yet? The fork in the socket ran too much voltage into my fragile foreign soul. Please, God, don't let it all end here. I plunged into the terminal and blurted out my story to the baggage manager. A man standing nearby said: "I can help." My gratitude began to well. "For a ten-spot." Jesus Christ, what had I learned in all this reporting? I was still the naive schmuck who left Tucson believing in fairies. Money.

My bags were safe. The janitor had watched them, he pointed out, extending a palm. Minutes later I arrived at Delta in a three-quarter-ton luggage cart, an express delivery truck and someone else got screwed out of something. I'd planned to pay overweight, what with books and papers, but needn't have worried about that either. "Lay something on me," the bagman said.

The other Portland is a wood-sided old sailors' city. But it is under heavy pressure. Developers discovered the Maine coast sometime back, and investors are locked in battle with authorities trying to preserve character. To some degree, it is like that all the way to Eastport. But Portland, like San Antonio, is already overlaid with an ill-fitting modern city that filters its charm.

I switched on the radio. "Well," said a down-home voice, "the tourists are coming. Time to park the Mercedes in the barn and get out the old pickup. . . . Time to practice up on the lingo, get rid of those r's. Talk slow, drive slow and, above all, don't take all their money. Leave some for your neighbor. Maine, a Fortune Five Hundred tourist state."

Down at the water a guy who might be Molly the Roofer's running mate was watering eight handsome dogs from a drinking fountain. He spotted me as an outsider and stood back, assuming I'd object or at least demand priority over the hounds. Then he nodded and kept watering. He had puffy eyes and a three-day beard and carried a giant pot of sesame tahini. I didn't recognize the dogs' breed. What are those? I asked. "Happy dogs." With a brief bow, he said, "I leave you to your drink of aqua pura."

At the old port downtown a weathered old supply store ran a marina for 130 yachts and fishing boats. Slips cost two thousand dollars a year, but there was a ten-year waiting list. I asked Bill Scherr, the manager, what he would advise if I had a boat to dock somewhere. "I'd say get here about five years ago." Marina space is rare in Maine and worse farther south. What little there is, yacht brokers grab. You can hardly sell a boat without a slip.

Thinking of France, and New York, I said people must sell their rights for a lot of money under the table. "Nope," he said. "Three things happen. They lose the money. They make me mad. They lose their space."

Scarcity seemed a good thing. The old port has become Old Port. Merchants replaced the original owners of the tumbledown district, and then developers bought entire chunks of the center of town. It is restored, but also gentrified, yuppified, plasticized and full of brass ship antiques made last week in Taipei. But Portland declared a five-year moratorium on the waterfront.

Like everyone else, I knew about L. L. Bean's twenty-four-hour gum boot emporium up the road in Freeport. But I wasn't ready for the Maine Mall, a spendatorium of Dallas proportions, with its own exit off I-95. And in Freeport the old Texaco station is a Ralph Lauren outlet. L. L. Bean attracts three million customers a year to its three-story department store, the key to which Bean threw away long ago. It does a third of a billion dollars a year in business, counting mail orders. With all that money in the wind, Freeport, a village of sixty-seven hundred, is a shopping mall.

DiMillo's is a lobster restaurant in a converted car ferry tied up at the main wharf. I went early and selected a table on deck. Perfect weather, light breeze, boats chugging by below. Like every seafront restaurant in the rest of the world, DiMillo's had figured out that the fresh smells were as much a part of a recipe as spices. And I could smoke a pipe in the sea breeze. When the waiter came, I asked for lobster. Did I mean a lobster roll? Anything but sandwiches, he explained, were served down below, with the nasty carpet and closed-in feeling of a restaurant in the Midwest. Or San Diego.

Up the coast, however, you can eat lobster outdoors until you drop. Some beautiful towns sit amid flowering trees and gleaming steeples. The Maine coast seemed to breed a healthy mix of body and spirit. In Camden, just off the waterfront, Lillian Berliawsky ran the ABCDeF Bookstore, more than a hundred thousand old volumes about everything. Near the town park the local Shakespeare Company packs the benches.

At nearby Rockport I talked to Peter Heimann, who retired from the CIA to settle in with his books and think peacefully about the world. He was active in a little foreign affairs club, the Mid Coast

Forum, which kept its membership to fifty, despite a long waiting list.

He loved the art and music and outdoor life, but he was troubled by the evening news. "We have no long-term perspective, only until the next election," he said. "But all of our problems are long-term. Sometimes it's possible to be very pessimistic about the future of the United States."

I walked around Camden pondering the future of the United States. Along Bayview Road huge old estates stretched down to the water. Their values had gone astronomically beyond what an old lobsterman might have imagined a generation ago. With so many things, like coastline, only so much exists of the good stuff. One might argue that money is no way to keep score. But a lot of the best things in life were getting more expensive by the week.

Down the road, at a farmers' market, I talked to some young guys who had fun raising vegetables. But I wondered how many sprigs of dill, as opposed to, say, phone calls in an arbitrage deal, it took to buy a chunk of the Maine coast. Somewhere, it seemed, the balance among production and service and professional flimflam had gotten seriously out of whack. And it seemed to be getting worse.

Diehard Mainiacs were distressed at a government decision no longer to man the historic old lighthouses along the coast. It was cheaper, and less complicated, to run them automatically. The beams and horns would still warn ships of rocks, and no one wanted to tear anything down. Nonetheless, it was sad to think there would be no one left to put a light in the window.

Finally, I went to see a guy who lived in one of the nicest places on the Camden beach. He had earned it. Ken Carlson overextended himself back when things were cheap. He loved the area, and he sat through its winters. He'd lived all over, and he made his money the American way.

Carlson imported the first BMWs, dealing with a Bavarian who liked to compare notes on the war; both had fought it. When Carlson discovered his customers were mainly wealthy young Jews, he figured the American market was capable of anything. He went into advertising.

For years now Carlson's main activity had been trying to save drug addicts. Out of maybe a thousand, he had a few victories. Much of his volunteer work was in New York. But a lot was in Camden.

Camden? The color negative for picture-perfect America?

"We have doctors, dentists," he said. "What I could tell you about the wonderful people who use drugs . . . This affects the richest along with the poorest." The difference, he pointed out, was that only the poorest get arrested. "There is a laissez-faire attitude; that's the way it's supposed to be. Talk about education. These kids don't understand anything because they're bombed out of their skulls."

Big unions had corrupted local police departments in Maine to ease smuggling, he said. Drug profits bankrolled larger bribes. Well-placed people could use influence to stop investigations. "I never realized we had that kind of corruption," he said, referring to more than Maine.

Neither did I. As I sat in his cozy library, in one of the last unspoiled extremities left in America, I found this a profoundly disturbing conversation. Carlson was no loonball foaming at the mouth. He worked in the streets. And the cream of the community brought him their bombed-out sons and daughters. He knew the cops. Suppose he was even one quarter right.

"We're wired," he said. "We're corrupt. We got cancer. Nobody knows who the bad guy is anymore."

I asked about his successes, and he showed me a photograph. Smiling blacks and Hispanics stood together in a team, wearing jerseys, ready for wholesome sport. Everyone had been a druggie, and most had kicked the habit. I said he must be proud.

"They're all crack dealers."

Crack dealers? They've gotten themselves off drugs, and they're pushing them to kids not yet addicted?

"That's how it works when you grow up with no values, no moral sense," he explained to me. "Getting off drugs is one thing. Hey, this is business."

CHAPTER

= 17 =

Below the
Beltway

Having started out with Liberty Weekend in New York, I wanted to end with Independence Day on the Mall. As it turned out, this Fourth of July provided more fireworks than anyone wanted. A news bulletin announced an Iranian airliner had crashed in the Persian Gulf with 290 people aboard; we were not responsible. Soon afterward an update followed. The USS *Vincennes* had shot down the Airbus 320, mistaking it for an F-14.

Not even Iranian hard-liners could have believed we did it on purpose. But in Washington and across the world, the question burned: How could it have happened? After days of conflicting reports and half-truths from the Pentagon, basic points remained in dispute. There was a tepid apology and quibbling over compensation. Honor was not the issue; it was blame. Those civilians were in the wrong place at the wrong time, argued no small number. They killed themselves.

Polls suggested most Americans were prepared to drop the issue. We did what we had to do. Why pay good money for nothing? When Teheran produced evidence that its plane had been on course and climbing, Washington refuted it. I watched a television correspondent lay out the two self-serving versions and conclude, "One side or the other is telling a false story."

He was right. Our credibility had been so battered by lies, distortions, "damage control," erased tapes, secret hypocrisy and broken promises that when it came to our word against Iran's, it was anyone's guess. We had come a long way from George Washington and his cherry tree.

Washington, at the time, was experiencing classical revival. I. F. Stone had covered Socrates' trial, which fitted right in since most people in town viewed the world from Plato's satirical viewpoint: reflected off a cave wall. But the most apt literary parallel was the simplest: Alice's Wonderland. The place was Never-never land, and reality was somewhere through a looking glass.

Not long before, as Gaza and the Gulf flared, mysterious hit men killed Abu Jihad, Yasir Arafat's alter ego. In Europe no one doubted who was responsible. Papers detailed how the Israeli cabinet made the decision to do it. But White House spokesman Marlin Fitzwater said the administration had "no information at all" from Israel on who was to blame. It had not asked for any. He explained, "We wouldn't get involved in internal affairs."

Out in the real world you had to wonder if those lunatic survivalists had made good their threat to spike the capital's water supply with LSD.

At that moment we were alienating the Western Hemisphere in a hamfisted effort to remove General Manuel Antonio Noriega by destroying Panama. We had ignored our Constitution and squandered our word to wage civil war in Nicaragua. Those were internal affairs. Splashing nitroglycerin on a Middle East bonfire was not.

In Washington the White Rabbit was no laughing matter. Few people tried to see themselves as outsiders might. Fewer still looked at foreigners as those foreigners might look at themselves. As a result, Wonderland became reality. And that guy yelling, "Off with their heads!" was not kidding around.

WELCOME TO THE MOST IMPORTANT CITY IN THE WORLD crowed a sign at National Airport. Riggs Bank had put it up, but it might have been almost anyone in town. A veteran news executive sneered when I mentioned that Washington reporters ignored the world. He had seen too many stories from foreign capitals giving other leaders' points of view. "Who cares?" he said. "It's Reagan who counts."

New York might dispute the most-important status. *Newsweek* devoted six pages and a cover to bickering between the two. But on any decent map of the world, Washington and New York are a quarter-inch apart. The whole country makes up only 5 percent of world population. We might have the most raw power, but we would have to drop a bomb to prove it. Meantime, one drug-dealing general in a small state we created beat us hands down.

Money, Donald Trump argued in *Newsweek,* is the real power. It is if that's how you keep score. But it might be wise to redo the sums. We seemed to be embarrassingly overextended.

If any country can be called the greatest, others have to bestow the title. Qualities like generosity, humanity, wisdom, leadership and courage outweigh the ability to exterminate people in absurd multiples. Smash-and-grab foreign victories run up our spirit at home. Abroad what counts is how we confront our own problems and our willingness to try to help others face theirs.

Deep into a presidential campaign, each party had seized the high ground. But greatness had little to do with elections. Few basic problems could be solved in four years, or even in eight. The question was who had the courage to apply sense over politics to keep what was good and throw out what wasn't. Nations who studied history knew greatness was a trait, not a track record.

I had all sorts of prejudices about how things worked in Washington, but I wanted a fresh look. After traveling the country as an inside outsider, I was going to its control center.

As the plane comes low into National, there can be no city anywhere more thrilling than Washington. The beauty is one thing. But you'd need Maalox in your veins not to get a rush from the white monuments spreading from the Potomac as it snakes among trees and stately structures. Red Square suggests menacing power. But the Capitol and the Mall promise more. The "city on the hill" that infests so much rhetoric, it is here. Especially when tinged pink in cherry blossoms, it is beyond thrilling.

Seeing the Jefferson Memorial, I thought of a Frenchwoman who had made a trip to Washington. "That is where you feel the strength, the depth, the richness of the American people," she told me. "Standing at night at that monument, I felt like bursting. You feel as if Jefferson is still speaking to you."

If you imagine who strode those streets, you see where this greatness idea starts. Even recently we were authors of the Marshall Plan, a welcoming asylum for refugees. We stood for right and good sense; we were the ones with *The Untouchables.* All over the world, I had met diplomats worthy of this heritage, with integrity and experience, who knew what we could achieve.

One of them was at the National Security Council. He worked in the Old Executive Office Building among aged wood and high ceilings in a setting that befitted a Metternich. Only the discreet computer screen suggested the nuclear age power at hand. He understood the world he watched and what his country stood for. Jefferson would have been comfortable there. Or maybe not. The same building had produced Oliver North.

In Washington the ghosts are always there to haunt. James Madison, for example: "I believe there are more instances of the abridgment of the freedom of the people by gradual and silent encroachments of those in power than by violent and sudden usurpations." Back then, when political wisdom went beyond "Where's the beef?" Founding Fathers worried a lot.

But in Washington, where most people's memory starts with the morning news, ghosts are easy to handle. You wrap yourself in their sheets and barn-burn your way toward the most questionable of goals. If you want to sell a disorderly band of cutthroats, you call them the moral equivalent of our Founding Fathers.

Early on I began saving string for this last trip to Washington. A piece by Arthur Schlesinger, Jr., in the *Wall Street Journal* described Reagan's foreign policy as "rigid ideological dogmatism with sublime professional incompetence." Schlesinger was among those who knew that a political murder started World War I and that apathetic ignorance drew out World War II. But Reagan recognized change in the Soviet Union, as Richard Nixon did in China, and anyone drawing up a balance sheet can find pluses to balance the minuses. The problem was systematic, cutting across party lines and administrations.

First, there was the logistics of it all, a shocking sense of ad hockery to what ought to be very serious business. For a *New Yorker* piece, Daniel Ford once visited an underground doomsday command post where a general showed off his phone to the President. If the Russians attacked, he would relay the warning. Let's see, Ford said. The general seized the phone; it was dead. After much fumbling, and discussion over which operator to dial, the free world was ready to defend what was left of itself.

The phone might work now, but that nagging discomfort remains. So much is based on technology that is only fancy machinery programmed by products of our school system. What if, for example, our best naval radar can't distinguish a small fighter from a passenger liner? What if it can and a panicky operator misreads it?

Worse, however, was the human part. Policy by amateur ideologues teetered on crude, simple pillars, such as "anti-Communist" and "pro-Communist." Diplomats knew, for example, that Renamo guerrillas in Mozambique massacred civilians by the thousands, bayoneting babies and burning families alive. They destroyed schools and clinics. Funded by South Africa to wreak havoc, they made no effort to win hearts and minds, unless you count removing organs with machetes. But they opposed communism. Jesse Helms called them "freedom fighters," and a staunch lobby, including Bob Dole and Jack Kemp, pressed Reagan to support them.

The warring rebel factions in Afghanistan took on the hue of Minutemen struggling for democracy. They hated the Soviet Union, but not because they loved us. They were fervent, conservative Muslims. In a refugee camp I visited, elders stoned to death a woman who let a male paramedic into her tent to treat her ailing daughter. Ed Cody of the Washington *Post* talked to a rebel leader about the Soviet-backed government. It's terrible, the Afghan said. It sent people from Kabul to teach village women how to read. "We will understand," remarked a Washington friend who knew Afghanistan, "when the Stinger missiles we gave are lent to Muslim brothers to shoot down Israeli planes."

The town is littered with good people who know better, tossed aside for telling the truth. Wayne Smith, an old pal from Argentina, was one of the best kinds of diplomats we produced. People trusted his judgment and his word, and his booming laugh melted ice. He was U.S. envoy to Cuba and the man Maurice Bishop hoped would find a willing ear in Washington. Smith explained why we had to talk to Grenada. Even more, he relayed Castro's enthusiasm to deal on broad issues. Reagan ignored him and misrepresented Cuba's position. Smith resigned in disgust.

I found Wayne teaching at Johns Hopkins. "The situation on the ground doesn't matter at all," he said. "What counts is how it's perceived here, domestic policy. The degree of imprecision is enormous. Decisions are made on the basis of no information. It's all there, but the higher the level, the more it is hermetically sealed. No one else even advises. It is on the basis of a one-page, two-page memo, which under the best of circumstances is read in the car on the way to the White House. More often, not at all, because somebody gets in the car to continue a conversation."

In Washington you got to be an expert on the world by talking about it, not by understanding it. In 1987 Helms, worried by Mozambique, pushed the Senate Foreign Relations Committee for an amendment banning aid to any African country with foreign troops on its soil. But, asked Daniel Patrick Moynihan, what about places with French troops, like Chad or Djibouti? Helms was puzzled. Djibouti? Moynihan bounded to the map, climbed onto a chair and stabbed a finger at the Horn of Africa: "Communists to the left; Communists to the right; Djibouti—right in the middle." Helms retreated but not, most likely, to an atlas.

Domestic policy was based on reasons far afield from national interest or even common sense. A bill confronting the greenhouse effect would not pass, I was told, because it upset too many "special interests." I wondered whose interests were more special than the general one, of keeping the earth's lowlands from withering while oceans rose to submerge them. Practical and philosophical differences were healthy in a democracy. But all over, I had found good people paralyzed by frustration at stalled legislation. When decisions were made, too often they confirmed Goethe: Nothing is more dangerous than ignorance in action.

As I moved from office to office, issues like smoking and speed limits sank to insignificance. We had bigger problems. If these loonballs running the country managed to get us into the next century, it would be a miracle.

If anything was clear, it was that Americans were worried about drugs. The health problem was one thing. Alcohol and tobacco took more lives. Marijuana smoking was a dubious risk. Fewer people were addicted to hard drugs than was widely believed. But the impact of a hundred-billion-dollar illegal industry staggered the nation. The corruption, the perversion of kids, the fear and hatred all ate away at our values. The whole business was bleeding us badly.

Users were not likely to stop without help. Telling an addict to just say no, Abbie Hoffman observed, is like telling a manic-depressive to just cheer up. Even with East German technical advice, we would not be able to seal our borders. Ideally we could ease the despair at the root. Meantime, drugs would have to be cut back at the source and intercepted en route.

With little thought to consequences, Americans were prepared to toy with their most fundamental freedoms. The greatest difference between our system and the Soviet Union's is that we are not bound by our own borders. We have the right to leave. But customs officials announced they would seize passports of people caught smuggling drugs.

On southern highways police stopped motorists who fitted a secret profile if they obeyed laws too scrupulously. There was talk of checkpoints. Arbitrary search, the hallmark of dictatorship, was part of the price. Congress voted to execute traffickers and to strip users of basic rights.

In every failed democracy the military first moved into law enforcement, adding a layer of martial law to balanced powers. We set up the National Guard as a buffer, for limited emergency use. But faced with drugs, we gave our armed forces civilian police power. That people dismiss this as an exaggerated concern is why it is so serious. Colonel North had a full scenario for what to do if civil order broke down.

As John Stockwell noted in Texas, and as anyone could see by looking closely, the corruption of institutions threatened the whole basis of our society.

Given all of this, you might expect Americans to be upset upon learning that people on their payroll were involved in drug traffic. But that was all too easy to ignore.

For years U.S. officials knew that our Central American policy relied heavily upon senior officers in Panama and Honduras who smuggled cocaine by the ton into the United States. By 1974 DEA officials were so sure that Noriega was running drugs, a classified Justice Department report noted back then, that some wanted to assassinate him. But besides helping the CIA, he informed on independent smugglers. In effect, he made the DEA an enforcer for the Medellín Cartel, his partners. In 1983 the DEA man in Honduras told Washington that military officers were smuggling drugs. He was not encouraged to act; soon afterward the DEA closed its Honduras office.

Unpursued, allies steadily stepped up their traffic. The more desperately the administration needed help in undermining Nicaragua, the more its peripheral vision seemed to narrow.

Meantime, the CIA deployed patriots and thugs skilled in moving things secretly. Many were Cuban-Americans from Rolodexes going back to the Bay of Pigs. Others were mercenaries scraped off the streets. When some free-lanced in drugs, CIA agents shrugged it off. Operatives cultivated traffickers who, after all, had contacts, information and experience at staying off main roads. CIA hirelings and the druglords washed each other's money.

The Nicaraguan counterrevolution was a loose amalgam of warlords. Some contras would not touch drugs. Others, for their war chests or retirement funds, relayed cocaine and marijuana in the same planes that brought guns south. "Black flights," unmolested by customs or the military, could land drugs directly into Homestead Air Force Base in Florida.

A few reporters began writing about this in 1984. By 1987 some books and television documentaries had appeared. But there was no resonance. When Watergate began to unravel, each scoop had provoked another, and the best people in town had fallen all over themselves for the next break. But only a hardy few stuck with this one, often to ridicule from colleagues not willing to pick up the scent. Editors worried about anonymous informants; sources, fearing for their lives, would not be named. It was classic catch-22. Official action would have given the story solid footing, but the story was that there was no official action.

The Christic Institute, an artisanal shop of lawyers and investigators who had won the Karen Silkwood case, assembled a convincing dossier. Most newspeople shunned them because Danny Sheehan, the director, swung a little wide. But he was not supposed to be a primary source; his files were a rich trove of unfollowed leads. When the Iran-contra hearings started, someone flashed a banner reading ASK ABOUT COCAINE. He was hustled away and jailed, and no one asked about cocaine.

About the only reporter who managed to get across the real sense of the story was Garry Trudeau in *Doonesbury*. And most people thought he was just being funny.

If journalists should have hit this harder, it was not their constitutional responsibility. Congress had no such excuse. Senator John Kerry, a Massachusetts Democrat who had rallied people against the Vietnam War, tried to stir reaction to the drug traffic as well. He found himself in a much smaller crowd. His Senate subcommittee on narcotics produced startling testimony, as did Representative Charles Hughes's crime committee in the House. But it was just more words for the Washington landfill. Too many senators and congressmen held back or even blocked action.

To find out why, I did some Washington reporting.

"It is simple," a Kerry staff member explained. "The administration denies it. So how can you investigate what does not exist?" Another added: "People didn't want to touch this for fear of what they'd find. Kerry took a lot of flak over this."

They were plainly right. It was an unpopular issue, however vital, so legislators stayed clear. The Justice Department, which reported to the President, had even less interest in making waves. When the Iran-contra scandal made headlines, thirty staff investigators were put to work. Kerry's subcommittee had one and a half, plus whomever he could spare from his own team. Out of twenty thousand congressional staff people with a billion-dollar budget, that seemed a paltry way to address a worst crisis. But staffs were busy finding out what their bosses were supposed to think.

Jack Blum, Kerry's chief investigator, a sort of lovable bloodhound with a wry wit and an abused sense of outrage, told me: "I'm impressed by the inability of the prosecutorial system to get information in an orderly fashion. I'm convinced there is a story here, but somehow it doesn't end up in the hands of the grand jury, especially when national security is invoked."

I saw him later, after the hearings. He was all but buried in his cramped little Senate office by enough sworn testimony and evidence to keep the Florida district courts busy for a decade.

"The essence is there was tampering with the prosecutorial system," he said. "The government processed information never passed along to the U.S. attorneys. . . . [I]n every situation where there was a clash with foreign policy, law enforcement was downgraded, something to use rather than take seriously."

But Blum was not surprised. He knew Washington. "There are separate worlds of law enforcement and intelligence, and the national security question is the interface between those two worlds," he said. "People who work for the CIA do not ever tell the cops, period, because a disclosure might compromise a later operation. A guy can literally get away with murder with the intelligence world watching, unless he stumbles and falls into the world of cops, in which case they walk away and let him fry. Or he decides to talk, and they feed him to the cops."

It followed logically from policy, Blum said. "The minute you've got a system for looking the other way, you've got a problem. You can't have off-the-books accounts, or they're not worth squat. If anyone takes the money and runs, they do nothing. There is an extraordinary unwillingness to come to grips with errant operators. When you add no-bid, highly classified, unauditable contracts, the fun begins. These people have their own agenda and are as likely to screw it up as do it right."

Essentially, Blum said, "we turn to fourth-rate killers without a second thought." Covert operators say the bizarre work demands it, and they do not look elsewhere. "It's a total distrust of everything that is honest and coherent," he said. "If it's straight up, it can't be right." And who can blame CIA officials in Virginia for abuses in the field? As Blum put it, "If you are a field manager and fucked up terribly, the last thing you're going to do is tell your boss."

Problems go to the top, sometimes to heads of state, Blum concluded. "We've developed an ability to tolerate high levels of corruption. You just hold your nose and look the other way."

Later I asked Kerry about the hearings. He said he found an "extraordinary dereliction of responsibility" of the administration to enforce laws and live up to its words. "Some contras, some parts of the contra movement were positively, undeniably and without any reasonable doubt benefiting from narcotics trafficking . . . and American officials knew it," he said.

But Kerry is a Democrat, I was told in Washington. What should I expect?

Our Central American policy outweighed the drug threat. If Nicaraguans made that two-day drive to Harlingen, Texas, we would be enslaved and would not worry about drugs. But that posed a credibility problem. The Nicaraguans, though Marxist-Leninists who preached revolution, were not especially harsh. On taking power, they executed only one torturer-killer. They closed newspapers but left presses—and editors—intact. Anastasio Somoza's old officers were let loose to form a guerrilla army.

"The obvious lesson is if you don't kill your enemies, the CIA will employ them and use them against you," remarked Robert White, yet another good man wasted. He was an ambassador to El Salvador who was not willing to help our friends there, the exemplary democrats, explain away twenty-five thousand death squad murders.

White took Wayne Smith's analysis farther: Reality was purposely skewed to fit the plan. We insisted, for example, that lack of censorship meant El Salvador had a free press. Newspapers fire-bombed mysteriously, and journalists murdered, did not count.

From the outside it seemed impossible that administration officials could wonder why allies were so upset. On a trip to Central America late in 1988, I met a senior Spanish diplomat who, it was clear, loved the United States and admired its people. But he knew the realities.

"How can you Americans make an enemy of Oscar Arias [of Costa Rica], who is more American than you are, and friends of Honduran military rulers, who traffic drugs?" he asked, before answering his own question. "You don't want friends and allies, you want serfs, so you are stuck with who you can buy."

Time after time I ran into people like him. They recognized our good intentions. But they blamed us for militarizing the region, driving Nicaragua into the arms of the Soviet Union, losing friends for the United States and, in the process, causing the deaths of up to a hundred thousand people.

Back home in America, that was a major surprise. Why weren't we wondering what any secret gang of thugs could achieve that was worth the smear on our name? Did we think no one noticed that we promoted democracy by bankrolling dictators? If we could warm up to the former Evil Empire, why were we obsessed with one of its distant clients? Suppose our contras won. Would that be progress, installing a bickering junta of former Somocistas?

In never-never land, questions like these take you armpit-deep into politics. Our system creates moral justification for damn near anything, if policy demands it. Look at Noriega.

When forced to be outraged about drugs, we picked on Noriega, who had failed to outrage us earlier. But we could not just run him quietly out of office, as the cynical French would do. We had to strike a blow for democracy. He was painted as an intolerable tyrant, thus sanctifying by comparison such moral equivalents of our Founding Fathers as Mobutu Sese Seko of Zaire. If Noriega's officers detained American reporters for three hours, he trammeled press freedom. The U.S. admiral off Grenada who held American reporters for a day was only a good host.

State Department officials announced Noriega would be gone in a few days. That was February. By July we were begging him please to take a brief holiday on his drug money, anywhere, as long as he was out of Panama by November. He did not go.

Any Nigerian cabby on Pennsylvania Avenue could have warned what happens in the real world. Panamanian officers who hated Noriega closed ranks behind him. Pressed for cash, he merely rang up Havana, Managua or Medellín. Panamanians suffered because of the *yanquis*. Americans were harassed at the Canal. We pushed a new president to declare himself, only to abandon him later; he had to govern from hiding. We flexed muscles we wouldn't dare use, but leaders across Latin America thought we might invade. However much they disliked Noriega, they opposed us.

Politicians got in their hot flashes. Alfonse D'Amato likened the administration to a man who puts out a fire in his hair by hitting himself with a hammer. But D'Amato was there with the matches at first, with everyone else. He ridiculed "that little pineapple," a reference to Noriega's pockmarked skin. Our public scorn made it impossible for the general to lose face.

The historically literate saw a variation on Teddy Roosevelt's dictum. We spoke loudly and clobbered ourselves with a big stick. But even those whose world revolves around celluloid should have no trouble with this one: When we turn Mickey Mouse into Mighty Mouse, we cannot step on him when he roars. If we win, we're bullies. If we lose, God help us all.

The Bomb Panama lobby, still blinded by the flash of glory from Grenada, champed impatiently. Some others applauded a law suggested by Neal Richman, a California writer. We should be prohibited from bombing anyplace most Americans cannot locate on a map. That covers about everywhere, including Canada and Alabama.

The real irony was that Noriega was indicted despite obstructions from Washington. "We got away with it only because evidence came to us from independent sources . . . without our having to cross swords with the intelligence community," chief Assistant U.S. Attorney Richard Gregorie told me in Miami. I made a brief trip there to confirm what colleagues had told me: American citizens, foreign allies, contra officials had smuggled narcotics with impunity, despite clear evidence against them.

"The problem is foreign policy," Gregorie said. "We aren't doing what we have to do. We close our eyes to the fact that someone who might be anti-Communist is running drugs on the side. We are tolerating it." He said the CIA and other intelligence agencies withheld evidence from him. He kept butting into an institutional wall. Other agencies seemed reluctant to help.

"There's no war on drugs." Gregorie snorted. "That's horseshit. They're thumbing their noses at us."

In Washington I saw the other side of what I'd watched so long from the outside. We still had noble goals, a wish to do right by our lofty standards. Americans left homes and friends to sacrifice their digestive tracts, often their lives for this purpose. That is what made it tragic.

The world still looked to us for leadership. Margaret Thatcher moistened Americans' eyes in a tribute to Reagan after the 1988 Moscow Summit. But our appeal was our potential to do good, in a broad sense. In specific cases, nations had their own priorities. We shunned allies who disagreed with us. And we were always surprised when they did not follow us up the hill.

Down deep, our posture toward the world had not changed in forty years. Defense depended upon nuclear deterrence and allies who shared an increasingly questionable view of the Soviet Union. For small volatile skirmishes in remote jungles or gulfs, we were muscle-bound. We were hardly more flexible than the British redcoats who could not subdue colonial guerrillas in America.

Foreign policy was shaped in large, awkward components, too unwieldy for the real world. When we got our teeth into something, a Vietnam or a Nicaragua or a Libya, common sense dropped away. Roles were sketched out for heroes and villains; when they inevitably disappointed, secret actors helped them from the pits.

Expecting others to think like us, we heard what we needed to hear. A Japanese minister would say, "I'll do my best," and it sounded like yes. In Japan that means "forget it." This was where that fourth grade in Tucson took meaning. Once you imagine a Blacque Jacque Shellaque, you assign him a behavior pattern.

When I was a kid, my scoutmaster showed us how to make a raccoon trap. You dig a paw-size hole and point a sharp stick down into it. Then you toss in a piece of meat. A raccoon grabs the meat and catches his fist. The harder he pulls, the more it hurts. He could let go and dig the meat out from another direction. Or just walk away, free. But he'd sooner chew off his own fist. As I reflected on Washington today, coon traps were all I needed to know about foreign policy.

When we change, we change fast. At the end of 1987, while the nation spit out presidential candidates like watermelon pits, I watched Mikhail Gorbachev occupy Washington. Nikita Krushchev had banged his shoe on a New York table, leaving Americans with a picture that lasted years. This time, in a summit with Reagan, Gorbachev did it our way. He kennedyed Americans with courageous words from the heart. He nixoned them, talking hard facts on world politics. He reaganed them with ad-lib quips, making them laugh. But above all, he johnsoned Americans, halting his motorcade to leap out and press the flesh.

On camera Gorbachev waded into Middle America. From Paris I saw it in as much detail as every other American. He had been head tyrant of the Evil Empire. I'd seen a sign on a lamppost: HONK IF YOU HATE COMMUNISTS. In the off-the-wall *Weekly World News*, columnist Ed Anger had suggested "blasting those Lenin-loving maggots to Smithereens." This time people beamed with pleasure. "The guy's a public relations genius," someone observed. With impulse buyers that is all it takes. After a fleeting handshake one woman gushed: "I'm not going to wash my hand for six months." I wondered if she knew where that hand had been.

There was substance in Gorbachev's blitz. Soon afterward he cut losses and pulled out of Afghanistan. It was the Russians' Vietnam, but they spared themselves the breast-beating. Gorbachev resisted the chance to exploit American folly in Central America and the Middle East. Reagan was welcomed on the air in Moscow. He quietly confirmed what the Russians knew all along: The downing of Korean Air Lines Flight 007 was not a deliberate act of murder. Our earlier histrionics came back to haunt us.

Americans saw Russians had real fears about what we might have in mind. Many realized for the first time that ten million Russians were killed on their own soil in this century alone. They would not let it happen again. Polls showed Europeans—and Americans—were nearly as likely to trust Gorbachev as Reagan. With an adversary like that, it was no time to look at presidential candidates like contestants on *The Dating Game*.

Here was our ethnocentricity again. From a country of 250 million people, the only candidate with real foreign exposure had shaped his view in the CIA. As Henry Kissinger pointed out, the White House is no place for on-the-job training.

Glasnost was promising, and I was happy we saw Russians as people. But all that enthusiasm for Gorbachev made me itch.

As always, there was the flip side. Marcel Marceau, in his role as my magic mirror, said he was overwhelmed by how Americans greeted Gorbachev. "The warmth with which they received this former enemy," he said, "the way they opened up to hear this man who wanted to speak to them from the heart, it was wonderful." But what about

Krushchev? "They understood him," Marceau said. "When he banged his shoe, like a peasant, the farmers all said, 'Aha, a peasant.' " But didn't he think Americans were seeing all this too simplistically? Marceau beamed in triumph. "Exactly." Take your pick.

Washington is a hell of a town under any circumstance. By day it vibrates to the low hum of copiers and shredders. The fun starts when the Yes Sirs go home to 301 and 703, area codes on phones in Maryland and Virginia which they hope won't ring before morning. At Dupont Circle people eat frozen yogurt and crowd bookshops deep into the night. Georgetown's classy yupperies throb with life in handsome old buildings on tree-fringed streets.

Some fine restaurants are in Washington, and Giorgio's Pizza is not one of them. It is a seedy little storefront on Twentieth Street with a staff from somewhere east of Athens. I love it. While Mike Dukakis pursued an American dream, Giorgio the Greek was hard at work on his own. "Hey, who else sells a seventeen-dollar pizza in this town?" he asked. "This is quality. All fresh, provolone, mozzarella." He meant that in Washington you had to be real good or awful. Since a crackdown on expense accounts, the trend was toward awful.

"You think some guy's gonna take his girlfriend to lunch for fifty dollars of his own money?" he continued. "He goes to McDonald's. The junk food places were supposed to stay in the suburbs, out of D.C. They ruined everything. I gotta friend, little pizza oven, a couple of gyro sticks, souvlaki, that's all. The landlord wants a hundred sixty-seven dollars a square foot. You gotta sell gold or cocaine for that."

A guy who liked his girlfriend could take her for lunch in Ethiopia, Jamaica, Mexico, France, Lebanon or a dozen parts of Asia within leaving Adams Morgan, a short trot past Dupont Circle. Top-end French restaurants were up to Paris quality, and prices.

Entertainment, though rich in the arts, leans heavily toward talking about the topic of the week. I went to a party not long after the Iran-contra hearings, and people were on to Judge Bork. A fetching young woman intoned the top forty words: abortion; packing the court; civil rights. I told a friend that she looked familiar. "Her?" he replied. "That's Fawn Hall." We talked briefly; she was just another bright woman, out of work in Washington. The sexy shredder had had her fifteen minutes, and it was someone else's turn at the Wheel of Fortune.

A desperate drug culture dominates neighborhoods over a wide sweep of the city. At more than a murder a day, Washington outpaced Detroit. Any congressman could take a distressing tour of urban poverty a few minutes away from Capitol Hill.

For the President, reality is even closer. Homeless men pause to rest at Lafayette Square, "Peace Park," directly across Pennsylvania Avenue from the White House. Police hustle bums along their way, but no one has been able to dislodge William Thomas and his permanent antinuclear vigil. As secretary of the interior, James Watt tried to remove the protesters until someone reminded him this was a democracy.

"We're here to reach people who think freedom means having a VCR," Thomas explained.

Back in New York, Sunrise the Rainbow had mentioned being arrested for camping. That was how police controlled the vigil. After jailing Thomas for three months, only to find him back again, they worked out a system. Signs could be only so big; they measure them. Someone must remain within a few feet of any sign. And no sleeping. That also applied to the homeless who might doze in the President's line of sight. One cop was famed for his habit of stamping on the legs of sleeping transients.

A lot goes right, one must always insist. But the little items were unsettling. There was Herman Rodriguez, who fled El Salvador in 1979 and settled near Washington, a self-taught mechanic who was raising a happy family. On his way home with dinner from McDonald's, someone dropped a thirty-six-pound boulder onto his windshield, from an overhead bridge, and it killed him. Why?

At school, kids under ten have a new playground game. With crushed chalk, plastic Baggies and Monopoly money, huddling around and acting quickly to foil observation, they play drug dealer.

All over town, energetic people in tiny offices were doing something about something. My favorites were Craig and Suzy Van Note in a bomb site walkup off Dupont Circle. Their organization is Monitor Consortium or, less formally, You Name It, We Save It. They link up a network of conservationists and ecologists, mailing out thick packets of press clippings, advisories, speeches and petitions. Craig, a former *Time* reporter and a politics junkie, puts people in touch with whomever they need to know.

"Bats!" Craig said, putting his hand over the phone as I came in to chat one morning. He was talking to Merlin Tuttle, the bat king out in Texas. "The next thing. Bats. You got to meet this guy, he's making bat houses and . . ." Earlier it was orcas. Craig was no fan of Sea World.

I'd met people from Brazil to Thailand who devoted their lives to serious environmental issues, but only in America are they a whole industry. A few did more harm than good, focusing attention on a single species, or a specific problem, while larger habitats headed to hell. But Craig and Suzy knew them all, and with a word in the right spot, or a full-bore campaign, they could paralyze threats before most people even knew about them.

A few blocks away something called AARP had established itself with blinding speed. Suddenly the American Association of Retired Persons was the second largest organization in the country after the Roman Catholic Church, twice the size of the AFL-CIO. When I first heard the name, I pictured a few old duffers handwriting letters. But twenty-eight million people on a mailing list are serious clout.

At feeding time in Alice's Wonderland, you never know what you will find. I had a drink with John Ehrlichman in the posh back dining room of the Madison Hotel. He was tanned and fit from Santa Fe, bucked up by his book royalties and status as a charming bad guy from Watergate. Had I been really lucky, I would have found G. Gordon Liddy, the burglar-celebrity with a license plate on his Rolls reading "H20," to whom audiences pay enormous sums to explain how, in America, crime pays just fine.

When memories are short, character blemishes clear up fast. But it was more than that. By the end of Reagan's administration hardly anyone could throw stones without smashing his own windows.

That was the strangest feeling, to come home among the keepers of the flame of liberty and find a chief guardian, the minister of justice, struggling to stay out of jail. Two steps ahead of a report that essentially called him a crook, Edwin Meese resigned in triumph. He had been "completely vindicated" because no one would try to convict him. Right and wrong had disappeared. In their place we had the concept of anything goes except what might be proved specifically unlawful. It did not matter that Justice Department doorkeepers reached the point of denying free speech, barring a messenger whose T-shirt said: "Meese is a Pig."

Washington seemed suffused with a cynical air, far removed from the people it was set up to serve. In any situation the first instinct was to lie. Orwellian concepts, like damage control and image making, were the accepted routine. Consultants wired electrodes to test listeners, focus groups, so they could advise politicians what was in their hearts and on their minds.

If you couldn't buy justice, you could buy attention. Toshiba spent nine million dollars persuading congressmen to overlook its technology sales to the Soviet Union. On a fight over a seven-day waiting period for pistol permits, the gun lobby outspent its opponents seven to one. Congressmen got the message.

On one trip I watched an owlish little poindexter, a man no one ever asked me to vote for, tell the nation where he thought their buck should stop. He gave "deniability" to the President, who declined to take the rap because he was napping. He said he dissembled "because I did not want any outside interference."

Worse, not many people seemed to care. Much of the nation cheered a marine colonel who lied to Congress—and then lectured senators. The basic issue, our ability to hold a moral position and negotiate effectively, was far more dangerous than Watergate. But people laughed it off. I asked Joan Mower, an AP reporter who covered Iran-contra, if she knew why. She shrugged. "Maybe because it's foreign. They can't relate."

North got a civics lesson from several senators. But before the graduating class of Jerry Falwell's Liberty University, he called the charges against him "a badge of honor."

Across the country I met people who had lost faith in the institutions meant to inspire them. For them, it was unthinkable to take the government at its word. They had to rely on their own consciences, not their leaders' example, to do what they judged to be right. No kid heading out in the world these days was likely to be the naive schmuck that I had been.

At the same time others clung to the belief that government must know best; it was easier that way. Rude reporters who shouted questions at their betters were simply looking for sensation to further their careers. Of course, America was the best. It always had been, and it always would be.

I wasn't sure which tendency was more disturbing.

During anniversary celebrations for the Constitution, Jane Pauley interviewed a Philadelphia student who helped write a modern version. Did she think her generation could have come up with such a document, Pauley asked, "or was it a miracle?"

Those four sheets of lambskin, if a fine piece of work, are hardly unique. I came across another constitution that leaves ours in the shadows. It not only guarantees free speech, the right of assembly, a free press and all the usual stuff but also assures a referendum on major matters. It stresses the sanctity of the home, including mail and telephone communications. Both sexes and all races and creeds have equal rights to basic needs. States can secede freely from the union. Try making it stick, however; it is the constitution of the Soviet Union.

If we are a long way from being Russia, it is not because of a piece of paper. A century and half ago De Tocqueville sniffed the wind and warned us: "Everywhere the State acquires more and more direct control over the humblest members of the community and a more exclusive power of governing each of them in his smallest concerns. This gradual weakening of the individual in relation to society at large may be traced to a thousand things."

A cool look today is distressing.

In early 1988 Europeans saw a CBS report on abuses by the Internal Revenue Service. A Denver couple had been ruined by an arbitrary seizure. "We could show exactly how it could be paid," a tearful woman reported. "But the man made it very clear. We don't want your taxes. We want your business. We've lost everything." Henry and Sally James were told they owed seventy-seven hundred dollars; a lien on their house ruined a clean credit rating. Months later the IRS admitted it was wrong. "I honestly felt that this must have been how it felt to live in Nazi Germany, to be treated like that," Mrs. James told CBS—and a whole lot of interested Germans. "We were guilty and had to prove our innocence."

Later the FBI admitted spying on two hundred organizations that questioned Central America policy, sneaking photographs, taping conversations and interviewing contacts. Reputations were damaged by what agents admitted later was false evidence. Not that long before, the FBI has assembled secret files on virtually every American writer of substance. More recently agents enlisted librarians to report on what books Americans read.

Federal agents are after spies, and honest citizens can help, the argument runs. But where does it stop? The Army circulated a flyer urging employees to dial 1-800-CALL-SPY if they noticed suspicious signs: "Do you know someone who makes frequent short trips—

unofficial—over long weekends—to places such as Canada, or Central or South America? Do you know someone who is called at work by someone with a foreign accent who refuses to give a name or leave a message? . . ." The number received nineteen thousand calls in a matter of months.

Democracy or not, we know only what comes to light. There was the case of Todd Patterson. When Todd was eleven in 1983, Nat Hentoff reported, he decided to write an encyclopedia of the world. He asked 169 countries for information, and many wrote back, including the Soviet Union. Soon the Pattersons' phone made weird noises. Todd's father said into the phone: If you want information, come get it. Two days later an FBI agent appeared. An explanation was not enough. In the following years at least fifty envelopes addressed to Todd arrived damaged or empty. In 1987 Todd requested to see his file; he wanted to work for the State Department one day and needed a clean record. It was classified, the FBI said. Finally, he got six pages, heavily blacked out. The rest was secret because of national security.

In Miami authorities seized eighty pages of notes from an American free-lance writer returning from Nicaragua. Anthony Lewis, in *The New York Times,* said the man's address books, notes and manuscripts were copied and sent to the FBI, the State Department and the Immigration and Naturalization Service.

What is it we think the Russians do?

Local police forces routinely overstep the limits, such as occasionally beating a prisoner to death. Corruption is far more rampant than we admit. At one point a tenth of the Miami police force was under a cloud. Whole counties were made safe for drug smugglers, thanks to generous sharing of the loot.

People told me such things were rare; no one with a clear conscience need worry. But rare instances were common. What about David Eugene Connor, a twenty-year-old worker arrested in Indiana on an Arizona warrant? He spent three months in jail, in Indianapolis and Tucson, before anyone got around to checking his ironclad alibi. As he had told them, he had the right name but a different birthday and Social Security number.

In Greensboro, North Carolina, Wayne Moorman left his wife at a Laundromat to get some gas. He also left his driver's license. Police held him incommunicado for three days, without a charge, until he persuaded a stranger to post a hundred-dollar bond. After the Greensboro *News & Record* reported the story, a woman wrote to say she had hidden the paper from her husband, a South African anxious to be an American. "I am at an utter loss to explain how such things happen in a free country," she wrote. "If it could happen to Moorman, it could happen to me."

More insidious are abuses that are not accidents. Americans who travel feel an unsettling twinge when foreign border police thumb through blacklists. But our own "lookout book" has two million names. When a Colombian named Patricia Lara came to New York in 1986, to receive journalism honors, she was seized at the airport, jailed and deported; no one told her why.

Only in late 1987 did Congress temporarily blunt the McCarran-Walter Act, which denied visas to journalists and thinkers who bore a suspicious whiff of un-American thinking. Canadian writer Farley Mowat made the silly remark that he would shoot down with a .22 any overflying U.S. nuclear bomber; he was refused entry on grounds that he advocated violent overthrow.

Junior INS officers still have what can amount to life-and-death authority over refugees seeking asylum. In 1988 hundreds of Soviet citizens, promised visas, gave up all means of support only to find the Americans ordered a three-month delay. That was explained as a mistake. But the problem is an arbitrary policy.

Margaret Randall, a U.S. citizen who gave up her nationality and then thought better of it, could not get a visa to stay in her native land. In the *Nation* her lawyer listed these grounds on which she was ordered deported: She was an admitted atheist; she had dedicated an issue of her journal to Huey Newton; she had written a poem called "Che"; she was a friend of the Nicaraguan culture minister; she interviewed Communists; she held certain Marxist historical views; she published cartoons critical of the United States; she ran an ad for a book by Karl Marx.

In a hearing an INS lawyer sought to show she should be deported as subversive for once editing a magazine described in print as a "revolutionary weapon." Randall said that was a metaphor. What's a metaphor? the lawyer asked. When Randall mentioned "many of the feelings" raised by her generation, the lawyer pounced. "Leftist feelings?" "Feelings." "Communist feelings?" "All kinds of feelings." At that the lawyer demanded: "I mean, did you ever have an article . . . extolling the virtues of the free enterprise system?"

According to People for the American Way, at least 780 books had been blacklisted by 1987 in different school systems because religious, ethnic or other groups put censorship above sensitivities.

Catcher in the Rye was widely shunned because Holden Caulfield went into a whorehouse, even though he chickened out. *Huckleberry Finn* was banned in Chicago, for Nigger Jim, whom Huck saved from slavery. Shakespeare is cut up from all sides. In Texas even the *Random House Dictionary* is forbidden. A slang definition for "going to bed" involves sexual intercourse.

Abroad we squandered our largest single asset, America's Word. Foreigners used to admire us for telling the truth, even if it hurt. In the long term, we seemed to understand, that worked to our favor. But zealous officials enlisted the U.S. Information Agency and the Voice of America in propaganda. The CIA used disinformation, yet another Washington word for lying, causing scorn abroad and blowback at home.

In Zaire, according to a secret memo that crossed my desk, the CIA promised to brief local officials on American reporters seeking visas and "mobilize all of its friends in the international press" to blur secret efforts to aid Angola rebels.

We cannot always stand up to comparison with the Soviet Union. Its system is plagued by long lines for simple things. Hard work seldom brings the rewards it should. But there are food and housing at the end of the lines. Health care, inferior to ours, is at least accessible to all. In America a man can earn twenty-five million dollars just for getting fired. But we fought hard not to force companies to give workers two months' notice before eliminating their jobs.

In Moscow you could pick up a newspaper that carried an editorial page piece about how an American hospital ordered a sick old person out to the parking lot, where he died, because of a question over payment. It was *USA Today*.

However we see ourselves at home, the world draws its own conclusions. A leader's ability to shape national image outweighs a nation's actual performance. The Russians are improving at this, and we are no longer the good guys by default. When the Korean plane was shot down, France's influential little daily *Libération* headlined the story COMRADE STRANGELOVE. When the Iranian plane went down, the headline said CITIZEN STRANGELOVE.

Deep in my clippings pile is a quote from Bernie Sanders, the mayor of Burlington, Vermont: "The most obvious weakness of our constitution is that the economic rights of our citizens are not adequately addressed. Freedom must mean more than the right to vote for a candidate for President. . . . One is not free sleeping out in the streets. One is not free eating cat food in order to survive."

True, there is at least a dazzling selection of cat food. But Sanders seems on to something. How can we live with ourselves when so many people have no decent income, shelter, health or old-age security? In the 1980's, while every other industrialized society went the other direction, we cut the federal budget for low-income housing from thirty-three billion to eight billion dollars.

Another couple of clippings added irony. With the equivalent of 11 percent of our defense budget, Census Bureau figures showed, we could place every family in America above the poverty line. What's more, Harvard researchers estimated that greater efficiency could cut 25 percent from our weapons program without reducing it by a single bullet.

The swiftest glance around suggests we could save that 11 percent with little loss. Just cutting back corruption would help. But far more is lost by sloppiness, ineptitude and patronage. The small things add up, like spending twenty-thousand dollars a year for playing cards and matchbooks on Air Force One and Two. Pentagon officials resist any cut in muscle, and that is fair enough. But a fort on the Chesapeake Bay in case the British come back? A cavalry outpost in southern Utah to fight Indians?

Just a little rational thinking would help. In Jordan I once met a U.S. liaison officer who watched the irony in action. "Americans out here can't wait for the next war," he said with a guffaw. "It won't be Israel against the Arabs, but McDonnell Douglas against General Dynamics."

It was Dwight Eisenhower, not Abbie Hoffman, who cautioned against the encroaching power of the "military-industrial complex." A few embarrassing details emerged from the Pentagon when our ships moved in the Persian Gulf. The Russians had four hundred thousand naval mines, and we had three thirty-year-old minesweepers somewhere in South Carolina. Why did the Soviet Union have a hundred times as many minesweepers as we? "There was no lobby for minesweepers," Congressman Charles Wilson of Texas explained to reporters. "No one ever got to be Chief of Naval Operations by service on a helicopter."

I raised these points with Jack Koehler, my last boss before I transferred to foreign service. Koehler was AP bureau chief in Newark,

New Jersey, then, but he surfaced briefly at the wrong end of the news. Reagan named him as White House communications director. He was out within a week. Reporters learned he had been a Hitler cub scout as a little kid in Germany before U.S. troops took him in and made him an American. It was one of those absurdities of a society that can't picture foreign conditions. Koehler's deliverance from the Nazis has shaped him into a concrete conservative, a devotee of the American way. But in Washington shorthand he was a Nazi.

By the time I talked to Jack he had calmly analyzed what he learned the hard way. "There is no patriotism, no loyalty to the President; everyone is out for himself," he said, speaking of the White House but broadening his judgment to much of Washington. As much as the public interest, government is influenced by leaks, logrolling and lies. At his first staff session with senior Cabinet people, he was told: "If you don't want what you say to appear in tomorrow morning's Washington *Post,* don't say it."

That was the atmosphere I felt in Washington. A lot of dedicated, skilled people did their jobs. Some sinister and selfish people preyed at the edges. But almost everyone was motivated by human nature, not by some conscious role in a great patriotic enterprise. The missionary class tended to head for Borneo. That all seemed perfectly natural to me. What did not fit were all those hypocritical speeches suggesting selfless perfection in the service of humankind.

This could be unsettling if you add this to the polls. A sampling for *Rolling Stone* found that only 60 percent of the upwardly mobile young professionals queried would enlist if North America were attacked. A quarter would not fight under any circumstance. In Japan, in someone else's study, young people were ready to take up arms in self-defense. But more saw their potential enemy as the United States than the Soviet Union. They seemed to fear the effect of unbridled greed directed aimlessly.

The Japanese were only reading the signs. The American Council on Education and UCLA researchers queried 209,627 students who would graduate in 1991, at 390 schools, about goals. More than three quarters said being financially well off was "essential" or "very important." Only 39 percent put emphasis on developing a meaningful philosophy of life. It was the lowest number since the question was introduced in 1967. Back then the figure was 83 percent.

James Bovard of the Competitive Enterprise Institute worked out why so few people feel connected to their government. An average

family's $4,722 tax bill goes for 524 drug tests for federal employ-
ees, or a U.S. Postal Service ad praising itself for providing the world's
best mail service, or selling six thousand bushels of wheat to the
Russians at subsidized prices, or a congressman's weekend in Jamaica to hear an hourlong lecture on growing marijuana in the Third
World.

We habitually blame all these problems on a lack of leadership,
Lewis Lapham remarked in an essay, and he observed: "If people
had the bad luck to come across a leader, they would find out that
he might demand something from them, and this impertinence would
put an abrupt and indignant end to their wish for his return." As
much as leadership, it seemed, we needed sensible followership.

A leader has to show people the basis for greatness, Lapham wrote.
"It has less to do with the making of laws than with the making of
words that allow men to see their immortality, not in the monuments or weapons, but in their children."

That made sense. If we are the best people in the world, it is
because of what we believe we are. When we begin to define our
superiority, to ourselves or to others, it melts away. All the talk of
our decline, real or imagined, has nothing to do with trade deficits,
and nuclear stockpiles and performances in Olympic bobsledding.
It has to do with what you can tell Thomas Jefferson alone at night,
on the Washington Mall.

Jefferson, in the end, had the key: "If a nation expects to be ignorant and free, in a state of civilization, it expects what never was
and never will be."

It was easier back then, when it took four days to make a copy of
the Constitution and trouble arrived in ships, with cannons blazing
to announce its presence. These days it is easier to miss a national
emergency and, once it has been identified, to bury it in words in
the hope it will go away. But Jefferson's point is sharper than ever.

By tuning out the world, we've lost our ability to hear when static
pops. Unless trouble blares out loud and clear—HOSTAGES SEIZED,
PEARL HARBOR ATTACKED—we hear only an annoying hum. We don't
see the need to know about a small place until someone, crazed with
frustration, puts a bomb in the subway to call our attention to it.
We can ignore bigger places until our economy is hopelessly dependent on them. How many people know that America owns only 4
percent of the world's merchant ships?

With little sense of our real power, we send out squad cars of marines and sailors and blame a hostile world for their inevitable failure. We twist our allies' arms to support us, seeming not to realize that public approval under duress worsens the real rifts underneath.

Our perceived decline is mainly because others, with our help, investment and ideas, have caught up. We have grown used to a World Series in which we provide the only teams. Now we have to prove that we're best rather than just say it. True, we spend more for defense than Japan and West Germany. Anyone over fifty can tell you why. The world has shifted again, and we have to find a sensible place in it.

It is true that in 1986, when U.S. officials decided to offer ten thousand special immigrant visas during a one-week period, they received two hundred thousand applications on the first half day. But we are kidding ourselves if we think that is more for love than opportunity. The American Dream is our biggest export. When we ignore Korea, we fixate on sacrifices made in another time. We don't hear rioting students: "Drive the American bastards home."

If we don't have to fight for our lives, we will have to fight for our jobs and our children's future by taking intelligent, far-reaching decisions. In this, Vanna White's bra size and the batting average of some guy named Catfood Hunter are not among the facts that will matter.

For a reporter who didn't come to preach, I was finding myself frothing at the mouth. Few people seemed concerned at what was plainly obvious to all: as a large nation in a complex world, the best we could hope to do was learn to recognize able leaders and then keep an eye on their judgment. Reagan had it right, even if he made a parody of the principle: Hire the best person for the job and let him, or her, get on with it.

We need to elect people on the basis of their good sense, solid character, world experience and courage to do what is best within a broad philosophy. We have to let them apply painful, costly, slow-acting remedies. We have to accept contradictions. But we have to watch them as if our lives depended on it. Our reporters have to shout at them and demand to read their mail. If they betray us, we must remove them fast. That requires us to take part as informed, patient followers, who know enough not to expect miracles and who can put aside narrow interests in the face of real problems. If we decide to depend upon their judgment, we have to give them time.

But politics by pollster works the other way. To be elected, a candidate has to anticipate our every prejudice, special interest and blind spot. We worry about where he comes from because that might give us an edge over others. We fret over ethnic background, religion or color, bank balance and bed partners. If a candidate cries, that is death: too human. A candidate who stops to think before speaking has no chance; thinking can eat up the full thirty seconds the camera allows.

World affairs turn on nuance, but an American leader must say yes or no, right or left, east or west—and fast.

Any candidate prepared to go through with this process, who emerges triumphant, can only hope for the sort of praise I heard all over the country: "I guess he's okay." Out of a quarter billion people, was this the best our system would allow us?

I realized, of course, I could get laughed out of Wonderland for this sort of simplistic stuff. Didn't I understand how things worked? Hadn't I learned anything in twenty years? In fact, I had found a whole country full of people who saw it the way I did. They were apathetic because they had lost touch with their leaders—and their values—and didn't know what to do about it.

And cynics be damned, it was simple enough. The ideals were there; we had to stop treating them like museum displays and sandwich them into our daily awareness. We had to help mothers raise children who have something to care about. We had to ensure that schools teach the basics a citizen needs to know. We had to get drugs and organized crime off the streets, by providing jobs on one hand and deploying police on the other. Better prisons . . . Oh, hell, any American knows this list better than I do. What I never understood was why we weren't doing more about it.

What stuck in my mind was that needlepoint motto in the galley of the *Star of India*, from back in the days when people weighed their words: "Do Right and Fear Not."

With any reporting job, it is handy to step away and let the strongest images float to the top. Here, especially, I needed a last look from the outside.

In Paris I talked to others who saw America with a detached view. Arthur Hartman, who had been ambassador to France and then to the Soviet Union, had just returned from a look around. His images were clear: "I was surprised; the country is very conservative. Reagan has convinced people of a lot of things that never really were. Consequently, they have not dealt with what is. The school systems are in shocking shape, and that, of course, is the end of democracy."

Idanna Pucci, my Italian friend who had adopted New York for its flair and vigor, was giving up on the United States. Americans, she decided, had lost their ability to extract flavor from life. They were too caught up in competition to appreciate what they were after. America had never learned how to live. "The mediocrity, the vulgarity, the lack of any greater vision of the world, I'm fed up," she said. "In Europe even a poor man has his little glass of wine, and he appreciates it. No matter how rich you are, a hamburger still tastes like a hamburger."

One day Richard Boardman appeared. He was always my barometer of America's lovable fringe. In Malaysia, as a junior diplomat, he had a chauffeur-driven old Jaguar and a sprawling colonial house with fanback wicker chairs and a Chinese marriage bed. Everyone loved him, from Malay sultans to Chinese noodle slingers. Richard was always up on the richest—or the most bizarre—new fragment of Americana. He had learned how to live.

Back in Washington, he was always just off to play a tree in an opera, or to the Aerospace Museum, or down to Haiti to scout for paintings. He loved the values that Reagan was supposed to bring back. At the U.S. Information Agency his job was to select American art for exhibitions abroad. He knew we had the finest in performing and visual arts, and the whole place excited him.

But he was moving to Australia. From being a quirky sophisticate with wit, he was just different in a society that tolerated no eccentricity. He missed etiquette, social graces and people who could laugh at themselves. He longed for dinner parties where, at the very least, you got a good meal. He was tired of women over forty who, let down by the feminist movement, ended discussions by saying, "You raised your voice at me."

He was unhappy over people chanting in the National Cathedral and ministers who attracted the faithful by saying, "Now, let's put aside this God business and talk about good fellowship." Television, his old joy, finally got to him: the greed and slapstick of game shows; the soaps that shaped so many lives; the Geraldo-Oprah formula that played on emotions—"He touched you *where*? Show me. . . ."

He had been to someone's fiftieth birthday party; the man was making a list of ten things essential to life. He had stalled after sliced salami and Beethoven, and he wanted guidance. "Remote," Richard suggested. Remote? the man asked. "You know, remote control, so you don't have to get off the couch to change channels." It was time for him to go.

Retired because of a medical problem from his time abroad, Richard was sick of Washington people insisting, "But what do you do?" He had been to Australia, where he found the values back where they had been decades ago in America. "I'm not fleeing the United States," he insisted. 'But there is an enhanced vulgarity about daily life there. I'm not at home anymore. I'd rather be in Australia."

Finally, Norma and Bill Greer came by on holiday. They were old pals from Tucson, salt-of-the-earth types who loved their country, on their first trip to Europe. At dinner we talked about the difference. A French friend laughed about his trip to Florida. He found a deserted beach and took off his swimming suit. Moments later the police arrived. Someone, peering hard through binoculars, was outraged. That launched Bill.

North of Malibu, he said, sheriff's deputies ride around on three-wheelers in shorts and golf shirts with .357 magnums hanging from their utility belts. They are the beer patrol. He had seen two of them harass a Mexican family, down to sniffing the child's lemonade container. "We were drinking a bottle of wine by the Seine, and two policemen walked by," Bill said. "I panicked, thinking of Malibu. But they just walked by, and I realized that having a drink with a picnic was normal. Now that's freedom."

At least it was part of freedom. Put all together, those conversations fitted in with my strongest impressions. In our desire to avoid risk and unpleasantness, we were giving up what was much more important. Vicarious living was replacing our reality. For $19.95 we could buy a videotape of a dog to experience, as the ad said, the joys of pet ownership without the mess and bother. We could buy a video child for the same price, and the same reasons.

Mainly, we escape, get away clean. We say we have no time to watch the world, but we play four hundred million rounds of golf a year. We can't afford to help hungry people, but our average child gets two hundred dollars' worth of toys a year, more than most Third World fathers earn to keep their families alive. Even our dogs are overweight. We are obsessed by AIDS because it touches us. Measles still kills thirty times more people. We spend twice as much on our lawns as on foreign aid.

And we had figured out what to do about worry; we took 330 tons of tranquilizers a year.

Something had happened to our sense of priorities and our attention span. The night Michael Dukakis was nominated to run for President, Governor Bill Clinton of Arkansas was roasted mercilessly. His nomination speech, people complained, went on and on and on. "I couldn't believe it," one woman told a television camera. It lasted thirty minutes.

As an outsider I might be getting something wrong. But why can't people who routinely sit still for an hour of *Santa Barbara* and commercials spend half that time listening to their handpicked spokesman present the man they want to guide the world for the next eight years?

The campaign was like that. When Dukakis was nominated, I watched frenzy on the floor but saw a picture in my mind of ice-blooded strategists engineering spontaneity off camera. When Bush named his running mate, to gasps of disbelief, the first forty words out of Dan Quayle's mouth invoked something or someone called the Gipper. It would be a long couple of months.

Beyond America, people waited for talk of philosophies for staying alive in a perilous age. They got simplistic couplets and triple talk. Voters showed interest in the economy, jobs, drugs and environment, not "foreign affairs." No one pointed out that almost everything was a foreign affair in today's tiny world.

Few realized they were choosing a President for five billion people. The standard bugaboo, nuclear war, was the least likely of assorted potential disasters. Candidates talked about Boston Harbor, not ozone. But unless some leader stood up to special interests, one day ships would be docking halfway up the Berkshires. Whether we noticed or not, the Sydney Opera House and Bangladesh would disappear under the waves.

I was in Stockholm the night votes were counted. As elsewhere in Europe, people watched all night. On a TV panel five Swedes droned on about Dewey and Dixville Notch with easy familiarity. People who snowshoe through blizzards to vote in simple referendums could not believe how few Americans turned out.

A defense expert I met, a visiting German, shook his head. "That shows what enormous liberty exists for the American people," he said. "They are free to hold a zero intellectual-level campaign. It should be funny, but it's not. It is horrifying." A day later in Oslo a

Norwegian at NATO's northern headquarters, put it: "I am afraid that if Americans have to learn history yet one more time, it will be the last."

But back home in America, the pros won by manipulation, not substance, and few people seemed to mind. A nation of onlookers kibitzed while the winning team shaped their candidates like lumps of clay, dressing them in cowboy hats or sweat pants. Computers worked all night to pick what record each candidate would play. Reality sometimes intruded. A girl of twelve asked Quayle whether he'd make her keep her baby if her father raped her. He swallowed; you could hear the needle scratch over the grooves. He babbled platitudes as the girl pressed on, composed and articulate. I wondered if she could pinch-hit on the ticket.

The campaign obscured most news but not the touching battle to free three whales from Alaska ice. One spectator was Terry Anderson, a friend and AP colleague, finishing his fourth year chained to a radiator in Lebanon. In a videotape he pointed out that no one showed such cooperative energy to free the hostages. Reagan said Terry was being used; he knew only what he was told. Except what he knew better than anyone: He was still there.

Beirut terrorists, with their handful of captives, held the honor and purpose of a nation that considers itself great. For a people who love symbols, Terry embodied what the election should be about, something more than Bush's flag factory or whether Dukakis knew how to double-clutch a tank.

I thought of this, watching a sidelight to the blaze of campaign coverage. A Republican ad smeared Dukakis with a photo of a furloughed convict, strumming the white man's nightmare of a black rapist on the loose. When people objected, the committee behind it produced a glowing letter from Quayle. But party headquarters had an explanation: The letter was written by an intern, using a signature machine. No one was responsible.

These days the buck doesn't stop anywhere. It passes from the evening news to *Nightline* to *Meet the Brinkley* and then devalues to nothing. We no longer hold anyone accountable.

The Iran-contra affair began as an effort to buy out hostages, blocking other avenues of approach and making our stand-firm policy so much hypocritical nonsense. Illegal arms proceeds were sneaked to contras in contempt of Congress by a man the President called a national hero. We know few details because many documents that weren't shredded are being kept from us.

But what finally happened? A congressional report said the White House had trampled on the Constitution and the President was "ultimately responsible." When reporters queried Reagan, he gave his charming smirk and said he had not read the report. When would he read it? "Let's just say, uh, sometime in the future."

We elected Bush with the question hanging: Where *was* George? He was next door the whole time, the resident CIA veteran and former ambassador. In 1983 he headed the South Florida Task Force to interdict drugs. If he did not catch on to the arms deals and guns-for-drugs operations, we were up Doo-Doo Creek. If he did, he lied to us. When Ted Koppel pressed him, Bush snickered at "two or three little issues gone wrong." This should have come up in the campaign. Where was *Mike*?

More to the point, where were we, the people?

I'd planned to end with an analysis of where we were headed. But I gave that up. I would have had to go on what politicians said, and I'd learned what that was worth. Bush swore he would not raise taxes. Even before he took office, his aides scrambled for synonyms. Polls suggested 73 percent of the nation expected the man they elected to welsh on them. Reagan went out in glory, all unanswered questions forgotten. Home in California, he declared he had won the cold war. And Nancy insisted that he had never napped in office.

There were ample grounds for hope. As this manuscript edged toward the presses, I squeaked in a look at Inauguration Day. A lovable mother figure was fluffing up the White House pillows, chucking out Nancy's froufrous. President Bush made some smooth moves. As he said, it was a new chapter.

But in my pile of leftovers, I found a *Harper's* index item: In nine of the last ten elections, we elected the man who had made the most optimistic convention speech. American pie was savored best in the sky. Jimmy Carter had insisted, "I will never lie to you," and we know where that got him. The 1990s, it seemed, would demand production, not process. But there was another index item: In Japan, the ratio of graduating engineers to lawyers is ten to one. In the United States, it is one to ten.

God bless us every one.

*

Before the election I made yet one more trip back. But by the end of that July 4 in Washington, I'd already seen enough. The sun was out, and the air was scented by flowering trees and some of the half billion hot dogs Americans would be eating that day. It was one of those moments when questions fall away and you know why you're happy to be an American.

I stood along Constitution Avenue, looking straight up to the White House, waiting for a parade to start. Down the road I could see those guys with the fifes and drum, limping along to remind us how it all started. The world felt good. Just then a woman police officer on a Japanese motorbike barked at the crowd. We moved back. A cop with a fat gut came up with a rope. "Get back," he said. I got back, but I stepped gingerly because of a small child in a pram directly behind me. It was not fast enough.

The cop shoved me in the stomach. "Don't push me on the Fourth of July," I said to him, politely but clearly. He stopped and fixed me with the kind of vicious stare I had not seen since a Bulgarian policeman caught me trying to outrun him.

But I wasn't arrested. I had a wonderful time and returned that night for fireworks over the Washington Monument. A half million people spilled onto the Mall, and I saw nothing aggressive among them. Families sat on blankets and ate their spinach pasta with plastic forks. At six o'clock the next morning an army of blacks and Hispanics cleaned it all up. The American scene.

The parade's grand marshal was Jessica McClure, the brave little Texas girl who had fallen down a well pipe and spent 58½ hours trapped there while the nation waited at the edge of its chair. She symbolized America's spirit, and the warmth toward her testified to the generosity we cherished. Her young parents were dignified in their pride. People who watched the parade felt as if they had had a hand in saving Jessica's life. They had forgotten the ignoble squabble over TV rights in her hometown.

But right down the street, carefully arranged on a dozen State Department shelves, were reports on hunger and epidemics that took the lives of fifteen thousand children a day. Americans could know this but chose not to. We were warm and generous, just inattentive. As a result, it was as if 275 school buses full of kids plunged off a cliff every day of our lives. Most of them were in Africa and Asia. Some were in South Texas, however, just down the road from the McClures' place.

The dramatic immediacy of a dark well makes a difference. But a child's slow death from an empty stomach is drama enough.

Hunger? A student in Jeffrey Barker's contemporary moral problems class, at Albright College in Pennsylvania, had asked: "Why do we have to study world hunger? We've already solved that problem. We had Live Aid. It's no longer in the news."

That was what I learned, back home in America. Long ago I'd read Michael Arlen's *Living Room War* on how television miniaturized what was real about Vietnam. I knew about our ability to switch off alarming news. But this was something new.

We, the people, now came equipped with control panels, like our television sets. We could select a channel, intensify the color, replay it and talk about it with countrymen from Jacksonville to Juneau. If we chose to ignore a channel, we could tell ourselves it didn't concern us, as though it really didn't. In all of my travels I got the clear feeling that not many people stopped to think that the real world has a way of changing channels and turning up the volume all by itself.

Like the man in Louisiana who thought garbage was the garbageman's problem, we rely unreasonably on the frontiers we define around ourselves. Borders are fine for Fourth of July speeches. In a world where missiles arrive in minutes and financial disasters in seconds, however, they mean little. In the end, all those ordinary differences we emphasize fall away to reality. There is no First, Second or Third World. There is only one, and we're just part of it.

But still. From the Embassy Row Hotel I caught a cab to Dulles International Airport. The driver had a strange accent I could not place. He was from Iran. That day, yet again, Iran was in the news, and I asked him about American policy. He was articulate, intelligent. We did not realize the intricacies of what we had gotten ourselves into. Americans did not understand the world. That was very dangerous, to everyone. Here was my last witness; I began scribbling like crazy.

As we cleared Arlington, he mentioned the American hostages in Lebanon. They were spies. I put down my pen. Terry Anderson was no spy, I told him. "Spy, all spies," the driver said, launching into a rambling tirade about Middle East politics. Angry, I tried to break in. There was no interrupting. "You Americans don't know anything about . . ." He had flipped out totally, stumbling over words.

"Listen, goddammit," I started, but got no further. He was half
in the back seat by then, taking both hands off the wheel to gesti-
culate. The lumbering old Chevrolet, doing 65 mph in heavy freeway traffic, veered toward the shoulder. I sat back, and we both
glowered in silence. At the terminal he started in again. I had no
idea about Lebanon. I pointed out that I'd spent a lot of time in
Lebanon; he'd never been there. "Doesn't matter," he replied.
"You—"

I informed him that he was a moron. "Racist!" he screamed.
"Typical American racist! You . . ." I added that he was a dangerously unbalanced moron. "Why do you Americans go to Lebanon?
Why do you go anywhere?" He paused for a final shot: "You should
stay in your own country."

Oh, boy. But I didn't say it. I paid the fare and shook his hand.
"I've got to thank you," I told him. "One thing I really love about
this country is that it still makes room for fuckheads like you. Have
a nice day." What a place. I got on the plane and smiled halfway
across the ocean.

Acknowledgments

This book took a lot of help, and the people deserving thanks number deep into the hundreds. It was not a project of my employer, The Associated Press, but the AP was gracious, and friends in the company were generous with their own time. In Paris, Charles Campbell edited the manuscript, with vital kibitzing by Sydney Rubin. Back home in America, Hank Ackerman, Woody Baird, Tad Bartimus, Mike Cochran, Richard Cole, George Esper, Andy Lippmann, Scott McCartney and Eric Newhouse were among many from whom much was asked and received.

Most sources are named in the text. Others are happy not to be. My thanks go to all. The following list, hardly exhaustive, includes old friends and people who lavished warmth and enthusiasm on some passing stranger threatening to write what he saw, no matter what: Willis Barnstone, Donna Chicklo, Ed Cody, Carolen Collins, Martha Craig, Jim Davidson, Judd DeBoer and the Browns of Idaho, Robert Feiner, Barbara Gerber, Barry Goodfield, Greg and Bubbles Guirard, Irv and Florence Hoff, Patricia Kempe, Ted Lempinen, Gary Marx, Jo Menell, Yvette Mimieux and Howard Ruby, John Nance, Butch and Mary Ann O'Neal, Nancy Pitt, Leslie Porter, the Sanderses, the Shlachters and Peiperts, Bob Stebbings, Gene Tice, the Van Notes, Bill Waller, Michael and Susan Wallis, Jan Warren, Marc and Ginny Wilson, Arnold Zeitlin and some people in Washington who would rather remain nameless. Olivia Shaije and Daniella Sprung helped with research.

Every book has an editor or two, and most have an agent; only the luckiest have Jim Landis, Jane Meara and Carol Mann together.

And for inspiration, and help in the trenches down to getting this sucker onto the Concorde to beat a deadline, Gretchen Hoff.